Ooh! I love this book, love hearir [barcode] and monsters. Filled to the bri beginners (and experienced writers because there is always something more to learn) a place to start, where to go next—and what might happen there. These essays are enabling and encouraging and useful. They speak not only to process but also to the life of the poet, the business of poetry and the need for literary citizenship and community. This is a book I'll return to again and again! Readers will, too. And get a fountain pen!!

—**Karla Huston**

The special pen, or sliver of eavesdropping, or the book that will change your life; the night table or bus ride where scraps of writings happen—these are just a few of the magical elements the practitioners gathered in this inspiring anthology call on to sing and to guide new poets inside the mysteries of poem-making. The marketplace of publishing beckons and glitters, but these poet-essayists remind us that the best feeling in the world is finding oneself in the middle of writing a poem. Humor, sharp prosodic strategies and prompts, advice about submitting, and some very cool personal anecdotes, alongside several daunting and stark accounts, hallmark every section of this anthology. There's wisdom and guidance in every essay. *Far Villages* is invaluable for beginners, to be sure, but also for poets teaching new writers, poets in-between poems, and poets who've been writing a while and are thirsty to refresh. This smart and unusually various academic and personal text serves as revivifying reminder that the welcome itself sustains new American writing.

—**Judith Vollmer**

Far Villages freely invites the novice poet into a company of friendly strangers who recast the anxiety of influence in terms of mentorship. Readers will find that the innovative chapter headings, beginning with "Hello and Welcome…" all the way to the final chapter called "A Way of Seeing the World" are likewise refreshing in the willing patronage the book offers to the apprentice poet. Drawing from diverse poetic traditions, *Far Villages* is a vital addition in the field of new and evolving poetics.

—**Claudia Keelan**

FAR VILLAGES

Welcome Essays for
New & Beginner Poets

Edited by
Abayomi Animashaun

Black
Lawrence
Press

Black
Lawrence
Press

www.blacklawrence.com

Executive Editor: Diane Goettel
Cover Design: Zoe Norvell
Book Design: Amy Freels

Copyright © 2020
ISBN: 978-1-62557-714-6

Published 2020 by Black Lawrence Press.
Printed in the United States.

for
makers gone
here and still to come

CONTENTS

Contemplating Form

Poetry Workshop

Publishing and the Literary Community

The Poet's Journey

"This poetry. I never know what I'm going to say.
I don't plan it.
When I'm outside the saying of it,
I get very quiet and rarely speak at all."

—Jalaluddin Rumi, *The Essential Rumi*

INTRODUCTION

At the heart of this anthology is the belief that poetry is open to everyone but also the recognition that substantial progress within it takes years of apprenticeship, of experimenting, of trying, of failing—that there's a difference between randomly picking it up and choosing to make it an essential part of one's life.

For a writer new to the craft, this can sound like a daunting task. And it is! Poetry is "connate with the origin of man", as Shelley reminds. Not only is it practiced the world over, in countries, among peoples, and tribes, it's also written and oral. There are so many voices, so many books, and an infinite number of approaches. Where does one begin? Yet, for many poets, the journey often begins with a perceived silence on the *what* and *how* of poetry.

This seeming silence often belies an on-going, sometimes fierce, conversation about what poetry is, what it should do, *and* how it should be approached and pursued. This conversation is as old as poetry itself. But, for those outside of it, this back and forth—to echo William Stafford—can be hard to see.

For some, this seeming absence of conversation about poetry can contribute to initial fear and paralysis due to the lack of know-how. For others, it can contribute to the idea that poetry has no other beginning and end than inside themselves, that instantly they know what they are doing, that they are masters with nothing to learn, and that the millennia worth of songs and works are secondary or in some cases irrelevant to their immediate concerns.

This is how many poets start out—with initial fear or with a self-assuredness that betrays a lack of understanding about the nature of poetry, how it refuses to be pinned down, how its landscape is greater than any woman or man.

These responses also point to foundational questions, among them: How does a poet become? And, in her journey, what markers should she take on, ponder, or avoid?

Questions like these, in the end, can only be answered by the poet herself. Given that, in poetry, there are no absolutes. What the poet knows as *truth* she must come to herself and mature into over years. Still, all new *makers* must learn from those that come before them, because poetry is among the oldest trades in the world and among the most traditional. Poets learn their art and craft by studying other poets' perspectives, approaches, and discipline.

Thus, this anthology is conceived in the spirit of other poetry handbooks and manuals aimed at demystifying the bewildering nature of poetic craft and the poetic life *and* closing the gap between beginners' passion and steady practice, so that the new poet can begin cultivating a viable path outside false confidence and initial paralysis.

Closing the gap, however, does not mean hurrying the journey or being a poet instantly. No manual can, or should, promise this. There is no "Easy Guide to Becoming a Poet." What's true is that by reading and listening to others, trepidations can lessen, false confidence can be managed, and the poet can, in time, slowly begin the climb into that inexact space where aesthetic principles inform artistic vision, where artistic vision shapes aesthetic principles.

Also true is that the new *maker* must start somewhere. And, in the first section of this anthology, titled "Hello and Welcome", a number of poets discuss initial considerations beginners may choose to take on. For instance, David Shumate, whose essay comes after Christine Riddle's welcome letter and Tanis MacDonald's prologue, describes a partnership with silence that's akin to "following the brush". In other words, following where the poem leads.

This theme of being open to the writing process, trusting one's intuition, following where the poem leads, and being careful of the over-determined poem is one that many poets hold true and one that runs through this anthology.

Another theme that threads through this anthology points to an earlier sentiment—there are no absolutes. Kyle Flak articulates this in his essay, when he says that there is no one "correct kind of poem." Rishi Dastidar takes this a step further by saying that "... there isn't one single obvious way of going about [being a poet]. You end up trying a lot of things, some of which are, in retrospect, ludicrous."

In addition, Michael Angel Martín reminds readers about the futility of trying to pin down something as inherently elusive as poetry with definitions. "Any ruminative pursuit about what poetry is will only lead us back to poetic language." "Any essay chasing a definition of "poem" would probably only have probed itself into either a poem or white space."

If there is no correct kind of poem and no correct way of being a poet, perhaps the point, as Flak suggests, *is* to "have fun" and for each poet to find what works for her.

Yet, beneath poetry's fractured overlay, along with its endless entry points, is a long and vibrant conversation about its praxis and nature. A conversation that, when embraced, allows the poet to develop principles, tastes, postures of mind, and marrows of similitude with current and ancient practitioners. Without this sense of tradition, if we draw from T.S. Eliot, the new poet runs the serious risk of being stunted at the start. "I don't read others because I don't want to contaminate my genius." "I *only* read my contemporaries." Sentiments such as these will only leave the new poet frittering away at the gates.

In the second section, titled "Some Essentials of Poetry", contributors discuss issues of craft and provide engaging exercises for beginner and experienced poets alike. David M. Harris, from whose essay the title of the section is taken, provides the reader with some essentials of poetry "in no particular order."

Among these essentials is that it's not enough to want to write. One has to actually do it. It helps too for poets to be open to accidents, while also being open to the various approaches and forms that have been used over time.

Poetry *is* about operating in that matrix where old and ancient works form a nexus with new and contemporary approaches. But, it is also about play—play with ideas and language(s). David Bergman in his essay, "The Pleasure of Reading", speaks partly to this when he calls poetry "the first Montessori school."

Playing with language(s) and ideas! For the new poet, it's a notion worth keeping in mind given that poetry requires doing, constancy, and a realization that our abilities will "evolve over time" as we grow "from the obvious to the more subtle in our younger years; from the literal to the more abstract and metaphorical as we age" as John Langfeld asserts.

This discussion of craft is taken further in the section titled "Contemplating Form", where contributors address a myriad of concerns—from Kelly Cherry's insights on style all the way to Nathan McClain's discussion of Elizabeth Bishop. And, again, one is reminded that poets with informed resolutions to aspects of craft are the ones most willing to study what other poets have said and are saying. Thus, these poets have more tools at their disposal, which gives them more to work with and more to talk about...

On the contrary, if a new poet, for instance, becomes resolutely married to the idea that representational poems that are confessional are the only real poems no *ifs*, *ands*, or *buts*, such a poet might altogether miss Zoe Brigley's well-articulated argument that "being honest does not necessarily mean having to confess" and that "dream-work can be particularly useful to the poet who wants to write about difficult, personal material."

Poets must remain in conversation with works of the past and those of their time. As Chaun Ballard points out in his essay titled "Peas in the Pocket: The Practice of Fixed Poetic Form"—"Exploring form gives me the opportunity to be in conversation with a community of poets, both past and present, and by reusing structures that had long been in circulation, I follow in tradition."

In order to gain mastery, Ballard continues, the poet's skills "must be honed and sharpened repeatedly...this comes through the reading of other poets, corresponding critiques, and the composition of a number of drafts and revisions." Ballard goes on to say that he approaches poetry the way an athlete approaches his/her sports—by practicing every day. "Poets" he says "must put in the time and effort."

For poets looking for a structured environment to put in the time and effort, becoming part of a literary community might be a viable choice. In the section titled "Poetry Workshop", contributors provide hands-on suggestions for the poet thinking of pursuing this option. Literary communities can be found, for instance, in cafés, retreats, workshops, and MFA programs. They can include hundreds of people or they can be a simple community of two. What matters is for the poet to find what works for her in tone, rigor, and dynamic while keeping in mind that to "enter the community of writing" is to step "into a living stream that has a long history—and an unknown destiny" as Thom Tammaro points out.

Also true is that after working for a while—whether alone or within a collective—the poet might feel compelled to send his poems into the world to be considered for possible publication. When he finds himself at this stage, the poet must be resigned to the reality of rejection. Difficult as it is, he must learn that rejection is the business of poetry. He must learn to see rejection as an opportunity to return to the tool shop and fine-tune his work.

What the poet doesn't want is to be distraught after each rejection. In the section titled "Publication and the Literary Community", Helen Ruggieri and Whitney Sweet discuss situations when the poet might consider "rejecting rejection."

Still, rare as getting published is, it happens! And, after publication, the poet will have to deal with the "Wow! Now What?" phenomenon. "Wow! Now What?" is the title of Laura M Kaminski's essay, in which she addresses this important question that often comes after one's work (whether a poem or book of poems) has been accepted by a literary journal or press. In addition, Joan Leotta cautions against success. With publication, the poet doesn't want to think of himself as "arrived". "The mountain of writing "perfection" has no summit—it's a moving target" Leotta says. Regardless of what we've achieved, "[w]e can always improve."

Writing is not all about publications, nor is it just about winning awards. Poets are part of a literary community. And, for someone like Nancy Reddy, poets should often ask themselves how they are contributing to the viability of that community.

However, just because poets are part of a collective doesn't mean all journeys are the same in poetry. If they were, then all the essays in the section titled "The Poet's Journey" would be on the same subject. Instead, we see Leonard Franzén take up the important question of when a poet might call herself *a poet*. After how many books published? After how many prizes won? After how many readings given or classes taught? Isn't it better to focus on the work than being hung up on the label?

On the other hand, Aaron Brown ponders if every experience can be made into a poem, while Jessamine Price talks about the beauty inherent in memorizing poems. For her part, Tanis MacDonald cautions against the mythologized image of the writer as a lonely genius. This notion (or image) of the writer living *completely* in the sealed world of ideas is, as Darby Price eloquently puts it, "bullshit!"

Each poet must walk his path and mountain pass as he tries to overcome limitations in writing as in life. Yet, some challenges can be difficult to overcome—especially, in situations where the scars of loss and trauma remain indelible. We see this with some of the essays included in the section titled "Reclaiming Artistic Space," which also contains essays by Megan Merchant and Claudia F. Savage about how the poet can preserve or reenter her writing space when that space is taxed by familial concerns.

For most poets, writing does not occur in airtight spaces removed from the demands of a world that daily seems on a downward spiral. Thus, poetry informs how many poets see the world and live in it.

In the final section of this anthology titled, "A Way of Seeing the World," contributors explore this connection between poetry and place, to echo Stephen Page, in a variety of ways. For Gillian Parrish, who introduces poetry to her students as "world-making", the actual *making* occurs in the "scarce between-times" of a "busy week". Todd Davis asks how best poets can "be in the world, present to the sacred and desecrated, witness to grace and suffering which...is at the root of poetry?" While, José Angel Araguz writes about how identifying as Latinx "is not the end of a conversation but the continuation of one."

The essays mentioned in this introduction are just a handful of the many in this anthology that provide insights into the art and the poet's life. And, taken together, the eight section-titles of this book (which are from contributors' essays) paint a rough picture of the poet's evolution—a picture, which suggests that there's no such thing as instant mastery, that poetry requires patience and discipline.

For poets unsure of who to read and how to begin, there's an extensive reading list at the back of this anthology where each contributor suggests up to five works that poets might find useful as they journey into the ever-expanding field of meaning-making known as poetry.

Moreover, the number and variety of books on the reading list also show that the new poet has before him a long road of apprenticeship. To understand that poetry begins but also does not begin with oneself is an essential step toward being a mature poet.

With this in mind, I want to believe that the poet is someone who has set for herself the lifelong task of being in dialogue with the dead and living poets of her country (or countries), while also trying to find her place in that conversation through her own unique idiom. It's precisely this conversation, however, that many poets avoid in their early years.

This notion of being in dialogue with the dead and living poets from one's country is itself not new. It's drawing from T.S. Eliot's century-old essay, "Tradition and the Individual Talent", in which Eliot argues that "[n]o poet, no artist of any art, has his complete meaning alone. His significance, his appreciate is the appreciation of his relation to the dead poets and artists..."

Of course, we must set the poet or artist in relation to living poets as well. But the point is not lost. And, this brings me to one of my takeaways from this anthology:

Rather than being overwhelmed with fear or being instantly sure of his own greatness, the new poet can begin by looking forward to his own limitations. He can take heart knowing that he has a long reading list, that while he'll not read every single book of poetry ever written, he's committed to reading and studying as much as possible while he breathes.

He can take his first steps into poetry knowing that some days will be better than others, on some days poetry will make sense, on other days it won't. He can proceed into poetry, this second country and the far villages within it, knowing that what matters is not how loudly he beats his chest and screams "poetry", what matters is his daily engagement with it.

He can relax in the fact that when it comes to his search for that union between artistic vision and aesthetic principles, he's in it for the long-haul. And, he can take those first steps as he is—whether troubled or bruised, kind or gentle, whether from Dakar, Paris, London, or Tehran, whether learned or new to the craft—especially if he's new to the craft! He should know that, since he'll grow from reading and studying others, how he arrives at the gates and what he brings are enough.

He can continue his devotion to poetry knowing that much of it is elusive and important to poetry is preserving its own mystery. What relief knowing that he doesn't have to be sure about all things poetry from the beginning, that he's allowed to practice, fail, and embrace *unknowing*.

And, he can look forward to studying the works and lives of masters— poets like Yeats, Stafford, Neruda. Glück, Elytis, Rilke—*makers* who found ways of placing poetry at the core of their lives, initiates who grew in their craft by reading contemporaries and studying prior masters.

Abayomi Animashaun

Prologue

Tanis MacDonald

THIS IS FOR

you, sitting in the back of your high school class, or maybe in the front, bored and barely passing or passing without trying and wondering why it all seems so formulaic. This is for you in the library, reading anything and everything you can get your hands on not because you are so fascinated, though you might be sometimes, but because you never know what book might give you the sliver of light, the key to getting out of this place, this school, this set of expectations, this impossible crushed-down spine of a life. This is for you who go to church or temple or gurdwara at your parents' insistence and get lost for a moment or two in the rhythm of the words or the music or the prayers or readings, or the harmonies of hymns you haven't believed in for years but still, they sound like leaving, sound like art that gets made somewhere far away from here.

This is for you, your hidden weirdo glory in your rural community, your town without a theatre, your small city with no writers, with your family who just wants you to study science and be a doctor who can move back home, serve the community, and yes, sure, you agree in principle, that would be good, but. For you in the suburbs, so close and yet so far from all the lights and colours, from art and its makers. This is for you, backstage crew too cool to go on stage in the high school musical and you're *more into Zeppelin anyway, man,* for you, yearbook staff, town head-banger, geek girl, girly boy, boyly girl, people who want to dance but don't know how, class clown and the shyest person in school. You who say *journalist* so you don't have to explain *writer,* you who say *commercial artist* to excuse your compulsive drawing, and so you don't have to say that you really want to leave this place and live in a garret far far away.

This is for you, first generation of your family to go to university with the weight of that privilege and expectation, all that money spent on you, all that guilt, all that future to fill, and you know you'll have to pay somehow but how? This is for you, thinking that you are too old to take a class now that you are thirty-five, forty-five or fifty-five.

I see you making art out of almost nothing, out of your sheer will to make something of your own, something different from what you see every day. I see you finding books, I see you sewing and singing and making collages, staying late in art class, playing the piano for Sunday school. I see you playing D&D and Second Life and RPGs for the pleasure of becoming someone else and you are relieved that you don't have to call it art and be shamed for it. I see you cooking and baking for the pleasure of making, I see you learning the names of birds and plants for their mellifluous tongue-tripping beauty and for God's sake never calling yourself *a birder*, I see you mucking out a calf's stall for the sweet smell of hay and baby animal shit, for the calf's tangle of limbs in the morning. I see you running to listen to the rhythm of your breath. I see you learning to speak the language of your ancestors, I see you saying the words "ancestors" with a dawning sense of history.

I see you saying nothing when someone calls you a dreamer or a pansy or a fag or an airhead, a fluffball, a slut, a flake, or just an idiot for thinking you could be more, do more, catch beauty in a jar, get out of this place, be something other than.

I am thinking of you making art in unlikely and sometimes stringent circumstances: writing on your lunch hour, or taking photos with your phone, or curating books and films and paintings to declare what you love, or saving old beautiful things from the landfill, or kerning the lettering on an event poster.

Special shoutout to those of you who have to listen all day to people who tell you that it's not art, that it's banal, that it's more useless information, that the care you take and attention you give will add up to nothing. I will tell you this one thing in hope that it will help sustain you: you know what needs doing.

I see you, fat or bone-thin or just ordinary invisible, I see you with your perfect skin that will never be perfect enough, I see you rebel with every cause about which you are not going to speak because what's the point, who would hear you, Cassandra, Philomela, Tiresias? I see you push back against the beast, I hear you fight to breathe. I see you clawing your way out of that lonely purgatory you fell into three or four or ten years ago when he hit you, or she left, or everyone laughed and never let you forget. I see you washing the dishes or mowing the lawn while he jeers, while she tells you that you are never leaving, while he tells you he's the boss and can do whatever he wants to you. I see you, and I tell you that you deserve a life, a way out, you deserve your body and brain working in concert with all the art ever made, every piece of music, every brushstroke, every high note, every leap into the air, every curve, muscle, swing, colour, shape and shadow. Every word.

Hello and Welcome

Christine Riddle

DEAR POET,

Welcome to the fellowship.

I mean that sincerely. Every writer was once where you are now. We poets share a common bond but we don't all fit in the same box—and that's a wonderful thing.

I've been asked to write to you about writing, to encourage you, to share what wisdom I've gleaned along the way and what methods I use. Well, here goes.

Writing starts with reading. Simply put, you can't write if you don't read. Virginia Woolf famously said, "Read a thousand books and your words will flow like a river." I can hear you groaning. No worries. If you're under 30, there's probably still time and you can read *while* you're writing. But if that milestone is in your rear-view mirror, well unless you've been an avid reader, or you were reading chapter books at the age of three, you're likely not going to get there. In my opinion, it's quality, not quantity that matters anyway.

Next get a notebook, and keep it close. Keep it on the kitchen island while you're cooking; keep it within reach while you're reading; keep it on the bedside table while you're sleeping. You can't count on that inspired metaphor that woke you at 3 AM to still be retrievable when the alarm goes off at 7. And never leave the house without a pen. It's impossible to predict when inspiration will hit.

You also need to be reading poetry—all kinds of poetry. From triolet to villanelle, haiku to pantoum, sonnet to cinquain. From Dylan to Dickinson, Frost to Forché, Williams to Whitman. There's something to be learned from each of them. Jump in. Take a class. Join a writers' group. Go to poetry readings. Immerse yourself, and just keep writing until you find your own voice.

Now for the act of writing itself. Since this is so personal and varies so widely among writers I can't recommend a specific formula. I know writers who treat the process like a job—same time every day, and others who stay up all night once or twice a week. It works for them. And that's the thing. Only you know what works for you. But I *can* say one thing with certainty: if you *don't* write, you'll never get any better at it than you are today.

Which brings me to my final point—rejection. It happens much more often than not. I find it helps to put myself in the judge's or publisher's shoes. And while they should be impartial, they're also human and for all I know, my poem is competing with the best poem ever written about a subject that they're absolutely passionate about. And that you have no control over. So give your poem another objective look. And, don't give up on a good poem. To paraphrase Stephen King: In the end, writing is about enriching the lives of those who will read your work, and enriching your own life, as well.

Yours truly,
Christine Riddle

David Shumate

THE PILGRIM OF THE POEM

Every morning I sit in a room, raise my poetic antennae, and enter into a partnership with silence. It's a contract we negotiated long ago. I make myself receptive to whatever might happen in that silence—an image, a character, a memory, a scene, a phrase—and the silence provides the stage. I write one thing down. Then another. And then I begin to play around.

Over the years, I have learned to be patient with a poem as it takes shape. I use a light touch. I don't try to impose my will on it. I heed the advice of the ancient Chinese painters who said to "follow the brush." So I seldom know at the outset where a poem will take me.

———

Whenever I teach a poetry class, I begin by highlighting two basic principles:

The stuff of poetry is everywhere. Pay attention.

An example—Forty years ago I was walking along the streets of Hannibal, Missouri, Mark Twain country, where my cousin, Kathy, lived and where I visited frequently as a child. She pointed up to a place ten feet up on a building and said, "This spring, the flood waters rose to that level."

Twenty-five years later while I was writing one early morning, her words returned to me. And they became the core of a poem, "High Water Mark."

The stuff of poetry is everywhere. Pay attention.

———

A poem can draw almost directly from lived experience, but it can just as easily be a kaleidoscopic collection of scenes and images, characters and events, some lived, some imagined, some borrowed, then passed through the prism of the imagination until a larger truth emerges.

In my work, when I write "I," the "I" does not refer to me, the writer. It is a fellow I set loose on a little adventure, my proxy, to see what mischief he gets up to, what truths he stumbles upon. He acts as the "Pilgrim of the Poem," the one who asks a deity a confounding question, the one who knocks on the witch's door and, like Odysseus, slips into her bed.

———

For me, a poem seeks to unveil the essence of a thing, its glowing core. I ask this of each poem I write. Sometimes I actually get there. Other times, I fall short.

———

While revising, I am guided by a phrase from the Uruguayan poet, historian, social critic, and grand soul, Eduardo Galeano, who said he was perpetually in search of "words that are better than silence." Let that serve as your poetic lantern as you put the final polish on your work. A line in one of my early poems, "What Hemingway Learned from Cezanne," reads, "Each word must be inevitable. Like a scripture you cannot erase." I strive to live up to my own lofty expectations each day.

———

If you are serious about writing, make it a daily habit. If you return to it only upon occasion or when you feel inspired, you will spend too much time re-teaching yourself the basics. But if you develop a habit of writing every day, probing the subtle depths of a subject, a funny thing happens. The mind, the intellect, the ego, the senses, the memory, and the intuition all begin to work in greater synchrony. A particular "posture of mind" born of this synchrony begins to take shape. It is a satisfying feeling, one you yearn to return to day after day.

Sometimes, when you write a truthful line, it may even feel like your fingertips have started to glow. Then, my friend, you're hooked.

Rishi Dastidar

HOW A BATHTUB MIGHT CHANGE YOUR LIFE

*The following is a mostly true account of my journey through poetry so far.
It doesn't have a straightforward argument or narrative; it's instead a series of
thoughts or vignettes about poetry—performing it and writing it—and some
of the overlap between writing copy for advertising (my day job) and writing
poems.*

*These thoughts might or might not hang together—so it might be easier to
just think of this as an extended poem.*

Part 1: A bathtub can change your life.

OK, not a bathtub as such but rather a poem about them. And I don't exaggerate when I say that the poem—and the book I found it in—changed my life.

The poem is called 'Bathtubs,' and both it and the book, *Ashes for Breakfast*,
are by a German poet called Durs Grünbein. Here's a little taste of the poem:

> What adorable objects bathtubs are, enamelled
> and sleek and altogether
> unapproachable with their
>
> heroic curves of wrought-iron
> old ladies still frisky
> after the menopause.

It was the spring of 2007, and I'd just come back from a weekend in Berlin
and was looking for something to commemorate the trip. In those days there
was still a Borders bookshop on Oxford Street, London's main shopping
drag, so I popped in there one Monday lunchtime. Going up the escalator,

my eye chanced upon this book. I picked it up, started flicking through it, and please don't laugh but honestly, it's as close to a religious moment as I'm ever going to have in my life. I vividly remember thinking—*what is this stuff? Why don't the lines go all the way to the end of the page? Why has no one told me you could do this with words?*

I knew at that moment that I had found my thing—the thing that I wanted to write, that I will spend the rest of my days writing. Which was quite useful, as I had spent the previous 14 years knowing that I wanted to write and be a writer, but not having any real idea of what to write.

Pretty much the next day I signed up to do an introduction to poetry course at CityLit, a college in London—and that was it. I've been trying to be a poet ever since.

Part 2: You sometimes have to stand on tables to get noticed.

What no one tells you when you start trying to become a poet is that there isn't one single, obvious way of going about it. You end up trying a lot of things, some of which are, in retrospect, ludicrous.

Very early on, well before I was even remotely ready, I agreed to go and do an open mic session at a pub in Hoxton, a grittily fashionable part of East London.

(A side note: I know everyone says you should take every opportunity, especially if you don't know how to do something; just figure it out as you go. But be warned—often the sole use of these experiments is to experience the burning pain of embarrassment, because apparently doing something badly is much more valuable than doing something well when it comes to learning.)

Anyway, I didn't ask any questions about it—another mistake—I just turned up...to discover that the place was absolutely rammed...with people watching soccer.

Three people had turned up for the poetry. And there was no microphone.

Now what I should have done was turned tail and fled into the night. Instead, I stood on a table, then bellowed—and I really do mean bellowed, to the point at which I had no voice for the next few days—some very bad poems at those three bemused people.

This was, in retrospect, an early taste of one of the secrets of poetry that people don't tell you until later—often you have to win over your readers one by one. I just didn't realize that that was literally going to be the case.

Part 3: You start more poems than you ever finish.

And that's ok. Poetry is a game of persistence. Often you have to wait for the poems to arrive—there's one in my book, *Ticker-tape*, called "These things boys do," which took about a year, from the moment I thought of the idea for it, to actually sending it to my editor. Speaking to some other poets, this apparently makes me a fast mover.

The point is that you have to hold your nerve, and trust your instinct that something will turn up. It normally does.

You have to wait on submissions too, hearing about whether you've had any luck in persuading a magazine to take your work. The only certainty here is that you will be rejected often, and have the pleasure of waiting a long time to find out.

And this is doubly frustrating because poetry is the only art where you can have a complete, finished piece in less than 30 minutes. It was said of Frank O'Hara—his "Meditations in an Emergency" was featured in *Mad Men*—that at parties you could challenge him to write a poem. He would then disappear to the bathroom for 20 minutes or so, to emerge triumphantly with a perfect, flawless piece.

An elegant party trick for sure, but as another of my heroes, Clive James, has said there is no greater pleasure than sitting down in a café with a coffee, knowing that even before you have finished your drink you could have written something that the world will be reading 500 years later.

So to continue to enjoy writing poems, you have to cultivate something I call "patient impatience." You have to be open to the image, the phrase, the conceit arriving at any moment, and yet you have to not feel—or be—panicked when nothing is coming, which can be—will be—quite often.

I'm not advocating being passive or doing nothing: you must always be reading, drafting, scribbling. But fallow periods, however long or short, are never just that—there is always something going on under the surface; it just might not seem like it.

Part 4: It takes about 10 years to get good at doing poems.

My labelmate at Nine Arches Press in the UK, the poet Jo Bell, has a theory that 10 years is the average time it takes for someone to be really ready to start publishing their poetry—the poetic equivalent of Malcolm Gladwell's 10,000 hours of practice you need to get good at doing anything.

Now, considering the lack of financial rewards on offer, and then the slow process of getting noticed by magazine editors, publishers, radio people, booking agents—basically, you have to really, really want to write poems. Which means that most poets you meet are, how can I put this politely, a little intense.

Poetry is the branch of the entertainment industry that is closest to a religious vocation—a calling rather than a 9-to-5, regular office hours way of making a living.

When you get a chance, ply any poet with alcohol—and trust me, it won't take much—and ask them why? Why do you write this stuff when you could be crashing out popular novels, TV series, Hollywood screenplays?

And eventually, after some faux modest huffing and puffing, you'll see the glint in the eye. The glint that says, "I really like making patterns out of words on a page; arranging language so that it goes into the ears and the eyes and then captures a heart. Yes, all you other writers can have success, but you do not have what I have, which is a power to change the very atoms of someone's soul."

I didn't say we were rational.

Part 5: Constraints are liberating.

You might have guessed by now that most poets are, in addition to everything else, masochists. We have to be, to do this slightly weird, semi-secret thing that we do. And then, on the basis of most contrary evidence, to expect the world to be interested in our outpourings.

And so here's one of the ways in which poetry and copywriting overlap—most poets love a tight brief, a constraint.

The thing I tell my students—which always makes their faces fall—is: learn to write within the forms, within the rules, because when you break them later, you will do so with a style and a flourish you might not otherwise achieve.

And as in so many things, someone else said this better first, in this case the Irish poet Paul Muldoon, who said: "Form is a straitjacket in the way that a straitjacket was a straitjacket for Houdini."

Part 6: The 17th draft may be the charm but probably isn't.

My claim here is that there really is such a thing as over-drafting. You can worry at and rewrite a thing so much that you can effectively kill it, or at least the energy it needs to animate itself, to live in the ear of the reader and the listener. Or you forget the impulse that caused you to want to write the thing in the first place.

It's a hard thing to spot, but you do have to learn to look out for it. What I'm trying to say is: yes, keep tinkering, keep tuning the words, for that is part of our craft—but part of our craft also has to be knowing when to stop and put down the pen. And I genuinely think that's something that's not said enough.

Honestly, the best writers are mostly lazy, and that's actually the secret of their success. Or am I just projecting here?

Part 7: Copywriting is the unacknowledged patron of contemporary poetry.

Genuinely, I can't imagine giving up my day job any time soon. Not just because I can't afford to—let me be candid with you here. No one ever lives off the money they earn from publishing poems, or even more rarely winning competitions or awards. Poetry is the ultimate 'slash' career—we are poets slash lecturers, poets slash teachers, poets slash civil servants and yes, poets slash copywriters.

But also because I think the poetry does make me a better copywriter. Because it does give me something that feeds back into client work. A desire to take a few more risks maybe. A greater ability to weigh up words perhaps. Bravery in choosing to use outlandish verbs, even. (By the way, using rare or unusual verbs is the quickest way to look like a genius, in poetry at least—this is advice to make the prose wallahs wince.)

And if you need convincing, let me tell you of some words in *Ogilvy on Advertising*, written by David Ogilvy, the founder of Ogilvy and Mather, still one of the world's largest advertising agencies. He quotes William Maynard as saying: "Most good copywriters fall into two categories. Poets. And killers. Poets see an ad as an end. Killers as a means to an end." And then, genius that he is, Ogilvy ads: "If you are both killer and poet, you get rich."

Well, it's something to aim for.

Kyle Flak

HELLO AND WELCOME: TOP FIVE SUGGESTIONS FOR POETS WHO ARE JUST GETTING STARTED

1. Be a secret agent.

The happiest happiness I know is the joy of writing whatever I feel like inside a secret notebook. I like to buy the cheapest notebooks I can find. Sometimes I just glue some birch bark together with school glue and throw that in my pocket before I leave the house.

You can write in your secret notebook while riding the bus to a dentist appointment. You can write in your secret notebook while a wild bear is stealing your sandwich in the woods.

The main thing is to not care if your writing is good or not. The main thing is to just have fun and write whatever you want to. The main thing is to never think about publishing or getting famous or getting rich or impressing anyone with your literary biceps.

Play with language. Examine the universe. Describe your secret crush's astonishingly normal ear lobes. Rewrite your favorite soup commercial as an English sonnet. Is the man buying fifty light bulbs at the grocery store a mad scientist trying to take over the world with an army of cute baby squirrels dressed in pale blue tuxedos? Write about it and decide for yourself.

But actually, poetry lives in the heart and soul. So, you could just carry around a secret notebook, never write in it, and still be a poet.

Look at the clouds. Listen to an owl. Take a nap. Read a phone book backwards. Sit around in a graveyard on a rainy day. Melt tiny chocolates on your tongue at the zoo while waving at rhinos.

Being a poet is fun. Don't care what other people think. Just carry around a secret notebook and glow with the knowledge that at any moment you could take out a pen and write.

2. Toothbrush Poet

Good news! You don't have to quit being a used car salesman / high school student / robot repair technician / award-winning physicist / tree surgeon to become a poet!

You can write poems while you brush your teeth!

Dentists recommend brushing your teeth at least twice a day for a few minutes, so, okay what're you thinking about while you brush your teeth? How about profound emotional experiences and transcendent beauty?

While brushing, compose a line or two in your head. Then, after you spit out that gross broccoli and pork-chop-infused foamy stuff, rush over to your secret notebook and write your words down.

Let's see. Two lines of verse per toothbrushing session times two toothbrushing sessions per day equals four lines of verse per day equals twenty-eight lines of verse per week equals two hundred and eighty lines of verse per ten weeks equals two hundred and eighty thousand lines per ten thousand weeks, etc.

So, yes, you could become a major world poet by just composing a couple of lines per toothbrushing session. Wow.

(Note: you could also write poems in your head while doing a different daily activity, like walking the dog, combing your hair, or eating raisin bran, etc.)

3. Be a fool and a buddy.

Have you ever been to an "open mic" night? These things are awesome. On a single night you might encounter a lumberjack who juggles fried egg sandwiches, a nurse who sings opera, a real estate agent who impersonates Woody Allen, and a baboon trained to dance the Charleston.

So, why not perform a few of your very best and gnarliest poems, too? Even if no one likes them, it will be exciting to say a few of your lines out loud. And most likely, some nice stranger will actually like what you're up to and say so, right to your face!

And isn't it nice to make a new friend who says nice things about your poems to your face? Why, yes, yes it is.

Many good and meaningful friendships can bloom and grow at open mic nights. You are all creative people and you are all interested in sharing what you do with the world. So, why not sip a pinot grigio or chocolate milk together and discuss the thoughts and feelings that brought you all to such an event in the first place?

Almost every town has some type of open mic night. They usually take place at a downtown bar or coffee shop. If your town doesn't have one, then start one. All you have to do is bring some extra business to a casual beverage establishment on a slow night and there you go: you've got a community.

4. Revision is a beautiful time-traveling device you can drive as much as you want!

Okay, so you're reading through your secret notebook and you don't like what you see. Do you throw the notebook into the sea? No! It's never too late to change a poem as long as you are alive. And: if you're not alive, just become a ghost and haunt a house where someone has a pen. Tell a living person what you would like your poems to be like and they will gladly make the necessary changes. No big deal.

Revision doesn't have to be stressful or terrible. Just reread your old poems and change whatever parts you want to change in whatever way you want to change them.

The only thing that could possibly make revision horrible is if you are telling yourself stuff like, "I've got to turn this 9,000-page poem into the greatest thing the world has ever known in the next ten seconds or else a fire-breathing mutant penguin is going to destroy the universe!"

In reality, there is no such thing as "perfection" or "greatness." Your poems can be whatever you want them to be.

Some good poems are small, quiet, and humble. Some good poems are big, wild, loud, and crazy. There is not one "correct kind of poem."

When you revise, just have fun and change things as much as you want until you like what the poem has become. In one mood, you might prefer a poem to be one way. In a different mood, you might prefer a poem to be a different way. It doesn't matter. You can revise as much as you want or as little as you want.

5. There are many ways to be a poet. Please just be yourself.

Gertrude Stein hung out with all the major artists of her time in Paris, France. Emily Dickinson rarely left her family home in Amherst, Massachusetts. Wallace Stevens worked in the insurance industry. William Carlos Williams was a doctor. Frank O'Hara worked at an art museum. Maya Angelou was the first black female streetcar conductor in San Francisco. Anne Sexton was a fashion model for awhile. T.S. Eliot worked at a bank in London for many years. Langston Hughes was once a busboy at a Washington, D.C. hotel. Walt Whitman was a volunteer nurse during the Civil War. There is no normal or correct way to be a poet. You could earn a living from any job on the face of the Earth, come from any kind of background, and have whatever kind of personality you actually have. The only important thing is to be someone who writes poems sometimes. You don't even have to write every day. You could write one poem on the last day of your life at age 97. Or you could write all your poems in purple crayon on your mom's walls at age 5. Or you could only write poems in the sky with a special kind of airplane smoke.

Get rid of all the "supposed tos" and "I shoulds." A poet is anybody who has ever written a poem. Even a secret unread poem hidden in a shark's belly counts.

So, get going. Write some poems. You might have fun.

Michelle Bonczek Evory

GETTING STARTED: EVOKING THE MUSES

Throughout history, humans have credited poems and other forms of art as coming from somewhere mystical, mysterious, and divine. We've envisioned angels, muses, embodiments of inspiration who have been gracious enough to bestow upon us the moments of clarity and imagination from which our poems have crystalized. In Greek mythology, the god Apollo was recognized as the God of poetry and music. In Norse, Bragi fills this role. Aengus is the Irish god of poetry to whom William Butler Yeats devotes his poem "The Song of Wandering Aengus." And if you had a very specific type of poem you wished to write, you could call upon the Nine Greek Muses (Calliope for epic poetry, Clio for historical, Erato for music, and so on) for inspiration.

Should you ever call out to one of these gods and receive no answer, however, I'd like to introduce you to alternative muses who have been known to grant poems consistently: journaling, collecting, reading, freewriting, moving, keeping a writing routine, creating a ritual, and dreaming.

Journaling

For many of us, a poem starts with an idea, a memory, a sound, an image. Or it starts when we finally take a pen to paper or sit at our computers and begin to type. But, actually, a poem begins way before we begin to compose that first line with words. As we move through our day, our mind sorts through experiences, sensations, feelings, images, and ideas and files them in our memory. And as time passes, we forget many of the memories we hold onto in the short term. Something we experience today and remember tomorrow may be lost in a year. It is one of the many reasons writers keep journals—to take notes, pay attention and observe, collect images, sounds, ideas and experiences as they happen before they are stowed away in the basement of our brains.

Perhaps when you were younger you kept a diary. One with a tiny gold key or an attached ribbon to tie around it. I remember writing in one first when I was in fifth grade. It was blue and came with a tiny lock. I used to keep a record of the weather and what I did every day. Then I formed a crush on an eighth-grader and I began to record our encounters in the cafeteria and in the hallway. I became an observer, and began to feel desire. Later, maybe in seventh grade, the purpose of my diary grew. I began to record not only my observations, but also my feelings and thoughts, and eventually I wrote my first poem. Who knows how this happens. We begin to indulge in writing and expression and soon we fine-tune our ears to the music, to the prosody, of language. We become ever more aware of the sensual power of language and tighten the connection between how we feel and how we place these feelings in words; between what we see in our mind's eye and what we describe through words on a page; between what words on a page describe and what we see in our mind's eye.

As we grow into adulthood, journaling takes on different uses than tracking weather and crushes—especially if we are writers, thinkers, creators. We might start our day writing as the Poet William Heyen has done for decades; it is such a necessary habit, he has said, that he cannot go a day without it. We might write down our dreams or initial thoughts for the day, our plans. We might reflect on yesterday's events or expound our ideas for our next series of poems.

———

Reflection: Keeping a personal journal is a basic practice encouraged in all sorts of writing and art classes. Why do you think that is? Have you ever kept a journal? For what purpose? Did it have an effect on your creative writing?

———

Keeping a journal works to encourage poems in mainly two ways. First, it provides us time to practice writing and to play with words, while at the same time uncovering potential material to bring to our poems. The poet William Wordsworth famously defined poetry as "a spontaneous overflow of feelings... *recollected in tranquility*". Keeping a journal encourages time for the second half of this equation. The practice of making time to write can sometimes be the hardest obstacle to overcome in our daily lives of work, school, and family responsibilities. Keeping a journal produces a routine that becomes easier to keep the more we do it, and it gives us a way to uncover material to write about.

Secondly, in many circumstances, keeping a journal can clear our heads of everyday concerns and frustrations—we can vent in our journals, unload our thoughts and memories that may be standing in the way of our imagination's flow. If we use the journal to essentially dump the tiny concerns eating away at us, we clear the path for new thoughts and relax enough to forget our worries and play.

If you are a lover of objects, one of the joys of keeping a journal is being able to purchase an attractive book in which to write. I find the feel of the journal, the smell of its cover and its colors to be enjoyable. It makes me feel special. Perhaps it's the ten-year-old me still dazzled by my first diary, but perhaps you, too, will discover this pleasure as you begin to keep your own. Of course, today, it may be more practical for you to type on a screen. And if that works for you, then by all means let it. I have actually experimented with both and found each to have its own advantages.

———

Activity: Purchase a journal or notebook and commit to writing in it every day for one week. It might help to schedule this activity for the same time each day. Try to write in a place that is quiet and pleasing—a coffee shop, a library, a comfy chair on the front porch. At the end of the week assess how your journal is working for you. Are you writing with the intention to create poems? Or are you venting? Either way, how has journaling affected your imaginative flow?

———

Collecting

A journal can be very useful in helping us to collect material for when we have time to and are ready to actually write. In our contemporary technological world of multi-tasking, our attention spans have been shortened. Sometimes, in order to maintain a writing lifestyle, it is more practical to work in bursts. And this is where we can remain attentive; we can catch moments—images, ideas, phrases—that we come across and write them down. Keeping a collection notebook helps us to remember the gems of images and sounds that spark poetry before we forget them. When you hear, see, or think something that sings, write it down.

As mentioned earlier, many writers keep notebooks or scraps of paper on their night tables, in their cars, in pockets and purses. As long as you have a pen and some form of paper—oh how many poets are surprised by pockets of words they find on napkins and pieces of envelopes!—you are equipped and can consider yourself to be a writer in the act of hunting. Then, when you sit down to write, you will not start from nothing; you can flip through what you've collected and build from there.

———

Activity: Carry around a small notebook and jot down musical or odd phrases or pieces of conversation you overhear throughout your day. Write down a new word you learn in biology class, or a funny sentence out of context you overhear while waiting in line at the dining hall. Write down a phrase you like from a poem or story you read, or capture an image you see while you're driving or on a walk: a shattered bluebird's egg, the greasy fingerprints of a child in a display window, a squirrel towing an apple down a neighbor's porch stairs. While having coffee, take your earbuds out and engage the world, mine it for language and images. Jot down strong memories. When you write, pull out your collection and begin a poem from one of the phrases or images, or insert one into a revision.

———

Many beginning writers make the mistake of trying to compose poems entirely in their heads, forgetting that as soon as we actually start writing the direction our words take are guaranteed to change. Keeping a collection notebook helps with these obstacles. Therefore, I encourage you to write things down and to not think too much about them. Do not try to write poems in your head—this is not *writing* poems; it is thinking poems. Allow your full imaginative process to come forth when you can actually write.

Reading

For me, the act of writing is wed to the act of reading. When I can't seem to get a groove on while writing, I read. Reading poetry re-patterns the rhythms in my mind and refocuses my attention on the craft of poetry. There are poets I turn to again and again, but I also read literary journals, magazines, new books of poetry, and essays on craft—anything to engage me in the contemplation of writing or inspire me to write. Usually it doesn't take long for me to be moved to write. Sometimes it does, and that's okay, too.

Reading is important to learning to become a good poet. It introduces you to approaches and moves that you otherwise would not have imagined or made. It introduces you to a wider world of the poetic imagination. And it introduces you to the standards of good writing. It saves you time by giving you your predecessors' experiences to build upon. Imagine trying to learn any art with no knowledge of what came before. Imagine playing the drums or piano and aiming to compose a symphony without ever having heard music or observing a musician at work, or being handed a pot and fork with the aspirations of cooking a soufflé but without ever having seen or tasted a soufflé before. We build upon the achievements of our predecessors and when you write poetry, you write on the shoulders of such poets as Walt Whitman, Emily Dickinson, and Shakespeare. You, of course, need not like all the poets you read, or agree with their writing philosophies, but it certainly helps you as a writer to be aware of them and to consider them. It helps you to learn to know your poetic self.

Activity: Begin to assemble your own anthology of poems that interest you. Either poems you enjoy or ones that puzzle you. You may include poems you do not like, too—it all adds up to your own poetic persona. How can you tell someone who you are as a poet and imaginative individual by simply allowing them to read your anthology? What poems will you pick to represent you?

When we read in this way, we say we are "reading like a writer." What's it mean to read like a writer? Well, for starters, it means we are actively reading, paying close attention to the decisions the poet made when composing and revising the poem as though we ourselves were the poet who wrote it. We consider the choices made concerning line, tone, image, diction, metaphor, form. We ask questions about its composition. Why did the poet choose this word instead of another? Why is this written in quatrains instead of couplets? Why choose to end on an image rather than a statement? Why choose to write this in third person rather than first? What does this title do for the reader's experience of the poem?

Asking questions such as these makes us think like writers rather than just readers. The hope is that we will learn some tricks to bring back to our own poems. An exercise that can help us to delve even deeper into the process of other writers is to write an imitation poem in which you mimic a poem's form and moves to create a new poem. The purpose of the exercise is to immerse yourself deeply and attentively into a poem and, following its style, produce a poem modeled after its characteristics. By unfolding a poem step by step and repeating its poetic moves you will see what it is like to actually make the mental decisions and leaps that the poet did. Some of the elements you will want to pay attention to include the following: form and line length; syntax and sentence structure; tone, voice, and mood; frequency of metaphor and images; use of punctuation.

Activity: Choose a poem you like and compose your own imitation of it. Moving line by line, note the syntax of each one—perhaps take notes in the margins—and then transcribe these moves into your own poem.

———

Now, reading need not be limited to poetry or literature. In fact, it must not be. When we write poetry we don't write about poetry (usually). We write from experiences either real or imagined and, therefore, reading books of all kinds benefits you by expanding the possibility of the experience and knowledge you bring to a poem. Personally, in addition to poetry and literature, I read cooking magazines, *National Geographic*, books about gardening, non-fiction books about many, many things—insects, salt, American history, mythology, religion, anthropology, crop circles, the topology of Montana. These feed my writing by providing me with new images, words, ideas, metaphors. Knowledge and experiences are the fuel on which our poems go.

Activity: Go to the library and find a book on a subject that interests you but that you know little about. Horses, the human brain, gemstones, Australian aborigines, astronomy, coral. Adopt this book or its language into your writing life by committing to write a poem inspired by your new knowledge.

Freewriting

In Peter Elbow's classic text on writing, *Writing Without Teachers*, the first chapter opens with an explanation of freewriting. What is freewriting? It is as it sounds. It is writing for a certain amount of time without stopping—it is writing down whatever occurs to you without being charged with having to be grammatically or syntactically or factually correct; it is writing with no barriers or taboos, it is free. Sometimes it is referred to as automatic writing and it is incredibly helpful for both loosening the imagination, warming up our writing brains, and as was the case with the Surrealists who loved such activities, freewriting allows us to capture what associations our minds are making unconsciously and bringing to light the unknown parts of ourselves.

When we freewrite we do not judge. We simply let what occurs to us in our minds come straight out to the page. If our minds go blank we may write "I cannot think of anything to write my mind is blank" and so on and forth until a new direction arises. The main point, however, is to not edit as we write—good advice for whenever we are writing anything, as writing and editing are two completely different steps in the process and should not/cannot be combined if either is to be successful. If we edit while we write we set up blockages. Rarely does any good writing take shape on a first try. As Ernest Hemingway so elegantly phrased it, "All first drafts are shit." Rather, we must work our way through ideas and words and ways of explaining and showing and revise to find the best words in the best order.

But I am already ahead of myself. Freewriting does not have to result in a poem. Rather, it is one step in the process of coming to a poem. You may do a freewrite exercise and simply feel more relaxed without any desire to sift back through what you wrote, like writing in a journal. And that's fine. As Elbow explains, if you undertake the act of freewriting frequently the practice allows you to form new habits of the mind resulting in an easier flow of words—the language will come quicker and more reliably. It is, in a sense, an exercise. Like playing scales on the piano or running sprints. Freewriting readies us for writing without judgment, for writing without editing ourselves while in the beginning stages in which wild, raw energy, uncovering connections, and risk are more important than properly constructed sentences, clarity, or cliché-free lines. To put it simply, it is a type of play.

I like to think of the results of freewriting as blocks of clay where we can shape and take whatever we want from them, or not. A block of clay may become a beautiful sculpture, but much work need be done before it emerges and is smoothed into art. So it is with our writing. You can't give up in the beginning stages or place the pressure of perfection in the beginning stages of creation. Give it time and attention and the poem will naturally evolve.

———

Activity: Choose from one of the following prompts and write for fifteen minutes without stopping or editing yourself.

Describe your ideal vacation. Where would you go? What does it look like? From a dictionary, choose two words randomly and insert them into the following sentence:
    Explaining _____ to a _____.
What did you dream about recently?
If I were any animal I'd be a _____.
Are you more like a river or a lake?

———

Moving

For some poets, it's not so much going in that helps them to write, as going out. Wallace Stevens famously composed poems in his head on his daily two-mile walks to and from work in Hartford, Connecticut, where he was employed at the Hartford Accident and Indemnity Company. It is reported that he liked to match the sounds and rhythms in his poems to his steps. Edward Hirsch shared similar feelings in a 2008 *Washington Post* article.

As he sums up, "Poetry is written from the body as well as the mind, and the rhythm and pace of a walk can get you going and keep you grounded."

In addition to keeping words in rhythm with your steps, walking is also useful for observing. Simply carry a notebook with you to collect images or ideas.

I'm not sure if this is due to the new heightened awareness to health in this country, but I know many writers who run 5Ks, 10Ks, half, and even full marathons. Maybe we naturally like to punish ourselves (writing can be so hard!) or maybe all of the oxygen in the brain is good for the imagination. Either way, creating opportunities for your mind and body to speak with one another is a proven way to inspire writing, and it's good for your health.

———

Activity: Go for a walk around your neighborhood and observe the day. What is happening outside your home? What are the neighbors doing? What is newly sprouted or drooped? Dictate what you are seeing in your mind and imagine it in rhythm with your steps. If you are a runner, do the same; go for a jog in the park. If you mutter something of interest do not be afraid to stop and jot it down.

———

Keeping a Writing Routine

There are no sure rules to being a writer, but whenever you write, it can be helpful to write at the same time and in the same way every day—even if it is only ten minutes. Like physically training your quadriceps for a marathon, routine trains us as writers to write well, to be prepared and ready to catch and develop ideas. Routine readies our mind to write.

Early Birds

When it comes to creating a routine, the poet William Stafford and many others will argue that writing in the morning is best. In his *Contemporary Authors Autobiography Series* essay Stafford explains that in the early morning hours "something is offering you a guidance available only to those undistracted by anything else." And he should know, as it is a practice he kept for over fifty years.

The morning has its advantages. It's before one is bogged down with responsibilities and also a time when the subconscious mind is closest to the conscious: upon waking. Writing in the morning might offer you deeper images and surreal subject matter.

Henry David Thoreau would also cast a vote for writing in the morning. In his book *Walden*, Thoreau praises and expounds on the high qualities of mornings and being *awake* both physically and spiritually.

Lunch Poems

In 1964, Lawrence Ferlinghetti's City Lights published Frank O'Hara's collection of poems entitled *Lunch Poems*. And as it sounds, many of the poems were composed during O'Hara's lunch hour while sitting in Times Square. Many are written in the moment and focused on events happening in the moment. The tone of the poems is conversational and easygoing. I don't think O'Hara only wrote during his lunch hour, but here it makes a point—write when you can, regularly. O'Hara built a collection of poems out of it and maybe you can too.

Another New Yorker who thrived creatively during the afternoon is Walt Whitman, who would extend his own lunch hour, taking notes as he observed the busy streets of Manhattan and all of its diversity and bustle.

———

Activity: Write your own series of lunch poems. Every day for a week, break out pen and paper or a keyboard and write a poem or notes toward a poem about what's happening around you. Describe the people and what they do. Zoom in on the scents and sounds. Recreate what you're eating on the page through language. Make your readers' mouths water. Yum!

———

Night Owls

Still, for others, it is easier to write at night, despite W. H. Auden's claim that "Only the 'Hitlers of the world' work at night; no honest artist does." And if you choose to give this a try, you will be joining Bob Dylan, Franz Kafka, and Ann Beattie. Similar to morning, the night can be quiet and solitary. The rest of the world asleep, you feel focused on your poetry, your job and responsibilities for the day done. Maybe you collect ideas throughout the day and pour them into your poems at night. It all depends on you and what works best for your schedule and for your senses—people's bodies are different and run on different schedules. For more on the issue, check out Kathryn Schulz who extrapolates on her own experience as a night owl in her essay "Writing in the Dark" originally published in *New York Magazine*.

———

Reflection: When do you find yourself writing mostly? Are you a night owl, early bird, or neither? What do you think the advantages might be to writing at these different times? Include in this discussion your professor's experience. When does he/she write and how did he/she come to do so?

———

Create a Ritual

Mason Currey's book *Daily Rituals: How Artists Work* chronicles the habits of 400 writers and their quirky rituals, many which include partaking in coffee, tea, sherry, wine, and tobacco. It is well known, but not known to what degree, that Samuel Taylor Coleridge wrote poems while on opium. The poet William Heyen lights a candle before he writes. Whatever the ritual, the purpose of it is to instill a certain mindset that arises from the act. As you may know, many athletes have rituals, too. Boston Red Sox third-basemen Wade Boggs ate chicken before each game. Among his many eccentricities, Turk Wendell insisted on chewing four pieces of black licorice whenever he pitched. According to David K. Israel, "At the end of each inning, he'd spit them out, return to the dugout, and brush his teeth, but only after taking a flying leap over the baseline." We need not be that elaborate, but of course, if it works...

Dream

When we dream, our brains make connections that our conscious mind does not make while we're awake. And sometimes these connections lead to eureka moments and new discoveries. For example, did you know that all of the following scientific discoveries were made in dreams: the periodic table; evolution by natural selection; and the scientific method? You can read about these and others at the website Famous Scientists. Or that Paul McCartney reportedly composed the melody of "Yesterday" in a dream? According to an article by Jennifer King Lindley, "Stephanie Meyer awoke from sleep with the idea for the *Twilight* series." And just imagine what effect dreams had on *The Twilight Zone* writer Rod Sterling!

Throughout human history, cultures have relied on dreams for knowledge and insight. Some Native Americans, for instance, believed that their ancestors visited them in their dreams. The Greeks and Romans believed that Gods and Goddesses visited them in their dreams. Many religions connected dreams with supernatural or divine intervention. And Sigmund Freud famously understood dreams to be an expression of our innermost desires and fears.

In recent times, scientific research and experiments have shown that while our bodies sleep, our dreaming mind sorts through the day's stimuli, not only organizing them, but developing them. In the article "While You Were Sleeping," Jennifer King Lindley explains how sleeping heals the body, enhances memory, reduces stress, and boosts creativity. Good news for poets!

John Steinbeck was right when he wrote, "It is a common experience that a problem difficult at night is resolved in the morning after the committee of sleep has worked on it." "When you dream in REM sleep, the rational control center of the brain is deactivated," says [Jessica] Payne. "This produces an amazingly creative state, and you are able to come up with ideas that you would not be able to when you are awake."

This knowledge must have been known to the group of French writers and artists who, in the 1920's, began the Surrealist Movement. Interested in turning away from logic and reason, the Surrealists turned toward the subconscious and inexplicable for content. They were interested in dreams, freewriting, random selections of images and phrases from various places that when juxtaposed would evoke a strange, unfamiliar sense of knowing that could not be explained rationally. Their work is surprising, startling, and captivating, and contemporary poetry has been very much influenced by their approaches and aesthetic. The poem "Couple" by Matthew Rohrer is a good example of a recent use of surrealistic technique. It begins: "A couple paints themselves like the sky so no one will see them." A couple painting themselves like the sky is, well, impossible in real life, but not impossible in a poem. It evokes the painting of René Magritte, himself a surrealist, and known for painting people who look like the sky. It is easy to imagine this leap of the imagination arising from a dream. Rohrer is a contemporary writer, but you can learn more about surrealism by researching writers at the roots of the movement such as André Breton, Stéphane Mallarmé, and Guillaume Apollinaire.

In addition to examining poems that use surrealistic techniques, you might consider also checking out art. One example of a piece of art that strikes me personally was crafted by Méret Oppenheim after a conversation he shared at a Paris cafe with Pablo Picasso and Dora Maar, who was wearing a bracelet covered with fur. The result was a teacup covered with gazelle fur, which is housed at the MOMA in New York. Their website is a great source for viewing surrealist and Modern art.

———

Activity: Keep a dream journal on the side of your bed and write down your dreams every morning before you rise for one week. At the end of the week, read through and select the best material to start a poem. Keep this practice up and when you need images or material, flip through your dream journal for ideas.

———

Activity: Consult a dream dictionary and look up some of the images catalogued in your dream journal. Blending the meaning and the images together, compose a poem in which a dream becomes reality.

———

WORKS CITED

"Aengus." *Wikipedia.*

"Apollo" "List of Knowledge Deities." *Wikipedia.*

"Bragi." "List of Knowledge Deities." *Wikipedia.*

Currey, Mason. *Daily Rituals: How Artists Work.* Knopf, 2013.

Elbow, Peter. *Writers Without Teachers,* 2nd ed. Oxford, 1998. 5-6.

Hirsch, Edward. "Walking with His Muse, a Poet Becomes His Own Destination." *The Washington Post.* Apr 20, 2008.

Israel, David K. "Top 10 Baseball Player Rituals." *Mental Floss.* 9 July 2009.

Lindley, Jennifer K. "While You Were Sleeping…" *Real Simple.* Aug 2014: 105-13.

Rohrer, Matthew. "The Painted Couple." *A Hummock in the Malookas.* Norton, 1995.

Samuelson, Arnold. *With Hemingway: A Year in Key West and Cuba.* Random House, 1984. p. 11.

Schulz, Kathryn. "Writing in the Dark: Confessions of a Literary Night Owl." *New York Magazine.* 3 May 2012.

The Doc. "7 Great Examples of Scientific Discoveries Made in Dreams." *Famous Scientists: The Art of Genius.*

"William E. Stafford." *Poetry Foundation.*

Jennifer Moore

FRANKENSTEIN POETICS

> *Invention... does not consist in creating out of void, but out of chaos;*
> *... [it] consists in the capacity of seizing on the capabilities of a subject, and in the power of moulding and fashioning ideas to suggest it.*
> —*Mary Shelley*

One way to think about poetry is as a practice of *construction*. Poets gather ideas, fragments, phrases, and other ephemera together to shape and transform language, a transformation that brings something new—a perspective, a way of looking—into the world. This essay explains this concept of poetic invention and provides a guide of sorts for new poets as they learn to read, think, and write. I hope to help readers better understand the art form and reflect on their own creative and constructive practices as poets.

1. Pheasant or Machine? What Poetry Is

Everything arrives from somewhere else. "I am a part of all I have met."[1] A poem is a patchwork corpus of your experiences, a voice speaking out, weaved from all the voices you've been listening to since you began to listen at all. A Frankenstein's monster of ideas, attitudes, and perspectives; the "Adam of your labours."[2]

The collage that will become your poem—and, by extension, your poetry— is an embodiment of the idea of *intertextuality*, a term that suggests relationships between and among texts throughout history. Intertextuality implies

---

1. Alfred, Lord Tennyson, "Ulysses."

2. From Mary Shelley's *Frankenstein*; one of the identifying phrases Victor gives to his creation.

interdependence, in that any text depends, in a sense, on those that have preceded it. A poem, a novel, or a song does not exist as an isolated object but as a network of quotations and references. Any text is the "absorption and transformation of another."[3]

In "The Ecstasy of Influence" Jonathan Lethem writes about this phenomenon, noting the "nostalgic" echoes between midcentury cartoons (*The Flintstones*, Rankin/Bass specials) and 90s series like *The Simpsons* and *South Park*, ultimately arguing that the latter would not exist without former. He looks at other historical "plagiarisms" when he points out the links between Shakespeare and Ovid ("Pyramus and Thisbe"), Leonard Bernstein (*West Side Story*), and T. S. Eliot ("The Waste Land"), using this network of connections to further argue that writers "find their voice" by way of other voices. He demonstrates this by folding into his own essay Mary Shelley's idea that "Invention, it must be humbly admitted, does not consist in creating out of void but out of chaos. Any artist knows these truths, no matter how deeply he or she submerges that knowing."

When you hear the echo of Shelley in Lethem, you are beginning to understand, to see the scaffolding on which all new art is built. What makes an aesthetic perspective unique is *how* it reveals the artist's idiosyncratic recombination of influences; it's the particular method or style of hybridization. As Henry James observes, "Questions of art are largely questions of execution."

So, what is a poem? We can start with etymology, the word itself. *Poeisis:* ancient Greek, "to make." To bring something into being that did not exist before. A physical construction, a building from materials; that's the *what*. The how, the craft, is called *tekne*. Bring the two together—the what and the how, *poeisis* and *tekne,* "poetic technique" as both process and product—and you have a sense of what *creation* and *creativity* might mean. Something that did not exist now does. As Dr. Frankenstein would say, "It's aliiiiive!"

But what is *it*? What does *it* look like, how does *it* act? We might take a cue from Shakespeare's *Hamlet* and think about a poem as infinite space contained in a nutshell. You are a king of this space. You build infinity in the walls of your shell, *shell* because a poem has formal boundaries, and *infinity* because "a poem [is] the act of the mind,"[4] and it exists in the minds

---

3. This phrase is found in Julia Kristeva's essay "Word, Dialogue and Novel."

4. Wallace Stevens, "Of Modern Poetry."

of readers so long as there are readers, which I will optimistically say will be for eternity.

But wait, you say, how does Hamlet's statement end? "O God, I could be bounded in a nutshell and count myself a king of infinite space, *were it not that I have bad dreams.*"[5] That's the *why* of writing; we'll get to that later.

Other *whats*: for Gaston Bachelard, the best poems create "intimate immensity";[6] an entire forest in a pine needle, a paradox of scale and emotion. William Carlos Williams says a poem is "a small (or large) machine made of words,"[7] emphasizing the *constructedness* of language, and Coleridge goes with "the best words in their best order,"[8] emphasizing selection and pattern. Viktor Shklovsky, theorizing the pictorial nature of writing, says that "poetry is thinking in images."[9] And in "Adagia," Wallace Stevens offers a collection of perspectives: "the poet is the priest of the invisible." A poem is "a pheasant disappearing in the brush." And what does the poet do? For Stevens, she transforms material: "The poet makes silk dresses out of worms."[10]

One way to think about poems is not as recollections of experiences, but experiences in and of themselves. Robert Lowell writes that a poem is not *about* an event, it *is* an event.[11] But, you say, you have been writing poems about events your whole life—isn't that what most of us do?—and you may ask, "what's the relationship between the event and its iteration on the page?" Eavan Boland asks a similar question: "So if I don't write poetry to express an experience, then why do I write it? I write it not to express the experience but to experience it further."[12]

The goal is not recollection—the goal is transformation. You're making something with your hands and your eyes and your ears. Because what are

---

5. Act II, Scene II, in conversation with Rosencrantz and Guildenstern.

6. From Chapter 8 of the mesmerizing book *The Poetics of Space.*

7. From the Introduction to *The Wedge.*

8. Coleridge places this definition in relation to that of prose, which he defines as "words in their best order."

9. "Art as Technique".

10. This curious text, featured in Stevens' *Opus Posthumous*, offers epigrammatic, lively, often enigmatic statements on the philosophy and practice of poetry.

11. This idea is discussed in David Wojahn's essay, "'On Hearing that My Poems Were Being Studied in a Distant Place': Thoughts on Distance, Difficulty, and Secret Address."

12. From Boland's excellent essay "Why I Am a Poet." Similar essays can be found in her book *Object Lessons: The Life of the Woman and the Poet in Our Time.*

we doing if not assembling fragments of a whole that never really existed in the first place?

A poem is what's possible.

2. Do I Dare/ Modify the Sahara? Why We Might Write in the First Place

> *In poetry everything is permitted. With only this condition of course; you have to improve upon the blank page.*
> —Nicanor Parra

Challenge: to create something from nothing. From chaos a voice, a thing. Novelist Thomas Berger asks, "Why do writers write? Because it isn't there."

Vincent van Gogh defies those who would dare us *not* to create: "If you hear a voice within you saying, 'You are not a painter,' then by all means paint…and that voice will be silenced, but only by working."[13]

Mary Ruefle gives us a similarly defiant perspective when she writes the following:

> It is irreverent to create that which doesn't exist; the newly made thing flies in the face of the already created and as such is based on negation (what already exists is simply not enough!), but born also out of the greatest reverence for all that already is. When Borges, visiting the Sahara, picked up a little bit of sand, carried it in his hand and let it fall someplace else, he said, "I am modifying the Sahara," and he wrote that this was one of the most significant memories of his stay. What Borges did is what we do when we write poems after millennia of poem writing. We aren't saving the Sahara, we are modifying it, and you have to be irreverent to think you can modify the Sahara in the first place, and sincere in your attempt to do so.[14]

Poetry is important for a million reasons (it creates a "twinship" between writer and reader, as Helen Vendler writes;[15] it gives us "fresh new ways of look-

---

13. Written in a letter from Drenthe, October 1883.

14. This passage is taken from her brilliant essay on irreverence and sincerity, "Kangaroo Beach," published in *Madness, Rack, and Honey.*

15. This twinship is a form of intimacy, for Vendler, partly possible because of the nature of the lyric speaker and addressee. The "I" invites the reader to take on the voice as if it were

ing at an ordinary-appearing world," as Ted Kooser writes[16]), but I find myself coming back to Wallace Stevens: art is "the imagination pressing back against the pressure of reality."[17] Allowing the imagination to "press back" against the various pains of daily existence is one way to deal with them. Ken Sherman talks about Stevens' idea of poetry as both "a shield and a sword";[18] art becomes important when we realize what we are capable of creating—on the page and in readers—and how the imagination, poetry in particular, can have an immense curative, restorative power in what is often an acutely anemic time.

You're putting your finger on the map, saying *I was here*. Writing poems is a way of shaking hands with a reader, a way of saying: *This is what it's like from my corner of the world*. A message in a bottle, a letter carried by passenger pigeon, always meant for readers, meant as a way to communicate in the here and now, and to do so after we're no longer here: *Remember me when I am gone*.

3. How to Begin: Generation, Inception, "Inspiration"

> So much has been done, exclaimed the soul of Frankenstein—
> more, far more, will I achieve; treading in the steps already
> marked, I will pioneer a new way, explore unknown powers, and
> unfold to the world the deepest mysteries of creation.
> —Mary Shelley

> You begin with the possibilities of the material.
> —Robert Rauschenberg

Art is about paying attention: to the world around you, to the fact that your perception itself colors the way you see the world around you. "Things seen are things *as seen*."[19]

When faced with a blank page: read. Read, read, read. Begin by immersing yourself in the language of others, jotting down words and phrases that stick

---

the reader's own, addressing an imagined or real "you." These pronouns create a closeness, a personal relationship, allowing us to step into the roles of speaker.

16. Kooser follows this observation by sharing a one-line poem by Joe Hutchison titled "Artichoke": "O heart weighed down by so many wings."

17. This is found in the final passage of his essay "The Noble Rider and the Sound of Words."

18. From "A Violence from Within: Poetry & Terrorism."

19. Wallace Stevens, "Adagia," *Opus Posthumous*.

with you. Read one phrase; write one phrase. Read one sentence; write one sentence. Cover the page; don't think twice. If you need a jump-start, write lists of words, A-Z. From lists come phrases; from phrases come lines, and from all of these sources you'll be doing the meta-work of thinking about relationships. How is *this* like *this*? (i.e., metaphor). Words on a page. You'll go back to them later.

Creative nonfiction author Janisse Ray visited my class a few years ago and, when asked what inspires her to write, she posed the following question: "What obsesses you?"[20] She then asked us to consider the things that turned us on, that kept us up at night, that we couldn't stop thinking about. So we wrote lists of our obsessions. A list like this might be a good place to start. (Note: if nothing obsesses you, write about that.)

But you may ask, "What about 'Write what you know?'" This is a tricky idea. It can be a helpful place to begin, but is also somewhat limiting (especially when we realize that our life experience thus far might not be all that interesting). What makes what *you* know something *everyone wants to know*, or everyone *should* know, is how you change that raw material into something electric, thrilling, imperative. So, a revision to the old adage: write *from* what you know *toward* what you don't. You have to let go of the wheel sometimes. Don't be afraid of the car that steers itself—it might discover it has wings and turn into a bird. In sum: not transcription, but *transformation*. Let it fly where it wants to; don't worry about where it lands.

4. Coal First, Diamond Later: On Drafting

One of the greatest pieces of advice on drafting comes from Anne Lamott, in a chapter from *Bird by Bird* called "Shitty First Drafts." Here the author gives "permission" to be awful:

> Almost all good writing begins with terrible first efforts. You need to start somewhere. Start by getting something— anything—down on paper. A friend of mine says that the first draft is the down draft—you just get it down. The second draft is the up draft—you fix it up. You try to say what you have to say more accurately. And the third draft is the dental, where you check every tooth, to see if it's loose or cramped or decayed, or even, God help us, healthy.[21]

---

20. Ohio Northern University, Creative Writing Workshop class visit, 2015.
21. *Bird by Bird*.

Writing is a process of sorting through the junk, but you have to write before you know what's junk and what's not. Put pen to paper before the pen can protest. You need something to work with before you can work with what you have.

In other words, coal first, diamond later. You'll get there, but you need time and perspective. "Writing a first draft is very much like watching a Polaroid develop. You can't—and, in fact, you're not supposed to—know exactly what the picture is going to look like until it's finished developing. First you just point at what has your attention and take the picture."[22]

What if your first draft feels like a failure? If your ideal poem resembles nothing like the thing on the page? Well, join the club. "My dreams were at once more fantastic and agreeable than my writings."[23] Keith Richards, lyricist and guitarist for The Rolling Stones, says writing songs is like "a jigsaw and a kaleidoscope put together except it's all through the ears."[24] Combining a jigsaw with a kaleidoscope—*process*, in other words—is part of the work of creating something innovative. Everyone starts somewhere; most of us start with failure. But it's a place to begin. You feel like a failure because you're looking at a lump of coal, or a car with wings, or a hybrid kaleidoscope-jigsaw. Welcome to the Island of Misfit Toys! Time, technique, feedback, revision: that's where the diamond comes from. And if you don't want a diamond in the first place, there are plenty of uses for coal, too.

Once you have a draft that you think might reveal something, leave it alone for a while. ("A while" is relative, and always depends on the piece itself.) Let it grow in your desk drawer. (Your head's also a desk drawer.) Then return with fresh eyes to see if what you imagined was there still is. If so, you've got something to work with. If not, back to the drafting table.

5. How to Make *Good* Art

One thing to do? Release your grip on the known and make your language strange. Hemingway says, "All our words from loose using have lost their edge."[25] This was a hundred years ago. How much loose usage has happened

---

22. Ibid.

23. Mary Shelley, Author's Introduction to *Frankenstein*.

24. Richards' claim is taken from Andrew Pettie's review of two Rolling Stones documentaries, published in *The Telegraph* (2012). The quote is followed by Pettie, writing "This struck me as the kind of insight only available to someone who has taken a lot of acid."

25. From Hemingway's nonfiction book *Death in the Afternoon*.

since then? Give your words that edge again by using them in unexpected ways. Viktor Shklovsky called this *defamiliarization*. Examples:

1) The weather fleured. They weakened all his eyes,
   And burning thumbs into his ears, and shook
   His hand like a notch. (John Berryman)[26]

2) Welcome to subverbia (Nikki Wallschlaeger)[27]

3) I willed my Keepsakes – Signed away
   What portion of me be
   Assignable – and then it was
   There interposed a Fly–

   With Blue – uncertain – stumbling Buzz –
   Between the light – and me –
   And then the Windows failed – and then
   I could not see to see – (Emily Dickinson)[28]

The snippets make the point. How does weather *fleur*? Are buzzes the color of *blue*? What and where is *subverbia*?

Effect on the reader: *Oh!* Surprise, the disarming use of language in ways other than expected. In French, this is called a *coup de foudre;* lightning, thunderbolt; love at first sight.

Then: *Yes, of course.* Such embodiment feels inevitable—that that's the *only* word that *could* work. Thrill plus recognition of the love for "all things counter, original, spare, strange."[29] Energy. Surprise. Snap-crackle-pop, then insight. The opposite? Generic, "one-size-fits-all" language. Energy gone; now we're flatlining. D.O.A. No fun.

Lucie Brock-Broido is a poet supremely skilled in defamiliarization. Take, for example, this section from her poem "At the River Unshin's Edge":

---

26. Berryman, from "Dream Song 8," *The Dream Songs.*
27. Wallschlaeger, from *Houses.*
28. Dickinson, from "I Heard a Fly Buzz."
29. Gerard Manley Hopkins, from "Pied Beauty" (*Poetry Foundation*).

Silique of mustards, briar, wrack,

Long after in the reeds of the long aftergrass.
A bastard schooner transgresses
The angelica, feverroot blisters, the hyssop
Flowers going on & on. The fireboat
Will slip its slip into the water's grave
Soliloquy. I will be drunk on it [...][30]

The final line break is evidence of the meaning-making powers of linea-
tion. See how we initially read this passage *simply* as a line?: "the water's
grave." That meaning is altered, is transformed, by what comes after it: "Solil-
oquy." What was a noun is now an adjective. Or rather, it's both. And this
doubling of meaning only happens because of that line break. These are the
moments of surprise that engage readers, that thrill us, and that you want to
think about as you revise.

Consider the following: where is the energy of your piece? How can you
illuminate it? Most important question of all: How do these writers make
such choices feel absolutely inevitable (in other words, perfectly natural and
exactly right)? Answer: imagination, practice, technique, maybe a touch of
zaniness and, above all, revision (more on that later).

Back to lively language. Mary Ruefle writes that a poem must rival a physi-
cal experience.[31] You have to make the "stone *stony*,"[32] make the words on the
page feel concrete, textural. Let them shimmer, resonate and be luminous.
Mina Loy's poem "Gertrude Stein" is a love letter to a poet who does just that:

Curie
of the laboratory
of vocabulary
she crushed
the tonnage
of consciousness
congealed to phrases

---

30. From *The Master Letters*.

31. From her title essay "Madness, Rack, and Honey."

32. Viktor Shklovsky, from "Art as Technique."

to extract
a radium of the word[33]

Tall order, I know. But don't despair: defamiliarization can't be the norm. It has to be the exception in order to work well. In other words, you can't jam a poem full of these kinds of oddities; you have to spread them out across poems. Balance is key. Yeats refers to "the numb line"—lines in poems that don't do anything particularly remarkable except create time and space between the zingers.[34] A poem can't be all zingers; numb lines are the tightrope you're walking on. You can't be a magician 100% of the time. A surprise is only a surprise if it surprises you.

6. Notes on Workshop

> Every real poem is the breaking of an existing silence, and the
> first question we might ask any poem is, What kind of voice is
> breaking silence, and what kind of silence is being broken?
> —Adrienne Rich

Workshopping can be a key element of poetic process, an essential step that brings excitement, perhaps some anxiety, and likely, frustration. This is because for the first time in its life, a new poem has *readers*.

Remember, first, that you want feedback on the gem, not the junk. Bring your absolute best to the table. Remember, too, that we all have an ideal reader, but the folks we sit down with in the classroom might not resemble that reader in the least. We can have an ideal, but at the end of the day, real people reading our work is what we want and what we get. "We are unfashioned creatures."[35] Give your peers your best, and they should give you theirs.

An ideal reader of poetry, though, is one who is, as Wallace Stevens writes, "susceptible to imaginative or emotional meanings" rather than "rational meanings."[36] We need to *read* most poems with an ear and a heart for their

---

33. From *The Lost Lunar Baedeker*, ed. Roger Conover.

34. This idea has been rolling around in my head since my undergraduate years, never having known from which source it sprung. I've traced a version of this idea to the introduction to Thomas Hornsby Ferrill's book *Westering*, written by John Williams. He writes that Yeats' "numb line," through its emotional and rhetorical "neutrality," is able to intensify the surrounding material, creating resonances it otherwise would not have.

35. From Mary Shelley, *Frankenstein*.

36. From his essay "Poetry and Meaning," *Opus Posthumous*.

imaginative, rather than rational, significance. This can guide the kinds of questions we ask of the pieces brought to us. When rational questions are asked of imaginative pieces—"But was it *really* 1976?"; "How could a car without wings fly in the first place?"—we might remember our ideal reader, or we might point our actual reader to Stevens, or to Mary Shelley's character Robert Walton, who has "a love for the marvellous, a belief in the marvellous."[37]

One thing poets like from any reader, ideal *or* real, is for them to meet the poem on its own terms, then ask how it can achieve its most fully realized form. This requires that we resist trying to explain what a piece means and instead ask how it's doing what it's doing in the first place. Susan Sontag writes about this in "Against Interpretation":

> Real art has the capacity to make us nervous. By reducing the work of art to its content and then interpreting that, one tames the work of art.
>
> Interpretation...violates art. It makes art into an article for use, for arrangement into a mental scheme of categories.... The aim of all commentary on art now should be to make works of art—and by analogy, our own experience—more, rather than less, real to us. The function of criticism should be to show *how it is what it is*, even *that it is what it is*, rather than to show *what it means*.[38]

Such a stance should be our goal as workshop participants: to describe what we see, describe what we hear, then discuss how the poem does what it does. None of this involves "interpreting" "meaning," and all of it (well, our *hope* is that *most* of it) will be illuminating to the writer. They are seeing their poem through your eyes; they then have the opportunity to maintain, clarify, or alter that vision (through re-vision).

A word on drafts themselves: too many novice poets make the mistake of giving readers a "down draft" in workshop, which is to say they have not yet cleared the brush away from the field. Tessa Mellas once talked about reading drafts littered with proofreading and grammatical errors as analogous to watching a TV show on a snowy channel: you can't see the picture through the blizzard.[39] We want to see the program; all we see is fuzz. If you give a

---

37. From Mary Shelley, *Frankenstein*.

38. Originally published in 1966.

39. Ohio Northern University, Creative Writing Workshop class visit, 2013. I revisited

draft to your peers which hasn't been read through—out loud, by you, many times—then cleanly presented, your readers will only zero in on the errors. "Did you mean to type *friend* instead of *frond*?" "I think you're missing a verb in this sentence." "The sisters misses teh Father?"

There's a certain amount of pride we carry with us into a workshop, and a whole lot of vulnerability, and you want to make yourself as invulnerable as possible to that which you *can* control: clarity, accuracy, precision in terms of grammar, punctuation, and proofreading. After you've got that down, you get to have fun. "Every English poet should...master the rules of grammar before he attempts to bend or break them."[40]

A few other things to look for in drafts:

a) Pattern and variation. Where and how is the writer creating these structures, and to what end?

b) The "diction universe" of the poem (a term from Anne Winters). Are there any words that feel so out of left field that they throw off the balance of the poem's universe? Do we want Astroturf in the middle of a meadow? Maybe, maybe not. What kind of universe are we in in the first place?

c) A helpful exercise from Elizabeth Robinson: try to identify the beating heart of the poem by isolating one line, one phrase, or one moment that the rest of the poem seems to revolve around or point toward. Then ask, "How does everything else work to illuminate that core moment?" If workshop members share, out loud, what they think this is, it can help the writer to understand perspective and focus, and give a starting point to the revision process.

If after a workshop session you feel drained of motivation, discouraged by surface reading or misreading, or commentary that's more critical than reflective, understand first that feeling drained is normal; it's part of the

---

Tessa's reading recommendation from this talk, David Michael Kaplan's *Revision: A Creative Approach to Writing and Rewriting Fiction*, and in the chapter titled "Revising Your Prose for Power and Punch," he writes that when you "fine-tune" your work, you omit any "glitches" that make the reader aware of the text on the page rather than the world being created. He illustrates this by developing the metaphor of the snowy TV channel: a bit of interference won't disturb your engagement with a show, but the more visual hiccups there are, the more distracted you become, and the more willing you are to simply turn the TV off.

40. Robert Graves in a lecture at Oxford as quoted in *Time* (15 December 1961).

process. Then, think of Susan Sontag: a goal for eventual revision might be "to put silence into poems and to reinstate the magic of the word."[41]

7. Re-visioning Revision: What Now?
It is perfectly okay to write garbage—as long as you edit brilliantly.
—*C. J. Cherryh*

Revision is a fundamental, foundational reconsideration of the original piece. As Adrienne Rich describes it, "Re-vision—[is] the act of looking back, of seeing with fresh eyes, of entering an old text from a new critical direction."[42] For some writers, the real generative fire happens at this stage. You get to play with the Play-Doh, tinker with the toys, make the sparks fly. For Laura van den Berg, "Revision is an invitation to return to an experimental space."[43]

This might frighten or destabilize you. For some novice poets, drafting is a process that moves one closer and closer to a finished thing, and a finished thing is a sign of accomplishment, an endpoint; *Voila!*: an opportunity to go do something else. "One of the biggest challenges in revision can be to escape the limitations we have constructed for ourselves in drafting."[44] Of course, we all want to feel as if what we've done is good enough, especially if our workshop peers were heaping praise on us. But if what you want is a *good* thing, this is the time to throw the recipe out the window and leave your original intention behind. And rewriting means trying out different ingredients.

One way to do this is to go back to the drawing board and start from square one, A-Z lists, a phrase on a page, that sort of thing. "The conscious application of technique—exercises, retyping, etc.—might feel mechanical at times, but the path to unconscious, spontaneous discovery (i.e., inspiration) is often built, in part, by conscious labor."[45] Inspiration doesn't arrive as a

---

41. *Against Interpretation.*

42. This passage is taken from Rich's essay "When We Dead Awaken: Writing as Re-Vision", a foundational essay for feminist literary criticism.

43. Fiction writer Laura van den Berg, tweeting @Lvandenberg, offered this insight and contextualized it with the following: "Last 2 weeks of classes have arrived! Here is an excerpt from one of my revision handouts (in which I challenged myself to list what I believe to be true about revision)" (29 November 2017).

44. Tweet, Laura van den Berg.

45. Tweet, Laura van den Berg

bird on your shoulder trilling the perfect song; you can only get that flash of insight if you sit down and do the work. It's *through* the labor we find what we didn't know we were looking for.

Mary Karr offers fantastic insights on the value of revision. In a Facebook post from a few years ago, she writes:

> Could Carmelo land a jump shot or Beethoven compose a symphony without thousands of hours at their separate enterprises? Vain, futile hours, they may seem to be. If you're uncomfortable, and you feel like you're failing, that means you're running with the big dogs. Discomfort = making hard choices.
>
> The answer is revision. Every great writer I've ever read starts dumb and refines it. (Teaching drafts of Yeats and Eliot this term, I thrill at how shitty many are.) "You ask the secret. It has just one name: again." Miroslav Holub[46]

The secret is there is no secret. It's sitting down, working and reworking, writing and rewriting. Gem from junk. Practice begets precision begets expertise. The more you write, the more you'll become a writer.

8. Why Keep Writing?

I used to think I wrote because there was something I wanted to say. Then I thought, "I will continue to write because I have not yet said what I wanted to say"; but I know now I continue to write because I have not yet heard what I have been listening to.
—Mary Ruefle

We've reached the end of our journey. We are in the Arctic Ocean and the icebergs are looming. What's that on the landscape? A figure, lurching. That figure is your ideal reader (or your possible poem, or both). Joan Houlihan says that we're looking for someone who "wants to be at least as engaged in a poem as in a successful magic act."

Are we looking for an audience? If so, what *is* an audience? Someone who listens, who pays attention. Ask yourself, Who are you writing for? You might

---

46. Mary Karr, Facebook post, 26 September 2014.

say, "I write for myself and strangers."[47] You might only write for yourself. You might only write for others. That's up to you. But if you're looking to publish your work, you might be faced with that initial question again: *What am I doing in the first place?* Again, join the club: "Very few writers really know what they are doing until they've done it."[48]

So now what? "The libraries of the world are thrown open to me—and in any port, I can renew my stock."[49] Reading and writing are infinite experiences. The world's an open library, containing too much to even contemplate absorbing. As readers, we're fortunate to have so many choices; as writers, we're fortunate to be able to do so in the first place. As a poet you get to create your own library, your own universe full of stars and silences and individuals to comprehend it all—you're building the world of the speaker. Look: *It's alive.* What wasn't in existence now is. And it's a marvellous thing to behold.

WORKS CITED

Bachelard, Gaston. "Intimate Immensity." *The Poetics of Space.* Boston: Beacon Press, 1994. 183-210.

Berryman, John. *The Dream Songs.* 1964. New York: Farrar, Straus and Giroux, 2000.

Boland, Eavan. "Why I am a Poet." Laois Education Centre archive.

Brock-Broido, Lucie. *The Master Letters.* New York: Knopf, 1995.

Coleridge, Samuel Taylor. *Familiar Quotations,* 10th ed., Ed. John Bartlett. 1919. Bartelby.com.

Dickinson, Emily. "I heard a fly buzz when I died." *The Poems of Emily Dickinson: Reading Edition,* ed. Ralph W. Franklin. Cambridge: The Belknap Press of Harvard University Press, 1998, 265-6.

Graves, Robert. "Quotes." Wikiquote. 10 May 2017.

Hemingway, Ernest. *Death in the Afternoon.* 1932. New York: Scribner, 1996.

Hopkins, Gerard Manley. "Pied Beauty." *Poetry Foundation.*

Houlihan, Joan. "Joan Houlihan and the Role of the Poet-Critic." Interview by Garrick Davis, *Contemporary Poetry Review,* 24 September 2012.

---

47. Gertrude Stein, *The Making of Americans.*

48. Anne Lamott, *Bird by Bird.*

49. Mary Shelley, *The Last Man.*

Karr, Mary. "Post." *Facebook*, 26 September 2014, 9:44 am.

Kooser, Ted. "A voice from the heartland." *The Baltimore Sun*, 5 September 2004.

Kristeva, Julia. "Word, Dialogue and Novel." *The Kristeva Reader*, ed. Toril Moi. New York: Columbia UP, 1986. 34-61.

Lamott, Anne. *Bird by Bird: Some Instructions on Writing and Life*. New York: Anchor, 1995.

Lethem, Jonathan. "The Ecstasy of Influence: A Plagiarism." *Harper's Magazine*, February 2007.

Loy, Mina. "Gertrude Stein." *The Lost Lunar Baedeker*, ed. Roger Conover. New York: Farrar, Straus and Giroux, 1997. 94.

Pettie, Andrew. "Rolling Stones: Crossfire Hurricane and Rolling Stones: Charlie Is My Darling, BBC Two." Review, *The Telegraph*, 26 November 2012.

Ray, Janisse. Personal interview. 11 February 2015.

Rich, Adrienne. "When We Dead Awaken: Writing as Re-Vision." *College English* 34.1 (October 1972): 18-30.

Ruefle, Mary. *Madness, Rack, and Honey*. Seattle: Wave Books, 2012.

Shakespeare, William. *Hamlet*. 1603. New York: Simon & Schuster, 2012.

Shelley, Mary. *Frankenstein*. 1818. New York: Bantam, 1991.

——. *The Last Man*. 1826. London: Wordsworth Classics, 2004.

Sherman, Ken. "A Violence from Within: Poetry & Terrorism." *AGNI Online*. 2004.

Shklovsky, Viktor. "Art as Technique." *Literary Theory: An Anthology* Vol. 2. Eds. Julie Rivkin and Michael Ryan. Malden, MA: Blackwell, 2004. 15-21.

Sontag, Susan. "Against Interpretation." 1966. *Against Interpretation and Other Essays*. New York: Picador, 2001. 3-14.

Stein, Gertrude. *The Making of Americans*. 1925. Champaign, IL: Dalkey Archives, 1995.

Stevens, Wallace. "Adagia." *Opus Posthumous: Poems, Plays, Prose*. New York: Vintage, 1990. 184-202.

——. "Poetry and Meaning." *Opus Posthumous: Poems, Plays, Prose*. New York: Vintage, 1990. 249.

——. "Of Modern Poetry." *The Collected Poems*. New York: Vintage, 1982. 239-240.

——. "The Noble Rider and the Sound of Words." *The Necessary Angel: Essays on Reality and the Imagination*. New York: Vintage, 1965. 3-36.

@Lvandenberg (Laura van den Berg). "1. Revision is an invitation to return to an experimental space." *Twitter*, 29 November 2017, 4:03 am.

@Lvandenberg (Laura van den Berg). "3. One of the biggest challenges in revision can be to escape the limitations we have constructed for ourselves in drafting." *Twitter,* 29 November 2017, 4:04 am.

@Lvandenberg (Laura van den Berg). "2. The conscious application of technique—exercises, retyping, etc.—might feel mechanical at times, but the path to unconscious, spontaneous discovery (i.e., inspiration) is often built, in part, by conscious labor." *Twitter,* 29 November 2017, 4:03 am.

Van Gogh, Vincent. "Quotes of Vincent Van Gogh." Wikiquote. 5 December 2017.

Vendler, Helen. *Poems, Poets, Poetry: An Introduction and Anthology.* 2nd ed. Boston: Bedford/St. Martin's, 2002.

Wallschlaeger, Nikki. *Houses.* Providence, RI: Horse Less Press, 2015.

Williams, William Carlos. "Introduction." *The Wedge.* 1944. The Poetry Foundation. 13 October 2009.

Wojahn, David. "'On Hearing that My Poems Were Being Studied in a Distant Place': Thoughts on Distance, Difficulty, and Secret Address." *Blackbird* 15.1 (Spring 2016).

Michael Angel Martín

WHAT IS A POEM? NOT SURE. BUT LET ME COUNT THE WAYS

One of the best lessons I have learned as a writer of poems is to know when to stop asking what a poem is. Trying to find the definition of "poem" inevitably fails as an intellectual pursuit because of the nature of language and definition. Literary theorists of all stripes have at least offered one sure piece of wisdom: to define anything requires words borrowed from other definitions made up of words ad infinitum. Although there are different names for this theory and different implications coming from different philosophers, you need only flip through a dictionary to see its truth. Because poems—and this is not a definition—are human monuments to the humanity of human language, one can begin to see that poems are better defined in the practice of poetry. Any ruminative pursuit about what poetry is will only lead us back to poetic language.

As helpless as it sounds, it is no less imperative to ask what a poem is. Every poet knows this imperative as soon as they sit at the desk to write a poem. Is this idea, this color, this cadence, line, metaphor, this musical itch I have to write on a page the stuff of a poem? At that point, the poet goes into the far reaches of their poetic tradition as imputed into the recesses of their mind for a working set of concepts—none definitive—to help them turn their strange linguistic urge into a poem. Looking back at how poems have been defined before, both in theory and in practice, helps the poet make their contribution either in deviation from or within the permeable boundaries of poetic tradition.

One sure way to look back to the tradition for key ideas about poetry is looking to the origins of a language itself. As a writer of poetry in English, it is useful to look far back to its elastic and absorptive origins. For now, I can offer a brief, grossly simplified, linguistic history: English began as an Indo-European language of West Germanic descent, or what is also called Low German. Because it was spoken by the Angle and Saxon tribes, the language became known and was characterized by hard, heavily accented monosyllabic Germanic words. This was spoken in what became England until the Norman Invasion of 1066, which introduced Old French, a Romance language with multisyllabic words, to Anglo-Saxon, and resulted in what we now know as Old English. The marriage of disparate linguistic origins (the Low Germanic with the Latinate Old French) resulted in the English we speak today, which possesses the largest vocabulary in the world. The sonic characteristics of each linguistic root is classed so that the hard, monosyllabic Anglo-Saxon words that remained were mostly ascribed to the conquered vocabulary of animal raising while the multisyllabic words of the Old French were ascribed to the sovereign positions and spaces of the conquerors. In modern English, the connotative differences can be heard when comparing Germanic words like "pig," "cow," and "sheep" to the French-rooted "chamber" or "cuisine."

Readers probably already knows this, but humor me: the dynamic of Old English can be seen and heard in what might be considered the epic ur-poem of the tongue, *Beowulf.* The poetry in *Beowulf* is deeply rooted in tribal Nordic tradition. These tribes would pass on stories, histories, and legends about who they were for future generations to the accompaniment of a drum. This tradition accounts for the alliterative and accentual constraints of the verse in *Beowulf.* The metric elements of each line mimic drumming by emphasizing two alliterative stressed syllables on each side of a caesura. The drum banged as the poem was recited. Unlike the quantitative constraints developed by Greek poets which measured the length of a syllable, Anglo-Saxon poetry lent itself more to the measurement of syllable accent or stress. After many centuries, modern English poets developed a system accentual-syllabic meter that measured the differences in accentual stress and the number of syllables to make up the line. Understanding how the poetic line as a musical intuition developed in English is a helpful point of entry for the poet asking what a poem is.

In *The Poem's Heartbeat,* poet Alfred Corn considers prosody, "the art or study of versification," as key to what makes a poem itself. In Corn's estimation, a poem's ability to transmit music and meaning through measurable systems of line and meter is not only intrinsically tied to its aesthetic value, but to what makes it a poem at all. Although there is some obvious truth to this notion, Corn's model accounts for only some of the poetry written in the language and only a small amount of how poetry is practiced. For instance, Alfred Corn cannot explain free verse, which does away with the systems of versification he considers necessary to make a poem. Corn seems unable to accept that a poem without a formal set of rules is also beholden to the mechanics of line and form, the results of which, in his theory, distinguishes prose from poetry.

The limitations of this model are most embarrassing when Corn begins to scan Walt Whitman with a persistence and desperation that only lets Whitman's lines burst from any models of analysis that are not sensitive to his deviation from formal expectations or his particular influences. It is no surprise that Corn is baffled by the prose poem, too, which he is sure to place under scare quotes, and even dismiss an explanation for altogether. Parenthetically, he writes, "prose poems" must "deploy special syntactic energies in order to charge their texts with the rhythmic intensity associated with poetry." How this is not also true of poetry at large is not at all clear, but Corn's insistence on the intrinsic value of and defining characteristics of rather accidental metrical and formal constraints for poetry in English would even mystify the masters of the tradition. It is no wonder Leftist poetic theorists, for all their sophistry, believe New Formalist poetry is the linguistic tool shed for Fascism!

William Wordsworth could probably not have imagined a poem without the formal constraints Alfred Corn clutched away from anarchy centuries after, and yet he had a more populist approach. In his preface to *Lyrical Ballads*, Wordsworth preemptively defends himself against charges that would question his poetry—the new lyric of Romanticism—to readers accustomed to Shakespeare, Dryden, and Pope. He even goes so far as to defend the right of his poems as poetry, imagining people who "would look round for poetry, and be induced to inquire by what species of courtesy these attempts can be permitted to assume the title." Unlike Alfred Corn two hundred years later, the problem for Wordsworth's potential critics was not a result of deviating from the metrical norms of English poetry preceding Romanticism, but "prosaisms" of subject matter and common language.

"If in a poem there should be found a series of lines," Wordsworth writes, "in which the language, though naturally arranged and according to the strict laws of metre, does not differ from that of prose" so that the critic is tempted to "exult over the Poet as over a man ignorant of his own profession," then the critic needs to challenge the definition of poetry. Wordsworth defends a "language really used by men; and at the same time, to throw over them a certain colouring of the imagination, whereby ordinary things should be presented to the mind in an unusual way." As a contemporary reader, it is not clear to me how Wordsworth commits "prosaisms" at all. The *Lyrical Ballads* contribute to elements that make up a still prevalent theory of the poet's subjectivity since Romanticism, so our ears hear no surprise. Still, it is telling how much more rooted in the mystery of poetry Wordsworth's "spontaneous overflow of powerful feelings" are than Alfred Corn's technical tests.

In Wordsworth's long lyric *Lines Composed a Few Miles Above Tintern Abbey, On Revisiting the Banks of the Wye During a Tour, July 13, 1798*, readers are able to see the subjectivity of the Romantic poet at work. As the title suggests, the speaker is revisiting the banks of the Wye, where he beholds once again "steep and lofty cliffs, / That on a wild secluded scene impress / Thoughts of more deep seclusion [...]" These thoughts are wrapped in the descriptions of his surroundings that follow, as well as his memory of the place, each of which display the working of the poet's mind in his given circumstances. The "beauteous forms," for instance, are rendered more deeply by having also been in memory:

> But oft, in lonely rooms, and 'mid the din
> Of towns and cities, I have owed to them
> In hours of weariness, sensations sweet,
> Felt in the blood, and felt along the heart;
> And passing even into my purer mind [...]

The poem displays the poet's mind working to make sense of his surroundings and his memory. At the same time, the poet presents philosophical intuitions within the confines of the poem as well: "A motion and a spirit, that impels / All thinking things, all objects of all thought, / And rolls through all things [...]"

With Romanticism, lyric poetry continues to include a description of the mind's process. The poet registers their world as a phenomenon of perception, memory, intellect, and emotion. Such a posture has become an indispensable part of poetry in English. Even if poets today have moved away from the explicit spiritual or philosophical conclusions of the English Romantics, most lyric poetry derives from the Romantic "blessed mood, / In which the burthen of mystery, / In which the heavy and the weary weight / Of all this unintelligible world, Is lighted [..]," as Wordsworth puts it in *Tintern Abbey*. In poetry workshops we always consider the speaker in a world. The dynamic between the two poles are put to language and are crafted into a lyric poem: The processes of intellect, perception, memory, and emotion in a poem, "[..] The mighty world / Of eye, and ear,—both what they half create, And what perceive [...]," as Wordsworth writes, have become the established ground from which lyric poetry springs.

Our current exploration into the definition of a poem is limited to the poetic tradition in English. This means the poem has derived most of its identity from the mechanics of a line, the interplay between meaning and music, and the subjectivity of the poet. Still, Europe alone has had entirely competing views about what a poem is that may or may not include some of the features discussed so far, or else have entirely new views. It is useful now to engage an entirely different paradigm. Poets have since incorporated ideas from different poetic traditions. Poets today especially have no compelling reason to think about poetry in their tradition alone. In spite of some dramatic differences, poetry in other cultures is no less recognizable. How can we know it is a poem at all if it operates under an entirely different paradigm about what a poem is? And yet we do. If poets remove themselves from their own tradition, they may begin to glimpse more crisply the elusive definition of what a poem is. One sure way is to risk shifting our focus to the east and explore haiku in comparison to the poetic tradition in English and how it has also influenced contemporary poetry.

I know my resource for discussing haiku is limited by translation and one contemporary westerner's particular scholarship, but I still believe it's useful. In his introduction to *The Essential Haiku*, Robert Hass explains how the form emerged out of the many kinds of linked verse practiced in Japan. Like much of Japan's classical poetry, the Haiku began with special attention to time and place, and most especially with the seasons of the year. The challenge from the start was to create an image so exact as to capture the spirit of the season in a place. The exactitude of image from common life also demanded a plainness of language. Basho, the oldest of the three masters Hass translates in this anthology, insisted poetry was a serious calling. He spent the majority of his life thinking about how to give resonance to the image and produced thousands of Haiku in his search. These images transmit a kind of mood that speaks to the transience of a life's moment in the world through time.

This insistence on time and place given over to a mood may not seem all that dissimilar to how poetry is written in English at first, especially in a time when the influence of haiku is taken for granted. As explained before, English poets since at least the Romantic period have left poets with a subjective rhetorical posture from which poetry emerges. Wordsworth even very directly calls this a "mood." As Hass writes, "When Wordsworth or Keats writes about being in 'pensive or wayward mood,' you know that they're doing one of the jobs of the artist, trying to assimilate psychological states for which the official culture didn't have a language."

The key difference is that Japan has a common language for the mood of transience that the haiku memorializes. When readers contemporary to the masters of haiku encountered a poem, they were not so much given a musical explanation of a poet's unique experience or a description of a poet's emotional or mental process—intuitions examined and conclusions about the world reached or pushed into further mystery; rather, the reader was called back to a common thought about the transience of things. "Swirling petals, falling leaves," Hass says, is more than a thought of poetry found in the mind of the individual poet, but rather a foundational "religious thought." The common seasonal reference in haiku—or a *kigo*—is not a universal in the Western sense. Instead, it is an anchor to the mystery of a single moment recorded for all of its impermanence. The haiku was thought incomplete without one because it is meant to connect to "a sense of exposure to the elements," as Hass puts it.

Because the seasonal references in the *kigo* were conventional and widely understood to most people in Japan, they, Hass says, "gave a powerful sense of a human place in the ritual and cyclical movement of the world." This is not to say the human individual was in any way central to the poetic enterprise as it is in the English tradition, as we see with Wordsworth earlier. For comparison, it is helpful to say that the "thought" behind a haiku's experience in nature is a Buddhist one and not of the Judeo-Christian origins audible in Wordsworth's "A motion and a spirit, that impels / All thinking things, all objects of all thought." Hass again:

At the core of Buddhist metaphysics are three ideas about natural things: that they are transient; that they are contingent; and that they suffer. Though the melancholy of autumn [for example] is as traditional an experience in European poetry as it is in Japanese, it is not fundamentally assimilated into the European system of thought.

There is no supernatural creator in this particular strand of Buddhist cosmology like those implied by the transcendental reveries of the English Romantics, no arbiter of meaning. In Wordsworth, nature reveals something more than itself and locates meaning elsewhere, which the poet transcribes. For the haiku meaning is beside the point.

The *kigo*, again, is a universal notion that anchors the human as a part of natural processes, but the crux of the haiku is actually in the uniqueness of "the moment seized on and rendered purely," as Hass says. This means that couched in traditional ideas about the seasons, the haiku gains its power not from the generalized image, but with their exactitude. The generalized image can only serve as a rhetorical or explanatory tool—analogy, metaphor, metonymy, etc.—each of which has its mysterious place in our European poetic tradition; the haiku has a different mystery in mind. As an example, let us look into a Basho haiku with a *kigo* that comes through clearly in translation:

> The crane's legs
> have gotten shorter
> in the spring rain.

The universal notion which the reader of haiku would be familiar with is most likely "in the spring rain." The precise record of perception and natural phenomena, however, is the crane's legs submerged in water. This brief image not only tells us of an individual crane in a single moment, but also transmits a phenomena of perception. Obviously, the crane's legs have not literally gotten shorter, but are being perceived as such. The image is reduced to phenomenology, recorded as it appears to Basho without any explanatory or mental interference on the part of the poet. To say the crane's legs have not literally gotten shorter is not the same thing as saying they have gotten shorter figuratively. The mystery of the poem is in that difference.

In some ways, the definition of what a poem is in the paradigm of haiku is even more elusive than when we looked for possible clues in the history of poetry in English. The haiku has its power in elusiveness itself, which has not only codified in its poetry for centuries, but in the religious traditions from which the form takes its cues as well. In either case, we have not even gotten close to probing all of the ways poetry has taken form and complicated any of the notions introduced in this perfunctory survey.

Any conceptual model or frame one devises to help define a poem is quickly precluded by another form or cultural experience of poetry. What about the poet writing in English today? If not metrics, then at least line and form as tools for meaning and music have, since our linguistic origins, continued to fuel our poems. Likewise, the subjectivity of the poet, which we inherit from the Romantics, remains the rhetorical posture of the lyric poem especially. Even in the case of this essay—which uses different conceptual models provided by poetry written in English followed by the haiku as a counterpoint—is rendered silent when considering contemporary poetry. Depending on the particular lineage or school a poet finds themselves called by, one poetic resource is privileged over another, but the image has surely become central. Any essay chasing a definition of "poem" would probably only have probed itself into either a poem or white space.

Some Essentials of Poetry

David M. Harris

SOME ESSENTIALS OF POETRY

Many people decide—usually in the first two years of high school—that they are going to be poets. A small portion of them goes on to write some poetry. Most of those never go on to write anything that is of any interest outside of a small circle of friends. These people dream of being poets in about the same way that I dreamed of being a pitcher for the New York Yankees: concentrating on the being, not the doing. Frankly, I'm not nearly as interested in people who want to be poets as I am in people who want to write poetry.

Any working writer has had countless encounters of the "I've always wanted to write a novel/screenplay/poetry collection" variety. And I've always wanted to play for the Yankees, or litigate a case in the Supreme Court, except that I haven't been prepared to do what is necessary to get there. There may be a gift for poetry which some people have and others don't, but great, or even good, poetry doesn't come from just spilling your emotions onto the page as you did in high school.

Part of the job of poetry is making the right decisions, and part of it is learning what you need to know before you can be a good artist. And part of it, of course, is just practice. Malcolm Gladwell said that it takes 10,000 hours of practice to make you an expert in anything. Gladwell is only right if your practice is directed intelligently. If you just keep practicing your scales for 10,000 hours, you still won't be an expert pianist. You have to deal with other essential issues as well.

So here, in no particular order, are some of the essential issues you have to deal with if you want to be a working poet.

Purpose

Decide why you are writing poetry. If it is for your own private purpose, such as therapy, then all the rest of this is irrelevant. All you need to do is go through the process of writing and get your work on paper. If you want other people to read it—that is, for it to be published—then you have to start worrying about craft. I'll mention a few useful books as we go along. But if you aren't interested in publishing, your job is finished when your last word is written.

And if you want to get published, it helps if you have some good idea of why you want that and what you expect from it. If you expect wealth and fame, you can find the name of a therapist in the Yellow Pages. Fame and fortune aren't part of poetry, unless you're a dying child, a movie star, or Billy Collins. My publisher told me that she would be thrilled if my book sold two hundred copies. So far, it hasn't.

Do you just think it would be cool to see your name in print, or do you feel you have something to say, or are you going to write no matter what and you might as well try to share what you produce?

This actually goes to the core of your relationship with writing. Before you can really produce what you want, you must know what you want. As obvious as this may sound, many new writers just start putting words on the page, or on the computer screen, without the slightest idea of their real intentions other than "to be a writer." It may be true, as Red Smith is reported to have said, that "You simply sit down at the typewriter, open your veins, and bleed" but even that only works if you have some idea what you are trying to write, and some idea of how to manipulate the words to get there. Starting to write and hoping for inspiration is the fast road to bad poetry.

If all you want is to see your name in print, you are fortunate to live in the age of self-publishing and blogs (which are, after all, online self-publishing). You can post your work and send links to your friends, or have a few copies printed and hand them to friends and families, without worrying about the intermediation of an editor.

Other people, of course, want the validation that comes from an editor's selection, and the somewhat greater visibility that goes with an established journal, whether in electronic or dead tree form. What you want will determine how you choose to present your work to the world.

None of these choices is intrinsically better or worse than any other. They suit different people differently. But you should know what your choice is, so you can act on it.

Form

Not all poems need to have rhyme or meter or a classical structure, but why not have these tools in your kit? You may come up with an idea that would benefit from being cast in sonnet form, or kyrielle, or sestina, and you can't take advantage of that if you don't know those forms and what they're good for.

There are two arguments against knowing the forms. The first is that they're old-fashioned. This works only if the people in the argument haven't read the New Formalists (Mark Jarman, Molly Peacock, Dana Gioia, Marilyn Hacker, Elizabeth Alexander, Andrew Hudgins, and many more), who are writing excellent formal poetry right now, as you read this.

The second argument is that it's much harder to write formal poetry than free verse. This one is true. But it's valid only if you think poetry is supposed to be easy. Good poetry is only very rarely easy.

The truth is that the traditional forms of poetry—or even new, invented ones—aren't really all that hard. Mostly, all they take is work and practice, and the practice can be fun. I worked my way through Stephen Fry's *The Ode Less Traveled*, which is informative and witty (this is the same Fry from *Peter's Friends* or the BBC *Jeeves and Wooster* programs) and came out with a notebook of formally correct but mostly uninspired verse and a few ideas—and the skill to use meter, at least, when a poem needs it. I'm still weak on rhyme. (I can make the lines rhyme, but not in an interesting way.) But I can recognize most of the standard forms when I run into them, and I have at least a rough idea of when I might want to try one of them.

For example, if you want to write a love poem, or something that plays against the idea of a love poem, a sonnet is an interesting form to try, since it began as a form dedicated to love poetry. Edna St. Vincent Millay made good use of this in sonnets such as "I, being born a woman and distressed." (Many sonnets are known by their first lines.)

Forms with repetitions, such as villanelles and pantoums and, to some extent, sestinas, can echo how our minds return to ideas or phrases, sometimes transforming them through repetition. Theodore Roethke's "The Waking" is a particularly fine example of the villanelle, in which he makes use of some slight variations on the form. You can also make variations, but you must understand the form before you can play with it.

Each form has a history and a function. They aren't arbitrary, except for a few of the more recently invented ones. Forms call on you to respond to them, to stretch yourself into new skills and new ideas. Looking for the right word to fit the meter or rhyme of a formal poem can lead you off into an unexpected direction, and as a poet you should be open to accident.

And you don't have to write every poem in a received form. You can write some free verse, some blank verse, and some strict forms. Most of my own work is free verse, but some of my best, and best-received, poems have been in forms.

Now, there are some people who argue that any piece of text that doesn't have meter and rhyme isn't poetry. They're just as mistaken as those who think that formal poetry is only for the fogies. The battle against free verse was lost long ago, arguably with the publication of *Leaves of Grass* and certainly no later than the Imagists, about a century ago.

A good reference book on formal poetry is *The Book of Forms*, by Lewis Turco. Miller Williams's *Patterns of Poetry* is also fine.

Work

At the beginning, I referred to the *job* of poetry. Like any art, and the sciences, it involves imagination and hard work. You remember what Edison said: "Genius is one percent inspiration and ninety-nine percent perspiration." Don't lose track of that ratio.

Over my desk I have a quotation from the painter Chuck Close: "Inspiration is for amateurs. The rest of us just show up for work." Under that I have a portrait of Anthony Trollope, who wrote most of his 47 novels while working for the Royal Post (where he invented the pillar box). Trollope got up early every morning to write, and wrote 250 words every fifteen minutes until it was time to go to the office. If you want to be a writer, the minimal necessary step is writing. And if you wait for inspiration, you are not writing. If I wait for inspiration to strike, I'm likely to be out on the golf course when it does, in a foursome that won't stop and wait for me to write an ode.

Inspiration does sometimes strike, of course. That's why I usually carry a notebook. (See **Tools**, below.) And if an idea comes to me while playing golf, I can make a note in my notebook or on my scorecard and save it. But ideas are plentiful, once you get into the habit of noticing them. I can't tell you how many times I've been told by non-writers, "I have an idea for a poem/novel/movie, but I don't know what to do about it." A writer is different from other people in sitting down and writing when those ideas come along.

A writer is also distinguished by not just noting those ideas, but developing them. And development doesn't come along on the wings of an angel; it is created ("creative" writing; get it?) through hard, concentrated work. Sometimes that work looks a lot like staring blankly at the page, or even like taking a long walk with the dog (this is why so many writers have dogs; that, and dogs aren't judgmental), but it's still work, and you have to do it to make progress as a poet.

None of this work is easy, but why should it be? Without hard work you'll never be a good tennis player or mechanic or painter or teacher; why should poetry be different?

Now, not all of a writer's work is sitting at a desk and putting words on paper (or on a computer). Some of the work is going out and walking with the dog, clearing the mind so that the new words (or the solutions to other problems) can have room. Some of the work is reading (see below) or research. (Yes, there can be a lot of research in poetry. You don't want to have an accidental reference to something that some readers will recognize as bogus, such as having wolves in Tennessee. I almost said badgers, but there are reports of badgers in Tennessee—see?) Sometimes you just follow a series of links in Wikipedia to see where you end up. And sometimes you do just sit and stare at the page and, every ten or fifteen minutes, write down a few more words. That may be how your process works.

When I was at Goddard College, there was a lot of emphasis on learning and embracing your own process. Your process probably isn't the same as Trollope's, or Billy Collins's (he writes a poem in the morning, polishes it, and never touches it again), or David Kirby's (he thinks about a poem for a couple of years, then writes it down, sometimes in as little as fifteen minutes), but it works for you, and part of your work is understanding how to get the work done.

Reading

I don't get specific ideas from other poets, but I get ideas about what can be done with language, or with poetry, or with ideas. I look at a poem sometimes to see how the poet got an effect, or how the images are put together, or how the poet has played variations and evolutions on a single complex image. (Go back to Shakespeare's sonnets for a lot of this, especially #18, "Shall I compare thee to a summer's day?") Sometimes I just get a particular inspiration (or reminder), such as that great poetry doesn't have to sound elevated, or that ordinary language can sound elevated if the poet is talented enough. (And, of course, I'm always trying to figure out how it was done.) For some years I read poetry on my radio show every Sunday morning, so I'm constantly getting new influences and new ideas.

But it's also useful to know what has been done; the converse is to have an idea of what hasn't been done. Ezra Pound urged us to "make it new," and we can't do that without knowing the old. (And "new" doesn't have to mean a subject that no one has considered before; it means expressing yourself in a way that no one else can, since they are not you.)

Besides, if you're interested enough in poetry to write it, you should be reading it for pleasure. Could you like only your own poetry, and not that of Shakespeare, or Auden, or Donald Hall (to mention just three of the poets whose work I am likely to pick up for fun)? If you don't get any pleasure from reading great poets, maybe you need a new hobby. (Unless, of course, you are only writing to express your inner soul and, maybe, to impress that cute guy in your English class. Then it doesn't matter if your poetry is any good—unless he's actually interested in poetry.)

And you shouldn't limit yourself to recent poetry. The genre wasn't invented when you were born, after all. Knowing what has been done in poetry means knowing Homer and Chaucer and Dante. Even knowing American poetry means knowing Phillis Wheatley and Anne Bradstreet, Poe and Longfellow, Whitman and Dickinson, and so on. Art exists in a context, and part of that context is history. Poems refer to each other directly and indirectly, a process called intertextuality, and you should want to be part of that conversation.

One of the great advantages you gain from reading the work of other people is that it gives you permission. If Maya Angelou tried something, you can try it, too. If, after learning how to write a conventional sonnet, Shakespeare could write sonnets that were thirteen or fifteen lines, so can you. You can experiment and expand your horizons, once you've learned where those horizons are.

Meaning

If I write a poem that is only about how bad I feel about my tight shoes, all anyone will get out of it is that I don't like tight shoes. That won't mean anything to the readers. If I use tight shoes as an image representing overcrowding in the schools, or the restrictions on our behavior imposed by social expectations (or both), then the poem has some real meaning. The trick is to take the triggering idea (the idea that gets you started writing; if you haven't read Richard Hugo's *The Triggering Town*, you really should; it's about getting from the first idea to the best poem you can make from it) and the generated idea (the one you come up with in the writing) and connect them to something outside your own consciousness. I think of it as universalizing, although I doubt it's ever really universal. But it is larger than my preference for shoes of the proper size, and more likely to touch the lives of my potential readers—to mean something to them.

This transition isn't easy, but that goes back to what I said about work. And it's necessary. Even the best light verse reaches out to something larger than itself; read some Dorothy Parker to see what I mean.

The concept of the generated idea implies that you do learn something while writing the poem. You are not writing to put pretty words together, you are exploring an idea and looking for a new idea.

But can't poetry just be pretty? No. There may be some people who will read poetry that is beautiful but meaningless language, but not many, and they won't really be touched by it. There was once a movement called "euphuism," spearheaded by the Elizabethan writer John Lyly. You've never heard of him? But you've heard of his contemporaries who wrote poetry that manipulated ideas at least as much as words. If you want to make real contact with real people, you have to give them something that connects with their lives. That's what I mean by "meaning." The purpose of any representational art, after all, is to provide meaning to life.

Besides, most of the truly beautiful language you can point to, in poetry or in prose, is beautiful at least in part (and in many cases mostly) because of the ideas it conveys. Martin Luther King, Jr.'s "I Have a Dream" speech isn't full of flowery language, but it is moving because it is full of evocative ideas, clearly and beautifully stated.

Indirection and Ambiguity

If all you do is write an essay and break it into lines, you can call it poetry if you like, but I usually won't call it poetry. (There are exceptions, like Marianne Moore's poem "Poetry.") We have to leave something for the reader to do, to find the meaning and make it personal. One of the ways we do that is by leaving something out, and also by alluding more than we state overtly. For example, in "Easter, 1916," Yeats never mentions the Rising in Dublin other than the reference to the date, but it's clear that's what the poem is about. It isn't right on the page; the reader has to get involved with the poem to see it, but it's there for every Irish schoolchild. The date and the names mentioned in the poem are reference enough.

We can also use ambiguity and surprise to make the reader think about interconnections between ideas and meanings. Words that have more than one meaning (most of them, after all), interruptions that suddenly lead in unexpected directions, and all sorts of ambiguities can get the reader involved in the ideas of the poem. Alicia Ostriker's poem "psalm," for example, is a series of rejections, preparing us for the greatest of all rejections at the end. But the closing line, "unless you ask me," is a potent affirmation. Another idea is drawn into the web of the poem without being stated overtly, and another layer of emotion is added to all of what came before. (Interestingly, this is the same mechanism that works in telling a joke.)

Imagery is a way of directing the indirection. Mary Oliver, in "The Black Walnut Tree," starts with the question of a large, old tree in the yard and uses its image to lead us to a meditation on family and ancestry and deep values. Look, for contrast, at what Joyce Kilmer did with a tree. Every image should mean something more than just the picture it conjures; ideally, all the images should work with and against each other, as in a collage.

One of our goals in poetry is to get as much information as possible into as few words as possible.

Lines

The line is a unit of its own, and it doesn't have to match a grammatical structure. Try always to have a line break do some work for the poem. (You won't always succeed, but every success will make the poem better.) Don't be afraid of caesura (a pause in the middle of a line) or enjambment (a grammatical phrase that carries over from one line to the next) or any of those tricks; they're just tricks, and you can use them when you need to. (A decent book of poetic jargon wouldn't hurt, either; the best is the *Princeton Encyclopedia of Poetry & Poetics*, but it is more than you need, and more than you need to pay. Edward Hirsch's *A Poet's Glossary* is more accessible. There are a lot of glossaries online, too, until you need something more elaborate. Poets.org is a good place to start for everything poetic.)

You can actually trace, in early modern English poetry, when people finished with end-stopped lines (lines whose grammatical structures end with the line) and started using enjambment and caesura. Today, some poems are spread out on the page in ways that it is hard to tell where a line begins or ends. No matter how we may feel about this technique, it gives a poet another tool for directing our attention to the relationships between ideas, between words, and between words and ideas. And that's what lines, at their best, do.

Too many contemporary poems are written in sentences and then broken into lines. But lines aren't just a way of organizing the words on the page so they don't look like prose. They are, or should be, units of meaning and of direction. They're part of the toolkit that a poet can use to teach the reader how to read each poem as it goes. A poem doesn't actually have to be written in sentences, but (except for prose poems, which we're not going to get into here) it does need to be in lines. So we have to start thinking in lines as we write. One way to practice this is to take a good poem that you don't know really well and type it into your computer without the line breaks. Then, a day or two later (when you've forgotten the original breaks) try to break it back into lines. Or have someone type it in for you. See if you can match the original lines, or see why the author broke them where she did.

Then apply those rules, or those instincts, to your own work.

Another way of manipulating lines is by making them longer and shorter. Most of the time, we use lines of consistent length throughout a poem, and long lines have a different effect than short ones. Consider the opening two lines of Longfellow's "Evangeline":

> "This is the forest primeval. The murmuring pines and the
> hemlocks,
> Bearded with moss, and in garments green, indistinct in the
> twilight . . ."

and how they have a different effect than the first two lines of Robert Browning's "Porphyria's Lover":

> "The rain set early in to-night,
> The sullen wind was soon awake . . ."

There are a number of differences, of course, but the effect of the longer lines in contrast to the shorter ones should be pretty clear.

Music

Hold on! Didn't I just say, a little while ago, that making beautiful sounds had no place in poetry?

Not exactly. What I said was that you should avoid beautiful language for its own sake. The music of the language can be harnessed in the service of the meaning; in fact, it should be whenever possible.

What do I mean by music? Organizing the sounds of the words. Sometimes, even often, this means choosing words for their sounds as well as their meanings. If you want to write that the trees are quite beautiful this evening, but you are working in iambic pentameter (if you don't know what that is, go to the glossary at Poets.org), you have to say "the trees are very beautiful tonight," or it won't fit the music you are trying to write.

Even if you aren't writing in a regular meter, you may want to have a section or a phrase that uses a rhythm or a sound for a particular effect. You can repeat a vowel sound (assonance) or a consonant sound (consonance) or start a string in a statement with the same sounds (alliteration). The sound of the words is another element you can manipulate to bring the reader closer to the experience you want to create in your poem.

Poe is the great example of how to do this, sometimes even how to go too far. But his poetry begs to be read out loud, and rewards the effort.

The Turn

This is just a technical term, but worth bearing in mind. Any good poem should have a turn, a point where the meaning shifts or the new meaning emerges. Look at most of Shakespeare's sonnets, and the turn is at the beginning of the last stanza, no matter which sonnet form he's using. In the works of Basho, the seventeenth-century haiku writer, it's often at the end of the second line. (He didn't have as much room to work with as Shakespeare had.) But most good poems will have a turn, and it's one of the elements we need to look for in our own work.

Let's look at an example from Shakespeare. All through Sonnet 18 he is comparing his beloved to larger and larger units of time, until he gets to "eternal lines of time." Then, in the final couplet, the comparison turns back on itself, so he is talking about the very poem that he is writing, transforming the meaning of everything that has come before.

The turn is like the punch line of a joke. Consider Henny Youngman's one-liner: "Take my wife—please." He starts off in one direction, and then reveals that what we thought was happening is not happening at all. You don't have to do this in every poem, but it's a very useful tool to keep in mind, if only because sometimes you need to change what you're writing about.

Revise

A first draft is just a starting point. I think it was Robert Lowell whose first draft was called "To Jean, on her Confirmation," and who eventually revised the poem into "To a Whore at the Brooklyn Navy Yard." My own "October 1979" ranged from six to two pages long at various points in the revision and was published at four. (And went through five or six titles, and was a story for quite a while.) Very often the only real function of the first draft is to tell us what we mean to be writing about. Then we need to make the poem be about that.

I could never have learned to revise poetry on my own. I needed lots of help, and was lucky to get it. (I didn't do poetry in my MFA.) I got a lot of guidance from my friend Michael Foran (who did do poetry at Goddard), and from my ex-wife, Judy, and I have been part of a few poetry groups that meet monthly here in Nashville. I can't overemphasize how important a good writing group can be. And it's a lot better than showing one person your work, unless that one person is a superb editor—sometimes even if that person is a superb editor—because people will get ideas from each other about the poem under discussion.

Finding a group can be pretty easy, depending, of course, on where you live. Start by putting "[town or county where you live] poetry group" into a search engine. If that doesn't help, expand it to include the nearest large town or city within reasonable distance, and I bet you'll have quite a choice. I found one of mine through Meetup.com. Or you may have to start your own, through Meetup or the local library or bookstore. Look for workshops, too; one of my groups grew out of a weekend workshop that was only supposed to last two days, and we've been meeting now for a few years.

Finding the right one for you is mostly a matter of trial and error, but you want writers who are at about the same level of craft that you are and who are looking to improve their craft rather than for a mutual admiration society. Those can be fun, but they won't help you grow.

And once you've got your critiques, of course, you have to do something about them. If you don't revise, you're skipping the real work of making the poem.

But you need to start revising before you get to the group. Part of what you learn from the group is how to see the flaws in your own work, by seeing the flaws in theirs.

One of the easiest aspects of revision, or easiest to learn, is deletion. Get rid of excess words. When I was working with Mary Jo Bang at Tin House Writers' Conference, one of her catchphrases was "What work is this doing?" Sometimes that meant I had to take out a stanza, sometimes just a word. But everything in a poem must be taking its share of the work of the poem. No decoration.

No decoration does not mean no beautiful language; beautiful language can be part of the work of the poem. It does mean no beautiful language for its own sake. Have I said that before? It bears repeating. Samuel Johnson said, "Read over your compositions, and wherever you meet with a passage which you think is particularly fine, strike it out." There is a kind of elaboration that distracts from the issue at hand, and that is the sort of decoration I ban from good poetry.

One of the most common problems that beginning poets face is their inability to delete or change what they have written. They remember exactly what they meant when they wrote those words or those lines, and they treasure the feeling that writing gave them. And that feeling, after all, is a lot better than the feeling of deleting those words or lines. Writing feels like success, and deleting feels like failure. At first.

But deleting, like all revising, is success. It's finding a better way to communicate your ideas, and sometimes we have to let the ideas stand in front, while we sit in the background like parents at a graduation. The poem should be more important than your ego; in the long run, a better poem will make you look better.

You can also save all the wonderful phrases that you delete; maybe there will be places for them in some other poems. Another of Mary Jo's suggestions was to save your deletions and look through them for the title of the poem.

Tools

I won't pretend that I carry my notebook everywhere, but almost everywhere. I have a plastic box with a clipboard instead of a handbag, and I have pens and a little notebook in there so if I get an idea I can write it down (and sometimes start drafting). In fact, I start all my drafts in the notebook. I also use only fountain pens, because I like the way they feel and how I can switch colors just for fun as easily as loading a different color when the pen runs dry, or by carrying a few different colors.

You don't have to use fountain pens. Some people prefer cheap ballpoints, or computers or their smartphones. But it's important to have tools that are convenient and that you like. If you like your tools, you're more likely to use them. (And if you want to get into fountain pens, you can get a nice Mont Blanc or Pelikan, or you can go to eBay, spend about the same amount, and get a double fistful of nice Chinese pens. They'll last basically forever, and even the best inks aren't very expensive considering how long they last. When I teach poetry, I give each member of my class a cheap fountain pen and a cartridge to get them started.)

There are some very elegant notebooks you can buy, or you can stay at the cheap end. It doesn't matter, as long as they come in a size that is convenient for you to carry. I know people who swear by the Field Notes or Moleskine notebooks that will fit in your pocket, and others by the Rhodia or Levenger versions. Use what pleases you, and if that turns out to be your phone, use it in good health.

The main point is to use it.

Honesty

All the rest of our craft is in service of trying to write the raw truth. I sometimes tell my students or workshoppers, "I want to see the blood on the page." Readers can tell when you're not being honest, and you're cheating them and yourself. After all, none of us is going to get rich writing poetry. We might as well learn what we have to say in the process of saying it.

And, in fact, your poetry doesn't have to be honest. This goes back to where we started, with your purpose in writing. I suppose not everyone wants to write honest and true poetry.

But everything I've said here assumes that you want to write the best poetry you can, and that is honest poetry.

What does that mean, "honest poetry"? What does it mean to have an honest relationship with your readers?

This is not a question of not lying to them. Sometimes you need to diverge from the literal truth in a poem, as when you relate a real event and add rain where, through an oversight, it had not been raining, or when you combine words in unusual and possibly illogical ways, such as "enlightened shoes." Those may be challenging, but they are not dishonest.

When you write a poem, you are entering a contract with your readers, or potential readers. They agree that they will try their best to understand what you are saying and give you the opportunity to convince them of something. You agree that you will offer something that might be convincing, and that you will try your best to present it in the most meaningful and interesting way that you can. Fulfilling that contract is writing honest poetry.

When you write about a subject that is controversial, or painful because it is deeply personal, and you find yourself turning away from the truth to protect yourself, you are not writing honest poetry. When you settle for the not-quite-right word, the lightning bug rather than the lightning, you are not writing honest poetry.

I don't mean that all poetry should be painful, or that it should try to bring the readers to tears. Sometimes, after all, the emotion we are trying to evoke is laughter, or outrage, or horniness. Whatever we are trying to do with each poem, we should try our hardest to do that in the best possible way.

Only then will we be truly honest with our readers and ourselves.

Michael Collins

FIRST LESSON

I love to teach poems that are intriguing and invigorating in their incarnations on the page while also providing models of strategies that can help the rest of us get started on new poems of our own. Below you will find one that I've enjoyed teaching for years, "What My Son's Haircut Taught Me About Flying" from *It Blows You Hollow* by Diane Seuss.

I would suggest reading it several times, at least once aloud. Pay attention to articulating and hearing the punctuation—the way a question mark sounds different than a period, the short pause of a comma, the interruption of a dash. One aspect of honing your practice of writing poetry is cultivating a heightened sensitivity to language, and carefully reading other poets is a great way to do so. Enjoy!

What My Son's Haircut Taught Me About Flying

The beautician's name is Robin Beebee. Wonder if her family
was from down around our way? There was a Beebee farm
where a sheep gave birth to a lamb with two heads. This was
back during the Civil War before medical science could have
kept a thing like that alive. They stuffed it looking in two
directions. Not many in this town talk about the connection
between that lamb with one body and two heads and the
Civil War, when the country was nearly split in half. It is not
a town for making sense of things like that—stuff it, put it in
the museum, go on with your life. When Robin Beebee cut
my son's hair and all of his curls went floating to the floor it
surprised me that I thought of these things. Wishing he could

have two heads, one for him and one for me. One with a real boy haircut, sideburns, straight line across the back, so he can feel good about himself, and one with the curls left alone, soft down his back like a little animal. We must fly in an airplane on Thursday, from up here in the cold to the warm south. The air is a place I do not want to be. I wish I had two bodies and could leave one behind here on the earth, sitting out in the cold cornfields watching the sky. But you can't have it two ways, that's kind of a town motto. Let the air do its business. Let Robin Beebee use her Beauty Academy schooling. Give your son to her. Her scissors are sharp as a taxidermist's and she has a smile on her face. "How's my little man today?" she asks. \There was a time that lamb lay limp in someone's arms, breathing with two mouths.

***

I like this poem for beginning poets because it flies in the face of some prominent myths about poetry. For starters, it lacks several traditional and often stereotypical elements of poetry.

Bullets!

Yes, italicized sidekick, welcome to the class. Try to be on time in the future.

I was stuck in a line.

Dude, we're in a book.

I KNOW. There are so many lines; it's hard to know which one to be in.

Of course. Here are your bullets:

- line breaks

- rhyme

- flowery language that sounds like the poet came directly from high tea with William Shakespeare and the Queen

Then, on the other hand, there are all of the things the poem *does* make use of that are *not* stereotypically "Poetic."

More bullets?

Sure, why not?

I think I'm going to call them eggs from now on.

Ok…?

It's a metaphor. I shatter paradigms; it's kind of my thing.

All right, well, do you, my friend. At any rate, the poem uses:

- the speaker's natural, daily voice—you might even say she highlights local dialect

- stories apparently from her own life, nothing grandiose or hard to imagine

- the speaker's own not overtly organized, subjective, associative thought process

I'm willing to bet that we each have these ingredients hidden away—or maybe not so hidden—in our own psyches. So, we each must be able to make poems in this way!

And tacos!

Yes, but, well, ok. I would like to focus on the associative thought process for a minute first because it's really a humble—yet fascinating—tactic for a poet to allow a reader to see them thinking—with all the messiness and leaping here—and there—that goes along with it. Let's go through the poem together. We begin:

> The beautician's name is Robin Beebee. Wonder if her family was from down around our way? There was a Beebee farm where a sheep gave birth to a lamb with two heads. This was back during the Civil War before medical science could have kept a thing like that alive. They stuffed it looking in two directions. Not many in this town talk about the connection between that lamb with one body and two heads and the Civil War, when the country was nearly split in half. It is not a town for making sense of things like that—stuff it, put it in the museum, go on with your life.

We barely begin the story about the speaker's son's haircut when a question intrudes. By associating Robin Beebee with the Beebees from the speaker's past, we are diverted to the Beebee farm, from there to the strange two-headed lamb, its time period (the Civil War), and the image of it eventually stuffed facing in two directions. That's a lot of mental leaps in a few lines! *And*, we have yet to hear about this haircut the title has promised! *And* we're not even finished with the associations! We proceed to connect the two-headed lamb with the Civil War splitting the country, and this leads us to the communal personality of the speaker's hometown, which avoids such complicated topics, preferring to "stuff it, put it in the museum, go on with your life."

Do you see what I mean about how the poem mirrors the messy ways in which we often think? Doesn't it seem that unanswered questions, associations with memories, and overpowering emotions guide the progressions of our consciousness as often as—or more often than—you know, logic?

They can't answer you.

That's what margins are for.

Oh, right. When do we make tacos?

Dude. Seriously. Let's get back to the poem and the ways in which it mirrors some of the ways we think when our thoughts are free to wander. In other words, this presentation of human consciousness would not be as applicable when we're directly focused on a task of some sort; then we think logically. Rather, this is how our minds "work" when we are in a more meditative state, sitting quietly drinking coffee in the morning, maybe commuting home from work—

Cutting vegetables, taking a shower, arranging the garden gnomes!

Yes, good examples. When we're not directing our thinking, it tends to proceed along less linear channels: One thing reminds us of another…and another and another and another. The interesting thing about this is that sometimes we make unforeseen connections as our minds associate one thing with another, connections that our logical thinking might ignore or bypass. In other words, writing associatively allows the writing to surprise us. Or, perhaps it is better to say that this kind of writing allows our deeper selves to surprise us through the act of writing. Let's see how some of these things manifest in what happens next:

> When Robin Beebee cut my son's hair and all of his curls went floating to the floor it surprised me that I thought of these things. Wishing he could have two heads, one for him and one for me. One with a real boy haircut, sideburns, straight line across the back, so he can feel good about himself, and one with the curls left alone, soft down his back like a little animal.

We're back in the literal scene again: Robin Beebee, the curls falling to the floor, the speaker and her thoughts. She even tells us that *she* was surprised by her chain of thoughts. Here, we're starting to feel located within the speaker's point of view again. However, right away, the reality of the son's haircut is fused with the image of the two-headed animal. This image, though, allows the speaker to express the central emotional complexity of the story: the tension between loving her son and wanting him to be happy about growing up and the desire to hold on to her little boy. Did this realization need to be coaxed out through thinking about the lamb in the Civil War? Or had the speaker been thinking about the implications of her son's haircut so much that these thoughts immediately attached themselves to the lamb her chain of associations arrived at? Either way, the final connection between the lamb and her son definitely comes as a surprise.

Surely, there must be something more to this! I mean, a haircut, really? Is it all that serious?

Yes, well, I'm sure you're right since you *are* a fairly transparent comic relief device and all.

If I'm so transparent, how can they read me, Mr. Letter Typer?

Life's little paradoxes.... Fittingly, I have a feeling more surprises are coming:

We must fly in an airplane on Thursday, from up here in the cold to the warm south. The air is a place I do not want to be. I wish I had two bodies and could leave one behind here on the earth, sitting out in the cold cornfields watching the sky.

New problems assert themselves here: an impending flight and the fear of flying it invokes. Again, this calls forth the idea of doubling: two heads, two sons' haircuts, and, now, two bodies. These separations have been previously associated with anxiety about the march of time and death, which corresponds directly with the wish to leave one body on the ground, just in case the plane was to crash. A link to the speaker's own fear of death explicitly enters the poem's chain of associations here, obviously much more serious than a haircut. Interestingly, although—or perhaps *because*—the speaker is expressing a personal emotion here, the poem offers a far more generally accessible point of connection: the individual's experience of fearing death. A reader who has not mourned a son's haircut has probably felt a twinge of fear during a flight at some point—or, even without flying, we've all feared the *reason* to fear a plane crash.

Perhaps because this fear of death is larger than the speaker herself, we return to the collective voice of the town:

> But you can't have it two ways, that's kind of a town motto.
> Let the air do its business. Let Robin Beebee use her Beauty
> Academy schooling. Give your son to her. Her scissors are
> sharp as a taxidermist's and she has a smile on her face. "How's
> my little man today?" she asks.

At first, there seems to be some comfort in adopting the more general perspective of the entire town, the conventional wisdom. But then apparently harmless Robin Beebee is compared to the taxidermist who stuffed the lamb, and her friendly greeting, "little man," reminds the speaker once again of his inevitable maturation—and everything we've seen associated with it. Corresponding with the speaker's fear of death in a plane crash, the son's growth and eventual death are inching together as well:

> There was a time that lamb lay limp in someone's arms,
> breathing with two mouths.

I think we get the mortal implication, seeing as the speaker has already compared the lamb to her son and herself.

I like haircuts, and they are not about death!

Fair point. But that isn't really all that the poem is about. It's more about the inextricable connection between love and the potential for loss, the complete embrace of life and, by extension, the death waiting at the end of it. But the death part wouldn't even matter if life wasn't incredible; sometimes even "errands" like getting a haircut or necessities like flying in a plane find themselves filled with connections, implications, and psychic energy. It's hard to get from a haircut to this kind of depth using pure logic—maybe impossible. That's why we need association to help us leap patiently from one thing to the next until we arrive at such discoveries.

You've been talking for kind of a long time.

Well, I was—

They bought a "poetry writing" book, not a "reading about every thought you type about" one.

Well, I mean, you could have been nicer about it, but, ok.

Anyway, isn't it about time we did a—

Writing Exercise

Bolding things makes it a little too serious.

I know, right?

But this exercise isn't meant to be too serious. Although we touched on some heavy topics in discussing the poem, one of the reasons I love this piece is that it manages to deal with such serious material with mental playfulness, meaning that the speaker feels free to leap back and forth between topics without any compulsion to spell out an explicit logical progression. She explores, waiting to see where she will end up.

For this exercise, I would like to give you the same associative freedom. Since starting a poem directly onto a blank page or screen can be unnerving, let's begin with something that isn't a poem, a *list*.

Take out a blank piece of paper. At the top of it write down something you did recently, it can be any regular old thing like getting a haircut, except that there was something special about it, something mysterious, unnerving, eerie, surprising, etc. You do not need to know precisely why you felt—or still feel—this way. Just follow your instincts and pick something you have a hunch about.

Next, write down your activity in a simple, clear sentence, for example: "I went to the farmer's market…"

Once you have done this, set a timer for ten minutes. During that time, make a list down the page of as many simple sentences as you can. Try starting each with a subject and verb: I ran…, I saw…, I knew… These sentences may begin by telling the story of your experience, but try to be open to associations as well: ___ felt like…, ___ sounded like…, ___ looked like…, ___ smelled like…, ___ reminded me of…

Let yourself follow any and all associations that present themselves. Whenever a line of associations has played itself out, go back to your original story and pick up where you left off. Write as many sentences as you can without any intent for them to make logical sense. Try to write without stopping, editing, or censoring. Just write, write, write.

Once you have your list, take a minute to reread it. Circle the most interesting sentence. Then, underline any sentences that connect to that sentence, either because they are part of the same literal story or because they are associated with it in some way for you. The reason for this association does not have to make logical sense, at least at this point.

Can we destroy something?

You're an odd little duck, Italisidekick, but it's uncanny how you seem to know my next move all the time.

Ok, so, everyone, find some scissors and cut out each of the sentences you circled or underlined. Lay them out on the table, and put the circled one on top. Then, arrange the others below it in whatever order you wish. Once you are finished, type them up, one sentence on each line. Then, reread it and add sentences in between the ones you have typed anywhere they seem to be missing. You may find some of the sentences that you didn't circle or underline useful at this point as well; take a look and see!

Then, try some or all of the following:

- Play with the voice of your poem. Rewrite some of the sentences in a regional dialect, or the voice of your workplace, your family, your anything. Make a sentence fragment here and there by leaving off the subject. Put some sentences together using "and" or "but" or "so" etc. Make a sentence into a question.

- *Use an exclamation mark!!!!*

- Take out the line breaks and make a prose poem like the one we studied above. Or arrange the lines into stanzas by hitting return in between them to create white space on the page in places where you would like your reader to pause for one reason or another.

- Reread the poem and think about the ending. Do you want to end on a startling image like the doomed lamb being held while it was still alive? Or an arresting sentence, a lesson your poem is desperate to teach your reader?

- *What about a question?*

Finally:

- Read the poem aloud to yourself. Change anything that your ear doesn't like, anything that doesn't mean what you want it to or sound how you want it to, any sentences that feel too long or short, any places where a word choice seems wrong, or you want us to pause for a line or stanza break—anything!

- Read the poem aloud to yourself simply to enjoy of the poem you have created.

Rob Carney

A FIELD GUIDE TO POEMS IN THREE PARTS

I. Coyote's Daughter, Raven's Son

The poem is a shapeshifter animal, a trickster.
One minute, it's a sailfish. The next, it's a hook.

One night, it's an alley cat, urgent to get you outdoors,
get you on the fire escape and screaming. Another, it sleeps.

I remember there was a great migration—
poems soaring home.

And I remember, too, when they used to thunder like trains,
crushing the grass. I watched as the herd turned into crickets,

then rain, then into kids in the backyard running for the house
before the raindrops turned into hail, and while I watched

I smelled my dinner burning.
Clever trick.

"Well, what's the good in that?" Not much.
"Then what the hell's it want?" I don't know—to astonish

like leaves do in autumn. To hope, I guess,
it says one small thing that lasts.

I'd prefer to leave it at that, to add nothing, since going on now means reducing the poem to an epigram, as if prose were really the bigger stakes work, and I don't want to concede that. But back in mid-September my friend Joe Roberts wrote me a note that I've been thinking about ever since. He said, "I have a question for you. I've been struggling to come up with a purpose for poetry as it is, as opposed to prose. What makes poetry's purpose distinctive?" Thank you, Joe. It's nice being thought of as a guy who might have an answer.

On the one hand, I'm not sure poems have to have a purpose. I mean, I'd rather have lamps be lamps and let poems be the occasional genie. On the other hand, I know that's ridiculous. Poems *do* have purposes, lots of them, and I shouldn't avoid adding my thoughts about what those purposes are just because doing so takes some work. I know this won't be my final answer—there will be days ahead when I think of others, then others after that—but here goes...

Joe said he'd been reading *Spring and All* (William Carlos Williams). He said Williams' ideas were pretty good. He said, "The definition I pulled from him is that prose is meant to serve the emotions and be representational. Poetry is meant to serve the imagination and create something truly new. It's not a mirror to hold up to nature; it is an addition to nature, a 'crystallization of the imagination.'" Now, I love Williams by the acre, the square mile, but I'm going to say I think he's probably wrong about that one. Take Faulkner's *Go Down, Moses*. It's prose not poetry, and it's truly new. And that's just one example. In fact, it's the first that popped into my head. Here's another: Pick any of a dozen albums by Bob Dylan; what's happening seems both true and new to me, and also different than a poem, or even a whole book of poems, since there's the added interplay of voice and instruments to go along with whatever story or character or philosophical headlock he's turned into lyrics. No, probably the rightest part of Williams' idea is the "crystallization" thing. Faulkner gives us whole caves full of stalactites, stalagmites, bats, pooling water old as Original Sin, and also crystals; yet love that as much as you want, you can't wear it around your neck. Same with Dylan. Sure, he's bardic, but how long do you think it took the roadies to unload and set up for every concert on, say, his Rolling Thunder Revue tour in 1975? What's different (distinct) about poems, I think, isn't fancy. It's that they're short.

I said this once to Tony Weller, a bookseller in Salt Lake City. At first he thought I was a spluttering dunce, or just being lazy about the question. But I halfway talked him around to my point of view: poems are short, even when halfway behaving like narratives, even when sharing a compact story. They're crystallized: Life's psalm, Heart's wind chimes, Gut's tattoo.

I'm saying—and yes, I started this by saying the opposite ("Do I contradict myself? / Very well then I contradict myself, / I am large, I contain multitudes"; Walt Whitman)—I'm saying that the distinction of poetry is *its ability to be epigrammatic*. You can carry a poem inside you like a talisman because you can remember it, completely, start to finish, word for word. And it doesn't need accompaniment, just you, reciting it for yourself or someone else, all the lines and the rhythms, all its images and meanings, meanings you might start to paraphrase then decide you don't really need to after all...

Lynx Music

The lynx knows all about quiet,
his ears grown long to hear more of it.

He sharpens his claws on the trunk of it,
hunts silence,

carries it home. And his paws
ghost over snowdrifts,

and lakes are asleep
under ice sheets,

and the stars seem frozen
like an orchestra, waiting to begin...

has anyone seen the conductor?
Where has she gone in her night tuxedo?

The lynx looks ready to tell us something,
but only in the speech of violins.

II. Raccoon Verses

There Used to Be a Time When Foxes Were Brown

In the Old Songs about Washington, a raccoon and fox had an argument,
each one bragging that he was the better thief.

The fox stole some colors from the sunset
and painted, for himself, the first flowers,

but the raccoon grabbed their pollen
and gave it to bees to carry everywhere.

The fox got mad. And more bold. He picked the lock and entered
the Land of the Dead: endless bones to gnaw on.

Quiet as a current, the raccoon followed.
Quickly, while the fox was eating, he took and hid the door,

and in the Old Songs, this was good.
It meant the living and dead could now speak.

The fox saw one last chance to even the score: He poked a paw
into Thunder's pocket, trying to swipe a streak of lightning,

and the flash, if you listen to the Old Songs,
burned his fur the colors of smoke and fire.

That's an origin story about the color of foxes, so the raccoon's just a minor
character. He isn't even the antagonist since the fox is really his own worst
problem. But the minor character is the one on my mind because the other
morning I saw a baby raccoon and was glad that I did. So were Jen and Quen-
tin and Jameson. And so were our neighbors who kept a kind of casual vigil
while he slept all day and evening in their tree.

He'd been moving around under some groundcover vines in this spot
where cats like to hide and ambush birds, so I figured he was just a cat until

he strolled out onto the grass: this baby raccoon. I got my boys to come and look, but by then he'd gone up the tree, walking up the branches the way that you and I would walk down the sidewalk. And that's where he was, still napping, when my wife Jen got home in the afternoon.

If he were a bird, so what? But he wasn't. He was rare. And I think that's what a poem is too: this unexpected creature stepping out from under our language and climbing up a tree. And you there to notice.

I like that definition: poems are raccoons. I like it for two reasons; first, because it's easy to remember, and second because it doesn't make sense unless you're thinking in metaphor and imagery. I'll bet you that's how Williams felt after he'd written his famous wheelbarrow poem. I mean, I don't know for sure, but it doesn't seem impossible:

so much depends
upon

a red wheel
barrow

glazed with rain
water

beside the white
chickens.

Thinking in imagery tells us plenty more, of course. For starters, the colors stand out in contrast—red and white and brown (there are chickens, so there's dirt around) and gray (it's drizzling or used to be, so the sky above is overcast, but the sun's coming through enough to light up raindrops) and even green (not pictured, but somewhere just outside the frame since a place with chickens would have crops or a garden and likely some trees as a windbreak). And thinking in metaphor, it's telling us how much we need poems—those well-made language contraptions—to bring us new encounters and experiences. A poem can haul a lot more than chickenfeed, and it's capable of taking daily crap-loads and rolling them away. That's some kind of wheelbarrow.

I'm going to try to imitate that same kind of balance now and circle back
to foxes and raccoons:

Why the Raccoon's Tail Has Stripes

A fox is a fox—bright
zigzag, cunning stomach—but who is Raccoon,

which way do his whiskers point?
You can knock all day on that question; nobody's home,

just a key beneath the welcome mat,
and inside,

hanging from his ceiling,
strange chandeliers:

arrangements of keys and hoop earrings,
loose change forever going missing,

the silver promises of corkscrews,
laughter, desire...anything shiny.

All those years spent collecting—
here they are.

He isn't a thief; he just looks like a bandit.
Take back whatever you like.

He knows his tail is a lesson in perspective:
Find it/Lose it, Have it/Vanish, making stripes.

III. Now It's Your Turn,

and to help you get started, here's an exercise. You might not get a finished
poem your first try, but that's okay; it isn't nice to be greedy. If people ever

tell me I'm a decent writer, I say, "No, what I am sometimes is a pretty good reviser." Anyway, what you *won't* have is just a blank page.

11 Tasks

1st stanza:
1. Start with something doing something impossible...
2. then continue that picture for us.
3. In the next lines, use two of your senses to describe where or when or how this is happening (and maybe mix it up/try using synaesthesia).
4. Describe yourself in a weird way.
5. Make the "I" say something that he or she desires.

2nd stanza:
6. Make an assertion that sounds true but couldn't be...
7. and now make a truer assertion.
8. Write a line describing another part of your setting, using one or two of the senses.
9. Repeat the initial image in line 1, but change it in a noticeable way.
10. Finally, write a line that continues the story or mood,
11. but cross it out and make it the title of your poem instead.

Melanie Faith

WITH PROMPTS AND PATIENCE: THE MAKING OF VERSE

I've taught writing since 1999 while also experiencing two huge life changes: going back to graduate school to study for my MFA in poetry in 2005 and becoming an auntie in 2012. These events dynamically added to my personal life as well as my understanding of what it means to be an artist and a teacher, a giver, and a lifelong student of life and love.

With each poem I wrote, each writing class and seminar I've taught, and each summer afternoon I've spent with my darling nieces who live too far away, from birth through their pre-school years, I've grown to appreciate the ongoing and ever-evolving path in this writing life.

I've gathered quite a few topics that my writing students of all ages, backgrounds, and skill levels grapple with, including: remaining productive despite life's endless stream of paperwork and distractions, figuring out how to write a title that gives enough information to lure in a reader but not so much that the whole poem is told right away, how to offer genuinely useful feedback in a workshop, why strict chronology might be for the birds, and how a POV change can dramatically alter a poem—for the better. The following tips are written with a practicing artist's concerns and joys in mind.

***

On Tenacity: 6 Tips for Increased Poetic Productivity

One of my favorite artist retreats has a fascinating podcast. Makers in many genres, from fiber arts to writing, photography, and pottery, are interviewed in a one-on-one conversation about their creative lives, how they make time for their art, life-work balance, their favorite themes, teaching and/or their small businesses, and how they get their ideas and develop them.

Recently, a painter discussed her journey from high-school-graduate in a corporate world to going back to college as an adult with grown children. As she described her personal renascence while pursuing her bachelor's and the excitement of being in a community focusing on personal cultivation, she discussed an assignment for one of her courses: to make sixteen paintings in four weeks.

Wow. That's four paintings a week. I've never been a painter, but I've known a few and that's a brisk pace, to say the least, especially when even commissions can take weeks if not months.

Then I started to think about it further, in relation to my own creative process. Yes, it's a lot of work, but on the other hand, all artists learn through practice. Not willy-nilly practice, but diligent and ongoing practice. The best way to get better is not to get precious about the work, especially in the middle of making it. That's one of the reasons why, when I was an MFA student studying poetry ten years ago, our groups were assigned a portfolio of new poems to workshop with our fellow grad students each month. A funny thing happens when you get an assignment to turn in eight or ten new poems, month after month—you start to pick up your pace and adjust.

Were they perfect, publishable drafts? Mostly not, but that wasn't the primary goal of the assignment. Writing that many poems, you begin to sharpen self-editing skills and also, from making comments on others' drafts, you develop ideas for your own future poems. You learn that the only way to increase your own skills is to work consistently, so you attune your workflow habits; portfolios written a few hours before deadline were likely not going to impress or make much sense.

One of my favorite professors told us, "What you learn in this poem might not help this poem, but it will undoubtedly be used in service of your next poems." That only works if you are routinely creating so that you're prepared when inspiration strikes.

That's one of the reasons I recommend to my own writing students that they take part in writing challenges. Every April, for National Poetry Writing Month, poets across the world take part in a daily challenge, writing a single poem a day. Some poets form groups or do informal swaps, as I've done, with poetry friends to encourage each other through the thirty days of the challenge and to share the daily draft with another practitioner. In fact, I highly recommend swapping work with writing friends as a practice that increases motivation at any time of the year. Even if you can only swap once a month or a few times a year, just knowing someone else is waiting for your latest work is enough to coax the muse into motion.

6 Ways Poets Stay Motivated:

- **Drafts don't have to be perfect. Realize that good enough is great.** Ever hear the aphorism "Perfect is the enemy of good?" If we seek perfection, it's likely we'd never write. On the other hand, a terrible first draft is material to work with and may be polished through several edits into a stellar poem. When in doubt, just begin: write something. It doesn't have to be beautiful or remain the first line or first stanza forever or even in the poem at all. All parts of a poem are malleable, but if you have nothing on your page or screen then there's nothing to work with and that's the real shame of sporadic writing.

- **Get into a writing routine.** You might pick a time of day. Perhaps at 3:30 am, before your kids need to get up for school or before you begin your daily commute. Or maybe you're a night owl who likes to write once everyone else is in bed and you're clocked out of your job(s) for the day. Or maybe you designate one day as your writing day—say Tuesday. Any time during that day, sit down to write. Or maybe you take a writing challenge—agreeing to swap work with a friend once a week or every day during NaPoWriMo. Write the challenge and/or the swap day in your day planner or online calendar—it's a deadline to meet and should be regarded as sacrosanct as paying your taxes (ugh) and going on vacation. Experiment with days, times, and ideas that work best with your schedule and commitments.

- **Speaking of vacation, replenish your batteries from time to time. Realize when it's time for a rest.** It may seem counterintuitive, but all writers need some breaks. I call them "replenishing the well." Whether that means a few hours or days, some of the best writing can come after a day off to take a walk, meet a friend, or just lounging with a magazine or book. Give your writing (and your mind) time to breathe. Set aside older drafts for new material once you're back into the groove of your writing routine. Before you take your break, though, make a plan for the next day you'll write, to ensure you'll have an idea in mind and motivation to return to your new project or draft-in-progress.

- **Read a lot of poetry.** Peruse your favorite poets' work (for me, a perpetual go-to is Mary Oliver) and find new favorites in literary magazines, both online and off, and at databases like The Poetry Foundation, www.poetryfoundation.org, which has a searchable database with poems of almost every theme and style you can imagine.

- **Find a writing partner to swap work with, join a workshop group (or start one), or take part in a writing challenge (or set up one of your own).** If the monthly NaPoWriMo challenge doesn't work for your schedule, agree with a friend to write a poem every day in November (which also has just 30 days) or another month that will work for you (a friend and I are currently doing a daily October poem swap), or agree to send each other poems every day for a week of your own choosing.

- **Return to older/earlier drafts. That's viable writing practice, too. Have several poems going at once.** I do this with many writing and photography projects. It works especially well since it's hard to edit or properly judge a piece when it's freshly created; once the rose-tinted goggles have cleared a few days or months later, I return to edit earlier poems and photos, especially on a day when I'm not sure what to write.

***

Try this prompt! Write a poem about your writing process; these are called ars poeticas. Go ahead, get friendly with your writing and what it means to you and how it interacts with your daily life. Personify all you want; maybe your muse wears a bright pink feather boa and has a raspy, comedic Phyllis Diller laugh or perhaps your writing mojo is a counterintelligence spy who speaks four languages and wears a black shirt and Ray-Bans, blending in so seamlessly passersby forget what his face looked like three minutes later. Throw in some alliteration and fanciful allusions to describe what it's like for you to write and maybe even what keeps you struggling to write what you want.

***

6 Tips for Crafting Snazzy, Meaningful Titles
"Cecelia?"

"I like it. Sassy, yet sweet. And we can shorten it to Ceci."

"I'm not wild about shortening it, though. Do you think everyone would?"

"What's wrong with shortening it? I think it's cute."

"Nah. What about Cali?"

"Too common. We know three Calis."

"True. Sarah?"

"Too plain. Artemis?"

"No. No way."

"But it's so pretty!"

"Artemis Cooper in third grade. She was rotten. You can't do that to your kid."

"That doesn't mean our Artemis would be rotten."

"Nope. It'll always bring to mind Artemis Cooper for me. Veto. How about Daphne?"

"Daphne? But you can't shorten it, unless you do Daph, which sounds weird."

"I thought you hated shortened names."

"I like nicknames; I just don't like Ceci. And Daphne sounds like the cartoon duck. Veto."

Sound familiar? A name, much like a title, is often the first impression a person presents to the world. It carries symbolic weight and hope and background—sometimes of the chooser's culture, heritage, education, outlook, politics, religion, generation, or personal outlook. As with naming a child, the creator usually gets the honor of bestowing the moniker on their creation, for the good or detriment of the creation.

It may seem deceptively easy at times to slapdash a few words onto the top of the page (and I've done so myself, often as a place marker to be replaced later), but an appropriate title is your editors' and readers' first introduction to the theme and/or tone of your work. [Big breath.] That's one of the reasons why so many writers find it challenging, to say the least, to know what to call their poems.

I remember attending a one-hour seminar in grad school about the challenges of giving titles to poems—it's the kind of topic that you will encounter throughout your life as a poet, whether you decide to write solely for yourself or, more likely, share your work with loved ones or a broader literary audience at spoken-word readings and literary journals. It's a big responsibility, but it also has potential for great creative fun.

As we venture into title-giving territory, here are some great ways to instill meaningful titles that will intrigue your audience and resonate with your poem:

- **Pick a line or phrase from the poem itself.** This is my favorite method of titling my own works. Is there a particular phrase or line that your writing group complimented or that you enjoy each time you reread the draft? Is there a combination that underscores the protagonist or a key idea in the poem? Choosing that excerpt could be a great option to clue the reader into the poem's subject.

- **Let your title mirror your theme.** Does your poem explore a particular main idea, event, or topic? Consider the title: "On _____." Many poems have been written on the topics of love, hate, graduation, marriage, divorce, and death. You may choose to add more than one detail to the title to personalize, such as: "On Returning Home Early from the Prom in 1997" or "On Descending Mt. Kilimanjaro with One Leg."

- **Place name, poem name.** Some poems are set in an interesting place or time. For instance, W.H. Auden's famous poem about the start of WWII in Europe is impactfully titled, "September 1, 1939." Instantly, the reader is aware not only of when this poem takes place but of a crucial historical event and milestone taking place in the poem.

- **If your poem has a protagonist or if the poem is addressed to someone in particular, name the poem after the speaker or addressee.** You might also throw in another intriguing detail or two to hook your reader, such as: "For Cole, Age 4."

- **Go against the grain.** Remain open to the possibility that your title might not have much to do directly with the content of your poem, and yet.... If the subtle approach is more your style, then this is the way to go. It might be that you choose an intriguing word that denotes emotional or figurative content of your poem, such as: "Miasma" or "Mystique" that could mean almost anything when combined with the body of your poem, and may just invite your audience to make intriguing close reads.

- **Read your poem to a friend or fellow writer.** What jumps out at her/him first? That's right: borrow from those creative minds around you. Poem titles don't always have to originate with their authors. I've bounced unnamed poems off of some writing friends and family members and found that they are great at suggesting titles that are relevant and intriguing but that I never would have thought of on my own.

***

Try this prompt! Pick three of these methods and give your poem a title based on all three. Compare and contrast, choosing the title that seems to fit your draft best.

***

A Green Eel Named Yellow: On (Suspending) Poetic Logic

My extended family visited the National Aquarium today with the visiting nieces, who had never been. Among the stingrays, eels, tortoise, myriad schools of fish, dolphins, simulated rainforest, ibis and other birds, there was the requisite stop at the gift shop.

Cora Vi chose the girly carnation-pink stuffed turtle with the shiny pink shell that matches her pink-striped dress while Sylvie Ro gravitated immediately to the electric eel in acid green.

"What have you named them?" I asked, as they clutched their new stuffed toys in happy hands.

"I call mine Pink Best Friend," Cora Vi says.

"Mine Yellow," Sylvie Ro announces, as she twirls the long, snake-like body around her neck and down her torso, winding it around herself like Sheena, Queen of the Jungle.

"He's green," more than one of us says.

"His name Yellow," Sylvie Ro insists, and we all smile, shake our heads a bit, and go along with it. One of my high school friends once had a yellow teddy bear named Blue. "It was just blue to me," I recall her saying, "so I named him that at the time." Who can argue with that kind of inspiration?

In poetry, there have been whole movements influenced by logic that was topsy-turvy, seemingly random, and intriguing. The Surrealists come to mind. Such poets as André Breton, Paul Éluard, Robert Desnos, Arthur Rimbaud, Max Ernst, Guillaume Apollinaire, and Federico García Lorca, wrote poems primarily between the two World Wars that were steeped in dream imagery and frequently in political resistance to such movements as Fascism. They lived in desperate, war-torn landscapes and times where basic institutions and any sense of stability were taken from them.

The unconscious as well as images of violence and decay frequently featured in their poems, as did a technique called automatic writing, where a person freewrites from the top of their heads without stopping to structure and without going back later to edit or formulate a logical narrative from the draft. Whatever shows up on the page of its own free will appears in the poem. As such, Surrealists juxtaposed images that are normally not blended or seen in everyday reality.

Certainly, not everyone was or is a fan of such works, although many poets find them refreshing and not dissimilar from the unrest within our own times. Dream imagery can be highly personal and political poetry is not to everyone's taste. Still, as poets we can learn much from Surrealists' approach to drafting poems:

- **Breaking the logic barrier can open us up to a new approach.** Ever say (or hear someone else say in a workshop or class), "But that's the way it really happened!" when someone suggests making a change, such as omitting details, compressing others, or rewriting a line or stanza for clarity? It may have happened that way, it's true, but the pacing of real life can be slow, tedious, and let's face it: boring. Many times, especially if poems are based on true events, we can get so caught up in the order of happenings that our poems bulge with unnecessary details.

- **Poetry with a strong focus on imagery, especially juxtaposed imagery, is powerful, vivid, and often succinct.** Poetry thrives on compression. Word-pictures are the best way to both interest readers and cause them to process the main themes and ideas in your work in a short space.

- **The unconscious is well worth considering and even writing.** Many of our dreams—whether at night or daydreams—contain our deeper fears and questions about ourselves, others, our culture(s), and the conundrums of living a modern life, which serve as interesting topics to explore.

- **Sharply focused, unusual imagery can be a great way to address big themes with resonance and without brow-beating readers or clotting drafts with clichés.** Recurring symbols, settings, people, and events might point the way to a deep subject you hadn't even realized you wanted to explore but that set the stage for poems that connect readers with writer, especially given that many human fears and frustrations are similar across time and place—such as defeat, death, hope and loss of hope, and fear of failure, to name a few.

- **Remember: poems mirror life and life is frequently messy, illogical, and strange.** Invite some clashing images and discordant themes into your poems and see what happens. It can also be fun to pick a stringent form, like a sonnet, and employ vibrant, expansive, opposing images, creating a natural tension between structure and content.

So, a green eel named Yellow? Why not?

∗∗∗

Try This Prompt! For a week, write down any dream imagery you experience or can remember upon waking. After a week, mix and match recurring images and themes to create a poem that doesn't read as true-to-life but that illustrates important views or lessons of life or your interpretation of it. Don't (over)explain—set discordant or strange images and symbols next to each other. For inspiration, I've included two dream poems I've written using this process from my book *Poetry Power.*

Ovum Dream

"(for don't we all crave beauty and contamination)" —*Priscilla Sneff*
For CB: friend, fellow writer, dream interpreter extraordinaire

I fissured the shells open,
exposing a magic act—
gushing moons, buttery discs,
from pastel Styrofoam
ruptured

one at a time. But from one ivory encasing
a ribbon of four yolks flowed, full-sized—
three of the yolks bright black,
inky eclipses. I did not marvel at this
multiplication,

this bounty from one enclosure. My worry:
to whirl together what was given
or pitch them and begin again?
I did not wear an apron, I was all hands
razzmatazzing runny fluid into a crock.
The black yolks suspended orbs,
beautiful dark buoyancy in the glass chamber.

Were these ova the obvious—physical fertility
for a woman without children, creativity,
transmutation from hunger?
Or that I'd made a scrambled
sandwich hours before turning in?

In this vision, questioning myself on
what to do: I kept cracking them open,
the kitchen counter slick with sunny morning.
To whisk or to toss not the question at all;

I did nothing but the one trick
I knew. Rift and spill, rift and spill.
Waking to continue on paper.

In Route

All the rooms were painted goldenrod,
            one after one after one,
and the buffet had many fruits whose names
            the Australians in line behind me
kept explaining to my clueless cohorts.

The dress I was wearing when I looked down
            a jungle green with jade and red
birds, the flounce of the skirt pretty and full.
            I was pleased. Everyone else
in khaki and a t-shirt. You would spot me

across the crowd. The beautiful petite woman
            scooping eggs. Where'd she come from? Your lover
I sensed. I still found the blue rubber-band at my nape,
            shook my hair loose. The china of the plate
so ivory my face almost disappeared on its surface.

***

The Art of Offering Feedback: Real-World Tips for Helpful Poetry Critiques

Writing can be a solitary craft, yet there are many great ways to connect with other poets and grow our writing skills in the process. Workshops. Classes. Beta readers. Poem-swap buddies.

One of the best ways to become better poets is to share our work regularly with other writers working towards the same goals of clarity, beauty, and fluidity. By offering suggestions on others' work, we writers learn more about how our own poems work, how current and future poems might be improved, and how our own poetic and editorial preferences in theme, tone, and style emerge.

What makes a great critique?

- **Honesty and clarity.** Don't compliment parts just to have something to say—instead, reach for an excerpt you truly admire and then briefly explain why you admire it.

- **Specify, specify, specify.** Choose one or two intriguing, fresh insights that the poem provides and articulate why those word choices, lines, or stanzas resonate with you as a reader. The more specific you can be the better. An entirely negative critique, a gushingly positive statement, or a critique that is vague ("Everything's awesome!" Or, conversely, "This is stupid.") won't give the author enough to begin seeing their poem as the reader does. Mention specific words, lines, or stanzas so that the author can reference the parts you found vague, the alliteration you liked, and the two lines in stanza four that were confusing.

- **Encouragement.** Even if this style of poem isn't what you prefer (perhaps it's a sestina but you write free verse) or about a topic you've read a million times, point out what the poet is doing well. There will be something in every draft—a beautiful title, a word choice, or a cool setting. Writers frequently realize drafts need improvement, but when making suggestions, do so with a professional tone. Respect that it is always the other author's work and that you are providing a supportive viewpoint.

Tips for offering helpful feedback:

- **Compliment a phrase or word choice(s) that resonates with you.** Say what it is you like about this diction choice. Specific feedback is most helpful.

- **Consider theme.** Does the poem explore a certain leitmotif? Is all of the language and syntax appropriate for the theme? You might want to begin your comments with: To me, this poem is about_____, which is a great way to show your fellow writer how you are interpreting what they've written, whether the way the poet had intended or not. This feedback will also give the writer an opportunity to adjust their draft accordingly.

- **Note the stanza or lines you like best.** Explain. Also, consider where stanzas and lines end. If you notice any patterns with line breaks or where lines begin (such as anaphora, the repetition of a phrase at the beginning of several lines in a row for artistic resonance and emphasis), note them. You might also offer suggestions for where a line or stanza might begin or end with more impact and why.

- **Comment on the title.** Does the title invite readers into the poem without giving away too much of the poem's plot? If not, look within the poem's body for another title or offer suggestions for other titles that might match the poem's theme better.

- **Does the poem employ a strong end rhyme scheme in the first few lines and not follow that pattern later in the poem?** If so, gently point it out.

- **Poems often make allusions to places, literary figures/celebrities/ artists, cultural icons, and even other poems.** Note any you spot, and explain if they are fitting or not.

- **Remember: poems share many literary similarities with their prose cousins:** What is the poem's setting? Does the poem have characters, including a protagonist and antagonist and/or supporting characters? What is the main conflict within the poem? List them, citing specific line references for your answers.

- **Jot any questions you might have about the poem.** Are there omitted words or phrases (which often happens in the heat of drafting)? Does the poem begin with one idea and then veer off into another without finishing the first idea? Do you wonder what happens to the protagonist in a certain line? Are there pronoun confusions or ambiguous references? Gently note them.

Keep in Mind:

- **These are drafts, so spelling errors, repetitions, inconsistencies, and such are likely.** You can point out one if you want, but don't nitpick on small errors that the author will catch on her own later. Think big picture: theme, character, setting, dialogue, conflict, and other literary devices or parts of a possible story arc.

- Many workshops use the "compliment sandwich method" of feedback: offer one compliment, ask a question or point out a confusing passage, finish with another compliment. You don't have to follow this format, but it's worth considering.

- Remember that it takes a lot of courage to share one's writing. Follow the Golden Rule, and don't dish out vague or purposely hurtful feedback you wouldn't want to receive about your own writing.

***

Try this Prompt! Make a poetry-swap friend at a workshop, class, or online. Agree to share work once a month. When you send your work, note one area that you're wondering about and one area that you feel went well with the poem. Consider using the above guidelines as you offer feedback, suggestions, and support to your fellow artist.

***

Will the Real Speaker Please Stand up?

When I was a teenager, there was a game show that aired in the early evening called *To Tell the Truth*. In each episode, a series of celebrity panelists, often including the comic Paula Poundstone or actor Meshach Taylor, would listen to three ordinary-seeming contestants, all claiming to be the same person.

Each of three contestants, two fibbers and one truth-teller, would begin with the same claim, such as: "My name is Kelly Burns, and my shop sells the world's largest cupcakes." The celebrity panelists would then ask questions—sometimes serious and sometimes outlandish—to gauge who the real person belonging to the attribute might be before making a guess before the studio audience. The celebrity might quip, "What got you into the cupcake game, sweetie?" or "What's your best-selling flavor?" or "Just how big *are* your cupcakes?" or any number of oddball and entertaining queries that may or may not make the contestants trip over their words.

Sometimes, based on body language, facial expression, or tone of voice, it was easy to pinpoint the liar. Other times, it was decidedly difficult, especially since even people telling the truth tend to trip over their words if they're not used to being on camera or if the question catches them off guard. Part of the fun of watching the show was listening to the strange questions. The other enjoyment was guessing right along, seeing if I could judge context clues, such as voice inflection, better than the celebrity panelists. I was often surprised at the results when the announcer asked the real so-and-so to please stand up.

Only as an adult did I learn that the show originated in the mid-fifties and lasted until the late sixties in its first run. There have been several reboots since, including the season I watched. Clearly, people have a natural streak of curiosity when it comes to matters of potential faking and fibbing. We all like to think we can quickly gather the clues and not be fooled, but most of us—at least a portion of the time—misguess and make errors in judgments when reading context.

When I was a grad student, we workshopped our poems once a month. One of the first rules when verbally discussing other poets' work was that we not assume first-person poems were describing the author. In fact, persona poems in first-person could just as likely be from a character's POV or another real-life person's POV speaking about his or her life experience. In order to address the poem's first-person nature, we spoke of "the speaker," instead of "you." This, at first, seemed a bit of sleight of hand and kind of clunky to remember to say, but in the long-term and as a teacher myself it is ingenious and handy, especially when approaching others' drafts.

What are the advantages to penning poems with a speaker not ourselves? First person is an immediate POV. It deposits the writer and reader inside the skin of the protagonist telling the poem. It is often dynamic and focused. Third-person is a bit removed; more like a well-informed announcer. It's the difference between writing a character and writing *about* a character. While third-person can be all-knowing, first-person includes a limited scope that readers find compelling often because of their myopia, partialities, and limited understanding and viewpoint. While consternating in real people, flaws are intriguing and often gripping on the page.

Even if a poem is based on real-life events, a poet should not be constrained to present a poem from her own viewpoint. "But that's the way it happened!" we're tempted to argue. True, but that one fact or event might just be the starting point with the entire rest of the poem made up; as readers it is not our business to know. There may be emotional truths equal to or superseding external truths and, as we all know from having played telephone as children, even facts can shape-shift when told from person to person, depending on which details are included or omitted.

As poets, we would be wise, both in our own work and in approaching others' drafts, to acknowledge that each poem has a narrator—a speaker— who presents the poem from a unique position which may be part, whole, or not at all the poet.

***

Try this prompt!: Choose three poems—new or old, written by someone you know or a poet you only know through their published work—and make a note about the speaker. Does the author use first-person? Second-person "you" (which can have a jarring, bossy tone that grabs readers' attention)? Third-person? What is the effect of the speaker's POV on readers? Which do you prefer, and why? Would the poem's tone, context, or content be different from another POV? Then choose a draft of one of your poems, and change the speaker of the poem. What does this new speaker believe, see, or feel that changes your poem?

***

A parting word of encouragement: Will change in your poems happen overnight? No, and that is part of the magic of this art form. Step by step and over the course of years, with the encouragement of fellow practitioners and with plenty of prompts (and patience!), you will acquire the skill and the spirit that makes of verse a sacred song.

Nancy Scott

NAMING YOUR POEM

What if your parents decided not to give you a name; you went through life as "that kid" or "hey, you." Names are important. Chances are your parents puzzled over your name for months, changing their minds multiple times until you arrived. I was told my parents exhausted the alphabet before I was born, but even so, my original birth certificate reads, "Baby Levinson." I never liked the name they finally gave me. I always wanted to be Elizabeth or Susannah.

Sometimes poets take this "no name" or "untitled" way out because finding the right title can be tough. When I start to write a poem, I use what is commonly called a "placeholder" name as a springboard to get me started, but it rarely becomes the final title for the poem. I may have a general idea of what the poem will be about, but very often I find that somewhere down the page, the poem begins to take on a life of its own and I merely become the transcriber of what it is trying to say.

Because there are various types of titles, it is not always a simple task to decide what will work best; that is, what title will do its job, so to speak. Sometimes a short poem wants a long title and vice-versa. There are no hard and fast rules, except maybe to alert the reader to "here's what I have for you" or "you're going to love this poem."

I wrote a book of retold fairy tales, *The Owl Prince*, and all the titles have two parts, as in "The Scrawny Chicken or Why the War was Finally Won." Someone remarked that the titles themselves were almost a poem. Often I use one word, "Nightmares," or two words, "Eating Chocolate," because that's the main idea of the poem. Some titles can also take a significant line from the poem that sets the stage for what follows, as in "Stay on the Path, Mimi," where, on a trail in the woods, my four-year-old granddaughter warns me that there are snakes in the underbrush.

Sometimes information, perhaps a location or a proper name that would take too much space explaining within the poem will fit nicely in the title, as in "Riding the Funicular with a Rugby Player from New Zealand." Or set a tone, as in "Playing Chess with the Muskrat" or "Cousin Leon and the Playboy Bunny." I also like to open some titles with "Why" as in "Why I Never Want to Fly Across Montana Again." Most of these examples were not the first, or even the second or third titles I tried out on the poems. Every time I draft a poem, I do several revisions, and each time I revisit the title and often change it.

Titles are not necessarily cast in stone either. I've had poems published with one title, and then for my book, *A Siege of Raptors*, I gave every poem a new title to fit the special format for the book.

Editors generally have preferences. As managing editor of a journal, we don't publish white space in lieu of some kind of title. If we really like the poem, we will ask the poet for a title, but an asterisk or some kind of wingding font will occasionally make it through.

Remember that your title is your best free advertising. We write and publish our work with the hope that someone will read it. When I pick up a new book of poetry, I scan the pages. There are two things that will make me stop and read a particular poem. First, the title, and second, how the poem is arranged on the page, but that is another issue. Make your titles do some work. Don't let them get lazy and just take up space. Yes, you can fall in love with a particular title, but make sure it headlines the right poem.

Jenny Ferguson

THE FIVE SENSES ARE IMAGERY/IMAGERY IS POETRY

One of the first things I ask beginner poets to do as they start their exploration of this craft is to sit down and define poetry—creatively. They find it awkward. Uncomfortable even. But, they play along, using words like "experience" and "meaning" and "poetic language."

We don't talk about these definitions. We use them as a starting place. We file these definitions away. The exercise is to try to define a thing we think we know with our words. This is our first attempt at poetry.

Then we close our eyes. In the classroom. At the park perched on a wooden bench. In the grocery store next to a wall of cereal boxes. We close our eyes often and we listen, we smell, we taste, we touch. As poets-in-the-making, when we rely solely on our eyes to explore this world, we forget our other senses. And while poetry is a visual medium—letters set on paper—poetry is also an aural art. This Jericho Brown reminds us in his TEDx talk "The Art of Words." Jericho Brown tells us how, for him, poetry is like sitting in the Black church, like the sermons, like the voices that will inevitably call out in praise. But, like a sermon and those voices praising God, poetry is above all an aural art. That is, it's an art we process through our ears—and an art we transmit through our voices. Beginning poets forget this important fact when they sit down with their computers, their pens and paper.

Of course, voice here is metaphor. You only need to Google ASL Slam Poetry to experience voice. Watch "Symbiosis" by Douglas Ridloff. Then compare it to Emi Mahmoud's fantastic spoken word poem, "Why I Haven't Told You Yet." What have you learned about voice? How do you understand voice through your senses—all of them? Spend some time here. Write a poem in which you try to define voice—even if your poem is a list, or comes out in a form that doesn't feel like poetry to you. Make sure you use the five senses as you sketch out your poem-definition.

Closing our eyes, and letting our other senses take over, rise up, explore the world we so often see but rarely hear, taste, smell,and touch, allows us to access the building blocks we use to experience life and the tools we use to write poetry.

Focusing on the ear leads us to these lines from Victor Hernández Cruz's "Here Is an Ear Hear": "Finally after so many generations he got/ to hear what he most wanted: the sounds made by flowers/ as they stretched into the light." In this poem we hear the minute, the almost-unhearable, and in that focus, we fall deeper into poetry.

One exercise that can unlock the five senses—can unlock imagery—is to take a poem you really love. It can be one of yours. It can be your favorite poet's opus. Take this poem and rewrite it five times, with a focus on one of the senses each time. Once you've got five different poems, with five different foci, you'll make one poem. Print your poems out. Cut up the lines. Spread them out on your table.

Now, make a new poem—on that draws the strongest lines, the sharpest images. What do you notice here? What senses are most vivid to you? And why? Try this exercise again and again until you start finding concrete answers, until you understand sight, taste, touch, smell, and hearing as a poet must.

This exploration of the senses, and therefore of imagery in its most complete form, opens space for poets to write their first ars poetica. An ars poetica is a poem about the art of poetry, about this art we seek to understand. This genre of poem, it's one you can return to again and again. First read Horace's "Ars Poetica," and then Czeslaw Milosz's "Ars Poetica?," and if you want to read one more, try Dorothea Lasky's "Ars Poetica."

It's important to remember, poets spend their entire lives studying this art. You are at the beginning. And the beginning is a wonderful place to be. Start with the five senses, this will lead you to a new understanding of imagery. And imagery will lead you further along the path.

One of the last things I ask beginner poets to do as they wrap up the early stages of their study of this craft is sit down and define poetry—creatively. Harnessing the five senses into imagery, these definitions become not about poetry—but poetry itself.

Whitney Sweet

STEP AWAY FROM THE DESK. IT'S DRAWER TIME.

If you are anything like me, when you write a new poem and you believe it's good, you get all excited. For me, this comes in the form of a racing heart and a feeling akin to going on a first date. Me and this poem are having a great time. We might even go out again. When I get this feeling, I want to shout it from the rooftops. Much like when I met my husband, whom I fell for instantly, I fall for my poems (the good ones in particular) the moment the words spill out onto the page. I want everyone I know to read them. I recite them to myself over and over, I email them to friends and family, I contact old professors.

After doing this, only to tire of the original adrenaline rush of writing something fantastic, I put my poem away for awhile, inevitably to return to it one day when trying to find a good contest to enter, or when assembling a chapbook manuscript. That's when it hits me. The sinking regret of over excitement. *Ugh, is that a spelling mistake? Oh no, why would I have put a period here? Why are all the lines capitalized at the beginning? Gross, look at the lining! And don't get me started on the use of white space!* Much like grabbing coffee with an ex, the reality of the poem in the daylight makes me question everything.

Many times, I have felt bad about myself and my skills as a poet when this has happened. I have learned that what I needed to implement is something I like to call "drawer time." I also recommend this to my students, or people who ask me to edit their work. It can be used for any type of writing, as it is a great way to find your mistakes.

How it works is simple; when you've completed a piece of writing, and you're in the midst of celebrating how amazing you are and how your brain is the best thing ever created, step away from your desk. Go for a walk, bake a pie, visit a friend. Do something else. The key to this is to give your brain something else to do, so that when you return, you have fresh eyes and a refreshed brain to catch your errors and all the places for you to improve your writing.

For me personally, I like to put a lot of "ands" in my writing, especially in the first drafts of my poems. Over time, I have realized that this is a place-holder for me, a place where my thought was interrupted or came to an end. It signals a turn in the poem, or a place that is unsteady and unsure. When I come back from a break of drawer time, my first task is to take out the ands. To achieve this, I always read my work out loud. Sometimes, when this gets boring, I put on a British accent to hold my own interest. If you're British, you can use a Canadian accent, which seems only fair.

This system of taking breaks and returning to your work with fresh eyes can work for any timeline. If you are trying to hit a contest deadline and the piece is due in today, take a short break. Even if it's only for a half an hour, stepping away from the piece and coming back with a refreshed viewpoint can help you write a better poem. Of course, it is better if you give yourself more time to review a piece before you declare it finished. What I like to do is try to plan for a week's worth of drawer time if I'm writing a piece that must be ready for a particular event or to be submitted somewhere. This way, I can take a few cracks at improvements. Reading it over once or twice a day is the key, without rushing, and without pressure.

The way to making drawer time as effective as possible is to read your poem aloud each time you make changes. Pretend you are performing the piece. If you need an audience, video chat with a friend, or ask a family member to sit for you so you can read it aloud. If you don't have a friend you can ask, read it to yourself in the mirror. Poetry is meant to be alive and to be read aloud. When you read it aloud you will hear the rhythms, and the timing of each word. Does it ring nicely in your ear? Does it feel right? Does your pulse leap? Your scalp tingle? Are you thinking about it later in the day? If you can say yes to these, then your poem is finished.

The great thing about poetry is that when given drawer time, it can some-times age like a fine wine or a great wheel of cheese. As you grow as a person or writer, you will return to the piece after you've declared it finished, and perhaps discover that it is in fact, not finished. Poetry is a living thing, not isolated alone in a dusty book. Since we can often look back at poems from the past and see their relevance today, the same can be said for your work. Don't be afraid to leave a piece for a few months, or a year, and revisit it again when the time feels right. Perhaps it will feel like an old friend, or maybe it will need more improvements that you could never have dreamt of if you hadn't been out there living life.

To sum up, the steps of drawer time are as follows:

1) Write a poem.

2) Step away from your desk. Leave your notebook behind. Put it in your drawer.

3) Go do something fun.

4) Come back refreshed, with new eyes to view your piece.

5) Read your poem out loud upon each revision.

6) Repeat until you think the piece is perfect.

7) If it doesn't feel perfect, put it away for a longer time. Repeat steps 1-6.

8) Save that beautiful poem and try to get it published!

That's it. Drawer time is a simple and effective way to improve your poetry by the elimination of errors over time. With the help of this method you can prevent premature gray hairs, biting of nails, and the excessive snacking that accompanies the editing process.

Barbara Perry

EXERCISES FOR INVITING THE MUSE

There is often the complaint that you can't find the time to fit in some writing. But, Gabriel Gudding wrote a book-length poem while driving his car from Normal, Illinois to Providence, Rhode Island, and back every weekend to see his daughter.[1] Sure there were lots of highway vistas in it.

However you do it doesn't much matter. So set your alarm clock a half hour earlier. Go to a dollar store and buy more socks and underwear so you can skip laundry this weekend. Sit in your car in the parking garage instead of traffic. Give yourself the time, and you will be mixing your mind with that time and place, and that will be a great start. That is all we are aiming for right now: creating the time for something to appear on the page.

Technique 1:
Trust the Muse

Flip through a book without looking and randomly point at 5 words (or phrases if you like their adjoining words.) Jot them down and use at least 3 of them in a poem without thinking too much. I lean on the visual side as most of us do, so I use a book with lots of nouns or terms, like an old high school science book or a handyman's catalog of some kind. But if you are more conceptual, you may like a philosophy or economics book.

It is important to feel this is going to be *fun*. So pick something that attracts or aMUSES you. Or if that is too strong of a word, pick a book that intrigues you, whether its style is light, dark, or technical. Not knowing the material can actually be of help here, as you will have to take leaps of imagination to use it.

---

1. *Rhode Island Notebook*, Dalkey Archive Press, copyright 2007.

Perhaps with you more conceptual types, it might be a good idea to use an additional book that has a bodily or sensory foundation—kayaking trips, cookbook, auto mechanic tips, fabric descriptions etc.—as one will need to bring the conceptual heady stuff into the senses or the body. We will be dropping a great portion of our conscious thinking and relying on our inner sense of things. Poetry is something we conjure in our head *and* our body. So we are going to let the psyche or our inner sense of things guide us. This is found in sensing deep down, or in our body before consciousness.

Try this:
You Are Just the Scribe Trying to Keep Up
Never judge what you have just written. It is not time for your editor's voice to be listened to—it is only time for an uncensored creative gush. This is a moment of complete liberation of the mind's impulses, so let it rip! Give yourself *complete* permission to write the weirdest, saddest, most nihilistic, confusing, or most Pollyanish etc., poem ever!

By letting go of yourself and your literary ideals—be it a desire for something pithy or soulful or epic—you can blow the doors off of any self-consciousness and create a potent and surprising experience. Sit back and enjoy the ride of no expectations—you are doing this to generate possible poetic material, not a final product—you are just the scribe trying to keep up with the barrage of uncensored thoughts, images, and phrases.

Try this:
Exaggerate to Reveal the Truth
Exaggeration is a most wonderful tool. You can stay with the original feeling, but by employing exaggeration you might unearth more passionate, unique, buried responses that are less self-conscious, and truer to your raw poetic reality.

I once wrote a poem that I thought was purely indulgent nonsense and upon rereading it, I noticed that the piece was working on another level—it had a dark undertow and told a difficult story in a fresh way because humor/detachment was accessed by not identifying with its pain, resultant of a bad break-up. I did this by (subconsciously) creating multiple players in the poem, who were amusing me. The main speaker of the poem was an exaggerated hot mess, which was fun to unleash. At its finale I used exaggeration to embody my cool logical side as a poet's attorney, which gave it closure. All of this happened because exaggeration overrode the self-conscious or self-critical voice.

Technique 2:
Swivel Points

If what you have just written has some zest or promise, but is like a stew that is missing some spice, write the missing spice on another sheet of paper. For instance, if the piece is too cloying or sweet, you might write "sour," "biting," "sarcastic," or "cruel." Then to set up this new swivel point, use a word or phrase that makes room for this, such as "But," "Unfortunately," or "In reality," etc. Or you can use any number of negating idioms such as "Who cares?," "Beats me," "Give me a break," "So what," etc. to ask a question or make a retort about this piece of writing—then write your bitter answer. This works to inject a surprise or twist to the poem, which can be like hitting pay dirt in poetry.

Technique 3:
The Present is Your Portal

You may even want to utilize on-the-spot present stimulus, such as your phone ringing, or hearing the blood whooshing in your head. Being open to underground musings is not so different from being alert to your sensory present. They are not separate in fact, but what you physically experience in the present (like that phone ringing) is in contact with the subconscious. Seeing, hearing, feeling etc., this moment can touch into your subconscious because you may not have solidified this experience yet into a thought or consciousness—it is of the same substance as the unbound material that is the swirling dreamlike matter of the subconscious—i.e. imagistic, or kinetic/bodily knowledge, but certainly not of language—yet.

Therefore you are immersed in the language of the subconscious when you are using the senses as your touchstone. As a result you are able to step into the flow of the subconscious with its many mirror-like images reflecting back up to you in glimpses of consciousness, somewhat like a Cubist painting.

Try this:
Be Aware of Your Exact Intersection of Time and Space

For example, you are sitting at your desk with the morning sun streaming in your window, noting the shadows, cool or warm air, sounds of children running, etc. At the same time, be on the lookout for inner images that pop up in your mind, or an elusive feeling that is burbling up. Start with this inner sensing and just unwind, run and romp through the proverbial field of thoughts, and the momentum or the unfurling poetic logic will appear. This is about freedom, experimentation, and unbridled voice. You may find that one angle of musing is particularly raring to go, fun or satisfying to expand on, and off you go with that voice. Let it gallop out as far as it wants.

Soon enough it is not yours anymore, this writing, but a message from the depths.

I once heard a Cambridge physicist say that we receive 150,000,000 impulses of information a second,[2] yet can only be conscious of perhaps seven in any one moment. So there is a rich storehouse of information that is your subconscious. Let's use it!

Here is an example of this type of writing:

Writing the Unknown

Tippy toeing in from the side of my head suddenly I have to quickly type a bridge for something to pass over or it will be gone, and I realize there always was a waiting mind wanting to reveal itself to me, as if I was some unknown planet within a vast galaxy I might like to explore, perhaps the vastness we speak of when Buddhist's talk of emptiness. But in that case I myself am this emptiness and in that space they also say, all is born. What is being born in the emptiness is a constant trust to step onto the next lily pad or asteroid, a moving-out-into act of mind that skips like a rock over a bone broth lake and sometimes you have to keep jettisoning those slim rock-words and connect them to this exact time of your serial tossing, trying to keep a constant flow because if you stop and doubt something you have then stopped the continuum. And that is ok too. But don't stop for long, keep unfurling or sparking, whatever it is in trusting this movement, this mind uncorraled by fear or hope. There is a feeling like there is a gift to unwrap at some point and

---

2. Jeremy Hayward, PhD in theoretical physics at Cambridge University. Lecture at Chicago Shambhala Meditation Center 2008.

it will be unwrapped either obscenely or demurely but it always moves; it is like a plateful of raw egg under fingers, but you are blindfolded, skimming along, not knowing where the center is or the end.

-end-

Try this:

Go Where the Energy Is

To deepen your trust and investigation of this process, go where the energy is—the place that sparks your mind like an energized conversation. You are in fact having a type of conversation between your subconscious and your consciousness. You are being attentive to an inner voice and thus responsive to it. Your consciousness responds with ideas inspired by the subconscious. The subconscious is coming up as the consciousness reaches down. They begin to blend. Sometimes consciousness is more akin to an inner wisdom than intellect at this point. And that can make for great poetry.

Do not let the conscious intellect stay above ground, so to speak—always listen for inner phrases or take note of any inner images or sensations—that is what you want to be in touch with. You must treat these visitations like honored guests that you are very interested in knowing and accepting. Accept and befriend the tokens of the subconscious. And most importantly *enjoy*, trust what is unfolding.

What often happens in this receptive space is an image, phrase, or sensation appears, and usually rather faintly. Yet still it is being offered. It will be a bit insistent, though you can't see how it has anything to do with what you are "trying" to write.

Let's say it's an image of a cigarette, or something sensorily remembered or presently felt, like the bright sun on your uplifted face. And certainly you can combine anything that comes up. In that event, the smoke may form hieroglyphics that swirl in beams of light above your head—you are free to muse what this may portend, or this may stay a mysterious, small image in the larger context of what you are building. Like an amusement park of no bounds, try anything you are curious about, and when any of this energizes you, then stay with that ride for as long as it lasts.

Never make the process hard or too highbrow—always allow yourself to feel *un*selfconscious, inventive. I have found the best headspace is when I am almost giddy with this place of freedom—because after all, it is elating to be writing quickly, catching those inner hunches as they bubble up, not feeling mired nor hesitant but accepting whatever floats up into your mind, and following the energy.

Our Many Inner (S)elves

We now know the key is to allow the subconscious into the process. We can also invite the subconscious up by setting parameters of ease, the same as wanting someone to feel comfortable around you—without hesitation, welcome any small gesture they make to communicate, encourage them by attentively wanting to know more about them. Treat them like royalty—but of course, this is really just being unconditionally accepting of anything that surfaces from your own psyche. The idea is to lose yourself to this conversation, become one with it. At some point a sublime twist of language will leech out, utterly without your thinking, and you will experience the serious payback of courting the Muse.

Below is an example of inviting my Muse to help me write a poem on this essay. I've included the whole unedited experiment so you can see how densely the ideas might flow in. If your head gets too scrambled in reading this, please simply skip down to the rough edit that follows.

Voice: I am waiting on the drywall guy.
You: Oh yes! And??
Voice: He's late. Maybe it's my cue to keep writing.
You: Please continue!
Voice: What is really on my mind is my hands are cold and I need to exercise. I can't find that switch that says "inspired". I think I will make a sandwich but what is starving more is my writing head. I say I want to live this life, which means "write," so here I am. But I don't know who I am as I am slightly, vastly, and randomly different every day. But there must be wisdom to all these branchings I suspect.

Who am I kidding? Usually I am asleep when I have my best ideas. So that takes care of that. Oh please elves of the dream place, come out and play with the premise of this day as a day for finishing this essay. Elfin essay about how I cannot fathom this but I still must imagine this could be. Help me just get on the sled and start sliding to this end, an ending that says all I want to say which I do not know—i.e. I think I want to *show* the way to the elves. Oh, that's it—show the form of a mind that opens and takes you on the journey of the elfin tale, the tale about how the pixies rise up from your brain and bring you bits of flowers and grain and images of their ancestors before them who died in battle with that brain. They are not mad at you though because they know they are also made by your brain and therefore know that they are here to help you solve your quixotic self. They know they are here to die or to continue transforming into other (s)elves. There will always be a (s)elf that brings biscuits and gravy to the table when there are lean pickin's. Stay with this (s)elf and down the road from there, there will come (s)elves donned with top hats, being drawn to higher aspirations, somewhat like a snake that comes out of the ground to warm itself under the call of the brilliant sun.

This becomes less of a peak experience and more of an illuminant way where you don't need a hole to call home, and you don't need a theory of ancestors or little outfits, lots of green or workshops but just that place that keeps unfolding and becoming, a dimension that is rising out of the present circumstances and is surfacing. Vast temples for worshipping and auditoriums for listening arise as the images, attitudes, and flashes of thought expand. It is a type of time surfacing that holds the future forms of the past, now. And the church bells start ringing as I know this, they ring like I will know this for a long time, and I want to say I feel I am on a sled in a field of snow in a Dr. Zhivago life and really that is too sad and I have to ask, doesn't this new time assure one of more possibility, more opportunity? Does the scene have to be so white and vast that ones dreams too can be lost here? Is life that big? I am blinded by the white opulence of choice whereas if I have a room with a warm body under the covers with me I think I am complete. The (s)elves say it's time to tie some Windsor knots and look for structure. But they also say "Beware, you can get lost there too."

-end poem experiment-

All these exercises and tips are meant to let your creative spirit densely etch its way up to the surface, without judgment. You want that, as it is easier to cut out extraneous bits than to write the perfect line again and again. In fact whittling down is an essential way we write good lines.

Below is the first rough draft of the poem. I started whittling away at the superfluous parts and playing with line breaks, to clarify the piece. I also might add words that help reveal the poem's true intent. NOW is the time to put on your critical thinking, not before:

Calling all dream elves—help me get on the sled
and start sliding to an end, an ending
that says all I want to say
which I do not know but shows
the form of a mind that opens and takes
you on the journey of the elfin tale
of how the pixies rise up from your brain to bring you bits
of flowers and grain and images
of their ancestors before them
who died in battle with that brain.
They are not angry with you though because
they are also made by this brain
and therefore know they are here
to help solve your quixotic (s)elf.
They know they are here
to die or to turn into other (s)elves.

There will always be a (s)elf that brings biscuits and gravy to the table
when there are lean pickin's. Stay with this (s)elf
and down the road they will become (s)elf propelled vehicles
drawn by higher aspirations
somewhat like a snake that comes out
of the ground to warm itself under the call
of the brilliant sun. This becomes less

of a peak experience and more of an illuminant way
where you don't need a hole to call home
you don't need a theory of ancestors or little outfits,
lots of green or workshops but just that place
that keeps unfolding a dimension
that is rising out of the present mind
of vast temples for worshipping and auditoriums for listening
as the images, attitudes, and flashes of thought expand.
It is a type of time surfacing
that holds all future forms and the church bells
start ringing as I know this

they ring like I will know this for a long time and I want to say
I feel I am on a sled in a field of snow in a Dr. Zhivago life
and really that is too sad and I have to ask
doesn't this new expanse of time
assure one of time fulfilled?
Does the scene have to be so vast that
ones dreams too can be lost here?
I am blinded by the white
opulence of choice

-end rough draft-

Often poems anchor around an image or theme. In this case the poem itself did not seem to start until the elves arrived on the scene. That is where the writing started to get energized and coalesced, so that is where I began the poem.

The experimentation continues, but we have now approached form. Whether or not this piece would hold more of its original power as a prose poem, try to put it in line breaks as that allows one to see the piece more clearly and edit out the detritus. Line breaks are also where creative stops and starts happen, at the beginning and end of lines. They can also make an idea clearer too if needed. The topic of line breaks and form could take up many books, but here we are concentrating on the front end of poetry making, the courting of one's Muse to release potent raw material.

As for knowing the poem's intent, sometimes the poet does not even realize the poem's true intent until they stop struggling with the poem and allow the poem to say what it wants—i.e. after editing out ideas that felt extraneous, the ending came as a surprise to me!

Try this:

Accept Everything

Think of yourself as an actor and not yourself—you are free to be or say anything. Certainly you do not confuse the real Brad Pitt with the guy he played in Fight Club do you? It is the same—these things you are writing are creations that give voice to the many (s)elves within you. Inhabiting a wildly different persona or attitude may initially feel like you have split off from a sane self, but by trusting this creative device, it will offer worlds upon worlds of combinations, intellect, and emotions to your process—as well as wild a*mus*ement.

So believe in your innate inner richness, allow yourself the sense of being on vacation where space and time is yours to fully sink into. You are rich in resources. What wonderful, sad, frustrated, fulfilled, painful, acerbic, or silly, etc., feelings can you allow up?

If what you have allowed up holds some psychic energy for you, then the next phrase, image, or piece of poetic logic will automatically come up from this. If your left brain tries to interfere telling you something is too silly, violent, grotesque, improper, verbose etc., ignore that part of your brain, just as you would some wacko yelling at you from a YouTube clip. They are not even in the same room as you, not even the same world—your world of indulging in the spontaneity and impulse of mind on page—they have nothing to do with this world of writing by the seat of your pants, accepting everything and anything that comes up, and following the energy.

Technique 4
Finding Your Authentic Start

You can write willy-nilly for an hour and never find your groove. In such a case it's time to don your b.s. detector to see if you are dropping down deep enough into the process or if you are still playing it safe. If you have been writing for at least 10 minutes and are not finding much of a flow yet, simply stop, take a deep breath, still your mind for a bit and say to yourself "What I *really* want to say is..." then dive in and don't look back.

Stopping and writing "What I really want to say is..." gives yourself a chance to drop any strait-jacketing logic you've written yourself into, or even poetic logic if it is drying up. Natalie Goldberg mentions this technique in her bestseller *Writing Down the Bones*, the bedrock book on finding your writing voice. By doing this, you leap over any self-conscious thoughts. These are put in place by the vestiges of our reptilian brain's commands to stay safe. You don't need these cautionary cues—you are not walking down a dark alley but rather touching into your unconscious impressions, where wisdom and poetry reside.

For example, by simply stopping, taking a long breath and checking into a deeper strata of your being, you realize you have been feeling sad all day. You remember a good friend that you lost a few years ago, and it is the slant of the sun this time of year that takes you back to this; you are able to feel the ways in which your body holds this, which can now can take shape on the page.

By stopping and checking in with yourself, you are returning to your genuine edge of self, taking the time to refocus on a deeper truth you can sense, where you can once again free-fall into the images and ideas that surround it. You are poising yourself to take a swan dive into your psyche's ponderous depths.

Like Dorothy in the Wizard of Oz, you've always had the power to get back to your true home, that deep self, that vast present and past sensory data of all you are. What you had to learn was to trust your inner Kansas, not rely on externalities to point the way: monkeys, witches, helpful Little People, none of these could take you to the source of your creative depths. In fact the path that your creative self takes was potentially shackled from mid-childhood on. I heard an advanced Buddhist teacher once say that around 6-9 years old, a certain spirit-like quality goes underground. So what we must do is begin to trust our inner sense of things as we did in our early childhood, and make that connection strong again.

In poetry you are recovering impulses born of the submerged syntheses of your life; therefore poetry builds a bridge to welcome this deep aspect of yourself to the surface.

It all begins with an image or inner sensing that faintly calls. Welcoming this fragment from your psyche, you catch a Cubist glimpse of a poetic reality. You encourage a deepening of this visitation by playful musing and startling honesty, as described in the techniques and tips above. Soon you are gliding on a slick track of writing until the image and/or inner senses exhaust themselves.

It is like a party where a song that you can hardly resist starts blasting, so you toss your pâté into the air and start moving couches aside, to dance like a possessed spirit. And that you are. Before that you were having a good enough time talking, noshing. But now something grabs you—so you throw everything to the side and dive in—body and soul.

Norman Minnick

AWAKENING THE DIONYSIAN NERVE: BRINGING POEMS OFF THE PAGE AND INTO THE BODY

Imagine taking a music class in which you are required to read the scores to music but never actually listen to music. Too often, this is what happens in the classroom when we are asked to read poetry. Remember your eighth-grade teacher telling you to turn to page 563 of your textbook, read a poem by Robert Frost, and then answer the questions that follow? You did as you were told, closed the book, and the poem was forgotten. Bringing poems off the page and into the body—in other words, memorizing and reciting poems—allows us not only to hear poems but also experience them, to learn *how* a poem means as opposed to *what* a poem means.

The best way to understand poetry is to experience it. This goes against the traditional approach of dissection and analysis. Memorization opens complex pathways in the psyche and, as Lucio Mariani says, "allows the Dionysian nerve hidden in each of us to surface and become stimulated so that [we] get to have the admittedly difficult but extraordinary experience of knowing a poem directly."[1] As John Ciardi and Miller Williams explain in their landmark book *How Does a Poem Mean?* "The common question from which an approach begins is 'what does the poem mean?'" In response, they write, "the reader tends to 'interpret' the poem rather than to experience it."[2]

The pianist will tell us that the arrangement of notes on the page is not the music. "The music," she will say, "is this…" at which point she will begin to play. The same is true for poetry. That is, the little black marks we call letters that we organize into words are like music notes; they are only notations for

1. Mariani et al. "Concerning the Diffusion and Re-Creation of Poetry: In Praise of the Lesser Players." *Literary Imagination.* 2005; 7.1: 95-102.

2. Ciardi, J. and Williams, M. *How Does a Poem Mean?* 2nd ed. Houghton Mifflin, 1975.

how the poem is to be spoken (or sung, as the case may be). The thing on the page we call a poem is no different than the score to a piece of music.

This, of course, applies mainly to free-verse poems that do not have an established meter, rhyme scheme, etc. Here are some ideas to consider when memorizing and reciting a poem:

Silence

Any composer will tell us that silence is equally as important as the notes. The same is true in poetry. This is why we have line breaks and stanza breaks. It is important to honor the silence in poetry.

As we speak we are breathing out or exhaling. When we inhale we are nourishing our bodies with oxygen. It is also impossible to speak as we inhale. Inspiration comes in the silence, in the breath, of a poem. The word inspire comes from the Latin *spirare*, "to breathe," which is also the root of "spirit."

So, what to do with line breaks and stanza breaks? No two line breaks and no two stanza breaks are treated the same. In other words, there is not a set length of time one should pause at the end of a line. It will vary according to the poem in question. With practice and attention, the poem will inform you how it is to be said. Denise Levertov, in her essay "On the Function of the Line," muses that the rhythm of a poem depends on "a sense of a pulse, a pulse behind the words."[3]

To get a feel for this "sense of pulse behind the words," try the second stanza from "To a Poor Old Woman" by William Carlos Williams (she is eating plums):

> They taste good to her
> They taste good
> to her. They taste
> good to her[4]

When you pause according to the "pulse behind the words," more emphasis falls on the word or phrase that begins the next line. Notice how the meaning shifts:

> They taste good to her
> They taste good

---

3. Levertov, Denise. *New & Selected Essays*. New Directions, 1992.

4. Williams, William Carlos. *The Collected Poems of William Carlos Williams: Volume I, 1909-1939*. New Directions, 1938.

to her. They taste
good to her

Wendy Bishop, in her guide to writing poetry, *Thirteen Ways of Looking for a Poem*, invites us to consider the way Sharon Olds breaks her lines in "The One Girl at the Boys' Party." Bishop suggests that you read the poem aloud several times and asks, "What do you make of (and how do you read) the several lines ending on 'and'—a coordinating conjunction that some poets feel does not belong at the focal point of a line break?"[5] It is a good question that hopefully gets the reader thinking about the line and line breaks. But she misses the point. By suggesting that the focal point is at the end of the line, she is not hearing the poem or sensing its pulse.

Sound

When we speak we emphasize or de-emphasize certain words to express what we are trying to convey. In linguistics, this is called "prosody," the rhythm, stress, and intonation of speech. To get a feel for the sound of words, we must forget for a moment what words mean, what they symbolize. Imagine a graphic equalizer on a stereo on which the bars move up and down with the music. Now imagine if you had one to represent your speech patterns. Let us take the first line of John Keats's "On the Grasshopper and Cricket."[6]

The poetry of earth is never dead

By stressing certain words, this line could take on varying shades of meaning. There are at least four.

The POETRY of earth is never dead
The poetry of EARTH is never dead
The poetry of earth is NEVER dead
The poetry of earth is never DEAD

Of course, this is the most basic illustration because more than likely we would stress more than one word in a line and unstress other words. For example:

---

5. Bishop, Wendy. *Thirteen Ways of Looking for a Poem*. Addison Wesley Longman, 2000.

6. Keats, John. *The Complete Poems*. Knopf, 1994.

The POETRY of earth is NEVER dead

or

The poetry of EARTH is NEVER DEAD

and so on. Readers have been struggling with this for centuries: "To be, or not to be,"

THAT is the question
that IS the question
that is THE question
that is the QUESTION

There is a wonderful line in Walt Whitman's "Song of the Exposition":

Behold, the sea itself...

For years I thought that the stress was on "sea." After all, it is the subject here. Later I learned that if the word "itself" is stressed, this would invite a more nuanced understanding that suggests what we are to behold is not the sea but the sea *itself*. The emphasis is made not by stressing the word "itself" but de-emphasizing the word. I discovered this through Ralph Vaughan Williams' Symphony No. 1 "A Sea Symphony," which opens as a brass fanfare in B flat minor, followed by a choir singing in the same chord, BEHOLD, THE... then the full orchestra comes in with a clash on the word SEA, which has resolved into D major followed by a barely audible *itself*.

Here is one more example:

Exultation is the going
Of an inland soul to sea -
Past the houses -
Past the headlands -
Into deep Eternity -

If this first stanza of this poem by Emily Dickinson were to appear in a textbook, there would certainly be a footnote or a sidebar with the definition of "exultation." Only after having memorized this poem did it suggest to me that the stress should be on "going." "Exultation" is significant, but as a noun that appears as the first word of the poem, it gets all the attention it needs. Here is the second stanza.

> Bred as we, among the mountains,
> Can the sailor understand
> The divine intoxication
> Of the first league out from Land?[7]

Poems are living, breathing creatures. The way a poem feels right one day may not feel right the next. The way you say a poem to an audience of strangers will probably be different than the way you would say the same poem to loved ones around the kitchen table. Also, the way you say a poem may not be the way someone else says the poem. This does not mean that one or the other is correct. To compare this to music again, let us take Bach's cello suites. Listen to recordings by Mstislav Rostropovich alongside Pablo Casals, János Starker, Yo-Yo Ma, Mischa Maisky, and Pierre Fournier. Although each cellist is playing the same piece, each will have a uniquely different sound. Musicians say that cellists "speak" the suites. Some will be warmer or more soulful while others may sound more detached and mathematical. Yet each is looking at the same score and "interpreting" the piece according to his or her unique sensibility.

The poem is not what is on the page any more than the score to a piece of music is the song. We must be careful when experienced poets and teachers instruct otherwise as Ted Kooser does in his *Poetry Home Repair Manual*. He advises his reader to squint so that the poem on the page is merely a shape and suggests that irregular lines distract the reader.[8] This would be like telling Thelonious Monk not to shift three steps in "'Round Midnight" and start the fifth measure in E because it looks strange on the page. It's a good thing Galway Kinnell did not listen to advice like this. Kinnell was a master at allowing his poems to come alive on the page and seek their own musicality despite how they appeared on the page. Take "The Bear," for example, and it's last two lines, "what, anyway, / was that sticky infusion, that rank flavor of blood, that poetry, by which I lived?"[9]

7. Dickinson, Emily. *The Poems of Emily Dickinson: Reading Edition*, The Belknap Press of Harvard University Press, 1998.

8. Kooser, Ted. *The Poetry Home Repair Manual: Practical Advice for Beginning Poets*. Bison Books, 2007.

9. Kinnell, Galway. *A New Selected Poems*. Houghton Mifflin, 2000.

We should let poems speak, sing, bellow, growl, whimper, or wail through us. Poems, if allowed to inform us, should not need theatrics to heighten the experience. Once we have become comfortable with the practice of memorizing and saying poems, the poems' meanings and nuances start to reveal themselves to us.

Bringing a poem off the page and into the body, not merely opening a book and reading it, is essential if we are to experience the poem. This is comparable to looking at a photo of a stained-glass window as opposed to standing before the window itself and basking in its brilliant colors.

Dike Okoro

JOURNEYS IN VERSE: DEREK WALCOTT

One of the first poets whose poetry left an indelible imprint on my mind
was Derek Walcott. As a budding poet, I was amazed at the ethereal nature of
the Nobel Prize for Literature laureate's verse. It wasn't just about his assort-
ment of images that evoked the natural wonders of the Caribbean. Nor was it
the meticulously selected images that betrayed the genius of a painter hiding
behind the beauty of words. Something puzzling and yet striking seemed
tailored to his diction. Perhaps it must have been my longing to unravel
whatever it was about the logic of the man from St. Lucia that planted in me
a yearning to discover the numerous ways his imaginative representation of
the cultural, historical, spiritual, and environmental ethos of the Caribbean
helps to situate the mental flights he undergoes during poetry composition.
Whether these flights are forms of resolutions remained for me unclear.

Today, we live in an age where the power of the word and respect for
the word keeps pushing poets to reconsider their relationship with words.
Perhaps in my recent ponderings on this matter I owe much indebtedness
to Walcott, whose intimation on his moments when composing a poem was
explained in an interview he granted to *The Paris Review*, where he states:
"Between the beginning and the ending and the actual composition that goes
on, there is a kind of trance that you hope to enter where every aspect of your
intellect is functioning simultaneously for the progress of the composition.
But there is no way that you can induce that trance." I agree with Walcott.
As a poet, I have also found the process of composition to be a journey that
doesn't afford one the benefit of a map. Which means I have had to sort
myself out when I figured the poem was not forthcoming. Put simply, I tend
to be patient and hope that my motivation for writing, which is to create
something meaningful out of words I do not fully trust, will lead me some-

where. This experience is quite like what Billy Collins tried to explain when responding to an interviewer's question in *The Paris Review*, when he was asked, "Could you go through the genesis of a poem?" and he responded, "There's a lot of waiting around until something happens.... Like most poets, I don't know where I'm going.... You're trying to discover something you don't know exists, maybe something of value." Precisely, I have had my share of moments when I didn't know where I was going while writing a poem. I went through each draft waiting for the finished product to emerge, much like what Collins says. Perhaps it was because I exercised patience that I was able to appreciate what I discovered in the end when the complete poem had been written.

Strikingly, I concur with Collins' claim that "the act of discovering something you don't know exists" is an experience a poet encounters when composing a poem. His statement echoes Walcott's inference that the act of poetry composition is like a trance one hopes to enter. Whether this experience works for every poet, both young and old, is something I do not know. Let me be frank: there is no shortcut in the composition of a poem. A poet must be disciplined enough to respect his craft and accept that art that merits value is produced through stages. Besides, the poet summons all kinds of influences when composing a poem, including language, memory, and sound. I bet this is US writer Ben Lerner's rather unambiguous admission in an interview with Kate Kellaway that appeared in *The Guardian*, when he contends that the materiality of language allows a poet to engage in a reciprocal experience where he or she speaks through language in much the same way that language speaks through him/her (Kellaway).

Lerner's words echo back to me one of the mysteries poets experience during the composition of a poem. The idea that writing presents a symbiotic relationship between the poet and language is true. For the poet, what is worth acknowledging is the fact that experience leads to both learning and being appreciative of the space of composition. But more than anything else, it provides a sort of open-ended explanation to what Walcott tried to adumbrate with his description of the composition process as a trance. Walcott and Lerner share a common insight in this regard, in that both poets agree that the poet has no control over the experience during composition. In other words, language takes charge and produces what eventually becomes meaning to both poet and reader.

Admirably, Walcott's contention is instructive in the sense that he is reminding poets that the art of composition is one that exerts its powers upon the limitations of the poet. Might this be the very idea behind his declaration that "there is no way that you can induce that trance"? Put simply, many poets, especially those distinguished in the art, have offered views that parallel Walcott's. Agha Shahid Ali, reflecting on the art of poetry writing, contends that such an experience as the kind posited by Walcott "varies from poem to poem," adding, "I am not one of those people who requires to be away from the world and be isolated and all that. I need chunks of time, which can be just one day or two days, but I don't need to go away to one of those places" (Gamalinda). Shahid Ali's preference for time over place, in relation to the composition of a poem, is an unalloyed reminder of what the poet Yusef Komunyakaa suggests when he, for example, claims in an interview he granted to the *Washington Square Review* that he marvels:

> at how poems reside visually beside each other to create emotional and psychological movement. The tension is within poems—word by word, line by line—but tension also exists within the silences and spaces between poems. We could say that a book is a compilation of shapes and sounds. The blend is natural. And one hopes that a collection isn't a house of cards, that it is a place where surprises are negotiated. (Isokawa)

Komunyakaa's contention that a poetry collection is "a place where surprises are negotiated" seems to parallel Walcott's claim that during poetry composition "there is a trance that you hope to enter where every aspect of your intellect is functioning..." The onus, I suspect, lies not only in the similarity in the poetic approach but also in the sharing of opinion indebted to experience.

Walcott's reflection on the intimacy shared between poet and poem is one that set me thinking. Much as I tried to believe the anecdote was one that could easily be applicable to any poet living, I am accepting of the possibility that, for all it is worth, the nexus remained both a tribute to poetry and an encouragement to the up-and-coming poet. Hence, I take it that one way or the other, what is registered in Walcott's quote is a subtle submission to the sanctity of the poetic experience. Walcott was obviously not an apprentice poet when he granted this interview. In his statement one can discern the essence of the poet's journey as a creator as well as the unspoken role of words as bodies that occupy a revered space in the poet's consciousness. Furthermore, Walcott's particularization of "trance" as a state the poet hopes to enter during composition offers a window through which a reader can view the making of a poem. That is, his acceptance that the intellect is functioning simultaneously for the progress of the composition is no routine appraisal but a focal point that reiterates something pivotal to every young poet and even the veteran poet. Poets do not write in a vacuum. Everything imagined and written acts as a co-participant in the poet's diverse but moderate efforts to experience writing in the very extremities that facilitate the composition of a poem.

Without even explaining the rationale behind Walcott's position, I think of the intimacy of the experience of writing and the inviting nature of words to the poet. When it comes to composition nothing seems to override the liberty "words" convey in ideas that evade human influence. These ideas are not far from the impartiality of words and the definiteness of their elicitation. So that when Walcott avers that there is "no way that [one] can induce that trance" made operative by a composed poem, the idea of the artist surrendering to the powers of his art immediately paves the way for fresh ways of rethinking the strengths of the composed poem.

To want to write a poem, a poet ought to experience some basic and expected feelings and respond to both the physical and the imagined. For Walcott, the Caribbean is not just physical space but a spiritual and psychological setting that helps him to fuse ideas that are consciously and unconsciously recreated in his imaginative works. When he evokes images of the sea and admits, "The sea is always present. It's visible" (Grimes), he is relating to his reader how his individual being responds to images through ideas of public and private spaces in him. Derek Walcott was born in the Caribbean. He grew up there and knew very well the physical and the psychic landscape of St. Lucia. That he chooses to foreground the Caribbean both consciously and unconsciously because it is the place he knows best and a familiar subject matter for his work goes to show how consciously he speaks not only of his familiarity with the spirit of the place but also his awareness of how rich and influential the natural environment can be to a poet's imagination.

When Walcott writes about the Caribbean, he offers his readers images that reveal his awareness of the place. In his verse there's the necessity of wanting to narrate a story about the place, the sea and the skies. The poet's ability to capture these experiences is very similar to what Maya Angelou attempts to explain regarding the process of poetry writing when she states that "You have to want to. You have to have sharp ears. And you have to not be afraid of being human" (Angelou). In the end, Walcott offers us something much more than a mere experience that shows us how he relates to poems. Rather, we can learn from his admission and take into consideration the practical aspect of the writing experience.

Put simply, Walcott's declaration that "there is no way you can induce that trance" also directs our attention to the certainties and the possibilities of the experience of composing a poem. To take it in a nutshell, he is giving the hard truth. Poetry composition requires actual experience; not some form of imaginary dialogue with the muse alone. Like a painter, the poet must know and be contained by his own time-related mechanisms and space, in order to effectively accomplish the composition of a poem. In a way, Walcott's creative approach evokes what W.H. Auden describes when he says, "One demands two things of a poem. Firstly, it must be a well-made verbal object that does honor to the language in which it is written. Secondly, it must say something significant about a reality common to us all, but perceived from a unique perspective" (Auden et al). In relation to the composition process, Auden's admission echoes Walcott's conclusion about the creative process.

Interestingly, Walcott was renowned for seeking metaphors from nature. This aspect of his writing emanated from the proximity his homeland of St. Lucia shared with the sea. Thus, when he told *The Economist* in 1990: "The sea is always present. It's always visible. All the roads lead to it. I consider the sound of the sea to be part of my body" (Grimes), he is explaining the complex but sensuous aspect of creating a poem from listening, especially to sounds from nature. Further, Walcott compares the sound of the sea to "part of his body" and adds, "And if you say in patois, 'The boats are coming back,' the beat of that line, its metrical space, has to do with the sound and rhythm of the sea itself" (Grimes).

Furthermore, Walcott's reverence for the sea is an attribute that is associated with many writers who seek inspiration from nature. For example, Wendell Berry asserts that "nature has a very high place in the poetic tradition," a complex but seemingly realistic response to a question posed to him as to how "the southern agrarians looked to religion to do what nature does—to be something all powerful and uncontrollable and mysterious" (Leonard).

This statement is similar to Walcott's admission about the sound of the sea. Walcott finds nature to be relevant to his imaginative process. Thus he spent his writing career seeing through the prism of a Caribbean world that offered him all the elements that he valued in the natural environment. He is not just an admirer of nature but also a painter of nature through words that sing the physical, visual, and spiritual connectedness of his home in his poetry.

In practical terms, Walcott's intimation that the sea inspires him to write is reminiscent of conclusions made by several great poets. Joseph Brodsky once stated in an essay he wrote in honor of the classic English poet, John Donne, that "The poet is engaged, in general, in the translation of one thing into another. He is curious about everything.... It is not that language is his instrument, it's that he is the instrument of language...the poet is the servant of language" (Pomeranzev). What Brodsky says here is marked by an impression that is rooted in interrogation. It is the same interrogative curiosity that one finds in Walcott's claim when he compares the composition of a poem to a trance-like state. In Walcott's verse one realizes the importance of the writer being born and raised in a place where physical and non-physical realities affect him or her.

In a published obituary piece that appears in *The New York Times*, William Grimes remembers Walcott and the significance of his place of origin, St. Lucia, to his poetry. Here is an example of what Grimes says: "In the poem 'Islands,' from the collection *In a Green Night*, he wrote: 'I seek / As climate seeks its style, to write / Verse crisp as sand, clear as sunlight...'" (Grimes). From these lines it is obvious the way Walcott's place of origin holds an importance place in his sense of nostalgia. Also, his diction is meticulously representative of the public and private ideas that are shaped by his familiarity with place, history, culture and aesthetic beauty of the Caribbean. Thus, for Walcott nostalgia is a source of inspiration and helps him to form an association with indigenous Caribbean background.

When Walcott suggests that a feeling that might arouse interest in a poet after composing a poem is situated in a trance, one can begin to understand that there is a kind of unspoken but understandable mystery in poetry composition that demands understanding. It isn't about something that is not known but more so about a certainty, especially as regards the clothing of pages with the liberty of words. Perhaps it is what Walcott attempted to say in the interview when he further declares: "What you are taking on is not a renewal of your identity but actually a renewal of your *anonymity*, so that what is in front of you becomes more important than what you are."

This, for me, brings back the idea of the journey the poet takes in the process of composition. And what better way for one to contextualize the process than Walcott's quotes! Or better still, one ought to remember that poets themselves are parts of poetic journeys, or mental flights, that inspire others to write poetry. Walcott is no exception to this journey or mental flight. His body of work has influenced many, including Jamaica's recently appointed poet laureate and University of Michigan Ann Arbor professor, Lorna Goodison, who upon accepting her new appointment reflected on Walcott's impact on her writing: "A lot of what I learned about creative writing is owed to Derek Walcott, so I learned from the best" (Goodison). Derek Walcott died on March 17, 2017, and ever since I learned of his demise I have been drawn to reading more and more of his poetry. And, looking through his works, especially his affinity to images of nature, especially the sea, I have come to understand that his work indeed represents journeys, not just about himself but also what he hopes his reader will grasp from the interaction between his mind and his muse. Hence, for the beginner poet, the word of advice I would give is "patience." This word unravels every mystery there is in the composition of a poem, however time consuming. Better still, it allows the beginner poet to gain a level of trust in his or her ability after several failed attempts at completing the draft of a poem.

WORKS CITED

Angelou, Maya. "Maya Angelou on How to Write—and How to Live." *Oprah.com*.

Auden, W. H. and George L. Kline. "The Poems of Joseph Brodsky." *The New York Review of Books*. 5 Apr 1973.

Gamalinda, Eric. "An Interview with Poet Agha Shahid Ali." *Poets &Writers*.

Goodison, Lorna. "Lorna Goodison—Poet Laureate, A Lover of Country, A Voice to Its People." *The Gleaner*. 19 May 2017.

Grimes, William. "Derek Walcott, Poet and Nobel Laureate of the Caribbean Dies at 87." *The New York Times*. 17 Mar 2017.

Isokawa, Dana. "An interview with Yusef Komunyakaa: Dana Isokawa." *Washington Square Review*. Issue 33. 17 August 2017.

Kellaway, Kate. "Interview: Ben Lerner: Poetry is this space where every single particle of Language is charged with the most meaning." *The Guardian.* 20 Nov 2016.

Leonard, Sarah. "Nature as an Ally: An Interview with Wendell Berry." *Dissent.* Spring 2012.

Plimpton, George. "Billy Collins: The Art of Poetry No.83." *The Paris Review.* Issue 59, Fall 2001.

Pomerantsev, Igor. "Brodsky on Donne: 'The Poet Is Engaged in the Translation of One Thing Into Another'". 24 May 2010. *RadioFreeEurope RadioLiberty.*

Walcott, Derek. "Derek Walcott, The Art of Poetry No. 37." 17 August 2017. Interviewed by Edward Hirsh, *The Paris Review.* Issue 101, Winter 1986.

Emily Stoddard

WRITING BY WATER TABLE

I grew up less than an hour's drive from Lake Michigan. When you spend summers with dunes over one shoulder and open water over the other, you quickly learn how the water table works. At a certain point in digging into the sand, every scoop is answered with a rush of water. Something deeper rushes forward to fill the gap where your hand or your plastic shovel has just been.

Early on, maybe for your first few summers, this is a curiosity. Will the water always be there? How deep can I dig before it disappears?

In the creative process, it's these deeper waters that I still do not entirely know or understand. It's these deeper waters, this source beneath the sand where I dig, that provoke me back to the empty page as a poet and writer. I do not exactly *navigate* them—instead, I begin digging, and eventually, they appear. They ride along the surface, feeding the images and ideas that show up in poetry. For me, they are both the spirit behind the writing and the reason for writing at all. I want to know where the waters come from, what secrets they carry, what vessel they might fill. To keep digging until a form takes shape. Some days the form is a castle, intricate and beveled with light. Some days it is only a smooth mound that casts a shadow, a cool spot where I tuck my words away from direct sun.

Early in the journey, and sometimes later when we face a block, it can be tempting to view this nameless, formless, shape-shifting creative energy with misplaced reverence. It carries so much potential and power—and it seems to operate so serendipitously or unconsciously—that we don't try to harness it. We approach it as though it's an enlightened muse. Sometimes, we treat it like a ferocious animal that leaps only when we aren't looking. The deeper creative flow is somehow the ultimate gift and the ultimate terror. To engage it directly, to count on it as a part of ourselves, might feel like sacrilege for some poets. If we *do* approach it directly, it's often with lowered eyes and a small bucket, expecting to receive only so much.

Because some of us hold a superstition, especially as we're beginning to trust the images, language, and sounds that roll through our poems: *If I use that stunning idea today, I accept that there may not be another for some time. So I need to covet that idea, treat it tenderly, and woo it into something greater. I'll give it only the "right" words at the "right" time.* How many poems have been smothered this way?

Some of us hold a fear: *If I tell that one story I've been carrying with me, the bucket will be empty. The water will run dry. I'll have "used up" my creative purpose. Maybe better not to start at all. Better to peek in the bucket from time to time and grieve for that lonely story. To walk in circles around the poem that might have been "the" poem.*

How many stories have gone silent because they carried the weight of an entire creative life? Who really knows what else lives in the shadows of the bucket, or in those deeper waters?

In this way, how we approach the empty page reveals how much scarcity is often woven into our beliefs about creativity and poem-making. Do I believe in a kind of divine and fleeting inspiration? Absolutely. But do I believe we must approach it with fragility? The more I write, the more I'm convinced otherwise.

Over a handful of summers carving at the sand along Lake Michigan, you begin to notice that the water will always be there. You develop a certain instinct for just how deep you must dig before it shows up. You even begin your digging with this knowing. You plan on the possibility of the water rising up to meet you. You imagine castles surrounded by moats and small rivers.

As a poet, it becomes one of the most irresistible parts of the journey: learning to trust that if you reach your hand down and open your palm, you can catch a word or an image from the deeper waters. It's a trust that doesn't leave much room for scarce thinking. Getting here is like learning to build more complex sand castles. It can take a few seasons to discover that this is a choice you can make. That this is not just a surprise gift from the muse, but an orientation to receiving the world—an orientation that a poet can actually practice.

This is ultimately a conversation with your own instinct. As May Swenson wrote: "The best poetry has its roots in the subconscious to a great degree.

Youth, naiveté, reliance on instinct more than learning and method, a sense of freedom and play, even trust in randomness, is necessary to the making of a poem." In my practice, I've sought ways to stay open to the conversation with instinct so that it becomes more than a passing hello. My hope is to make instinct's presence more real, to let those deeper waters know that my hands are open, and to give those waters a home when they show up.

Most helpful has been what I call the "raw material practice." This is my bucket, my shovel, my place in the sand. My raw material has a physical space on my computer (as a document), in a notebook, and in an app on my phone. It's the place where *all* bits of instinct go. Here are the types of things that, for me, have instinct's presence all over them: any image, idea, phrase, or spark that pops into your head as you daydream or brush your teeth or get your groceries. Anything that snaps into your dreams, or catches your eye or ear as you move through the world. A moment that makes you laugh very hard or tear up. A passing glance that catches you off guard. A sound that startles you.

These signals are easy to ignore, because sometimes they come with only one word attached. We tend to like instinct that feels like an Idea with a capital I. Anything less seems worthless, questionable, or silly. We like to know where it's going before we trust it. This is how we begin to pull our hands out of the sand, away from those deeper waters.

Writers' notebooks are nothing new, of course. For me, the most important part of this practice is not the tool but how I relate to it. I've traveled with the practice for a few years, landing in it intuitively and trusting it more over time:

First, I keep the tool itself simple. My raw material "bucket" is never a pretty notebook. It's not an elaborate system. If any part of it feels too special, then it will probably feel like only special ideas may go in it. I like to confuse my inner critics by making this tool so plain and practical that they don't even notice when I use it. It lets me receive the gifts from the deep waters with less hesitation.

Next, I actively refer to this as "raw material," even in conversation with fellow writers. I find that naming the home for this connection to instinct makes it more real and tangible. The name "raw material" also helps me detach from what it might or might not become. I do not have to know if an image belongs in a new poem, a second draft of something in progress, or if it could be the seed of an essay—it's just raw material. I can simply receive the gift of the image and stay open for more.

Finally, I add to this as often as I can. Any time an image, idea, question, or resonant moment surfaces, I drop it in this spot. It doesn't have to be a complete thought or sentence. After a year or so of trying this practice, I began accepting *anything* that floated in, just to see what would happen. That meant that even when it was just one or two words that surfaced, I said yes to the gift and put it in my raw material. I was surprised by what the experiment revealed. In one instance, the words "magpied fields" were in my mouth one morning as I woke up. There was no reason for those words to be there. I had no context for them, but I knew I had a place to put them. Into the raw material file they went. A year later, I understood a little more where the deep water was leading...as I stood in Taos, New Mexico, marveling at a field full of magpies. Shocked that my instinct had somehow been a kind of premonition, I returned to my raw material. I found animals and birds of all kinds waiting to speak. A poem surfaced that brought them together. It was as if they had been waiting for me to get the signal and notice the poem that had been drafting itself all along.

Raw material also doesn't have to be strange, unusual, or abstract. Maybe you're seeing an image of your mother's hands. You're brushing your teeth one morning, and suddenly, there's the image in your mind. You might grab your phone, write a note to yourself, and tag it "raw material." It might say: "Mom's hands. Holding hose. Summer." And as you type that, the image might flow a little more. Suddenly you might feel the urge to add: "Sunflowers, so tall that year. She finally figured out the garden. Green thumb after that summer."

See how far it will take you, and just get it down. It might bubble up all day, and you might write more that evening. Or it might rest in your raw material for months and come back when you're looking for something to write about in the future. You might ask, "Why *did* that garden matter so much to mom?" and suddenly, the waters will rise up again.

In my own practice of staying with the deeper waters, the more I have said yes, the more that has shown up. It's become a resource I can carry through quieter creative seasons, like a personal trove of writing prompts. And it has become a way to avoid the superstitions of my inner critics. While they guard the front door, I'm busy digging my way through the back, one bit of raw material at a time.

Jason McCall

FINDING COMFORT IN FINDING YOUR COMFORT ZONE

In grad school, I wrote the same poem for two years, and I am a better poet because of it.

No, I did not rewrite every word over and over again like Bart at the beginning of *The Simpsons*. The titles of the poem changed. The words changed. The subject matter changed. The acceptance rates increased, slightly. Sometimes, the poem was celebrated in workshop classes. Sometimes, it was derided in workshop. But it was always the same poem.

Of course, I did not realize I was writing the same poem. I did not see it until one of my advisors made me print out the first draft of my graduate thesis and look at how one poem followed the next poem in the draft.

Two ten-line stanzas. The first stanza was an observation or visual description. The second stanza transitioned into a revelation or personal epiphany. There was a reference to a biblical or mythological character. There was a strong enjambment to move the reader from the penultimate line to the closing line of the poem. My thesis was sixty poems long, and this poem made up over half of the poems in the first draft.

My advisor told me my manuscript moved in circles. She said my manuscript kept coming back to the same spot, the same poem. She told me that I had mastered that poem. She told me to look for ways to move on from that poem.

At first, I was surprised and ashamed. I couldn't help but think of myself as a villain from *The Scooby-Doo Show* who had been unmasked to reveal the fraud, the trickster underneath my poetic facade. However, the more I revised my manuscript and returned to the conversation I had with my advisor, the more my emotions changed. My advisor told me to grow, evolve, and move beyond the poem I had become so comfortable with. However, she told me to move beyond the poem because I mastered the poem.

I never imagined anyone would call me a master of any element of poetry when I started writing in the ninth grade. The closest I'd ever come to feeling like a master in anything was winning my third-grade spelling bee. I love poetry partially because I have always seen poetry as an act of failure. Poetry, to me, is always the act of trying to hold the sun in place, trying to make an echo last a second longer. All Poets are Pandora. All poets are Orpheus in Hades, trying to peek into the forbidden even though we've been warned by the gods. (See, the mythological references will not stay away.) When my advisor told me to move on, it was both a stern critique and a genuine compliment.

Along with the constant challenge and failure of poetry, I also love poetry because of its diversity. There are thousands of ways to play with form, meter, diction, and spacing on the page. Poets are often told to explore new techniques to get out of their comfort zone or to think outside of the box. However, poets have to develop a comfort zone before they can get out of their comfort zone. Poets have to find a box before they can think outside of their box. Shakespeare wrote over a hundred sonnets. Rumi wrote more than one ghazal.

For poets at every level, it is important to experiment. Poetry is a buffet, and poets are cheating themselves if they do not sample what poetry has to offer. Poets should attempt a sonnet. Poets should pat themselves on the back after completing a villanelle or sestina. Poets should seek out new forms like bop poetry or kwansabas. Poets should see what happens to their voice when they revisit a poem written in quatrains and break the quatrains into couplets. These are just a handful of the near-limitless experiments poets can attempt. However, one of the most important poetic experiments is the experiment of repetition. Once a poet finds a form or subject that feels comfortable, the poet should exploit that comfort. Poets should not be afraid of doing what they do well. Too often, I see poets who abandon their strengths. Too often, I see poets who are ashamed of their strengths. There should not be any shame in returning to the sonnet, the couplet, or the love poem. Poets should write the comfortable poem until they understand why the poem is comfortable. They should write the comfortable poem until they know they can write the poem effectively and understand why they can write the poem effectively. Once poets understand why a certain type of poem works for them or why they keep returning to a certain type of poem, then they can build on that poem. They can find other forms and subject matter to complement their favorite type of poem.

I am lucky. I have been lucky enough to teach creative writing to great students at great colleges and universities. I have been lucky enough to find mentors and friends in the writing field who are greater writers than I would ever even dream to be. I have won a few awards and published a few books. However, as a poet, I know that most of my luck stems from the confidence I gained from my advisor's critique of my graduate thesis. I know that I can write one good poem, and knowing that has given me the confidence to keep writing the next poem. And the next. And the next.

Tara Skurtu

I DON'T LIKE POETRY, I'M NOT A POETRY PERSON

Every time I hear someone say *I don't like poetry* or *I'm not a poetry person*, I think the opposite is true. I believe everyone is a poetry person. Poetry is just a form of storytelling, and we're born to tell stories.

Last year, at a bistro in Romania, I was rearranging the order of my manuscript, yet again, when a little girl wandered over to me, looked at my laptop screen, and rested her chin on my table. I asked her in Romanian if she knew about poetry. *Yes, yes,* she said, *I know poetry. I like it.* Kids get it.

I once read Elizabeth Bishop's "The Fish" to a ten-year-old girl. We were talking about how a simple moment can be a poem. I told her I was going to read one that was just this. I wasn't sure if the length of it would hold her attention—Bishop poems are so patiently written, and reading them requires patience. (I often tell my students that her poems are like beer—sometimes an acquired taste.) Also, based on my own experience googling several of the boat terms toward the poem's end the first time I read it—bailer, thwarts, gunnels—I knew she wouldn't understand all of the vocabulary.

"I caught a tremendous fish..." As I read it, she sat quietly, looking from one object in the apartment to another. I couldn't read her face, but she didn't look particularly interested. "...And I let the fish go." I looked at my young friend, who sat without talking for a moment. *You know what?* she said. *You're right. It's about something so simple, it's like it's not even worth it.*

I probably shouldn't have, but I felt a little bummed out. I knew she was just a kid, that this was just a poem. But then, she continued, *she makes it worth it.* The moral of this moment? Children teach us about poetry.

Somewhere along the way—usually around high school, sometimes college—a lot of students (mainly the ones who aren't writing poems) become intimidated by poetry. They associate it with archaic grammar, rhymes, rigid form. It has to be understood one specific way, becomes something that can't be penetrated.

A teenager once raised his hand and asked me, *Do we just write, or do we write in the form of a poem?* Returning to poetry is just like trying to use a second language you haven't spoken or heard in a while: you may be out of practice, but the essence remains intact. It's all about getting started.

I like to write "Poetry is..." on the board. Each student comes up and writes a word. *Fear, feelings, imagination, story, fiction, life, art, analyzing, communication, nature, reality, honesty, mystery, melody, limitless, unknown, dreams, freedom, love, hidden.* Sometimes unlearning is the simple act of realizing again what you once instinctively felt.

I like to begin each semester with an in-class guided writing exercise on memory. I have the students think of a moment in which their perceptions—of themselves, their world, a person—changed. Another person must be present in this memory. I tell them to use specific details (and that detailed doesn't necessarily mean more words) and not to worry about complete sentences. Twenty lines max. I give a series of directions while they write, and I interrupt them constantly with these instructions—because this is how memory works: seemingly unrelated moments are triggered by senses, place, story. The whole thing takes about ten minutes.

My current version of this exercise, simplified, is:

1. Where are you? Write the place of this memory.
2. What is happening?
3. Zoom in on something you notice, one thing that stands out.
4. Who are you with?
5. This person reminds you of someone, something. Relate this person to another person, image, object, sense, place, etc.
6. Change a detail (because memory is a narrative, and narratives can be altered).
7. You hear (or smell, or taste, etc.) something. What is it?
8. Change another detail.
9. Someone says something. What does this person say?
10. Change another detail.
11. You do something. What do you do?
12. You notice something you hadn't noticed before. Zoom in on it.
13. Change one last detail.

Before they know it, they've drafted a poem that has place, metaphor/ simile, character, dialogue, the senses, action, image. And, most importantly, something is at stake.

I once asked my students in Transylvania if they knew what "at stake" meant. They didn't. We broke it down, delved into etymology: a pole, a stick. We discussed "burned at the stake," "impaled on a stake" (the latter is easily understood in Romania, whose history includes the likes of Vlad III of Wallachia).

Sometimes language requires demonstration. I placed a printed poem on the table, then held a pencil above my head. I stabbed the poem, pinned it to the table, tore a ragged gash through the middle of the page. I asked them to give me some words to describe what this poem just went through. *Danger. Limit. Loss. Risk.* Yes.

There's only one poem I can think of that comes close to defining the essence of poetry, and in it there's a literal stake. It's Heather McHugh's "What He Thought," and at the end, Giordano Bruno, in an iron mask, is being burned at one in Campo de' Fiori, 1600: "poetry is what // he thought, but did not say." This is the definition of poetry at risk: it employs the limits of language, endangers the realm of the comfortable, approaches a silence or loss we feel yet can't explain.

Recently, I decided to take this stake exercise one step further. I had everyone take out a sheet of paper. *Think about what writing poetry means to you now, what it represents.* I told them to do something, anything, to their sheet of paper. I immediately heard a page being crumpled into a ball. Without hesitation they each knew exactly what to do. I participated as well. I poked a near-perfect hole with a pencil through the middle of a blank page.

When everyone was done, I told them to turn their creations into words. I went first. I told them that writing poetry, to me, is like looking through this small hole in the page at a distant object—first with one eye, then the other—the process of discovering your dominant eye over and over again. Their turn: *equality, sadness, a boat that stops at the shores of emotions, frustration, many fragments put together to form something magical, a crown that makes me feel fabulous, a flower or a tree, an airplane, something useless that becomes beautiful, a butterfly on the way from one flower to another.* Finally, they are poetry people again. Finally, no fear.

David Bergman

THE PLEASURE OF READING

The poem is an experience of language that gives one pleasure; that is, one reads it for the pleasure of the language. Most writing isn't designed to give you pleasure—notices of eviction, laboratory results, directions for installing an app. These, too, may give pleasure—for example, the lab report may come back with the result that the tumor is benign—but it's not the *language* that is producing the delight; it's the information contained (or not contained) in the report. But the literary experience is different. In prose you may not be aware of the pleasure of the language. You rarely notice the skill of the writing in a good page-turner—you're too busy turning the page. But poetry will not permit you to ignore the language. The language is everything, or almost everything.

Many years ago, I took a walk with a friend's son, Guthrie, who was three years old at the time.

"What is that tree?" he asked. "It's a string-bean tree," I answered, but he very vehemently replied, insulted no doubt by my childish answer, "No, no, no! It's a ca-tal-pa." Slowly pronouncing the word so that I could learn it. He was delighted with himself. First, he was right; it was a catalpa. Second, he could show off his superior knowledge. But finally Guthrie was delighted with the word itself—*catalpa*. He took the opening syllable deep in his throat, luxuriously rolled his tongue over the middle syllable, and then hit the final syllable with a decided pop. *Catalpa*. It is a beautiful word, and he took enormous pleasure in saying it. Such incidents are not unusual for children. Most of them not only love the sound of words, but the way their mouths move making them. As they grow older, however, many seem to lose the delight in language. *Catalpa* has become a fact rather than a joy for the mouth to produce, an occasion for aural and oral pleasure.

Part of what gets in the way of the pleasure of language is the belief that every experience must have its take-away, some lesson that you could apply elsewhere, a useful factoid, a guide for self-improvement. Most poems don't have them (and you should be suspicious of those that hand them out). The source for me of the pleasure in most poetry is participating in the poem's performance. Sure, poems tell us certain things, give us certain information, present adages and shibboleths. But they do so far less than you think. Instead, and this list is hardly complete, they rage, they woo, they seduce (or try to), they curse, they praise, they honor, they mourn, they calm, they comfort, they excite, they disparage, they pray, they forgive and petition for forgiveness. My pleasure is to see language in action, performing on us and with us. It is more in the movement of language than in its meaning of language that I take delight. That is why patter songs and rap lyrics so please their respective audiences—all those words running together, finding their place in the pattern of syntax. It's thrilling and exhausting.

Poetry isn't an acquired taste, but for many it is a re-acquired taste. No one has to push children into enjoying Dr. Seuss or Shel Silverstein. Playing with words was as keen a sport as kicking a ball. But at some point, we are taught to mock the punster and the riddle-maker. We come to believe that there is something to be avoided in playing with words. And we get hung up on meaning.

I won't go so far as to say that meaning doesn't matter—of course, it does—but there are poets we read not for what they say but for the pleasure of how they use the language. Ezra Pound, for example, has always been a problematic American poet—one of the most important innovators and one of its vilest characters. Here is one of many racist snippets from *The Cantos*. At this point in his life, Pound has been arrested for treason and jailed in a cage in Pisa without anything to write on. Out of kindness, a black soldier makes him a table. But no good act goes unpunished, and the soldier even when praised by Pound is made to appear less than human:

> What counts is the cultural level,
>   thank Benin for this table ex packing box
>   "doan yu tell no one I made it"
>   from a mask fine as any in Frankfurt
>   "It'll get you off n th' groun"

Pound doesn't thank the soldier, whose speech he mocks, he thanks the civilization of Benin who produced such a good servant. Servant? The soldier is reduced to a mask in the Frankfurt museum, part of the stolen loot of imperialist exploitation. What Pound does in the passage is despicable; in the guise of praising the soldier, he finds the opportunity to complain about his mistreatment. Still one can take a certain pleasure from the vitality of his language. Pound frames the incident between the phrases–"cultural level" and "off n th' groun." Pound does not mean *level* to suggest equality or evenness, rather he is placing himself at a higher level and that, luckily, the soldier, although black, is of a sufficient cultural level to recognize his betters and raise Pound "off n th' ground." The soldier, the heir to the great culture of Benin, intuitively feels what his buddies were unable to feel: that it was wrong to leave Pound in the dirt. (We are open to side with his buddies.) As much as one might hate Pound's politics, one cannot ignore the subtle way he frames the incident. And then there is his obvious skill at playing with sound. In "the table ex packing box," he cleverly alternates between Bs and Xs and gracefully sequences the vowel sounds. Then there's the echoing of "mask" and "Frankfurt."

I'm not certain, in fact, that agreeing with a poet actually helps us enjoy what they say, at least it doesn't help me. When we think we agree with a writer, we are usually projecting on to the work attitudes and beliefs that are not contained in it. One of my favorite poets is W.H. Auden, who says lots of silly things. (He also says many wise ones.) In his poem "Their Lonely Betters" he argues that humans are alone among living creatures in possessing language, and that it's "only proper that words / Should be withheld from vegetables and birds." Technically he is correct: birds do not speak words, but they do possess ways of communicating to each other. But who or what is withholding language from plants and animals? It's as if Auden were imagining Mother Nature teasing turnips by dangling adverbs out of their reach. In any event, Karl von Frisch published his study *The Dancing Bees* in 1927, decoding the elaborate signs of their dance, and by the late 40s, when the poem was written, it was fairly well known. In short, humans are not quite superior as Auden suggests they are. But does this matter to the pleasure of the poem? Does bad science harm a poem? I think not.

To be fair, Auden doesn't present the linguistic superiority of human as either firm science or as a benefit. In fact Auden seems envious of the amorality of flora and fauna. The poem places the speaker (let's call him Auden for convenience) rather casually listening "from a beach-chair in the shade / To all the noises that my garden made." It's a lazy spring or summer day, and Auden doesn't have anything to do. Unsurprisingly, his mind turns to sex. In Auden's case the sound of the "rustling flowers" suggests that the plants are waiting for some "third party" "to say which pairs, if any, should get mated." The garden is a veritable orgy room where pollen and pistil fall upon one another through the intercession of some six-legged procurer. Auden's language, to be sure, is a good deal more discrete than my own—and that's where the language becomes fun. Discretion is a set of social rules about what should and should not be said. Auden likes playing with those rules, saying as much as he can without overstepping a social boundary, which because it is never explicitly defined, is all the more fun to play with. The poem then takes a much more serious turn:

> No one of them was capable of lying,
> There was not one which knew that it was dying
> Or would have with a rhythm or a rhyme
> Assumed responsibility for time.

Without language animals cannot lie; they cannot break oaths; they cannot fail to communicate when they said they would. (They can even have sex without shame since they live without the word *sin*.) Finally flowers and birds don't know how "lonely" they are because they cannot pledge their love or fidelity. The poem concludes:

> Let them leave language to their lonely betters
> Who count some days and long for certain letters;
> We, too, make noises when we laugh or weep:
> Words are for those with promises to keep.

Poor Auden. Now we see that he's been only trying to cheer himself up and polish the silver lining of his disappointment. The incapacity of "vegetables and birds" to communicate is merely a way to handle the frustration of being ignored by someone he cares about, someone we may assume has promised to write but hasn't. Auden keeps his language impersonal—those "lonely betters" could be anyone—but we have become used to his discretion and know that he is the person who is counting the days in hopes of receiving a long-anticipated letter. He's not enjoying his garden at leisure, as we first thought, but he has retired there feeling very much alone and ignored, worried perhaps that some third party has interfered with (rather than assisted in) the mating that he much desires.

I think that in order to enjoy this poem, one has to put away Auden's dubious distinctions between human and non-human animals (what the poem is saying) and look at what the poem is doing. And what it is doing is marking time in the hope that promises will eventually be kept and the increasing wariness that they won't. Auden is a better person because he has "with a rhythm [and] a rhyme / Assumed responsibility for time," but his sense of responsibility is tested by being left alone in his garden, with no company but the birds and the bees. The rhymes are all pure; the rhythm quite regular. He keeps everything in order. But beneath that order, there is loneliness and anger and an awareness that his emotions need to be kept in control because rage will do no one any good. Auden's acceptance of his subordinate role is directly addressed in "The More Loving One" in which he writes, "If equal affection cannot be, / Let the more loving one be me."

My students are often perplexed by this poem. In their world of Jerry Springer-like reality television, they find Auden's discretion not just of little value, but generally incomprehensible. In their minds, poetry is for fully expressing emotions, not holding back emotion or dancing around one's feelings. They prefer the cut-and-burn strategy of Sylvia Plath's more famous poems. What they ignore is that venting doesn't always make the venter feel better, and it's not especially enjoyable to watch. Our appreciation of what poems do is culturally determined. There is a fine line between discretion and repression. But the point I want to emphasize is that one should not pay too much attention to what poems say and enjoy what they are doing and how their performances place both the speaker and audience. Auden is performing in the poem. He is comforting himself, perhaps guilt-tripping his would-be correspondent while grabbing hold of the cultural level that will keep him out of the dirt. Archibald MacLeish argues famously that "a poem should not mean / But be." It's a rather passive role for the poem. I'm suggesting that to gain pleasure from a poem we should attend less to what it means, and more to what it does to us—we must put ourselves into the drama that it performs.

It's time we read a poem for pleasure. The poem I have in mind, Larry Eigner's "the music / in air," is extremely spare—a mere sixteen words long—and I worry that by examining it closely, I could clobber it to death. I'm hoping that although short, it is lovely and sturdy enough to bear my fumbling. I like to think of reading a poem as a kind of lovemaking. Most poems want to be made love to—they want a lot of foreplay, and—to paraphrase Marianne Moore—if you're interested in foreplay, you're interested in poetry. Even poetry slams, where words come loud and quick, are mostly foreplay—rough foreplay—but foreplay nevertheless.

I've chosen to start with "the music / in air" for another reason: it's virtually absent of ideas. I want us to try to enjoy a poem for what the language is doing. Believe me in this poem there's no big philosophical message to get in the way. Here's the entire poem:

> the music
> in air
>
>   the bows, trumpets
>   moved
>
>   and the red sunset
>   out
>   by the window

The big idea behind the poem is that while it's easy to imagine music in the air coming from bows and trumpets, it takes a leap of the imagination to hear "the red sunset / out / by the window." Not much of an idea. What kind of music does a sunset make? you ask. I imagine it has some of the blare of trumpets and some of the grit of a fiddle bow. Maybe even the sizzle of a drumset. Eigner has turned the visual into the auditory. There's nothing particularly unusual about such synesthesia. We experience them all the time; we speak of a "blue note" or a "hot pink" or even an "icy stare." For Eigner, the red sunset is part of the "music / in air." For so short a poem, such a delight is enough, and you are excused from further discussion.

But we might expect a poem about music to be musical, and one of the first things you might notice about "the music / in air" is that it doesn't contain the most obvious musical element—rhyme. Or does it? There are two near rhymes:

bows/window and *trumpets/sunset.* These echoes would be more noticeable if the poem hadn't matched the plural *trumpets* with the singular *sunset* or the stressed syllable *bows* with the unstressed *dow.* The poem has muffled the music so that instead of the rhyme's calling attention to itself (as rhyme frequently does), we are only dimly aware of a music floating around us.

This effect of a music that seems to hover just out of reach seems beautifully appropriate to the poem. In fact, the poem is constantly playing with the difference between the specifically locatable and the ambient. Take the title: "the music / in air." The article specifies a particular music, but *air* has no article. *The* music is dissipated through the general air. Let's take a look at where Eigner uses articles and where he's left them out.

> *the* music
> in air

>> *the* bows,   trumpets
>> moved

>> and *the* red sunset
> out
> by *the* window

Although we get specific bows (and bows by themselves don't make a sound), we are left with less locatable trumpets, which make the trumpets more airy. We don't *see* the source of the music until the last stanza when "*the* red sunset" is placed very specifically "out/by *the* window." The window locates (frames) the sunset within a new domestic space which is very different from the ethereal "music / in air" with which the poem began.

The way the sound of Eigner's poem hovers is emphasized by the way the poem appears on the page. The near rhymes don't always fall in the places usually reserved for rhymes. (Although *trumpets* and *sunset* are placed at the ends of their respective lines.) The poem is sprinkled across the page. The first two lines establish a margin, a base. All but one of the lines start at the right of the margin. The exception is the word *out*, which ironically sticks out by returning to the margin. The words *trumpets* and *the bow* float in the middle of the poem like muffled music in air. It is as if the music "moved" from the unlocatable air to the specific window, just as the poem loops around, but refuses to settle back at the margin. The poem maps the music on the page.

I suppose there are those who will take no pleasure in the way Eigner has constructed this poem. They do not care about echoing sounds or the placement of word on a page. Some people think words are useful only insofar as they represent an object or idea; some don't even find words useful for that. But that is the very nature of pleasure itself—those who don't experience pleasure don't see the point of it. The very best wine is wasted on me because I don't have the palate developed well enough to appreciate the subtle differences in aromas. "Originality," as John Stuart Mill points out in "On Liberty," "is the one thing that unoriginal minds cannot feel the use of." And pleasure is the last thing anesthetic minds want from their language. But the pleasure is there open to anyone who will take the time to feel it, to let go at last of the need to get "a meaning," whatever that is.

We could go further into the poem and look at the heteronym *bow*, a word that can be pronounced as both *boe* or *bough*. What does such uncertainty do to the poem? What would have happened if Eigner instead of *bow* substituted the word *violin*, which is a better parallel to *trumpet*? But exploring these questions brings up the speculative, and although the speculative has its own pleasures, I'd prefer to stay a moment longer and sop up the text. I admit I take the same pleasures listening to the sounds of language that dogs get from rolling around in some indiscernible scent. I rub my back against the poem; I fold my arms and feet joyously into my body as I scrunch down.

Up until now, I've limited the discussion exclusively to the pleasures of the text without recourse to any background material. But Larry Eigner was an extraordinary person, hardly the type we think of when we think of poets. Eigner was born in 1927 with cerebral palsy and lived with his family for most of his life in Swampscott, Massachusetts. His first poems were dictated to his mother because his disability made writing impossible, and she was among the few who could understand his slurred speech. For his Bar Mitzvah, he got a typewriter, and it liberated him. (One might say it made a man of him.) With the two fingers he could control, he produced a prodigious body of work. His collected poems fill four volumes. In his poetry he rarely, if ever, refers explicitly to his disability, or to being Jewish, or even to Swampscott. But for Michael Davidson, Eigner's cerebral palsy is at the center of the work even though "he seldom foregrounded his mediated physical condition." Davidson, therefore, believes "Cripping Larry Eigner allows us to read the body of the work in terms of his 'different' body." My aims are more modest than Davidson. I ask simply: how does knowledge of Eigner's cerebral palsy affect the pleasure of the poem? What I want to avoid is the cloyingly sentimental impulse to see him as a heroically disabled body. There's nothing heroic or disabled in "the music / in air." Indeed it rejects the heroic for the domestic. Like so many of Eigner's poems, it is a "record [of] real-time perception and observation" (Davidson). It records at first a music in air that seems unconfined, but the final lines that refer to the sunset seen through the window begin to close in the poem's space. How can we not read this movement as an attempt to escape Eigner's relative immobility? For Eigner sometimes what is close (bows and trumpets) is out of reach, while what is distant (the sunset) is just "out / by" the window. Much of the joys of life float around him impalpably, while others are easily discernable. Indeed, one might say that every one of Eigner's poems is an attempt to move beyond certain confinements or to discover new corners within them.

It may also help us appreciate the movement from the unlocatable music to the locatable sunset. The subject of the poem—the voice suggested by the words—is at first as hard to locate as the music.

The poem may represent a "record [of] real-time perception and observation," but where is the subjectivity that is observing and perceiving? As Charles Bernstein points out "Eigner rarely uses the conventional 'I' of lyric poetry." Where is the Eigner body? We might demand a writ of habeas corpus. For while the sun may be "out / by the window," Eigner's body is not so easily located. The problem is one of proprioception—awareness of the position of one's own body. Because Eigner was differently bodied, it takes him longer to locate the source of the music "out/by the window." Only by locating the source of the musical pleasure (which is also a visual pleasure) can Eigner locate himself by implication *within view of the window.* I would not go as far as Bernstein and say that "these poems are grounded not in the poet's expression but in each reader's perception"; rather I'd say that the poem invites the reader to share in the discovery of where music derives, that is by placing one's body in relation to sources of pleasure, which is not an easy thing to do for anyone, but particularly not for someone with cerebral palsy. The poem allows readers to locate themselves pleasurably, and knowing something about Eigner increases that pleasure in proprioception.

The language used in a poem also places it almost bodily at a certain time. "The music / in air" is written in a simple vocabulary. No word is more than two syllables, and those words—*music, trumpets, sunset* and *window*—are hardly esoteric. Big words draw attention to themselves, and Eigner is careful to keep things plain. The only adjective, for example, is "red." You'd think he'd come up with something more vivid or more musical, but he keeps it unobtrusive. But that doesn't mean there isn't a particular pleasure in his language. I was struck by "out / by," which grammarians call a double locative, two ways of situating the sunset: outside and by the window. The combination although not unknown in England (there's an Anglo-Saxon version from 845) is really an Americanism that peaked in popularity between the wars. Today, it's still used but not as often. Although not proscribed by careful users, it has a particular folksiness. An advertisement in an Austin, Texas newspaper, invited readers to "Enjoy exotic game, excellent steaks and attentive service in this unique and lovely setting out by the lake." Eigner wants exactly this trace music of understated folksiness to fill the air (and ear). Bows and trumpets are fine, but the most powerful music comes from the more commonplace "red sunset/out/by the window." This is a relatively quiet poem, and only in such a quiet environment would we have a chance to hear this rather homespun (but not vulgar) American language. There's a pleasure in hearing this sort of language.

It places the poem in the same way the poem places the sunset "out/by the window." This is an American sunset, framed in an ordinary American window. For me the poem has an innocent sweetness without being sentimental or mawkish. A rarity.

I want to suggest another matter we hardly ever consider when speaking of poetry: the technology of writing. Eigner could not write in long hand. His works were composed on typewriters, and that means that the carriage inexorably moving to the right with every letter. Consequently many Eigner poems begin at the top left and end in the bottom right corner of the page. It must have taken particular effort for him to bring the shift bar all the way to the left. For me Eigner is always contending against a rightward force that he can only partially resist. In some way he must resist the force that is taking him away from "the music / in air" and assert his right to the left-hand margin. All these thoughts increase my appreciation and pleasure in reading this poem and excite my admiration for its balanced joys.

Bernstein also tells us that Eigner's work "is an extension of the poetics associated with Mallarmé, Stein and the Objectivists." No doubt he is right.

There are people who would take a certain pleasure in such knowledge, and it would help them enjoy the poem more. Indeed, some would place this pleasure of literary historical knowledge before the textual pleasures I have noted. But the academic delight in such matters have made it harder for most readers to enjoy reading a poem. It makes them think that they need to be very knowledgeable to read poetry. My own feeling is that the poem offers its reader a field to play with language. One just needs to grab hold of the toys the author offers us. For the pleasure of a poem requires us to join in the play of language, to participate in what it is doing, and not be so concerned with what it means. We may need to get down on the floor to play with what Yeats calls his circus animals and leave the thin atmosphere of pedantry. Sometimes, it takes a person rooted to a particular place to discover where "the music / in air" comes from.

***

What a poem does and what a poem says are two things, and they can be radically different. What Paul Goodman's "The Lordly Hudson," asserts repeatedly is that the Hudson River is far better than any river in Europe or Asia. Whether this assertion is true is beside the point since Goodman doesn't try to argue it. Nor is it very interesting to those who study estuarial waters. "The Lordly Hudson" has even less of a lesson to teach than "The music / in air." Again we need to look at is what the poem is doing, and what it's doing is very strange.

Like many poets, Goodman places us immediately into a dramatic scene. We're thrust into a taxi cab and the fare, although he knows the answer, asks the driver "what stream is it?" This is not a rhetorical question. The fare, whom I'll call Goodman, is pretending to be an out-of-towner learning the names of the major geographic features, just as a clueless tourist might ask a Parisian cabbie, "Is that the Seine?" Calling the river a "stream" is another sign of the passenger's naivety. But why does Goodman, who was a lifelong New Yorker, play the part of provincial rube? The answer seems to be to get the cab driver to reaffirm what he knows, to say what he is reluctant to say himself. The poem is an act of reaffirmation. And it works. The driver repeats almost word for word what Goodman has in his mind.

Reaffirmation is an odd performative. Although J.R. Austin notes that performatives are often ceremonial as in marriage vows, once performed they seem to be done. Why repeat the performance? Yet religious and political life are filled with reaffirmations. We recite the Pledge of Allegiance on important national holidays; Catholics repeat the creed at every mass. We repeat "I love you" to those we love although we've said it hundreds of times before. Reaffirmations serve the purpose of comforting the reaffirmer as much as those reaffirmed. But beneath the celebratory impulse lies anxieties. Reaffirmation reveals some gap in the connection or a lessening of affiliation. Goodman presents himself to the driver as out-of-towner because he has been out of town and fears somewhat playfully of having lost his connection to his birthplace.

Reaffirmations like the pledge of allegiance or the Boy Scout Oath are usually in a heightened formulaic language suitable to their sacred purpose. The diction of "The Lordly Hudson," too, is elevated and filled with repeated formulaic phrases; in fact, the last stanza is made up of snippets from the previous three stanzas. Some are quite beautiful. Goodman floats out a stately pentameter in "It is our lordly Hudson hardly flowing." I'm touched by the possessive *our*. The taxi driver and all New Yorkers possess a share of the aristocratic "lordly Hudson." This call and response between Goodman and the taxi driver has so stirred Goodman that he must quiet himself. His reunion with the Hudson is more intense than he first imagined. "No one needs your passionate / suffrage to select this glory," he tells his heart in rather grand language. No one needs his vote when it comes to the beauty of the Hudson; an overwhelming majority already affirms it. Yet Goodman nevertheless needs to have his say. The self-consciousness of the language alerts us to the ecclesiastical use of *suffrage* as an "intercessional prayer." The Hudson becomes a god-like figure that Goodman asks to intercede on his behalf. Goodman poses one more question:

"Driver, has this a peer in Europe or the East?"
"No, no!" he said. Home! Home!
Be quiet, heart! This is our lordly Hudson
and has no peer in Europe or the East.

For Goodman, it isn't enough to feel an attachment to the Hudson or to appreciate its beauty; he must also rank it above other rivers of the world. He must be reaffirmed its greatness. Only when the driver agrees that it has no peer does Goodman call out "Home! Home!" The call is explosive, and he immediately has to quiet his heart, calming it with the knowledge that they are in view of the river.

Yet the cry "Home! Home!" has always disturbed me. For a long time I didn't pay attention to the punctuation, and I thought that he was directing the taxi driver to take him home. (Having reaffirmed his bond to the river, he is ready to face that more difficult reunion with his home.) But all the dialogue is in quotation marks, and the call *Home!* isn't. So he couldn't possibly be addressing the driver. I now realize it is his heart calling out to him, as if his heart were a separate passenger in the car. Yet why does Goodman try to quiet his heart? Is it demanding to be taken home while Goodman wishes to stay by the river, or is the heart saying our home is the river? I can't tell. Nor can Goodman, which may be one of the reasons he wishes to hush his heart.

And while we're at it, another thing disturbs me about this passage: the relationship between "No, No!" and "Home! Home!" The first, of course is the driver's answer to Goodman's question; the second the outpouring of Goodman's heart. Yet the two are linked by being placed on either end of a short line, by being rhythmically identical spondees, and finally, by their echoing O sounds. Is the poem rejecting the river and demanding the home, or is it suggesting that there is no home but the river? The pleasure of the poem is that we do not have to choose among these alternatives and that they can circulate together. The very need to reaffirm suggests that the bonds are not a tight as they might be. The reaffirmation recalls what might be forgotten or what can never be recaptured.

It's time we face yet another teasing riddle to this poem, Goodman's use of *hardly*. In what sense can the Hudson be said to be "hardly" flowing? According to New York State hydrologists, the Hudson discharges approximately 21,400 cubic feet of fresh water per second. That's a lot of water. Goodman could mean that because the Hudson is so wide and stately, it doesn't look as fast as smaller streams and rivers. But I doubt it. The diction suggests that Goodman is playing with older meanings of *hardly*, "with great exertion or effort, stern, severe, not easily" and "with trouble." The Hudson is flowing with effort, uneasily, and with trouble. Goodman tries to make the Hudson appear as "hardly flowing" (in the modern sense) to disguise how much effort it takes to flow (in the older sense). For if the river is one's home, then one's home is disappearing at the rate of 20,000 cubic feet per second. Home, instead of being fixed, solid, and permanent, is fluid, unstable, and constantly in flux. It is particularly fitting that the end of the poem is made of recirculated parts of the poem, for the unquiet heart is swirling like the poem. The composer Ned Rorem, who was Goodman's lover, set many of Goodman's poems to music. In his setting of "The Lordly Hudson," voted in 1948 the best published song of that year by the Music Library Association, the last words "Home! Home!" grow to fortissimo, but then diminish in volume even as the singer step by step reaches the piece's highest note. Rorem understood that the poem needed to move in opposite ways at once. The affirmation needed to bring the performer to his or her limits. It is a thrilling and dangerous conclusion when performed by the right singer.

My pleasure comes from the poem's "passionate suffrage," its intense (if staged) joy of seeing the Hudson again. (I must say I have always found the Hudson an extraordinarily beautiful river as it slides by Manhattan.) I like the way the poem starts in humor (Goodman's performance as an ignorant out-of-towner) but ends up almost in choked excitement declaring himself home. These are pleasures from reading the poem dramatically, which is to say, attending to what the words do. The reassurance that Goodman tries to give himself is a complex speech act whose dangers include over excitement as well as misunderstanding. I take pleasure in the way the poem muddles his reactions. And this is the key to taking pleasure in poetry and why it is so difficult for so many. We enjoy certainty. "The Lordly Hudson" begins with a gesture of establishing certainty; the passenger wants to hear from the driver what he already knows: "It is our lordly Hudson hardly flowing." But that gesture of certainty is tellingly introduced by the question "what stream is it?" Goodman finds himself quickly tangled in various streams of emotion, various uncertainties, aporia and ambiguities. Our certainties are lost. When we ask, "What does a poem mean?" We are asking for a simple message, a certainty that we can comfortably take away and easily use. What we can't easily use is this experiential muddle. And yet that is exactly what we need to find pleasurable and learn to enjoy.

There are parts of the brain that are concerned with finding comfort with uncertainty. It is easy to understand why primitive homo sapiens needed such a function. Danger threatened them from every step; their lives were uncertain, feeble, and short. But you cannot live always ready to hit the panic button. Today, our dangers and uncertainties are different. Some people—the readers of poetry—live in unprecedented safety. Yet depression, generalized anxiety disorder, and OCD are growing phenomena. Even as existential threats have diminished, we are rattled more and more by ambiguity, ambivalence, and indeterminacy. The safest places to develop the skills for handling such uncertainties is literature and particularly poetry, but it asks more of us; it asks us to enjoy that uncertainty, to relax in such uncertainty ("be still, my heart") and may be, in the end, to invite such uncertainty into our homes. (That taxi driver is going to get a big tip, I bet.) Poetry doesn't teach us a lesson; it provides us with toys by which we may learn how to be in the world. Poetry is the first Montessori school. Let's pretend this block of wood is a taxi, and this blue stripe in the rug is a river. "Driver," you ask, although you know the answer already.

"What river is this?"

John Langfeld

READING IT HE CHANGED ALMOST INTO ANOTHER MAN

Reading ethanolaminephos-
photransferase in German
or trying to elocute C_2H_7NO and
$NH_2(CH_2)_2OH$ in English
is like insisting on solfège from
folks with good ears.

Part the First: The Referential "Rule of Five"

1) Traditional language reflects the things around us we have *words* for, assuming we have words for things.

2) Traditional language reflects the things around us we have *feelings* for, assuming we have words for feelings.

3) Traditional language reflects the things around us we have *words and feelings* for, assuming we have words for both.

4) Traditional language reflects *how we think* about things and words and feelings.

5) Traditional language reflects *how we think about thinking* about things and words and feelings.

Our skills in using and responding to traditional language evolve over time—from the obvious to the more subtle in our younger years; from the literal to the more abstract and metaphorical as we age. We begin our journey toward literacy by exploring the outward appearances of language (*the obvious*) and continue that journey by exploring underlying forms (*the more subtle*). With a little help from our parents and books and a nurtured propensity for curiosity, we become more sophisticated the more we practice using and responding to language.

For example, we initially learn *to read* from "the outside in." When it is age-appropriate and necessary, we learn *to parse* from "the inside out." When we are facile enough with both reading and parsing, our ability to create meaning improves. Eventually, we learn to parse both directions responsibly—before synthesizing, generalizing and forming opinions; i.e., making meaning.

Example 1: Linear Reading and Parsing

- Outward Appearance *before* Underlying Form (*reading*)
- Underlying Form *before* Outward Appearance (*parsing*)

Example 2: Reading A Linear Poem
Outward Appearance *before* Underlying Form (*reading*)

Villanelle for the End of Days 21113 9/17/15	*Exaggerated, meant to seduce?*
Mindless repetition at the end of the day is like watching the same story on six different shows, realizing talking heads have very little to say.	*Pundit bashing, apparently the point*
It is likely not easy getting ready for the fray, with make-up on your face and powder on your nose, mindless repetition at the end of the day.	*How do you take this seriously with powder on your nose while you recite?*
You suppose they have chins up and before each take pray that the cue cards are ready and the bosses have toes, realizing talking heads have very little to say.	*blind-faith trusting the guy holding the cards; you aren't holding the cards, heh*
You suppose they try hard not to stutter, not to bray but to meet the high standards of the scripting they chose, mindless repetition at the end of the day.	*phony baloney; mindless high standards = sarcasm*
You imagine their bosses with feet of clay, with nary a vision but a sense of what flows, realizing talking heads have very little to say.	*Bosses who read polls to assess success, don't trust the "star"*
So forget heads and toes, choose a different caché, read a book and relax that who knows this knows mindless repetition at the end of the day is like watching the same story on six different shows.	*caché…double meaning get informed by reading, not TV* *really!*

Example 3: Parsing A Linear Poem
Underlying Form *before* Outward Appearance (*parsing*)

Villanelle for the End of Days	*title sounds traditional and*
21113	*biblical; implies formal*
9/17/15	*structure; better check*
	rhyming and repetition
Mindless repetition at the end of the day	*1a*
is like watching the same story on six different shows,	*2b*
realizing talking heads have very little to say.	*3a*
It is likely not easy getting ready for the fray,	*4a*
with make-up on your face and powder on your nose,	*5b*
mindless repetition at the end of the day.	*1a*
You suppose they have chins up and before each take pray	*6a*
that the cue cards are ready and the bosses have toes,	*7b*
realizing talking heads have very little to say.	*3a*
You suppose they try hard not to stutter, not to bray	*8a*
but to meet the high standards of the scripting they chose,	*9b*
mindless repetition at the end of the day.	*1a*
You imagine their bosses with feet of clay,	*10a*
with nary a vision but a sense of what flows,	*11b*
realizing talking heads have very little to say.	*3a*
So forget heads and toes, choose a different caché,	*12a*
read a book and relax that who knows this knows	*13b*
mindless repetition at the end of the day	*1a*
is like watching the same story on six different shows.	*2b*
This writer is making fun of TV pundits in a rigorously clas-	*Okay I looked up Villanelle;*
sical way. An ironic (funny) use of a tricky form that sounds	*five 3-liners; one, 4. last*
very serious in the reading, but the point is a "poke." Juxta-	*stanza is supposed to be*
position heightens the point and the poke.	*"abaa." Writer broke form*
	intentionally. usual poetic
	trick; complicated form!

Examples 2-3 reflect a linear reading and parsing of a very linear poem, and that brings up some good questions:

- What if we find something to read that is totally "off the wall" and impossible to fathom at first glance?

- How do we create meaning when confronted with language that is abstract and non-linear—things with only a few (if any) of the usual associative verbal clues and contexts?

- What if the parsing skills familiar to us are not helpful when confronting language that does not reflect the world of words as we know it?

- How do we respond to language that demands parsing skills we simply do not have?

Answers:

- We have to change the expectations we have for language and respond differently.

- We need to practice reading and parsing language, especially when it looks odd on the page and particularly when reading it aloud isn't helpful.

- We need to think about how we think about the words and ideas that seem to have been spilled randomly on a page but surely must mean something don't you think?

- We need to practice reading and parsing writing that includes more space than ink.

- And so on.

Part the Second: The De-Generative[1] "Rule of Five"

1) Words do not have to adhere to syntactical rules or accepted conventions.

2) Words do not have to be "inked" left to right for traditional reading.

3) Words can be meaningless fun and/or meaningful challenge.

4) Words can be *spellused* incorrectly on purpose [*sic*].

5) Words can be used purely for the sounds they make.

When it comes to reading and parsing linear writing in general, some people believe that words live in the air more importantly than they do on paper. Some people believe in both paper and air; some only paper. When it comes to reading and parsing non-linear writing, however, consider the following:

> Reading de-generative, non-linear language fairly assumes that the competencies needed for the application of *The Referential "Rule of Five"* are in place, particularly Rules 4 and 5.

Reading and parsing non-linear writing cogently takes seat-time. If our intention is to respond to what we read seriously, we should read language like we look at paintings in an art museum. We sit down on a bench (or stand still if it's crowded) and ponder as much of the "information" on a canvas that we can; i.e., the overall scene or image, the choices of pigment, the framing of content, the implications of symbol, etc.

In non-linear writing, the smallest of clues may yield many thoughts. We merely have to notice everything, then wonder a while and see where each clue takes us. More importantly, we need a laser-like focus on implication and inference: What might a writer mean by this or that? How many ways can we feel about this or that? Is there a point of view to discover, or is the lack of a point the point? The Taoist answer: "The only parsing is every parsing."

---

1. This "de-generative" is not based on the root word, "degenerate," but generative art. It sounds a bit odd, which is the point of course. A thesaurus wasn't helpful; thus, the coin.

Example 4: Non-linear Reading and Parsing
Mulling and Lateral Drift

- Outward Appearance (*reading and parsing implications, inferences and sundry clues*)
- Underlying Form (*reading and parsing implications, inferences and sundry clues*)

For the classically "stuck," perhaps this might help:

Part the Third: The Brevitist[2] "Rule of Three or Four"

1) Not every short poem is a ditty.

2) If you don't know a word, look it up.

3) The shorter the poem, the longer the sit.

Oh.

4) And don't be afraid to stand on your head, seek a spotter.

---

2. Epigrammatic writing (a term joined at the hip with "aphoristic" and "apothegmatic"; i.e., short and pithy) is a scholarly term. That's not a bad thing. "Brevitist" is easier on the tongue.

Example 5: Reading and Parsing A Non-Linear Poem
Implication and Inference

Line Dancing   *(is this about country music or poetic lineage?)*
19274
7/22/09

line can

      destroy the music *(is there such a thing as atonal poetry?)*
      remember the ear   *(oh I get it, word placement can make you hear words better)*

      changethepaceoftheread   *(aah, rhythm is important, too)*
      slow
              the

                      progress

                                    of

                                          context
    (reading too quickly means you might miss some things)

      make images POP   *(stand out)*
      make images   *(as in construct?)*

    (making the point elusive? it's lonely being an artist, romantic claptrap?) lonely

  (I guess this is a visual representation of the important of pace in reading aka dance!)

Part the Fourth: "I will be deaf to pleading (and excuses)"[3]

The processes presented above can and (and should) be applied to the visual arts as well. Consider *White Painting,* those three panels of white by Robert Rauschenberg so easily dismissed by those in a hurry. Sit down. Take a gander. Take three. A subtle presentation of color (color?) can speak to you if you attend as you should and apply the gist of Parts One, Two and Three.

What about the time arts, like theater and dance? Same thing... but with the added challenge to notice things more quickly, down-stage and up-, applying the gist of Parts One, Two and Three.

And so on.

---

3. *Romeo and Juliet*: III, I (parentheses mine)

Example 6: A Linear, Non-Linear Poem

Work this out on your own. Remember. The only parsing is every parsing.

If a digit falls in the forest

If goatskin, or sheepskin, or lambskin were used
for taking on pigment from quills or a press

and cellulose, vellum and pulp were recused
from bettering the fettering and misering the guess,

this poem might look pretty for some time to come,
all squiggles and curls, all in love with itself,

but it's likely to crumble and finally succumb
like the rest of us fading up there on the shelf.

Get a grip.

Digits make noise.

Gutenberg
2013

185

ADDENDUM

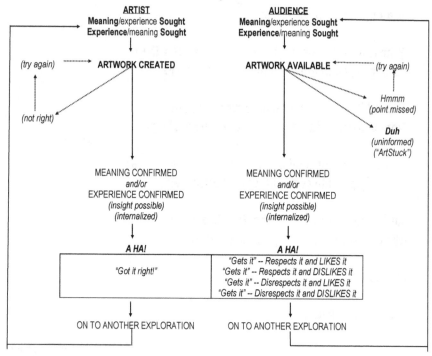

CONCEIVING, MAKING AND PERCEIVING THE ARTS
A Metacognitive Model

ARTIST	AUDIENCE
Meaning/experience **Sought**	**Meaning**/experience **Sought**
Experience/meaning **Sought**	**Experience**/meaning **Sought**

(try again) ⟶ **ARTWORK CREATED**   **ARTWORK AVAILABLE** ⟵ *(try again)*

(not right)

Hmmm
(point missed)

Duh
(uninformed)
("ArtStuck")

MEANING CONFIRMED
and/or
EXPERIENCE CONFIRMED
(insight possible)
(internalized)

MEANING CONFIRMED
and/or
EXPERIENCE CONFIRMED
(insight possible)
(internalized)

A HA!

A HA!

"Got it right!"

"Gets it" -- Respects it and LIKES it
"Gets it" -- Respects it and DISLIKES it
"Gets it" -- Disrespects it and LIKES it
"Gets it" -- Disrespects it and DISLIKES it

ON TO ANOTHER EXPLORATION   ON TO ANOTHER EXPLORATION

Investigating the creative uses of SIGHT, SOUND, MOVEMENT and LANGUAGE in this way can lead to a new and deeper appreciation of a piece of music, an artwork, a person, etc. It is a metacognitive adventure.

Criteria (words and questions) to use in evaluating the integrity of conceptual, formative and perceptual experience:

Imaginative	*Is it clever? Does it stimulate questions? Can you compare it to more commonplace things?*
Sensitive	*Is it mindful of context? Is there appropriate creative tension? Does it tap feelings? emotions?*
Skillful	*Is it technically proficient? Is there evidence of care and ability?*
Authentic	*Is it original? Is it genuine? Is there a personal voice? style? point to make?*

Contemplating Form

Kelly Cherry

STYLE IS THE STRUGGLE FOR CLARITY

Almost the first thing a reader notices about a piece of writing is its style—unless the style is transparent. Transparent prose is prose that lets you see the object before you. It has often been referred to as a window, for the window in no way obstructs your view. Indeed, it *serves* the view, quite as if it were a humble attendant.

When we speak of style, then, we usually mean prose that *obstructs* the view. But of course, we do still see something of the object in our line of sight (i.e., the sense of the sentence). How, then, is the object—the view, the sense—obstructed? By details of the sentence that yank our attention away from the sense, if only momentarily. Puns, alliteration, syntactical flourishes, words that call our attention to themselves are some of the details that can do this. Such details are, of course, snappy, playful, poetic, even enlivening, and the reader who reads them, if that reader wishes to be a writer, is apt to think, I'm going to get me some of those!

And why not?

There is no reason why not. But the getting of them is harder than one might think.

This is because no human being is exactly like another human being. Even if all the human beings involved are writers.

Ernest Hemingway could write, in *The Sun Also Rises*, his first and arguably best novel, this description of Basque country:

> ... We walked on the road between the thick trunks of the
> old beeches and the sunlight came through the leaves in light
> patches on the grass...

Suppose he had instead written this:

...As we walked on the road between the old beeches' thick trunks, sunlight came through the leaves in light patches, lingering on the grass...

My version is shorter, and introduces only one new word: "lingering." It's likely that someone would say my version is more "feminine" than Hemingway's, and perhaps it is. At the same time, my version is more efficient, and efficiency is sometimes considered a masculine characteristic. But I don't want to get into the gender wars here, only to understand what Hemingway was doing when he wrote that passage.

A writer whose style seems almost the opposite of Hemingway's is F. Scott Fitzgerald, whose closing sentence in *The Great Gatsby* is "So we beat on, boats against the current, borne back ceaselessly into the past."

In Fitzgerald's sentence he gives us a metaphor ("we" are "boats") and the metaphor is active (the boats are fighting the current unsuccessfully and being brought back into the past). The sentence is not terse in the way Hemingway's sentences above were terse. Here is another quotation from *The Great Gatsby*:

That's my Middle West—not the wheat or the prairies or the lost Swede towns, but the thrilling returning trains of my youth, and the street lamps and sleigh bells in the frosty dark and the shadows of holly wreaths thrown by lighted windows on the snow. I am part of that, a little solemn with the feel of those long winters, a little complacent from growing up in the Carraway house in a city where dwellings are still called through decades by a family's name.

We're not looking at it for what it says about the speaker or the Middle West but for the sentences. We have adjectives here, and sibilance ("Swede," "street," "sleigh," "shadows," "snow") and subordinate clauses that mimic the "long winters." There is music here, too, but nothing martial. "Dwellings" and "decades" alliterate. "Thrilling" and "returning" both end in -ing. Double "l's" appear in "thrilling," "bells," "holly" and "dwellings." "Bell-" rhymes with "dwell-." The passage is lyrical, approaching poetry. Did Fitzgerald work hard to produce the musical notes it contains? Probably not. He may have stopped to notice what he was doing and added or deleted a word or two, but on the whole, this is simply how he wrote. He may even have thought he was writing transparent prose, but because of the music in that paragraph it would be more accurate, if a cliché, to say that it is "crystal clear" than to call it "transparent prose." It was George Orwell, in his essay "Why I Write," a few decades after Fitzgerald and Hemingway published their first novels, who proclaimed, "Good prose is like a window pane." Neither Fitzgerald's prose nor Hemingway's is like a window pane, yet both have written good prose. We may prefer one over the other, but preference is merely preference, not universal truth.

And this is the point. Two writers, friends of a sort, published books, Fitzgerald in 1925 and Hemingway in 1926, and their styles are nothing alike. Is a writer in search of a style to choose one over the other? Which, and why?

Let's look at an earlier fiction author, the great Henry James, born in 1843, in America, though later he would become a British citizen. James was wonderfully prolific, writing novels, stories, plays, criticism (of literature and art), travel memoirs, and autobiography and thousands of letters. His work is not admired by everyone—there are some who have found it too fussy—but pretty much everyone recognizes it as a mainstay of the literary canon. Over a long life, style may shift, but this paragraph from *The Portrait of a Lady* can be taken as a fair example. A young American heiress, Isabel Archer, has arrived in England.

> She had been looking all round her again,—at the lawn, the great trees, the reedy, silvery Thames, the beautiful old house; and, while engaged in this survey, she had also narrowly scrutinized her companions; a comprehensiveness of observation easily conceivable on the part of a young woman who was evidently both intelligent and excited. She had seated herself, and had put away the little dog; her white hands, in her lap, were folded upon her black dress; her head was erect, her eye brilliant, her flexible figure turned itself lightly this way and that, in sympathy with the alertness with which she evidently caught impressions. Her impressions were numerous, and they were all reflected in a clear, still smile. "I have never seen anything so beautiful as this," she declared.

In an article in *The New Yorker*, "Out of the Frame," Anthony Lane rightly waves a yellow flag of caution. "The beauty of the telling," he points out, "should not be confused with the loveliness of the scene, whatever the enticement of the greensward; hundreds of writers have tried their hand at Old World pastoral and got stuck in a sentimental mud." Nevertheless, we are intelligent readers and can separate the description from the scene described.

One aid to reading James is the punctuation, which may seem a bit old-fashioned but is very useful to modern readers. Breathe when the punctuation advises you to, and the words become clear, the sentences sensible. Any notion of fussiness disappears. Note too the uppercrust diction, the multisyllabic words, and the attractively juxtaposed simple words like "reedy" and "silvery" and "little dog." The first sentence is not short but it is broken by a semicolon. The second sentence also uses semicolons, which contemporary American writers are often afraid to use, but they helpfully link moments that seem to want to be linked, moments that are of a piece. Although the paragraph is about a sitting woman, we see that she "scrutinizes," is "excited," takes actions of "putting away" and "folding," and "turning" and "declaring." There is a little alliteration, and the rhythm is subtle and varied. When we encounter Isabel's "clear, still smile," we know that she is good-natured, alive to life, and confident.

And now, to examine an entirely different style, consider this line from Ben Marcus's experimental and lovely first novel, *The Age of Wire and String*, published in 1995. The author's postmodern premise is that when we look at an object, our desire destroys it. He includes a kind of mini-dictionary with which we can interpret the very short stories in eight sections that make up the book. Sadness, the dictionary tells us, "can be eradicated with more of itself, in which case the face results in a placid system coursing with water, heaving." A "wind bowl" is a "pocket of curved, unsteady space formed between speaking persons." "The mother" is "the softest location in the house."

Clearly, the supplied definitions are not the usual kind of definition; they mirror and magnify the novel, or "catalogue of the life project," so that the reader can follow the plot, which is an assemblage of details that prompt the reader into thought and philosophical analysis. (He may have come up with this idea from reading Wittgenstein.)

Well, postmodern or not, we have a paragraph, and it consists of two long-ish, though not very long, sentences. There is alliteration ("project," "prosecuted," "placements," "perimeter," "program") but it doesn't really stand out, maybe because the diction seems to be that of someone who works in an office. It's there, though, bolstered by "temporary" and "dispersed," and it unifies the passage. There is less action here, and no metaphor, but I think we hear a quiet, supporting music. And the entire book is more or less a metaphor for life.

We can now see that all four writers rely on similar devices to define their styles, even the last, whose paragraph might be said to be transparent prose. Does this mean that all a writer has to do is use these devices to develop a style?

It's not that easy.

Might a beginning writer merely mimic the rhythm, punctuation, and diction of one of these published authors?

It doesn't hurt to try. In fact, mimicking great novelists and poets and essays is an excellent way of improving one's work—it will sharpen the attention one pays to it—but it won't turn you into a Hemingway, a Fitzgerald, a Henry James, or a Ben Marcus.

It won't turn you into an Elizabeth Taylor (brilliant British novelist) or Olivia Manning (another) or an Alice Munro (Canadian story writer) or a Lynda Schor (contemporary American story writer who writes wickedly funny stories about sex).

The reason it won't is that all four of our excerpted authors are struggling for clarity. Each is trying with all his might to set down exactly what is in his mind to set down. This is very difficult to do: the mind is cloudy and drifts; this idea approaches while that one turns to mist, dissolves and disappears; and is that district crowded or barren, are those big beeches comforting or gloomy, is the Thames silvery or the gray of metal, is the Middle West in sharpest focus in winter or during haying season? The right word, the right punctuation, the right rhyme or near-rhyme, the right rhythm, the right length: every choice *is* a choice, it is made more or less deliberately, and the purpose of the choice is to record what is in the writer's mind. What the writer feels in his mind, because if it were already clear and exact in his mind, he would not hesitate, but writers hesitate. Writers hesitate and revise, seeking to come closer to the imperfect vision in their minds.

Out of this struggle comes that which we call *style*. Style cannot be imposed upon a work; it grows out of the work. It is therefore personal, unique, and identifiable. It is developed by the writer in the process of writing.

I should add that it is developed by the writer in the process of writing *the story*. The story must be apparent at all times. Murk will sink it. Obscurity will deter the reader. Fudging, or smudging shade into the story to disguise plot points or blocks of time or motivation will make the reader throw the book across the room. The story must shine.

What I have said about fiction is equally applicable to poetry. Poetry thrives on clarity. That does not mean spelling out what is behind every line or leap; it means making sense. At the current moment, it is true that there are poets, possibly a school of poets, who try very hard *not* to make sense and often succeed. Unfortunately, there is no point to poetry that does not make sense. Such poems may seem brightly new, but they have been written by various experimental poets over centuries, and the audience for them eventually wears out because most readers want something that makes sense to them. Besides, there are other ways of writing brightly new poems. The best is to pursue the poetic ideas that interest you as carefully and as far as you can. You will be surprised at what turns up. To write is to use your senses to convey an idea. The reader cannot see what you are describing; he or she can see only the words you have put on the page. How you use those words will determine what the reader sees. Pick the right ones and use them carefully if you want to get your idea across.

The beginning writer will stumble if he or she tries on a style. Better to be patient, then discover that a style has wrapped itself around you. A style has pieced itself together from the thinnest threads of thought, from awkwardly angled mistakes and even from indecision, and—hey, look at this: it has become a garment of meaning and, perhaps, some radiance. This is true whether you write novels, short stories, flash fiction, formal poetry, free verse, essay, memoir, criticism, biography, or book reviews. It is true whether you write literature, mystery, sci-fi, romance, or young adult.

For another strong paragraph, here is the first in "A Good Man Is Hard to Find," one of Flannery O'Connor's best-known stories:

> The grandmother didn't want to go to Florida. She wanted to visit some of her connections in east Tennessee and she was seizing at every chance to change Bailey's mind. Bailey was the son she lived with, her only boy. He was sitting on the edge of his chair at the table, bent over the orange sports section of the *Journal*. "Now look here, Bailey," she said, "see here,

read this," and she stood with one hand on her thin hip and the other rattling the newspaper at his bald head. "Here this fellow that calls himself The Misfit is aloose from the Federal Pen and headed toward Florida and you read here what it says he did to these people. Just you read it. I wouldn't take my children in any direction with a criminal like that aloose in it. I couldn't answer to my conscience if I did."

In a horrible irony, we'll find out, of course, that the grandmother's self-serving desire to visit relatives in east Tennessee will result in her not being able to answer to her conscience. And that's the least of it. This heart-rending, perplexing story is said to demonstrate the depth of O'Connor's Catholic faith, but I wonder if it does, given that the end of the story is written into the beginning. (That is to say, it is predetermined, as grace, presumably, is not.) Nevertheless, the paragraph is superb. We hear the grandmother's voice. We also hear Bailey's silence. We see that orange sports section. We see the grandmother's bullying stance contradicted by her "thin hip." We see that Bailey ignores her. We learn about the Misfit and have a sinking presentiment that he will reappear somewhere, somehow. The primary device in this paragraph is rhythm: declarative sentences seem to whip the very air of it; they shove us into the story without preamble. Of course, the vivid details set the scene: Bailey at the edge of his chair, the grandmother standing and waving the newspaper, the grandmother's demand of Bailey that "just you read it." We have been thrust into this scene and can barely catch our breath. Perhaps this is the paragraph that comes closest to transparent prose, though the diction and the speed—and a sense of chaos and loud clatter that seems to surround the scene even unmentioned—definitely set the paragraph off from Hemingway, from Fitzgerald, from James, from Marcus. There is, in other words, style here, as well as in those other writers' work. It's a different style, but still a style. Flannery O'Connor did not pull it down from a shelf and try it on; she wrote and wrote and wrote and found herself covered in powerful language that let her get close to her own understanding of what she wanted to write. She could do it. So can you.

J.G. McClure

IN DEFENSE OF POEMS THAT MEAN

Pick up any fashionable poetry journal and you're likely to see an example of what Tony Hoagland has called the "Skittery Poem of Our Moment." Such a poem does not simply lack coherence; it actively resists it. In his essay, Hoagland gives as an example Rachel M. Simon's poem "Improvisation," which opens with a dizzying series of seemingly unrelated ideas and images, including (among others): human nature, the physical dimensions of small talk, veins seen through translucent skin, a skull, voices aimed at targets, cities and their suitability for feet, and why, in light of the unpredictability of friendships, one should never buy a door smaller than a tuba.

The characteristics are familiar: leaping from thought to thought, sharply-written-but-largely-nonsensical phrases, quirky humor, an assertive-yet-evasive voice, and so on. We move from talk to skin to cities to tubas to friends, never afforded the chance to stop and consider any one element. The mode is so widespread as to be instantly recognizable: it is what many readers likely think of immediately upon hearing the phrase "contemporary poetry." In Hoagland's words:

> "Improvisation" is a quintessential Poem of Our Moment: fast-moving and declarative, wobbling on the balance beam between associative and dissociative, somewhat absurdist, and, indeed, cerebral. Much talent and skill are evident in its making, in its pacing and management of gaps, the hints and sound bites which keep the reader reaching forward for the lynchpin of coherence. One admirable aspect of the poem is the way it seems capable of incorporating anything; yet the correlative theme of the poem is that all this motley data—i.e. experience—doesn't add up to a story. Even as the

poem implies a world without sequence, the poem itself has no consequence, no center of gravity, no body, no assertion of emotional value.

The logic behind this aesthetic is clear enough: it implicitly believes that in order to confront the fragmented nature of our postmodern world, we need fragmented, postmodern art. Narrative is viewed with fearful distrust, and is equated with deception and rigid authority. The skittery poem makes no claim to impose any kind of order, so it does not aim to deceive or control us. The problem, as Hoagland explains it, is this:

> Elusiveness is the speaker's central characteristic. Speed, wit, and absurdity are its attractive qualities. The last thing such poems are going to do is risk their detachment, their distance, their freedom from accountability. The one thing they are not going to do is commit themselves to the sweaty enclosures of subject matter and the potential embarrassment of sincerity.

By presenting itself as a performance of ironic wit, the poem ensures that it won't say anything disagreeable. The trouble is, though the language is well-written, the poem won't sincerely say anything at all.

What does such a poem really mean for us, aside from reminding us (yet again) that we live in a fragmented world and that our narratives are insufficient to remedy it?

But this isn't news: even Frost, poster child of the old guard, described a poem as "a momentary stay against confusion," a description that presupposes that everything outside of the poem is in a state of unending disorder. The skittery poem constantly reminds us of this confusion, while the Frostian poem works (momentarily, provisionally, insufficiently) against it—but in either case, both reader and writer understand that confusion is the state in which we live and from which we work.

It's worth noting that well before the burgeoning of the Skittery Poem of Our Moment, writers were engaging with similar issues, using similar techniques. Take, for example, the fragmented "Wandering Rocks" episode of *Ulysses*, in which we're bombarded with so much raw data, all of it potentially meaningful, that it eventually all becomes equally meaningless while almost-forming an almost-narrative that never quite seems to cohere.

Or take the Chilean poet Vicente Huidobro, whose brilliant book-length poem *Altazor* (written, like *Ulysses*, in the early 20th century) shows a world so chaotic that it eventually leads to the dissolution of the very language used to build it. Though these experiments were revolutionary in their moment, and are deservedly revered, by now their techniques have become familiar. Today, such techniques are no longer truly an experiment per se, but rather a genre trope. Simply claiming "experimentation" isn't enough to justify them.

By no means do I intend to suggest that the techniques that define the Skittery Poem of Our Moment—intelligence, evasiveness, absurdity, fragmentation—are valueless. Quite the opposite, some of the most moving poems we have use these devices heavily. Rather, I wish to suggest that these techniques must be tools used in service of something deeper. They need to be grounded in a foundation of emotional/moral/human stakes. The moment that these techniques become an end in themselves, as in Simon's poem and so many like it, is the moment in which they are reduced to mere linguistic showboating.

For an example of Meaningful Skitteriness, I want to turn back to Huidobro's *Altazor*. The first canto establishes the terror of protagonist Altazor's world:

> Altazor ¿por qué perdiste tu primera serenidad?
> ¿Qué ángel malo se paró en la puerta de tu sonrisa...?
> ...
> ¿Por qué un día de repente sentiste el terror de ser?
> ...Estás perdido Altazor
> Solo en medio del universo
> [Altazor, why did you lose your first serenity?
> What bad angel stopped in the door of your smile...?
> ...
> Why one day did you suddenly feel the terror of being?
> ...
> You're lost Altazor
> Alone in the middle of the universe]

From the beginning, we see Altazor in the throes of existential dread. The center can no longer hold, and he finds himself adrift (quite literally: he's presented as endlessly falling, strapped alone to a parachute). As the poem progresses, we realize that he no longer believes in God, no longer believes in any of the old structures of meaning, no longer knows what to believe in, and is terrified and miserable to the core.

Halfway through the book, Huidobro has Altazor utter these wonderful lines, a small but crucial gesture that firmly grounds all of the linguistic experimentation that is to follow:

> Y puesto que debemos vivir y no nos suicidamos
> Mientras vivamos juguemos
> El simple sport de los vocablos
> [And since we must live and not kill ourselves
> While we live let's play
> The simple sport of words]

This passage gracefully casts all of the nonsensical word-games that Altazor will play as a conscious evasion of his existential dread, the only way to avoid killing himself in an absurd universe. Even the wildest experiments are thus given a heavy emotional weight. So when Huidobro gives us, for instance, a solid block of approximately 200 consecutive puns on the word "molina [mill]," we understand why he does it: it becomes a poignantly obsessive mantra to stave off suicide.

When, eventually, Altazor's words begin to break down—leaving us with chopped-up, spliced-together terms that look like but are not words—we continue to sense the human stakes. Words, the one thing left to Altazor, are beginning to fall apart too. By the end of the book, we're left only with howling nonsense syllables, vowels combined and recombined:

> lalalí
> ....lo ia
> i i i o
> Ai a i ai a i i i i o ia

That final line is pronounced, more or less, as "ay ahh eee ay ahh eee eee eee eee ohh eeyah"—that is, screams. As strange and experimental as this ending may be, it's still grounded in a very human pain.

(It's worth noting that there is another important critical tradition regarding this poem, which sees the ending not as a howl of pain but as a song of triumph. Either way, though, the point remains: we are able to locate the emotional experience that necessitates the technique.)

That notion—that in order for a work to be moving there must be an emotional reality that necessitates its techniques—holds true today. Consider Dean Young's excellent poem "Afterward (Little Evening Sermon)," which begins:

> By the seventh time the story was told,
> the girl stood naked in the sprinklers
> and the fighter pilot had flown on E
> through Russia. The bear could almost talk,
> the crippled dog could almost run and we
> could almost love each other forever.
> Funny word, forever. You can put it at the end
> of almost any sentence and feel better about
> yourself, about how you've worked in a spray
> of sparks accomplishing almost nothing
> and feel that's exactly what the gods
> intended; look at the galaxies, spilled
> milk, their lust and retrograde whims.

The zaniness of the first sentence is enough to keep us sufficiently interested to continue reading. But that zaniness alone would not be enough to carry the poem: if Young merely kept naming strange and unrelated components of the story, we might get a chuckle or two, but that would be the end of it. Instead, Young includes the crucial phrase "and we / could almost love each other forever."

In an instant, we understand why the speaker's voice must be so skittery: his zaniness is a desperately manic attempt to avoid thinking about the pain of losing his beloved. The speaker starts to dwell on those painful thoughts, musing about how "forever" is a word that you use to "feel better about / yourself," but quickly he turns away from the relationship again and wildly reaches for anything else: galaxies, gods, milk. The poem continues:

What was it you were promised? I'm sorry
if it turned out to be a lie. But the girl
really did drink fire from a flower,
the dog did leap a chasm...

Here the line breaks enact the speaker's pained evasion. The speaker begins an apology—to his lover?—but then retreats to the vague deflection of "if it turned out to be a lie." Then another turn toward the lover—"But the girl"—and another turn away, back to the skittery images: "really did drink fire from a flower, / the dog did leap a chasm." Since we understand what's at stake, each of these leaps carries with it a powerful emotional resonance: we feel poignantly what the speaker will not allow himself to say.

I am not suggesting that a successful poem must indicate its emotional anchor so clearly, or that it must clearly contain some archetypal narrative like the breakup in "Afterward." Think of Vasko Popa's wonderfully strange poem "Ashes," as translated by Charles Simic:

Some are nights others stars
Each night sets fire to its own star
And dances a black dance around it
Until the star burns out
Then the nights divide themselves
Some become stars
Others remain nights
Again each night sets fire to its own star
And dances a black dance around it
Until the star burns out
The last night becomes both star and night
It sets fire to itself
And dances the black dance around itself

Though there's no explicitly stated human narrative here, no obvious allegory, we nonetheless recognize and are chilled by the actions: we see some version of ourselves in this ritualized, frightening, exuberant violence and self-destruction.

Now compare Popa's poem to an excerpt from the Skittery Poem of Our Moment that opened this essay. Though the Skittery Poem's phrases are evocative, there's nothing to emotionally ground them. Okay, sure, the reader is likely to feel, I accept that you won't buy a door smaller than a tuba—but so what? Why should I care about your taste in doorways? The poem is too successfully evasive: it evades us so thoroughly that we are not allowed to feel anything.

Michael Ryan once said that we come to poetry because we want to feel what it's like to be human, for ourselves and for others. Why else would anyone bother to read or write it? In an age where fewer and fewer people read poetry, we're certainly not writing for the money or the fame. Nor is anybody reading poems in order to have some good water-cooler talk.

If our goal is nothing short of communion, of sharing how being human feels to us—and to my mind that's the only good reason to be writing poems at all—then we can't depend solely on language games or fashionable skitteriness. We can't be afraid of consequence, sincerity, or emotion. We can't be afraid of the poem's humanity.

Stacey Balkun

FAIRY TALE AS TRANSFORMATIVE POETICS: AN INTRODUCTION

> *Nobody can write a new fairy tale; you can only mix up and dress up the old, old stories, and put the characters into new dresses.*
> —Andrew Lang, *The Lilac Fairy Book*

> *You have to fight magic with magic. You have to believe That you have something impossible up your sleeve.*
> —A.E. Stallings, *"Fairy Tale Logic"*

Fairy tales offer poets not only language, form, and familiarity but also structure, making them the perfect starting point for new poets. Fairy-tale language offers safe passage into the realm of the imaginatively possible as well as a chance at transformation: of the tale, timeline, speaker, setting, diction, or even poetic form. When a reader hears "Once upon a time..." or "There was once..." a door is opened; a new expectation is set, preparing readers for the magical and priming them for a leap. A poet can follow with "a jackalope-girl brushed her teeth" or "Gretel went to the mall" and the reader will not be surprised because the first few words have indicated that the world of the poem is no longer the world of our reality. As in fairy tales, the fantastic enters naturally and the rest of the poem rises to meet it, altering or destabilizing reality to allow for true emotional resonance using not only content but also form. Kate Bernheimer names four elements of such a fairy-tale form: flatness, abstraction, intuitive logic, and normalized magic, all of which are transformative. From incorporating these elements to embodying a familiar character or merely letting a little magic seep into the logic of our fabricated worlds, fairy tales can teach us how to write transformation and how to let form amplify our poems.

Not everything in the real world makes sense. Intuitive logic is "a sort of nonsensical sense" in which the story "tells us that first this happened, and then that happened. There is never an explanation of why" (Bernheimer). We can use this logic in an imagistic way, making associative leaps the reader must accept or creating narratives that mirror the inconsistency of difficult concepts or emotional situations. We can seize that irregularity, letting our poems break from the real and transform into beautiful if illogical beasts. We can trust our poems' intuition, no matter how strange it may seem. For example, in Ansel Elkins's "The Girl with Antlers," our speaker tears from her mother's womb because simply, "[t]here was no other way to arrive in this world" for her. A woman finds the girl and raises her without much ado, and, despite her antlers, our speaker becomes part of the household, claiming the woman even "hung the wash from my head." Here, feelings of awkwardness or exile transform into a magical character. The leaps between logic are treated as completely normal: normalized magic, "the day to day collapsed with the wondrous" (Bernheimer). A poem doesn't have to be set a long time ago in a land far, far away; rather, we can incorporate such magical elements into our otherwise realistic poems.

Another option for exercise is to draw from familiar tales, telling the stories from an alternate perspective or adding a plot twist. Using the reader's familiarity with a story, a poet is free to manipulate setting or character. She can tell old stories in new ways, especially those with difficult subjects. By letting a familiar tale do the narrative work, the poet can explore character more deeply, perhaps drawing from personal experience or taking a political stance. Louise Gluck's "Gretel in Darkness" looks back on the tale of "Hansel & Gretel" from the perspective of a future Gretel. In her poem, Gluck highlights the emotional damage Gretel has suffered in her plea to her brother: "But I killed for you." Gluck gives a deeper insight into Gretel's character, who is heartbreakingly lonely: "Nights I turn to you to hold me / but you are not there." With this poem, Gluck writes a sort of sequel, imagining the actuality of Gretel's "ever after." We can learn from this technique by trying our hands at sequel or even prequel poems to fairy tales. What led to the events within the story? What in the poet's past could be transformed, told as a fairy tale about to happen?

Since intuitive logic is already established by the introduction of a well-known fairy tale character, a poet is free to use as much or little of the tale as she wants. She can collapse realism and non-realism, letting the mundane mix with the magical. She can place the characters anywhere: grandma's house, Starbucks, the mall. Since the reader will have conflicting expectations for both the character and the setting, this tension can power the poem.

Janet McNally uses this technique to bring a mature voice and sense of darkness to the story of Rapunzel by placing her character in New York City. "Rapunzel on the Observation Deck of the Empire State Building" immediately situates us in a specific place, though we're surprised to see a fairy tale character in this space. The poem's form on the page echoes a fall: something that, like "a feather, a piece / of ribbon" does "hang in the air / a moment / before" it drops. Changing the setting of a well-known fairy tale frees the poet from the constraints of familiarity.

Transforming a familiar story can be a way to reclaim it by asserting agency. Vievee Francis's "Bluster" re-tells the story of Little Red Riding Hood in a way that puts Little Red in charge: "I knew the path and what was on it. / I wore his favorite color." Francis's retelling shows Little Red purposefully making the decisions that lead to her wolf encounter. To Little Red, the wolf uses the linguistic register of a family member to speak an ominous threat: "I could just eat you up." She's aware of his threat, though, and notes that acts as if she were a girl "whose cheeks he could pinch into blush." The poem reconsiders the color red: skin, lips, blood. The poem hints toward a sexual encounter and ends with a return to the fairy tale, imbued with new meaning: "I was my grandmother's granddaughter after all."

Francis's poem is neither prequel nor sequel; it does not modernize the tale nor change the setting exactly, but it offers a change of perspective. Little Red is not the helpless child blindly obeying her mother. Rather, Francis gives her agency, charging the reader with accepting female empowerment and bringing the issue of consent into play. We're reminded that not all monstrosities are as obvious as the wolf attack. However, not all young women need rescue.

Similarly, Anne Shaw wishes agency upon the helpless fairy-tale protagonist in her poem "Dido to the Little Matchgirl." This poem takes Hans Christian Andersen's "The Little Matchgirl" and merges it with the mythology of Dido, queen of Carthage, who slew herself upon a burning funeral pyre. Shaw takes these two familiar characters and creates a completely original situation with a strong, unique voice. Shaw's Dido urges the girl to listen to her, arguing that she can't "just sit there freezing / by the wall." Our speaker also knows desire; what it's like to "tie yourself to the bed because it burns." Here, Dido is candid with the young girl, explaining things beyond her six-year-old scope of experience. By showing her a future, she never quite freezes to death against that wall as she does in the fairy tale, having burned all of her matches to sell in order to experience visions of family and warmth.

As if the story of the matchstick girl wasn't heartbreaking enough, Shaw amplifies the distress of her situation, adding ,"But once it starts, a heart will not stop / breaking, that's the thing." Not only is this interpretation of a fairy tale poem rife with pain and disappointment, but it alludes to the happy ending that neither woman will ever know:

> Because the more you practice giving up
> the readier you'll be. You won't be twirling in a dress
> singing, *make me a match.*

Shaw refocuses the story to show how such "happiness" is rooted in dependency. Here, neither Dido nor the little match girl *needs* someone to fix their futures; they are each powerful in their own ways. Shaw rewrites Andersen's tale in a way that, like Francis's take on Little Red, frames that power and agency, darkly. Shaw brings this poem together with her stunning final line: "the place / for a woman who burns is in the fire." In a way, this line simplifies the poem because we're reminded of the connective thread between the two stories; however, fire is imbued with new meaning. The matchstick girl, like Dido, transforms completely—beyond death and beyond rebirth.

Like Shaw, we too can give ourselves the freedom to let different stories mingle within our poems. By widening the scope of a tale and letting distinct characters meet, something utterly new is born. As Marie Tatar says, "[f] airy tales have long created potent cocktails of beauty, horror, marvels, violence, and magic." We can use the techniques outlined here to create similar cocktails of our poems, whether we focus on a single fairy tale, blend several, or rather just let the familiar world lean towards the magical.

Some successful fairy-tale poems operate just beyond the world of realism, taking the form, language, and tales that are so familiar to us—ingrained since childhood—and giving them new life through imaginative or contemporary settings. Some fill in the gaps. Others adopt the elements of fairy-tale form to create their own magic and wonder. We don't need to retell a fairy tale to write a fairy-tale poem but rather consider its elements and form as a diving board for us to get started. Could a taste of normalized magic or a twist of intuitive logic free us from the pressure of a blank page? Could using a familiar character as a persona be a fruitful exercise for poets unsure of where to begin? I'm convinced that if we look at fairy tales as a method of transformation, of moving from the blank page to a fresh poem, telling a familiar or unfamiliar tale in either a magical or domestic setting, with characters who may be well-known or just our own, simple selves, our poems will be fresh and unique, right from the first draft.

Zoë Brigley

ON DREAMWORK AND NOT CONFESSING

In the autumn of 1921, a young man waited nervously in the waiting room of Dr. Sigmund Freud's Vienna office. On finally being admitted, the young man talked awkwardly with the doctor about poetry, about the power of dream language, and its possibilities for humankind. The doctor was perplexed, and before long he brought the conversation to a close, dismissing the young man, and moving on to a waiting patient.

That young man was André Breton, poet and founding member of the French Surrealist movement. Breton, who was introduced to Freud's *Interpretation of Dreams* during his World War I service as a psychiatric aide, remained fascinated by the idea of dreamwork, but he maintained a combative relationship with Freud. While Freud thought the language of dreams could be used as therapy, Breton saw a potential philosophical key to the human condition. Inspired by free association, Breton created automatic writing, defined by Aaron H. Esman as "an entrée to the wellsprings of creativity in the unconscious and, ultimately, to the liberation of the individual from the constraints of bourgeois society." In dream language, Breton saw a remedy for human despair, and the use of techniques like automatic writing certainly allowed a fantastic escape from the mundane cruelties of everyday life. The commentary and workshop to be outlined here considers how worthwhile dreamwork might be for the writer who wants to represent trauma, pain, or violence, whilst escaping an obvious confessional mode.

Poetry is often invoked as a catalyst for metamorphoses from despair to hope, from desperation to redemption. David Wojahn traces a vein of poetry about depression, noting the "tradition of mad British versifiers' from John Clare onwards, contrasting the British lineage with the American 'middle generation'"—Sylvia Plath, John Berryman, Robert Lowell *et al*—who all "suffered bouts of acute mental anguish resulting in extended hospitalization." Forerunners of confessional poetry like Walt Whitman or Allen Ginsberg were self-mythologizers, but the Confessional movement of the 1960s was different to what had gone before. Michael Schmidt explains in *Lives of the Poets* that Confessional Poetry was among the first to "deliberately deal the pay-dirt on themselves." While Schmidt admits that "[p]oets have always complained and settled scores and licked their wounds," they have "not for the most part opened their wounds and probed them before their readers."

What does it mean to confess? "Confess" is a nuanced word, originating in the French *confesser* and thus to the Latin *confiteri* or *confessus* with the synthesis of *con* (signifying completeness) and *fateri* "to confess" from *fari* "to speak." Complete speech, complete honesty is the origins of the confession. It conjures the booth of the Roman Catholic confessional in which one is cleansed of sin, or it recalls lurid tabloid stories in which the reader is a voyeur on the misdeeds or peculiarities (often sexual) of celebrities and stars.

Poetry as therapy for the writer is hardly a new idea. Discussing poetry and catharsis in the context of work in American prisons, the writer Lisa Rhodes describes how inmates "wrote their poems as a vehicle to reclaim their lives and to find a rationale for their existence." For such women, poetry was "the catharsis to help them through their struggles, the door in which they can recreate their life." To confess then can be to acknowledge wrongs, to own up and admit to the past, and to make known one's failings, often in the hope of some faraway redemption. Confessing might be the act of revealing oneself with the hope of receiving grace and forgiveness in return.

Such an opening up, however, can be dangerous in other ways for the writer. Confessional poetry is still regarded in some critical circles with suspicion. The poet Pascale Petit seems to sympathise with such a predicament in "Private and Public Wars," when she describes the supposedly awful femininity of Sylvia Plath. Petit notes that Plath made "the personal into her own symbolic language, a new mythos," but she regrets that, "one of the disadvantages of confessional poetry in the work of male and female poets is that its sensational content can attract too much attention so that the quality of the writing is neglected and Plath has especially suffered from an undervaluing of her original and vital style." Deryn Rees-Jones in *Consorting with Angels* suggests that such doubt about confession stems from a view of emotion in poetry as a kind of failing, and she goes on to note that such weakness is associated with "the awfulness of femininity." Heteronormative attitudes seem to inflect the reception of confessional poetry, and in such a situation, Wojahn's questions about the problems of writing the suffering of self become even more pertinent: "How do you write poetry at a time when even tying your shoes seems a Herculean labor? And how do you talk to someone about such a frightening predicament?"

What role does the reader play in all this? And why is confessional poetry still so popular in spite of critics' suspicions and derision? There is a kind of power in playing the priest, and taking up a judgmental role can create a feeling of authority. There is voyeurism too, as the poet might allow a lurid glimpse of an inner life behind the mask. Yet there is something more redemptive about reading a confessional poem too: the possibility of mutual understanding and sympathy. Between the writer and reader, there might be a kind of interaction that admits the frailty and weakness of human beings and a shared sense of how vulnerable we are—each to the other.

In *Weakness: A Literary and Philosophical History*, Michael O'Sullivan explains that human beings "must accept that there are certain human values, such as love, or *philia*, that leave us vulnerable to risk and luck" and he notes wryly that "Greek dramatists had been staging the most extreme forms of this vulnerability for some time." In ancient Greek tragedy, family ties easily become a weakness—Medea murdering her own children to avenge herself on her husband Jason, for example, in Euripides' play. Similarly, daring expressions of love can become moments of horror, so in Sophocles' *Oedipus Rex*, Oedipus self-inflicts his own blindness: the punishment for having been intimate with his mother/wife. To blind himself, Oedipus uses the pin of his mother's brooch, an act that signals the terrible surprise of innocence turned to taboo, the enchantment of love turned to an unspeakable act. For how easy it is for the tools we use in artistry, craft, and love to become weapons. In *The Body in Pain*, Elaine Scarry makes the illuminating observation that "[i]f one holds the two side by side [. . .] a hand (as weapon) and a hand (as tool), a knife (weapon) and a knife (tool), a hammer and a hammer, an ax and an ax—it is then clear that what differentiates them is not the object itself but the surface on which they fall."

The overlap of vulnerability and intimacy is at the heart of Greek tragedy and such mythical dramas reflect a very human anxiety about opening up and being intimate with others. "Because intimate life entails a vulnerability to radical misrecognition," Gregg M. Horowitz explains, "the prospect of trauma shadows our most intimate experience." The only antidote to such anxiety, Horowitz suggests, is to reach out to others: "The endless vulnerability of human life needs intimate communication without end."

Anxiety about vulnerability extends too to the act of writing, most especially confessional writing where the poet probes their most intimate, often painful moments for a public audience. Imagining and pain are two ends of a spectrum. As Elaine Scarry states in *The Body in Pain*, "pain and imagining are the 'framing events' within whose boundaries all other perceptual, somatic, and emotional events occur; thus, between the two extremes can be mapped the whole terrain of the human psyche." Scarry's analysis is useful here when she suggests that pain can actually enable a kind of imagining, because its estrangement demands a new lexical set, new metaphors and new comparisons to express it. In such a healing vision of literary practice, "to describe one's hurt in an image of agency is to project it into an object which, though at first conceived of as moving toward the body, by its very separability from the body becomes an image that can be lifted away, carrying some of the attributes of pain with it." Poetic speech then might have a special status as a means of overcoming traumatic suffering. As Horowitz notes, "Poetry, it turns out, plays an irreplaceable suasive role in the expanded sphere of ethical life by engaging us in intimate communication undertaken in the shadow of trauma." Poetry, however, does not have to be straightforward confession, though outright confessing is sometimes a first route into poetry for young or new writers. I emphasize, however, to my students that being honest does not necessarily mean having to confess, and this is where dreamwork can be particularly useful to the poet who wants to write about difficult, personal material.

Since the publication of Sigmund Freud's *The Interpretation of Dreams* in 1899, human culture has been informed in its understanding of dreams by the notion of the unconscious, a region of the human mind that acts as a repository for repressed sexual and aggressive thoughts. Much of Freud's writing was devoted to uncovering how such repressions emerged in dreams, slips of tongue or jokes for example. Slips of the tongue reveal our hidden sexual or aggressive thoughts, so when George W. Bush was giving a presidential address to a group of teachers, instead of thanking them, he announced that he would "like to spank all teachers." Similarly thought-provoking is the humor of the Marx Brothers, which often reveals latent aggression. "Don't look now," says Groucho to a pompous ambassador in *Duck Soup*, "but there's one man too many in this room and I think it's you."

What the dream, the joke, and the slip of the tongue all have in common is that they are related to thoughts and feelings that we repress in everyday life. Desires and fears reveal themselves in glimpses via dreams, jokes and slips of the tongue, and dreamwork can be useful in finding new ways to deal with personal material in poetry beyond the obvious confession. The unconscious is supposed to be an unknowable force within us, and yet the fact that Freud identified it is a contradiction. Like poetry, the unconscious is slanted and slanting, knowable and yet able to surprise and confound. Hélène Cixous goes as far as to say that writing "poetry involves gaining strength through the unconscious [...] because the unconscious, that other limitless country, is the place where the repressed manages to survive."

In *The Interpretation of Dreams*, Freud describes two types of dreamwork: condensation and displacement. Condensation describes the phenomenon in a dream where people and places overlap, so to use a hypothetical example, a building in a dream may have the stairs and hallway of your childhood home, but the walls and frontage of your current workplace. Similarly, a figure in a dream may have the hair and clothes of one person and the glasses and beard of another. The parts of the composite may seem random and unimportant, but Freud emphasizes that where two parts—places or people—are drawn together, the dream is usually signalling another commonality, an important parallel which the unconscious is working out through dreaming. Analyzing his own dreams, Freud finds that a composite figure is made of two authoritarian men about whom he feels a similar kind of anxiety.

The other type of dreamwork is displacement, a phenomenon when, as Freud describes it, "one of the dream thoughts seems to have entered the dream-content, but then to an undue extent". Freud gives the example of a patient who dreams of climbing up and down stairs; Freud diagnoses her dream-thought as related to desiring relations with someone of another class, so part of the dream thought remains (i.e. the movement up and down) to an undue extent. A symbolic movement in class relations becomes a physical movement.

Displacement and condensation can be seen at work in the famous dream sequence of Alfred Hitchcock's thriller *Spellbound*. The dream sequence sets were designed by Surrealist artist Salvador Dalí, and the dream itself is extremely Freudian. The film narrative is seen from the perspective of psychoanalyst Constance Peterson (played by Ingrid Bergman), who is trying to help a man accused of murder suffering, but suffering from amnesia. Calling himself "John Brown (played by Gregory Peck)," but not even knowing his own real name, the man tries to unravel his amnesia by telling his dream to Constance and the Freudian father figure, Dr. Alex Brulov. The dream begins in a gambling house, where, as "John" describes it, "there weren't any walls, just a lot of curtains with eyes painted on them" The scene is dominated by a man with a pair of giant scissors cutting the curtains and the eyes in half. Wish fulfilment comes next, as a woman enters the scene: "a girl […] with hardly anything on […] walking around the gambling room kissing everybody," and "John" admits that the woman looks a little like his current lover/psychoanalyst Constance. The dream moves on to a game of cards played with a bearded man, who might stand in for the murder victim, but also for Freud himself. The Freudian card player certainly seems to be in control, as he declares, "That makes 21 - I win," but when he turns over his cards, they appear to be blank. "John" has no chance to react before the proprietor of the gambling house, his face featureless and blank too, appears to accuse the card player of cheating: "This is my place, and if I catch you cheating again, I'll fix you." Memory, or the inability to remember, are represented by the blank cards, and the blank face of the angry proprietor.

The dream moves now to the sloping roof of a high building, the backdrop behind dominated by huge Dali-style faces puppet-like or melting in style. "John" calls to the bearded card player who is standing on the roof, but he falls slowly into the abyss below. Behind the chimney, the blank-faced proprietor hides with a small wheel in his hand, and suddenly "John" is shown running in the shadow of a huge pair of wings that almost catch up with him before he wakes.

By the end of the film, it is discovered that all the answers to the murder mystery lay in the dream. The win with 21 at cards is displacement of a place: the Twenty One Club where "John Brown" visited with the murder victim. The pair of wings is displacement for Angel Valley, the site of the murder. The turning motion of the wheel refers to the turning of a revolver, the murder weapon. Apart from the symbols that are explained in the film narrative, other images conjured by Dali linger to convey disturbing feelings. The eyes on the curtains might signal the feeling of being watched, but the cutting of the eyes with scissors, not only recalls the shock value of Surrealist film *Un Chien Andalou* (1929), but is also a classic Freudian image of castration. The blank cards are echoed on film by the proprietor's face being completely blank, signaling perhaps his lack of humanity, or even his amorality.

By the end of the film, it emerges that the man sliding down the roof to his death represents not only the murder victim killed on a ski slope, but the brother of "John Brown" who died as a child in an accident." The guilt complex has emerged because "John Brown" pushed his brother down a sloping wall where the brother was impaled on a set of railing. The act of sliding down and falling brings together the recent murder and the originary "Cain and Abel" narrative. A suitably grisly Hitchcockian backstory is slowly revealed through the film through Dali's artistry and the Freudian screenplay by Angus McPhail and Ben Hecht.

The concepts of displacement and condensation play an important part in Freud's ideas about dreamwork. Theorist Jacques Lacan, however, made a connection between dreamwork and poetry. Lacan compares condensation with metaphor and displacement with metonymy, an intervention that is interesting for the poet. The exercise that follows seeks to perform an act of transformation so that personal or difficult raw material is disguised following the example of dream work.

Preparation

Take a clean page in your notebook and be prepared to write down some personal material. Remember that it will be private, and you can destroy your notes later if necessary.

- Describe a person that you secretly admire and explain why.
- Describe a person that you secretly dislike and explain why.
- Write down a secret aspiration that you would not want anyone else to know.
- Write down a secret fear that you would not want anyone else to know.
- Describe a moment from childhood when you were very happy.
- Describe a moment from childhood when you were very unhappy.
- Describe a time when you were glad for someone else's misfortune.

- Take a few lines to describe a moment of shame.
- Take a few lines to describe a moment of elation.
- Describe something you have done that you should not have.

Writing Exercise

Your task is to write a poem in dream language. It should use difficult or personal material, but it should not be a confessional poem. Just as dream language scrambles latent thoughts, so this poem should use condensation and displacement, metaphor and metonymy, the symbolism of dreams, to disguise the content of the poem. What I am suggesting is in fact an act of translation, where the feeling of the personal material remains, though in a disguised form.

Final Thoughts

For a long time, as a young poet, I wanted to write about difficult and personal material, but I was unable to do so in an obvious, straightforward way. I was not ready for confession, and what is a writer to do when they need to put down experiences in words, but at the same time cannot reveal their deepest intimacies? In my own process, dreamwork was an answer. Playing himself in the film *Waking Life*, the composer-actor Guy Forsyth analyzes the power of dreams and considers how the creative process of dreaming might be brought into our everyday existence: "The trick is to combine your waking rational abilities with the infinite possibilities of your dreams. Because, if you can do that, you can do anything."

WORKS CITED

Cixous, Hélène (1976) 'The Laugh of the Medusa', trans. Keith Cohen and Pamela Cohen, *Signs* 14: 875-893. 879-880.

Esman, Aaron H. (2011) 'Psychoanalysis and Surrealism: Andre Breton and Sigmund Freud,' *Journal of the American Psychoanalytic Association*, Feb; 59(1): 173-81 p. 174.

Horowitz, Gregg M. (2010) "The Homeopathic Image, Or, Trauma, Intimacy And Poetry." *Critical Horizons* 11.3: 463-490. (p. 464).

O'Sullivan, Michael (2012) *Weakness: A Literary and Philosophical History*. London: Continuum International Publishing. ProQuest ebrary. Web. 15 May 2015. p. 11

Petit, Pascale (2011) 'Private and Public Wars,' *New Welsh Review* 72: 11.

Polizzotti, M. (1995) *Revolution of the Mind: The Life of Andre Breton*. New York: Farrar, Straus and Giroux, pp 162-163.

Scarry, Elaine (1985) *The Body in Pain: the Making and Unmaking of the World*. Oxford: Oxford University Press, p. 165.

Rees-Jones, Deryn (1997) *Consorting with Angels: Essays on Modern Women Poets*. Tarset: Bloodaxe, p. 25.

Rhodes, Lisa (2002) 'Poetry and a Prison Writing Program: A Mentor's Narrative Report,' *Journal of Poetry Therapy* 15.3: 163-168 (168).

Michael Schmidt, *Lives of the Poets*

Wojahn, David (1995) 'The State You Are Entering: Depression and Contemporary Poetry,' *New England Review* 17.1: 110-123, p. 113.

Jena Pincott, 'Slips of the Tongue,' *Psychology Today*. <https://www.psychologytoday.com/articles/201203/slips-the-tongue>.

Sigmund Freud, *The Interpretation of Dreams*.

Chaun Ballard

PEAS IN THE POCKET: THE PRACTICE OF FIXED POETIC FORM

1. How We Met

I would like to say that poetry was a beckoning, some desire in my unconscious spirit longing to break free. The truth is, for many years I avoided poetry like the uneaten peas my father-in-law hated to eat and stuffed in his jean pocket as a child.

In fact, the genre of poetry was the Achilles heel I kept secret. It represented one of my many flaws I wanted to strengthen the most. I thought that if I had this knowledge, I would no longer feel fearful or threatened by the English classroom. I wanted to juggle well-known references to canonical poetry and toss them around like everyday catch phrases. I wanted desperately to develop a love for reading poetry, to read poetry well, to know what I was reading, and to discuss poems like a well-studied student: I wanted to develop what I lacked; and, at the most basic level, I did not want to feel stupid.

My formal introduction to poetry finally came in the fall of 2009 after my wife and I completed our undergraduate degrees at the University of Hawai'i at Hilo. We were newlyweds, three months into our marriage, and we had just begun studying for our certificates in teaching English as a foreign language. I needed one more credit to maintain financial aid eligibility, and the opportunity to enroll in an English 286: Introduction to Poetry course presented itself. In this class, I came face to face with the various aspects of the genre from which I had shied away, much like the peas in the pocket of my father-in-law.

The only thing my father-in-law and I never bothered to consider was that eventually those things we sloughed to the wayside would again appear: his, in the form of miniature tennis balls floating in laundry water; mine, in the practice of the poetic tradition of form.

2. Becoming

In the Book of Genesis, the author says that the earth was formless and void, and that the spirit of God hovered over the face of the waters, and out of nothing God created the world.

For me, form—poetic form, that is—is like following in the footsteps of God. Like God, who employed the already-made dirt and dust to create humankind, poets can use the grains of form to create something new, something beautiful. We, as poets, hover over a blank sheet of paper with the desire to create something living and vivid. We want our creation to tell a story. We want to bear witness to the beasts in the field, the fish in the sea, and the birds in the air: literally and figuratively. We want our waters to produce land, but most importantly, we want them both to be teeming with life.

Exploring form gives me the opportunity to be in conversation with a community of poets, both past and present, and by reusing structures that had long been in circulation, I follow in tradition. Of course, form alone cannot make a poem successful, just as creating a landmass out of water does not make a planet teeming with life. There must be other elements present and working in unison.

Poetic form is simply the bare bones, the structural foundation, the broken branches along the flattened trail of grass our minds and hands follow down the page, or, as poet and professor Zack Rogow writes in an entry titled "Using Poetic Forms, Part 4: The Ghazal" on his *Advice for Writers* blog: "…sometimes form is exactly what you need to give shape to the feeling or idea.… The form becomes a perfect container to hold what's teasing your mind." As writers, our minds are often filled with sound bites and images from life's experiences. To me, it is important to organize these thoughts, especially when I am unsure of the direction a poem should take. Form is that container that aids me. It is that reusable, ever-trusty tool in the shed that can build a house, a fence, or any other structure that needs to exist.

3. Why Form?

Poets write in fixed forms for a variety of reasons. The ability to write in fixed forms affords me the opportunity to explore various poetic techniques, such as meter, rhyme, and repetition. In addition, fixed form also allows me an opportunity to distance myself from emotionally-charged subjects, containerize ideas, play with line structure, divert from my natural hang-ups and tendencies, and participate in a dialogue with both contemporary and historical poets, as well as providing me a freewrite kick-start.

The ability of a poet to write in fixed form also displays discipline and a showcase of mastery. In Kwame Dawes' online essay "Suffering and Form," he states, "Form is a [necessary] product of routine, a reflection of rituals of existence, the hallmark of which is dependability, predictability, and the familiar." In her article published with the Poetry Foundation, poet Rebecca Hazelton echoes Dawes' theory that form is a necessary product. She writes, "When we think of mastery...In poetry, one of the best ways to practice technique is to write in traditional forms." As the popular adage goes, practice makes perfect. Hazelton adds:

> When we think of mastery, we think of practice, and when we think of practice, we often think of repetition. Violinists spend much of their early years running scales before their fingers automatically and thoughtlessly assume their proper positions on the fretboard. Ceramicists must learn to wedge clay and center the clay on the wheel before they can successfully make pots...basketball players put in countless hours perfecting lay-ups, ballet dancers' toes bleed inside their pointe shoes, and swimmers crisscross the length of a pool countless times hoping to shave milliseconds off their time.

These examples Hazelton provides explain how mastering fixed form should play a significant role in the growth of a poet. In order to gain said mastery, poets must cultivate a routine that is grounded in the foundations of their skill and focus. These skills must be honed and sharpened repeatedly. For poets, this comes through the reading of other poets, corresponding critiques, and the composition of a number of drafts and revisions. Practicing fixed form develops the fundamentals of poetic structure and allows poets to play within the set guidelines: rhythm-counting, rhyme-finding, repetition, voltas, stanza structure, and more.

As a former athlete and a poet, I understand the benefits of developing my craft. The same approach I take to sharpening my basketball skills—whether it has to do with dribbling, lay-ups, or jump shots—is the same approach I take to writing poetry.

As with any other art or discipline, poets must put in the time and effort. The result of this dedication to traditional forms will provide a foundation for innovation in the future. Hazelton further explains:

> Many forms that sharpen skills are useful [also] in free verse. Forms with repeating lines, such as the villanelle or the triolet [or the pantoum], help train poets in the power of repetition and refrain in free verse and how a phrase can be recast through shifting context. . . . The ghazal, whose couplets can operate autonomously, is a lesson in juxtaposition. The possibilities aren't limiting; they're endless.

To help clarify this relationship between fixed form and free verse, I will use Hazelton's previous example of basketball. Writing in free verse for novice and seasoned poets is the equivalent of athletes playing pick-up ball on an outside court. It is just pick-up ball, so there are no referees, which means everyone is free to make their own calls.

Fixed form represents the athletes who join an organized league and are introduced to a system of guidelines. The athlete, therefore, must conform to the rules of the organization in which he abides, an organization that has a rich traditional history. Some athletes succeed in these new confines. Some walk away feeling they have had greater success outside tradition. Others test the boundary and push toward the limit.

Athletes figure out how to work within set guidelines by understanding the rules and using these guidelines to their advantage by pushing toward the edge: evoking change, just as poets do, when they use fixed form to springboard future innovation.

Fixed forms are needed as foundational tools; without the understanding of these forms, I as a poet cannot stretch beyond into uncharted territory. If I want to develop my poetics, I should be fluent in the guidelines of form, just as I, as a basketball player, am in tradition and organization. In this way, the significance of fixed form serves as an organized structure that I may either bend, trend, or break.

It is form from which the poetic foundation of all centuries past and present have invested in and have creatively partook. By keeping in the tradition of fixed forms, we are creating new conversations.

Form, by merely existing on the page, evokes a conversation, because the form itself holds a message. Each form carries with it an expectation of structure, sound, or historical genealogy. For every form, there are undercurrents of significance, all of which build up a basis for the reader, as Edward Hirsch explains in the *Poet's Glossary* about the legendary sonnet: "The sonnet is a small vessel capable of plunging tremendous depths. Something about the spaciousness and brevity of the fourteen-line poem seems to suit the contours of rhetorical argument especially when the subject is erotic love." Hirsch here confirms that a fixed form like the sonnet serves as a message-bearing bottle for the reader. When I read a sonnet, my mind will come to expect certain particulars regarding stanza length, rhyme, turns, and subject matter aligned (or not) with tradition (read: love, requited or unrequited); and if I read a ghazal, I will come to expect something different in regard to form (including a series of independent but interrelated couplets, a refrain and internal rhyme) and perhaps something similar in regard to subject matter, as there is often an "atmosphere of sadness and grief that pervades the ghazal..." and a "dedication to love and the beloved" (qtd. in Ali 3). With each form, whether a sonnet, ghazal, or any other fixed form, expectations are carried alongside it due to its traditional usage.

4. A Marriage between Form and Tragedy

Recently, my wife asked me why I write so many of my poems in fixed form, more often than not returning to the pantoum and ghazal. As I look at my work, I realize that approximately 46 percent of the poems are in some type of fixed form. To answer my wife's question truthfully, I believe that I must first examine the subjects which my poems tend to engage. Many of my poems are written about the tragic events to which I am exposed, events that I see on the news, both in the United States and in the Middle Eastern countries in which I have lived. Stories that I am affected by—whether the tragedy revolves around issues such as skin color or violence stemming from political and religious conflicts—are the stories that turn into poems. When I pore over the growing number of drafts I have written in fixed forms—sonnets, pantoums, ghazals, et cetera—there is a definite trend. When I want to write about tragedy, whether personal or political, I turn to form.

As I begin to draft a poem, I ask myself the following questions: What will this form do for my subject matter? How will this form allow the reader time to connect emotionally? How will the form heighten my content?

I notice that many of the forms I use have some sort of repetition or refrain, such as the pantoum or ghazal. As a rhetorical device, the use of repetition can heighten tension and build up to a climactic moment. Repetition plays a key role in setting the tone for a poem, which—when it comes to grief—can be imperative. One well-known example is found in Dylan Thomas' villanelle "Do Not Go Gentle into That Good Night," where there are two refrains used throughout the six stanzas (qtd. in Gwynn 220-221). The repeated lines are found in the quatrain that follows, where they close the poem:

> And you, my father, there on the sad height,
> Curse, bless, me with your fierce tears, I pray,
> Do not go gentle into that good night.
> Rage, rage, against the dying of the light.

These two repeated lines ("Do not go gentle into that good night" and "Rage, rage, against the dying of the light") emphasize the emotion found in loss: the speaker's helplessness in a situation he can do nothing to fix. The repeated lines serve as a cry or plea to fight against the inevitable. Thomas' use of repetition creates tension similar to when we grieve, or when there is something fiercely desired, and we find ourselves repeating the same prayer-like phrases: God, please; God, please; please, God.

For me, fixed forms can also serve to create distance when emotions run high. When something is tragic and requires a high level of emotion, it is difficult for me to write about it effectively without waxing dramatic or falling into a rant, especially when the subject matter leans toward that of political engagement. The draft can then be too raw, emotionally, and scare off most readers, perhaps rendering it an ineffective poem in that regard.

To better clarify this concept, I will compare and contrast a poem of mine that began as free verse and was then revised into fixed form. The free verse poem "What Would You Say If You Were Tamir Rice & You Had Two Seconds—," is about the twelve-year-old African American who was shot and killed by a police officer in Cleveland, Ohio. Its entirety is as follows: "Too late, / you're dead." My reason behind writing this poem was in attempt to give a near-realistic account of time, and to leave readers feeling the same way I did after watching the video of the twelve-year-old's death: shocked. For me, this poem was not about taking sides; it was about illustrating that near-realistic account of time.

However, after writing the poem, I found myself battling with its free verse couplet. It seemed too emotionally raw and one-dimensional for the weight of the subject matter. To further investigate this instinct regarding the couplet, I chose to write about the same situation in a fixed form. I wanted a form that would force me to write within its rules and restraints and would effectively give my brain some other element on which to focus. I also wanted to create some distance between myself and the subject matter, but not between the subject matter and the reader; I knew that if I took a step back, I would be able to let go of my initial reaction and allow the poem to do the work of creating empathy. To achieve this, I knew I had to select the right form. I knew it had to be a form that would allow me to participate in its creation as a surveyor and a reader.

The idea of the pantoum was presented to me as a writing prompt by the poetry group to which I belong. The form's qualities can lend themselves to the elements of a story, allowing the poet to present a setting, an exposition, and a rising action though the build-up of anticipation—set into place by the form's repetition and interlocking stanzas. An example of this can be found in Eva Saulitis' pantoum, "The Clearing," where she writes:

> It would be spring. I'd be out walking.
> I'd stumble across a field in a clearing.
> A shock in the woods I thought I knew.
> There'd be my mother wielding a hoe.
>
> I'd stumble across her in the clearing.
> Smoke from a stovepipe: her sister cooking.
> There'd be my mother wielding a hoe.
> She wouldn't be wearing a slip or stockings.

Here Saulitis sets the scene for her readers; she includes a place and time, and I am introduced to the characters and their actions, reinforced by the repetition between stanzas. As the poem continues, Saulitis presents the source of the conflict, but not the conflict itself: "As if there'd been no reason to beg. / They wouldn't be raped—they'd be safe. / Under her dress, my mother's strong bare legs." Though the act itself is not portrayed, the final two stanzas conclude by alluding again to the conflict and returning to the beginning:

Beside the door, a man's shoes.
Where have they gone, those men?
As the kindling popped and the tea cooled.
Song of a night-jar, song of a wren.

It would be spring. I'd be out walking.
A shock in the woods I thought I knew.
I'd stumble across a house in a clearing.
My mother stepping into the sun.

As seen in Saulitis' poem, the pantoum's repetition gives the poet time to reinforce this story-like structure, and it gives the reader time to reflect on the significance of a moment, rather than an act; and since narrative was the driving force behind me creating another piece about Tamir Rice, I felt a second draft, as a pantoum, might yield some success.

Narrative poems are always difficult for me to write in free verse—I tend to gravitate toward my typical habits and hang-ups, where I lead the poem instead of the poem leading me—so it made sense to lean toward the pantoum. The pantoum forced me to move away from my first reaction and concentrate on creating the narrative instead of the act that spurred it, balancing story elements with introspection. It also allowed me to create a more empathetic piece, as opposed to the earlier, shockingly brief, couplet, as the form's refrains helped to restrict me from saying too much.

The history of the pantoum can be traced back to its Malay beginnings. According to Hirsch, the pantoum was intended to be "[s]lowly sung, with a long chorus or refrain after each line." By the time the pantoum reached the West in the nineteenth century via Ernest Fouinet and Victor Hugo, its song-like qualities were abandoned (Strand and Boland). The attractiveness of the pantoum is simple; the form allows the reader an opportunity to participate in its dance as the interweaving quatrains insure that "[t]he reader always takes four steps forward and two steps back" (Hirsch). This is because the second and fourth lines in the stanza repeat as the first and third of the next stanza continuously until the last stanza of the poem. As the reader, I follow the poet's dance, forward and back.

As a pantoum continues, the last stanza completes itself by inserting the unrepeated lines one and three from the opening stanza, thus, "circl[ing] back to the beginning like a snake eating its tail" (Hirsch). This circling-back technique is well-portrayed in John Ashbery's "Pantoum," evident in the first stanza where Ashbery provides images grounded in the human and the natural world—with eyes, snow, and clay pipes—and in the last stanza, where the same images concludes the piece. The perpetual snake eating its tail is seen through Ashbery's pantoum as he circles the lines back to the beginning, tying the necklace closed, thus reaffirming what Hirsch writes about the pantoum: "the poem is always looking back over its shoulder, and thus it is well-suited to evoke a sense of times past. It is always turning back while moving forward; that's why it works so well for poignant poems of loss..." What rings true here, and is poignant for me, is that often poetry is too late, as events that I write about are already in the past, though I as a writer write in the present. I want my readers to be in that present with me, experiencing what was lost even as the poem is read in the here and now.

The pantoum, at first glance, may appear to be easy to write in the sense that the poet will always have two lines to carry over in the succeeding quatrain. However, it is this repetition that allows the direction of the poem to take an unexpected turn and can contain the form's greatest challenge; the repeated lines must be used or read in different ways because they are located between a sandwich of new material. Whatever the line was in the previous stanza, and how it was used, will change in the next. This feature of the pantoum demands more work, focus, and finesse by the poet because the poet must continue a narrative that has been rerouted in an uncharted direction. The repeated lines from a previous stanza must act as the poet's only navigational tool to ensure that the subsequent stanza will mold and mingle flawlessly with two new lines: evolving as it reflects, looking both forward and backward, as present in the pantoums of Saulitis and Ashbery.

The pantoum takes usually no less than three quatrains to complete the slow circle back to the lines in its first stanza. Where the sonnet and the villanelle are limited in their line count (with fourteen lines and nineteen lines, respectively), the pantoum does not bear this restriction. It can go until the poet has exhausted him or herself on the page.

As I revised the free verse "What Would You Say If You Were Tamir Rice & You Had Two Seconds—," it made sense to follow the pantoum's fixed form, as it would highlight the narrative elements I desired, including the slowing of time and a look into the past from a present lens in the hope that it would create a more empathetic piece. I titled this revision "Let Us Believe," and the poem cast Tamir Rice, as well as Trayvon Martin, Michael Brown, Sandra Bland, and a host of unnamed deceased in a different light:

Let us believe for a moment that
in this poem there is no suffering,
and the white sheet is still freshly folded,
tucked away inside a dimly lit ambulance, because

in this poem there is no suffering,
and the boy wearing his hood is enjoying his Skittles,
tucked away inside a dimly lit ambulance, because
he is receiving a generous ride home.

And the boy wearing his hood is enjoying his Skittles
next to the young man from St. Louis.
He is receiving a generous ride home
as well. Paramedics are joking with the boy wearing his hood

next to the young man from St. Louis.
One says: *What do you call a freshly folded white sheet?*
Paramedics are joking with the boy wearing his hood
as another man enters into the ambulance. He overhears as

one says: *What do you call a freshly folded white sheet?*
The joke is interrupted
as another man enters into the ambulance. He overhears as
the paramedic repeats the question.

The joke is interrupted.
A young lady enters, says she wouldn't be caught dead for failing to signal.
The paramedic repeats the question.
A twelve-year-old boy asks for a ride. He sits down next to

the young lady who said she wouldn't be caught dead for failing to
signal.
She whispers the answer to
the twelve-year-old boy who asked for a ride.
He says: *I know the answer,*

whispers the answer, too.
Let us believe, for a moment, that.

In this pantoum, Tamir is still present. What is absent, however, is the event
itself, and the certainty of the last line of the free verse poem: you're dead. In
the pantoum, the readers experience a what-if scenario or even a room-like
purgatory, where life and death are indistinguishable and multiple lives are
intertwined.

The pantoum form drives this narrative, and I am a participating sur-
veyor mapping its coordinates down the page. These individuals were in
my mind already—from a myriad of newspaper articles and clips watched
on television. Their presence manifested themselves in the poem through
their relationship to one another, each having experienced similar causes
of death. For these now-characters, the stanzas illustrate an exposition and
a rising action much like a short story, which builds an expectation for the
reader, a tension of what could come next. The repeated lines allow me to
share, without telling too much at one time: this form requires the plot line
to be patient in its development.

This poem is not true to the pantoum entirely because it has been bent
to suit the poem's content. The last stanza ends in a couplet, rather than the
pantoum's standard quatrain, because I wanted to visually illustrate loss; by
not including the final two lines, I aim to demonstrate the loss of life and the
loss of the answer. With the pantoum not being whole, or complete, those
final two lines leave the reader space to feel the weight of what is not present.

As much as the pantoum is effective in helping me to deliver content,
the ghazal was the first fixed form to win me over. Agha Shahid Ali's "In
Arabic" came to me at a time in which I did not yet have much exposure to
modern-day uses of fixed form. The ghazal was something new to me, and
it drew parallels to my years of living in the Middle East. An excerpt of his
ghazal reads as follows:

Majnoon, his clothes ripped, still weeps for Laila.
O, this is the madness of the desert, his crazy Arabic.

Who listens to Ishmael? Even now he cries out:
Abraham, throw away your knives, recite a psalm in Arabic.

From exile, Mahmoud Darwish writes to the world:
You'll all pass between the fleeting words of Arabic.

The magic of this fixed form lies in Ali's ability to reuse the word "Arabic" in a variety of different ways without making the lines sound forced or childish. The repetition of this one word becomes almost incantatory, and in its repetition the word "Arabic" becomes both expected and revered, like a prayer heard throughout the years.

In a ghazal like his, the repetition offers predictability in a way that becomes grounding, but not redundant. Each couplet gives me a new story, moment, or image to digest, though it is built around the refrain. With Ali's work, his material is often grounded—as in this example—in the cultural Middle East, which is emphasized by his use of the historically Arabic-Persian form; as such, the ghazal in its history and tradition is supportive of the content, and vice versa.

As Agha Shahid Ali explains in his anthology titled *Ravishing DisUnities*, a ghazal is written in couplets. The poem may be composed of an unlimited number of stanzas. The first two lines repeat the refrain at the end of both lines. Every subsequent couplet repeats the refrain in the latter line. There is usually an internal rhyme included in front of the refrain. An additional element of the ghazal is that the poem's stanzas are not required to follow a narrative sequence; with the ghazal there is no unified plot. Each couplet in the poem should be able to stand independently, like an island in an archipelago, as the reader "should at any time be able to pluck a couplet like a stone from a necklace, and it should continue to shine in that vivid isolation, though it would have a different lustre among and with the other stones" (Ali). The connection between the couplets—or, as my MFA thesis advisor, poet, and professor, Elizabeth Bradfield, explains it: a "loose gathering,"—comes from the overarching internal rhyme and the refrain's words—whatever those words might be.

It is said that, with every ghazal, "there is a cultural unity—created by the [shared] assumptions and expectations" (Ali). In this, the ghazal bears regional significance and highlights the repetition found in the Arabic language itself. The form sounds and reads recognizable to those with exposure to this culture and place. In the Arab culture, there are set phrases I must say when I greet someone in the morning or evening, where I would say, "*Sabaah al-kheyr,*" or "Morning of goodness," and the other will respond, "*Sabaah an-nour,*" or "Morning of light." The same is true for other repetitive phrases when I enter and exit a room, when I ask how someone is doing, and when someone gets a new haircut. As a new student of the language, I am prompted to meditate on ritual greetings such as these, and the assortment of consistently repetitive phrases stand out to me.

In addition to these internal rhymes and repetition, the ghazal mandates that the poet must insert his or her name within the last two lines of the final couplet, as Ali does in his ghazal "In Arabic[:]" "They ask me to tell them what Shahid means— / Listen: It means 'The Beloved' in Persian, 'witness' in Arabic." The placement of the poet's name in the last couplet serves as a signature. It locates him or her in the poem, tying them directly into its content.

In the ghazal, while I can predict the repeated word's coming, I cannot predict the lines that follow, the images that follow, the resulting revelations: a combination of expectation and surprise—similar to the pantoum. As I revise my ghazals, I often find myself shifting couplets around, moving the stanzas above or below one another, listening to hear how the sounds and images bounce off one another like a bat's echolocation system, trying to find the right balance of predictability and surprise.

In fixed form, there is a definite purpose to the repetition embedded within its structure, and it aims to serve its purpose: to heighten tension, as utilized in my own "Let Us Believe"; to emphasize emotions like those found in loss, as in Thomas' "Do Not Go Gentle into That Good Night"; or to create a song-like incantation, as in Ali's "In Arabic."

5. Conclusion

I was a student-athlete: a basketball player by trade. With basketball, fundamental elements were necessary, and appropriate, in order to establish foundational skills. Again, I return to Kwame Dawes: "Form is a [necessary] product of routine, a reflection of rituals of existence, the hallmark of which is dependability, predictability, and the familiar." Whether it is through hours of practice perfecting lay-ups or in drafting different forms, I understand that there is a foundation that demands mastery.

Form organizes a poem through shape and structure. While free verse may borrow and highlight aspects found in a fixed form, it is not bound by the same rules. I am therefore free to let the poem develop and move in its natural rhythm where refrains and patterns occur organically, but the influence of fixed form hits on my subconscious. Now, when I find myself writing, somewhere in the poem, I am called to repeat a specific line, to create a cadence as if I were creating a song. As the draft continues, or maybe looking back in its reflection, I realize that this repetition, or structure, springs forth in particular sections, areas, and stanzas of importance. I understand that these are characteristics of fixed form, and they permeate even my most free of free verse poems.

In all, these things are evident: poets will always find themselves hovering over a blank page like the spirit of God hovering over the face of the waters; forms are perfect containers to hold what's teasing the mind; fixed structures may bend, trend, or break; a landmass out of water does not make a planet teeming with life; by reusing fixed forms, we create new conversations; testing the boundaries of tradition leads to innovation; and my father-in-law still won't eat peas.

In other words, practice makes perfect.

WORKS CITED

Ali, Agha Shahid. "In Arabic." *Call Me Ishmael Tonight*. New York: W.W. Norton & Company, 2003.

Ali, Agha Shahid, ed. *Ravishing DisUnities: Real Ghazals in English*. Connecticut: Wesleyan University Press, 2000.

Ballard, Chaun. "Let Us Believe." *FLY ash*. Master's Thesis. University of Alaska Anchorage. 2017.

Ballard, Chaun. "What Would You Say If You Were Tamir Rice & You Had Two Seconds—." *Rattle*, 22 Nov. 2017.

Bradfield, Elizabeth. Message to the author. Spring 2017. E-mail.

Dawes, Kwame. "Suffering and Form." Web log post. *Harriet*. Poetry Foundation, 30 April 2010.

Gwynn, R.S., ed. *Poetry: A Longman Pocket Anthology.* New York: Longman, 1998.

Hazelton, Rebecca. "Why Write in Form?" *Poetry Foundation.* Poetry Foundation, 10 May 2016.

Hirsch, Edward. *A Poet's Glossary.* Boston: Houghton Mifflin Harcourt, 2014.

Rogow, Zack. *Advice for Writers.* Blogspot, 12 Sept. 2012.

Saulitis, Eva. "The Clearing." *Many Ways to Say It.* California: Red Hen Press, 2012.

Strand, Mark and Eavan Boland. *The Making of a Poem: A Norton Anthology of Poetic Forms.* New York: W. W. Norton & Company, Inc., 2000.

Michael Rather, Jr.

CONTEMPLATING FORM

If we begin with Lewis Turco's definition of poetry as "the art of language" in *The New Book of Forms* then form must also be assumed as necessary to a definition of poetry. This does not necessarily mean all poems must follow a fixed form, but it does imply that it is impossible to conceive of a piece of writing being labelled a poem if form did not play a part in its construction. I suppose this discussion requires an additional definition. "Form" as a construct must be defined. What do we mean by "form"?

In art, in particular, form may best be equated with determined or realized shape. The artist takes materials and organizes them according to some sort of sensory guidelines. What are the materials without the form? They are "nature." Again, let me explain. Objects without a conscious form are existing in a natural state. Art must be objects or materials shaped by an intelligence.

I am certain that many critics may disagree with this idea and have ample evidence to support the fallacious nature of my claim, but it seems to be a difficult idea to escape. Art requires that a consciousness (whether it be the observer or the artist) shape it. This shaping is done to evoke our primary senses.

Therefore, it seems important to see poetry as "shaped language" and the act of composing a poem "the art" of "manipulating symbols" in order to create greater connotative meanings. Certainly in our contemporary era we have more symbols than ever to use. Our shaping of language used to be limited to the few alpha-numeric figures and punctuation marks developed to express our spoken language. Now we have a number of what are referred to as emoticons and emojis, unique spellings based on the medium, and cross-cultural vocabulary transfers to provide us with a greater palette of visual symbols than ever. Poetry is increasingly evolving as a visual art form even if "sound poetry" was the furthest we could really go with it as an oral art.

What this amounts to is that we have a greater number of materials that are acceptable to use, but those materials and objects still must be placed in a specific shape in order to be useful or to create heightened meaning for our readers. For what is the purpose of poetry if it is not to somehow make language or symbol systems evoke emotions with greater force than common speech or prose? Why write poetry if no "art" is being attempted?

To attempt to write a poem is to attempt to shape language. This language may be organized through rhythmical, sound, or spatial considerations. Traditional fixed forms developed during the late Middle Ages and European Renaissance used all three elements to shape a poem, but more weight was given to rhythm and rhyme during this period. Poetry was more often than not encountered through a speech. It was not until the advent of the printing press that spatial considerations began to carry equal weight with rhythm and rhyme. In our present era what we have come to call "open form" poetics has developed. These are poems whose language is largely formed through spatial considerations: line breaks and stanzas. At its best though, open form poetics still balances all three elements. Take the piece "A Story of Mixed Emoticons" by John Rives as an example. The performance video done during a TEDtalk is available online at: https://www.ted.com/talks/ rives_tells_a_story_of_mixed_emoticons.

It is quite amazing what he is doing here with shaping language, and particularly the new symbolic language of emoticons, which has created for English an ideogrammic language previously lacking. Basically, Rives illustrates that the ideogram has developed in contemporary English and that even in ideogrammic language there is form. The full poem appears at 27 seconds and it looks like this:

O}-<Q<=10018MTW<u>TH</u>F
02.28.08 7:55p,|$\overset{**}{\_}$| Q<=
O}-< ½?...1/256? Omg! <3
Lol!{u}(_)3=<">+H$_2$07xNaCLl
yllambywlaw Q<+"?" O}-<
.._.etc jv*\o/* #*@%!"— —"
aabb O̶}̶-̶<̶ : (|) xXx })i({ SW.+
5th/42nd __^{O}__No.2 -➔]?

This is hardly what an Elizabethan poet might imagine poetry's evolution to be, but there it is. And the key concept to keep in mind is that this is a shaped object. These are materials, letters, numbers, symbols that all exist also in our consciousness and in our ears as sounds that refer to objects in the world. When placed together these sounds create an effect. The effect is for some reason greater than if the story had been told in a prosaic style or had been told simply in pictures.

When I get the opportunity to teach poetry, students often comment on discussion boards with the question, "Why can't a poet say what he/she means?" This is a myth of course. Poets almost always are writing "what they mean." But in doing so they are paying attention to the connotative possibilities of symbol and shape and sound and rhythm that language written, pictorial, or auditory evokes. A poet is focused on the shape of language. A poet is focused on form.

Think about all that is involved in Archibald MacLeish's "Ars Poetica." A cursory glance of the poem does not reveal any fixed form. The poem does not show the regular interval refrains of the villanelle, the six words in different order repetitions of a sestina, or the traditional fourteen-line structure we assume sonnets have. There does not seem to be a regular rhythm here either. It is not structured around a dominant metrical foot or a dominant metrical line. Some lines are only monometer. Other lines are hexameter. There isn't standardization in that sense, but a closer inspection of the poem does find a shaped structure. Every stanza is a couplet. The poem is divided into three groups of four couplets. It is separated by asterisks rather than Roman numerals or Arabic numerals or simply white space. There is something hinted at by absence in this poem. The couplets alternate between short lines and long lines. While no set metrical pattern exists in that alternation it is clear that the poem is intentionally lineated in order to emphasize certain statements. The end-stops fall on very specific instances. Almost every line ends in a rhyme and there are internal rhymes. Words mutate connotatively and create sonic repercussions. Look at "leaf, leaves, leave, and leaving" and how that plays sonically and visually with the other "l" words we encounter "leaning" and "lights."

Looking at this poem one cannot help but to see it as a shaped thing. It is language that is shaped. It has form.

Poetry, all poetry, has form. It is the only real division between poetry and prose. It is not that prose ignores the essential elements of language. Language is central to prose as well. Prose does not emphasize it in the same way that poetry does. Many poems ignore logical meaning in favor for lexical or sonical meanings that are evocative. Burnell Yow!'s "Sound Poem" available on You Tube is an example. Yow!'s "Sound Poem" does not mean anything in our understanding of logical and rhetorical discourse, but the poem does have formal structures that create meaning. It is shaped. If language or sound or image is intentionally shaped it is becoming "poetic or artistic."

Poetry is form then. The two are inseparable. As Ezra Pound tells us "Literature is language charged with meaning." How does language receive the charge? Language has inherent energy, but unless that energy is harnessed through some sort of medium (form) it dissipates. If we want language to retain its charge we must shape that language.

The best poems shape language in a way that its shape seems natural rather than contrived, but naturalness is a matter of taste. I find the three poems presented prior to these statements as utterly natural, and yet many of my students cannot tolerate Burnell Yow!'s poem. Many students find MacLeish's poem obtuse. Many students enjoy Rives's poem but are unclear as to what it is supposed to illustrate or what makes it a poem.

What makes all three poems poems is that they are formal, that means they have shape either visually or sonically.

Form helps writers maintain language's charge. When a poet (at least for a time) frees himself or herself from the shackles of logical or rhetorical meanings in language and focuses instead on the visual, auditory, and oral aspects of language he or she will possibly find out they have more to say than logic can tell. Take the following poem as an example:

[in Just-]
by e.e. cummings

in Just -
spring   when the world is mud-
luscious the little
lame balloonman

whistles   far   and wee

and eddieandbill come
running from marbles and
piracies and it's
spring

when the world is puddle-wonderful

the queer
old balloonman whistles
far   and   wee
and bettyandisbel come dancing

from hop-scotch and jump-rope and

it's
spring
and

    the

      goat-footed

balloonMan   whistles
far
and
wee

As William Carlos Williams states in the opening to *Spring and All*, "There is a constant barrier between the reader and his consciousness of immediate contact with the world. If there is an ocean it is here." The barrier of which Williams speaks is our intellect, our logical facilities. They serve their purpose when we are problem solving and when we must construct a structure, but when we are interacting with art, which demands immediate experience, too much logic can destroy the experience.

Do not suppose that form is logical. Logic is implied in form because it finds its roots in rhetorical conventions. The sonnet was created by a lawyer. Its initial structure is that of an argument. This is why it insists on having a volta. If the sonnet writer ignores all other rules of the sonnet (whether Shakespearean or Petrarchan) it must contain its volta to rightly be a sonnet. The rhetorical or logical structure is essential to that form, but logic can be illogical. See Lewis Carroll's writings where logic can sometimes create more uncertainty than madness. What I am emphasizing here is that form is not logical though it is a structure. It may have rhetorical movements and turns, but that does not mean those rhetorical forms are logical. Paradox is an illogical construct yet it finds its place in rhetorical theories and art.

Form can be illogical. Form can create emotion. Start where Pound would have us start, "Dante says: 'A canzone is a composition of words set to music.'" I would argue against the logic of music but not against its immediacy and not against it being a shaped object…a form.

Let's return to Cummings' poem. It uses shape to attempt to overcome the barrier between a reader and his consciousness of immediate contact with the world. It enacts form's power to control the charge of language and deliver it effectively. Even if intellectually a reader may be confused by this poem. Even if it takes multiple reads to understand the poems logic. The poem's form reveals the sinister nature of our Pan carrying balloons. Now, that is not to say that this poem would not benefit from some exercising of the intellect. But that is only because as we move further away from the mythological constructs of the past such references as "goat-footed" lose their allusive and connotative strength. My students think Cummings is talking about Tumnus from *The Lion, The Witch, and The Wardrobe*. They do not realize the satyrs of Greece were horny old goats. When I explain this (in less disturbing terms) the poem opens for them.

Form is how poets contain the charge in language. It is how we make language meaningful. This is not "meaning" as in providing a poem with a thesis. This is meaning in the sense that a poem affects its reader in an almost inexplicable way. The best poems affect us inexplicably. As Donald Hall states in *Goatfoot, Milktongue, and Twinbird: The Psychic Origins of Poetic Form*, "A poem is one man's inside talking to another man's inside.…This inside speaks through the second language of poetry, the unintended language." It is my belief that this "unintended language" is only possible through formal constructions. That form is the "Second Language." The second language is only understandable and achievable through an awareness of what Pound calls, "phanopoeia, melopoeia, and logopoeia." That is, a word is used to do one or more of the following things:

1. Throw an image upon the reader's eye,
2. Charge the reader's mind with the memory of some sound,
3. Group words in such a way that either an image or sound is evoked.

That is, without form there is no charge. The letters c and a and t mean nothing on their own, but when we give them form they suddenly begin to be charged:

cat
CAT
TAC
aTc
ATC
cta
Atc
tcA
ACT
act
ACt
A
C
T
TAC
A
C

This is all nonsense in the logical sense. In the phanopoeic sense meaning can be construed. If read as a "sound poem" this might have melopoeic power. The "T" and "C/K" sound may affect us. This might sound little more pleasant than a cough or a hack, but the point is three letters that mean nothing but three sounds do not have a charge until some intelligence gives them shape and form.

Form equals meaning. Form is the second language. Form is Poetry, so in order to write poetry a poet must at least begin with a rudimentary understanding of form.

Studying form, sound allows one to manipulate materials to create charged language that has the elements Pound found necessary for language to have any worthwhile meaning.

There is no sublimity without the nuts and bolts of form being understood. In short, no transcendence without the mechanics of wings. The goal is to make the wings disappear into the sky's blue or black or white (depending on clouds, dust, time of day, etc...) though sometimes it is good to see the mechanics of the wing. What beauty would there be in a bird's flight if the wings were not visible?

Sometimes the awareness of form itself is what creates the sublime. Would we not appreciate beauty in the human form if it did not have shape?

Why not language? Why not a poem?

We must know form to create it.

A form can be a theory of poetics. A form can reveal what a poet values in language and particularly in charged language. This is why so many academic poets seemingly frown at the performance poets, the old "raw and cooked" dichotomy Robert Lowell set up. It isn't an accurate dichotomy (no dichotomy is accurate), but it helps us understand the conversation a bit better. Performance poets often have not considered all the elements of a poem's form when they are constructing the composition. (Post-first draft...form should not typically dictate the first draft [and sometimes the second draft.]) Some performance poets or amateur poets who are enamored with the mystical aspects of poetry, who believe wholeheartedly Wordsworth's definition that poetry is the "spontaneous overflow of powerful emotions recollected in tranquility," often choose emotion over craft. They only think about form in terms of rhyme and if we are sometimes lucky the line is considered. What is most important to these poets is "truth." Art is not important and it could even then be argued that what these people are writing is not rightly called "poetry."

I cannot go as far as that. I will go far enough to say that until form is considered by the poet in the composition process what the poet is constructing is closer to rhyming prose or lineated prose. I will let others with much more understanding (and earned credibility) make the argument against writing that is not constructed with a mind/ear for how melopoeia, phanopoeia, and logopoeia differentiate poetry from our other written art forms. Louis Zukofsky, in his *A Test of Poetry*, is particularly forceful in the importance of formal elements to poetry's existence. He writes, "Prose chopped up into 'verses' of alternately rhyming lines of an equal number of syllables is not poetry.... The music of verse carries an emotional quality; when the music slackens, emotion dissipates, and the poetry is poor." What we do with language then, according to Zukofsky, is attempt to shape it in a way that heightens its musical qualities. I would add to that idea the element of space or shape and emphasize it as becoming even more prevalent in an age where symbol/sound texts co-exist with ideogrammic texts and our language seems poised to move to some sort of hybridization between the two.

Shape and sound. Sound is made of rhyme, alliteration, anaphora, assonance, and rhythm. I explain rhythm to students as the drum in a band. Rhyme, alliteration, anaphora, assonance...these are our other instruments. A drum line is evocative, but if all we have is the drum there is often something missing. If we want the full effect we need an orchestra. There is something beautiful in the minimalism of just a drum beat though.

This may be why some poetry forgoes any consideration of sound altogether in its composition. I'd argue that logical writing cannot ignore rhyme, alliteration, anaphora, assonance. That English is a language built around these things because that is also how children learn words, expand vocabulary, and compare/contrast the world. There are exceptions to every rule. I am no linguistic historian. I am making assumptions based on my own observations of young children, children's shows, and my vague memories of learning language.

I learned through rhyme.

Any Dr. Seuss book is built around rhyme.

Shel Silverstein = rhyme.

It is all rhyme. Nursery rhymes. Lullabies, Say goodnight...

Form existed even in those early days and the form helped to teach, transmit knowledge, and develop our comprehension. We learned early that "hen" and "again" had a sonic resonance. So that we could interchange the multiple versions of the last verse of "One, two, buckle my shoe..." We learned words and sounds through *Sesame Street* expanding vowels and consonant clusters and putting them together in unique ways. Phonics education was the norm in my elementary days. Sound it out. Rhyme was one of the first ways we learned language could bring pleasure. Matching rhyming words was a game. Such a great game.

Form, even in early life when art is dipping our hands in paints and running our soaked palms along the wall.

John Robinson

BEAUTY AND THE NATURE OF THE IMAGE

A poem is a work of art. As such, the idea of beauty plays a central role, both in creating and in the nature of the poetic image. Logically, however, not all poets have the same interest in the conveyance of the beautiful or even utilize this Romantic, poetic influence in the same way. Because of this difference and the general multiplicity of individual aesthetic sensibilities, I cannot say there is any single standard. I can only attempt an outline of my own poetic sensibilities and how I have been influenced in my life through theories of the past and life experience. Two informing ideas through the academic study of poetry and the theory of poetry remain a strong sense of Realism and an informed use of the Romantic image as understood in the works of the English Romantic poets: Wordsworth, Keats, Shelley, Byron, and others. The critical ideas that have refined my use and understanding of the Romantic image, the beautiful, exist primarily through the *Claims* poets and the literary criticism of Cleanth Brooks, Wimsatt & Beardsley, or the primary works of the Romantic poets themselves. Here, I only make an argument for myself, and hope to clarify how I understand and have been influenced in having my own artistic objectives.

The beauty of poetry is grounded in various aspects of pleasure. These concepts include, though are not limited to, a sense of gestalt for the poet as creator of the work of art and catharsis for the reader. However, these forms of pleasure remain in effect "caused" by something; they cannot just simply exist as a factor in all poetry. What creates pleasure in poetry are literary conventions such as rhythm, rhyme, metrical feet, line breaks, refrain, metaphor, image, simile—the sound pleasure of words and language. In Donald Hall's *Goatfoot, Milktongue, Twinbird: The Psychic Origins of Poetic Form*, he characterizes poetic pleasure of sound and rhythm with the last two terms, "milktongue" and "twinbird." The first involves "primitive pleasure of assonance and...consonance...and alliteration." When resolution has been achieved, then the second term, twinbird, comes into play. In one sense, the pleasure created by gestalt remains mostly artistic in concept—it pertains to the pleasure of the sense of the whole work of art; a poem, a painting, for example. In this sense, if rendered well, the observer knows immediately because the mind is captured, drawn into the work through the coalescence of the whole form, what some *Claims* poets call "the sensual body" which is the poem itself. In the Wordsworthian sense, the work holds attention. In another sense, the pleasure created by catharsis remains mostly internal, psychological or is mostly emotional in that the effect it creates relates to a reader's sense of somehow identifying with the poetry.

Far more central for the poetic process remains poetic experience, which serves as the ground from which all material arises or is churned up through contemplation of sensory phenomenon. When beauty exists most cohesively in a poem, all preconceptions of created-ness will not seem to exist. The work will operate or "function" a certain way, seem organic, though will not be purely functional even though it is something composed of parts. The elements of the poem in this sense will come together like the Keatsian analogy of leaves to a tree ("Letter to John Taylor"). Regardless of the number of drafts that create the final work, the poem still retains its power. It is our shared experience of natural beauty that makes this possible. Wordsworth says that the poet works to achieve a synthesis in a heightened state of mind "because in that condition the passions of men are incorporated with the beautiful and permanent forms of nature" (Wordsworth). I don't believe it is as if a unity of these two aspects exist in today's poetry. I cannot say for certain that I write with the idea of beauty at the forefront of my imagination. Perhaps most commonly, one would find through comparison some sort of truth synthesized with attention. However, for my own work, I believe the role of natural beauty in some sense always remains an influence or a factor. I don't feel that it is necessary to "paint with words" in every poem.

The idea of the natural setting, however, remains not without conflicts or problems, even though I share the essence of the following statement. In "Some Self-Analysis," Roethke writes, "I can see the moods of nature almost instinctively. Ever since I could walk, I have spent as much as I could in the open. A perception of nature—no matter how delicate, how subtle, how evanescent, remains with me forever" (Roethke, "Some Self Analysis"). I don't necessarily believe nature can have a mood, though the rest of the quote remains salvageable. In my own thinking, nature is indifferent. God is not indifferent, though I truly want to avoid any kind of religious or ideological, even deconstructionist discourse, because I don't find my own non-fundamentalist, spiritual views directly relevant to the work of poetry or literary criticism. My discourse in this writing *is* a work of literary critical thinking. In a postmodern society, some of those political or religious thoughts and questions aren't as justifiable as they once were, nor are they easily expressed in terms of condition, struggle, or consequence. Attitudes may be intuitively grounded because of what we see or experience, though ultimately all those perceptions originate from our own inwardness, our own senses, our private understanding of the true nature of reality and that the ultimate ground of reality is unknown, one of the great mysteries of life. However, while its source is a mystery, its nature is known and continuously being examined through the senses, through the various sciences, and cannot exist to such a Romantic degree as we first conceived. The harder facts remain: the truth of human knowledge and the problem of human suffering. The general run of life seems to counter the notion that some benevolent entity watches, much less controls, from beyond, or that omniscience ever was a trait of the sacred. We are faithful that given the instruments of intelligence and faith our conditions will improve. Someday, we will know a greater part of that mystery and I truly believe that this knowledge will make us more whole as people.

Truth as a poetic objective or value possibly originates from the influence of the writings of Plato, specifically his dialogues. Perhaps our strongest influence in this sense remains the Romantic poets with their sense of realism or use of the material from daily life. Truth is a way of grounding the work in something concrete, real and tangible, the experience of the every day. Note that in this sense the work may contain a fictional element and exist as a truthful account of some aspect of the human condition. Much of the time poets reside much closer to this truth and draw more directly on experience for material of the work of art. In "Theodore Roethke," he writes: "All such details, and others like them, seem particularly trivial and vulgar in my case because I have tried to put them down in poems, as barely and honestly as possible, symbolically, what few nuggets of observation and, let us hope, spiritual wisdom, I have managed to seize upon in the course of a conventional albeit sometimes disordered existence" (Roethke, "Theodore Roethke"). A statement like this could have been written by any of the *Claims* poets. This notion of truth remains the same for myself as in Roethke or Wordsworth's preface. For Wordsworth, the poet was to write using common language and everyday actions as they would normally appear to common people. Also, the material of the poem included any scientific subject or concept.

The image plays a central role among all these aspects of poetry because it can be located within the material of the work of art itself, regardless of one's concept of the meaning of the word. Louis Simpson's "Images" raises several important thoughts on the meaning, nature, and role of the image in past literary movements in poetry. The word "image" for many of these past groups was not synonymous with the more common term "picture." An image was not the subject of a poem: a thing. Second, an image was not adjective nor descriptive, ornamental qualities of language. An image was also not something synonymous with artistic vision; the informing, shaping sensibility of the poet. Consistent with Hall's concept of totality of form, Simpson says an image is the total sensory impression we experience from reading a poem primarily engaged through visual perception and description, the representation in writing of the whole inner workings of various literary and grammatical elements in the representation of human experience. While many *Claims* poets conceive of form as "the total interactive functioning of content and language, including every contributing element," the image is not characterized as an object in a jar, as perhaps many people would conceive (Levertov). A better analogy would be to say an image is not a noun or adjective in a sentence and does not function in such a way either. The *Claims* poets also tell us form always involves "physicality" or "energies" which find their creation through conflicting or a questioning of content and form or emotions. To say that an image is "the total sensory impression" is to make a similar claim for images because an image is more than a person, place, thing, or idea stated or described in a poem. An image may be symbolic, though always conveys more than what is represented through its variations of form and content.

Simpson says in his essay that there are three dominant concepts of the image: Imagist, Surrealist, and Symbolist. The Imagist conceives of the image as "a moment of perception. A movement of some sort. It is not just a sensation, a thing perceived by the senses." For the Surrealist, the image serves as a way to draw attention, to discard dissimilarities and in this sense shares much with the Russian Formalist notion of de-familiarization, or "making strange." The Symbolist image trains attention to what exists beyond detail, regardless of whether the part represents the whole or the reverse exists in the work or the poet's mind. In America, these three remain the prevailing sensibilities regardless of the descriptive terms of a poet's writing: formal, free-verse, or language poetries. Simpson concludes after comparing all three of these concepts that no matter what happens, the poet's task is always "perceiving affinities" or "a significance" which illustrate "metamorphosis, the changing of one thing into another." Something always happens.

In Robert Bly's thought, such affinities were found through the illustration of the poet's seeing a sameness, a similitude, even in Wordsworth's sense, among intuitive forces and impulses of the human psyche—usually between human experience of the poet and subjective content of the poet's intellect. The psychological "leaps" in this context consist of the making of associations wholly within consciousness. "Associating" serves as a way of perceiving, opening up, of going inward, realizing those affinities and illustrating their significance. In his essay, "Looking for Dragon Smoke," Bly says that "in the United States" we "poets have struggled primarily for freedom from old technique." Simpson says that the practice of writing the "deep image" is no different than the images of Williams or Pound. Bly objects and says this assumption remains too simplified. He says that the poetry of the third and fourth generation free verse "tends to restrict itself to certain mapped-out sections of the psyche." As their works illustrate, these poets often write in modified, though patterned lines, what Marjorie Perloff later calls the non-linear poetries.

Perhaps one of the best discussions of inwardness and the role and function of the image in correlation with Simpson's thought remains the Robert Bly essay, "What the Image Can Do." In this essay, he discusses numerous powers of the image. One of the most important aspects to understand is that the "image belongs with the simile, the metaphor and the analogy as an aspect of metaphorical language." This remains consistent with the concept of "totality of form" previously discussed. The image may seem like something finite, singular or isolated, though it's true nature and role remains very different. Bly says that "human intelligence in the image joins itself to something not entirely human. The image always holds to one of the senses at least," because an "image" always "keeps a way open to" those "certain energies that do not flow from a source in our personal life."

In theory, the idea of the image is what makes both the activity of the poem and the ever-unfolding action of its presence become the work. The image is the concept which allows us to perceive and understand what is communicated. This ingrained way of understanding the image as a thing, a picture created in the mind, is not easy to distinguish in the mind. If I have an image in my mind of a person, perhaps a more limited notion of image comes to serve the purpose. The more abstract, however, the idea seems to elude this ease of illustration and the affinity takes a different form. As we see then, the nature of the image may be said to have a dual role; one descriptive and the other, some sort of communicable property beyond that of mere details. In "A Wrong Turning in American Poetry," Robert Bly writes that "the image, being the natural speech of the imagination, cannot be drawn from or inserted back into the real world. It is an animal native to the imagination" and "cannot be seen in real life. A picture" however, "is drawn from the objective 'real' world." An image only provides faint insights and glimpses into consciousness. The image in the whole poem defines context and shapes meaning toward a specific end.

Cultural changes in the status and role of the work of art have transformed our collective understanding and therefore the general disposition of the poet. Hegel writes in his introduction to *The Philosophy of Fine Art*, "we are beyond the stage of reverence for works of art as divine objects deserving our worship. The impression they produce is one of a more reflective kind, and the emotions they arouse require a higher test." If it is true that the problem in the American past has been lack of inwardness and a materialism which results in the production of commodified types, then the lack of any widespread aura or valued standard produces tremendous independence. The resulting inwardness and real contact with authentic emotions exists as a positive aspect of this situation. The problem still lingers and exists as a major issue for poets: how to determine the quality of the communicated emotion when reading the poetry of other people as well as achieving the same standard in our own writing. We know from these essays the areas of life they have chosen to illuminate, yet this still does not solve the problem of what provokes thought or catharsis in the reader. Here, we are faced again with the notion of readership or disposition of the writer as the factor which determines these ends.

In use of the word "quality," I don't mean its evaluative meaning. I mean that when a poet communicates an emotion, no two readers share or read that emotion as it was intended, or at least, not unless the subject happens to be very generally shared among the readership. Again, this reflective condition you could also call almost meditative, self-conscious to the point of introversion, though not to the point of self-absorption. The reflective condition communicates emotions which originate from the unique intellect of the individual which becomes part of the problem solved by the good poem—transcendence of this condition. How to communicate what is felt from an understanding not wholly anyone else's except your own. We never know that we felt what the poet felt, that we even understand exactly how they communicate in their work. Even the reading process is a kind of groping for meaning, in a sense.

Before reading Louis Simpson, I never understood the idea of the image as actually "doing" anything. I equated the term "image" with "picture" or "idea." The word was specifically descriptive and I understood the term *only* in its adjectival sense. If we take this into account, it is possible for a person to have written poetry in two of these senses without even knowing there were theories or qualities that describe each, or one that remains fairly stock-and-trade coordinated by other concepts or techniques. Without formal training, without any comparison or discussion with other scholars and writers, your own work could exist as an example of either type without even knowing. Thinking back, I have been in the habit of falling into this intuitive mode in such a way or to such an extent that I have rarely been conscious of the maneuvering or theoretical positing of the poem, so to speak. After reading Simpson's comparisons in college, I knew I had to go back and make a comparison in some sense to what I had created. In certain works, I could see the influence more clearly of one or the other. I never knew what "Imagist," "Surrealist," or "Symbolist" poetry was until I went to college. I could see something was happening in the poem, though I had no name for the activity. Is it possible that these poets were not really breaking any new, theoretical ground and were perhaps just doing what poets have been doing for centuries? This is what Simpson suggests concluding his essay.

These three ideas then seem to be important to me in poetry because I think they play the most central role: beauty, images and emotion. If we had no sense of an informing aesthetic when creating a poem, something that not only pleased the maker, but also the reader of poetry, I don't think poetry would exist. It certainly wouldn't be what we have come to know it as and it certainly wouldn't have some of the qualities it has been known to possess for so long. How would we know or have an idea of what is cliché? Even if a work does not involve the description of some object of beauty, there still exists some sort of plan or statement. If you write a formal poem, then your goal is to achieve the requirements of that form. Passions, rather than emotions, is Wordsworth's term, though they are essentially synonymous. Poetry can express emotion and feeling or address the intellect.

As a personal goal, these elements should fuse or merge together, though this does not always happen. These elements should coalesce: truth, beauty, images, and emotions. Realizing, of course, it is always easier in retrospect to say what a poet should have accomplished and how such elements should theoretically involve or incorporate each. All theories in poetry are evidence of this fact. Keats honored the influence of Wordsworth, though felt his work characterized an "egotistical sublime." Robert Bly felt entire generations of American poets were misguided in their writing ("A Wrong Turning in American Poetry"). The central and guiding reason for their lack of quality, he felt, was their disposition toward outer things and not inwardness, having emotions as their substance. Even I happen to share a similar disposition; I am open to the fact that not everyone possesses the same sensibility. I don't enjoy writing from the same approach in every poem. Marvin Bell says in one of his essays that there comes a time when poets must choose between tendencies of mind; are you a poet of ideas, like Wallace Stevens, or are you a poet of images, like William Carlos Williams? Theodore Roethke writes in "Five American Poets" that "there can be no ideal instance of the purely intuitive poet... or the completely conscious and resolute writer, at the other extreme, who moves easily through the geography and climate of ideas." At this point, I still politely disagree with Bell. I don't believe in the insisting of a choice between or among styles. Maybe John Crowe Ransom was accurate in his description of "true poetry" in *The World's Body* as a balance of these two tendencies of quality or substance in poetry.

Because the image is a product of the imagination, it cannot be said to explicitly derive from anything individual and detached from human experience outside the self. Again, this is not contradictory for the same previous reason, that the image as a literary creation remains imaginary. As a product of the imagination and human intelligence, Bly says "the true image has thought in it; complicated analogical, even logical, perceptions are called in, and imagination fuses them to make a strong image." The Imagist image is interesting in concept, though failed to sustain itself in any credible way. Simpson says that for the Imagist, "the image is a quick opening into another order of reality. Then it closes again" with the intention "to show you something" so that "it is to be an "intuition" ("Images").

Romantic poets traditionally conceive of the purpose of the image as something to convey experience as well as beauty—sometimes of beauty itself, though often whatever subject preoccupied the poet's consciousness. American poetry still illustrates this tendency, though this use or influence of the idea of the beautiful primarily exists in Formalist or image-oriented free-verse. You will find the nature of the image challenged in avant-garde or recent language poetries. In my own work, I have attempted to blend these two tendencies, though only when it feels appropriate. Some poems attempt the address of experience of beauty in nature, though these poems remain few. I have noticed mostly a tendency of the brief, descriptive image as detail or accent of human meaning.

In the Hegelian sense, poetry is one of the high arts (Hegel). Cultural and curricular changes have influenced the nature of higher education toward an accelerated rate. Still, a strong sense of the value of the basic humanities remains within university programs throughout the United States. Typically, this takes the form of an emphasis on research in craft writing and the discipline of literary critical writing. I feel that because there exists no single aesthetic, guiding and shaping the students of today, one cannot say what the standard is or should be for all students. People come to the university from a variety of cultural and religious backgrounds. Because of this awareness, my understanding and concept of the place of poetry and critical theory of literature remains somewhat generic, though for good reason. Poetry is an expression of human emotion and feeling or thought created with a set of standards established by the artist. The university and its environment play a central and shaping role in the development of the informing sensibility of the poet. There remains a large segment of American society that rejects any serious self-consciousness of poetry or theory about poetic writing, that I believe could be improved upon through basic and rudimentary study. Regardless of this condition, my sense of beauty as an aspect of writing remains one influenced by an interest in nature. I never set out to make the beauty of nature a standard or any necessary element of a poem. Every writer writes from whatever aspect of life that influences them or provides a sense of fulfillment. I can only say that I attempt to convey through my art what is true to my experience and in doing so, certain aspects of the beautiful naturally emerge as simply what they are in terms of natural landscape or objects of beauty in and of themselves.

Beauty remains a purely subjective term, though exists as something that the poet conveys in different ways throughout his work. First, within individual works, being preoccupied and influenced by specific settings, "the local," as Creeley and Hugo would say, or even objects. Second, as an art, beauty exists through more general reference concerning the conventional forms considered art forms or structures. This even applies to elements within that system of knowledge and norms shared by all poets from life or poetic practice through knowledge of literary conventions and elements. In its simplified meaning, beauty consists of those visual and verbal elements of a work which remain most pleasing to the poet.

The relationship of beauty to other aesthetic values is that it remains one among many aspects that comprise the work of art that is the poem. Although it is not necessarily required for the work of art to be successful, in the broader sense it exists as one of those values established by what constitutes art in the academic sense. Beauty, even in a generalized aesthetic, has a different manifestation in comparison with something like visual art, or for example, Realism. Without lessening the meaning or importance of beauty as a value or standard, essentially this idea can be understood as one component among many, though in talking about beauty this way I realize that I risk sounding too functional or utilitarian. The other aesthetic values remain determined by the nature of poetic sensibility in question, both in terms of general typology and treatment of material. Not that there exists a hierarchy of form or that works that aspire to incorporate beautiful and pleasing subjects or imagery are *more* beautiful than others, only that formal works, simply because of the history of their existence, carry a sense of difference in their created-ness. This difference primarily resides in a fact of structural unity which plays a central role in the success or failure of the given work. Beauty was and still is an integral and evaluative element, though lesser now, of whether a formal work is good or bad.

The source of aesthetic enjoyment remains personal, though only widely shared by the larger subcultural reading or academic audience of the arts.

Each of us carries within our own artistic senses that feeling which urges toward creation of the work of art. Perhaps this is all that can be said without splintering the thought into various aesthetic groups. All poets share the experience of poetic process to some degree. For the present context of poetry being written in America, I feel assured to claim that many people writing literature have serious, academic interests in poetry and are indeed conscious of the psychological processes within themselves to a reasonable degree.

Beauty is an aspect perceived through the senses as a correlation of and among elements in an academically influenced system of aesthetics. Even though this system remains personal or individual and is never communicated to the reading public doesn't make it any less meaningful. However, the poet's use of detail should not become elaborate or risk the ornamental. Beauty resides in the successful coherence of the gestalt aspect, as previously stated. Theodore Roethke says in "The Beautiful Disorder" that:

> It's the shifting of the thought that's important, often—the rightness... of the imaginative jump. Many modern poets still are content only with the logical progression, or with metaphors—often beautiful, elaborate, fresh—but these consisting of appositives. In the richest poetry even the juxtaposition of objects should be pleasurable.

For myself, art and beauty arise from the impulse to create emotive and intellectual expression as art and can possibly include striving to achieve a standard of form consistent with poetic traditions of the past. These aspects remain an integral part of poetic process, though the impulse exists as independent, initially, then typically evolves and forms a direction through thought and drafting.

WORKS CITED

Bly, Robert. "A Wrong Turning in American Poetry." Hall, *Claims*, University of Michigan Press, 1982. pp. 17-37.

—. *Talking All Morning*. The University of Michigan Press, 1990.

—. "Leaping Up into Political Poetry: An Essay." *Talking*, pp. 95-105.

—. "Looking for Dragon Smoke." *Seventies*, no.1, Spring 1972, pp. 3-8.

Hall, Donald, editor. *Claims for Poetry*, University of Michigan Press, 1995.

—. "Goatfoot, Milktongue, Twinbird: The Psychic Origins of Poetic Form." Hall, *Claims*, pp. 141-150.

—. "More Notes on Poetry: The Act of Writing." *Goatfoot, Milktongue, Twinbird*; *Interviews, Essays, and Notes on Poetry, 1970-76.* The University of Michigan Press, 1975.

—. "More Notes on the Act of Writing." *Goatfoot*, pp. 102-103.

Hegel, Georg Wilhelm Friedrich. *Aesthetics: Lectures on Fine Art*, trans. T.M. Knox. Clarendon Press, 1975.

Kizer, Carolyn, editor. *On Poetry & Craft: Selected Prose of Theodore Roethke.* Copper Canyon Press, 2001.

Keats, John. "Letter to Benjamin Bailey, Saturday 22, November 1817" and "Letter to George and Thomas Keats, Sunday 21, December 1817." *Major British Writers*, enlarged edition. Walter J. Bate, editor, vol. 2 Harcourt, Brace and Company, 1959, pp.358-361.

Levertov, Denise. "An Admonition," Hall, *Claims*, pp. 250-253.

Ransom, John Crowe. *The World's Body.* Kennikat, 1938.

Robinson, John T. *June's Fisher of Solitudes.* Unpublished poetry collection.

Roethke, Theodore. "Some Self-Analysis." Kizer, *On Poetry*, pp. 17-19.

—. "Theodore Roethke." Kizer, *On Poetry*, pp. 27-29.

—. "Five American Poets." Kizer, *On Poetry*, pp. 161-163.

—. "The Beautiful Disorder." Kizer, *On Poetry*, pp. 193-203.

Shklovsky, Victor. "Art as Technique." *Russian Formalist Criticism: Four Essays.* Translated by Lee T. Lemon and Marion   J. Reis, University of Nebraska Press, 1965, pp. 3-24.

Simpson, Louis. *The Character of the Poet.* Ann Arbor: The University of Michigan Press, 1986.

—. "Images." *Character*, pp. 186-188.

Wordsworth, William. "Preface." *Lyrical Ballads. Major British Writers*, edited by Elizabeth Drew. Harcourt, Brace and Company, 1959. pp. 18-29.

Jaydn DeWald

IN PRAISE OF CONSTRAINTS: INCITING THE UNEXPECTED

Language is a box you wear over your head.
—Nona Caspers

Several years ago, I began to write poems whose lines were of uniform length. I must admit that, in the beginning, this constraint constituted a poetic manifestation of obsessive-compulsive disorder: I loved the way a poem composed of conventional spacing could, without resorting to justified margins, resemble a near-perfect rectangle. But I also loved the contrast between the subjectivity of a poem and its objective appearance on the page. Even though most of my early attempts suffered as a result of this constraint—I often sacrificed words and images for the sake of satisfying a line-length—I continued to write these "rectangles" obsessively. Then, after a month or so, I began to notice that, when I was stubborn enough, when I had worked a line until I was pleased both with its length and its poetic value, this constraint was a reliable way in which to incite arresting, largely unexpected results. Like established formal constraints (rhyme, meter, syllabics, etc), an arbitrary, uniform line length could, I discovered, force a poet to go beyond normative language and familiar sensory experience. I was forced to explore the possibilities of a given line, and this often meant radically altering—not simply expanding or contracting—the language. Just as a line of Creeley's will, with his emphasis on the breath, "say as much as it can, or as little, in the 'time' given," so a line of mine attempts to say as much as it can, or as little, in the *space* given.

This is slow, often tedious work. I wrote well over 10,000 words before I placed the final period on a recent 164-word poem entitled "Ritornello (or, Landscape with X)." Worlds apart, in short, from Ginsberg's famous dictum: "First thought, best thought." Still, I very much enjoy my strange, idiosyncratic constraint: it is an engaging game; there's nothing static about it. Indeed, my experiences trying to "find" lines of particular lengths have inadvertently become some of the most surprising and affecting of my poetry-writing life.

Importantly, though writing poetry can be a mental, emotional, and imaginative workout, to write with constraints is not simply to use and abuse a certain set of muscles; it is also to discover fresh, inventive ways in which to compensate for what's lacking, for the proverbial arm tied behind one's back. Despite the general slowness of the process—or perhaps precisely *because* of its slowness—the trick is to keep moving, to trust that movement in due course will end in discovery. Or else to trust that movement is itself the discovery. The parallels with trends in twentieth-century art, particularly Abstract Expressionism, are striking. "At a certain moment the canvas began to appear to one American painter after another as an arena in which to act," wrote art critic Harold Rosenberg. And this, for me, for my rectangles—a canvas inside the larger canvas of the page—is generally the case. I write a lot and I discard a lot, but deletion is as active and as productive a gesture as writing itself. I simply keep moving. Keep moving…

Now, years later, continuing to work with rectangles, I have come to care less about the appearance of the poems—that is, line-length uniformity—than the unexpected results this constraint incites. "A writer is not so much someone who has something to say," said William Stafford, "as he is someone who has found a process that will bring about new things he would not have thought of if he had not started to say them." In fact, I have come to rely upon this process as a means of igniting my imagination, of "inviting the muse," of digging deeper, of losing and discovering (in semi-equal measure) the self. I suppose I am, in Denise Levertov's words, "as enamored of the process of making as of the thing made." This essay will examine how certain other contemporary poets—Truong Tran, Christian Bök, Charles Wright (briefly), and Harryette Mullen—have imposed a variety of similar, seemingly arbitrary constraints to alter, in a variety of unexpected ways, their own poetry.

***

Because a constraint can, relative to its invasiveness or its level of difficulty, moderately or radically alter a poem, it's fruitful to look at some book-length constraints—or, at least, some individual poems within those books—to appreciate the spectrum of alteration that's not only possible but also sustainable. Let us begin with a fairly moderate example: Truong Tran's *four letter words* (2008), a collection of mostly unpunctuated, uncapitalized, untitled prose poems, which he calls "bricks."

> this poem the line every single word the slanted rhyme the image the red bird the boy the color grey the space in between the words the letters wondering the wanderings the illusion of a brick this book the title its reflection in the mirror the page the act of turning turning back the tide the apple the core this poem is everything the box the poem a lie written a lie in response if the you fictitious are looking for look in the folds where paper meets spine where the edge is contained where nowhere is a place to look to go look just beyond the last line written look in between that space in between

To omit punctuation is to omit sentences and clauses; and yet, because our mind tends to organize, Tran's poems remain quite readable. To omit punctuation, however, is also to allow for chance error—"chance to break the spell of our habitual literary expectations and to approach the condition of what has been called 'free imagination,'" as Charles Simic wrote in "Negative Capability and Its Children." Tran is allowing, in other words, for multiple, unintended meanings. Consider this (from Tran's *four letter words*): "boyish he responds to the boy baffled i've been in exile the word is my house imprisoned as if it is at the edge," which can be read, if punctuated, a number of different ways: "boyish, he responds to the boy, baffled: 'i've been in exile.' the word is my house, imprisoned, as if it is at the edge"; or, "boyish, he responds to the boy. baffled i've been. in exile, the word is my house, imprisoned, as if it is at the edge"; or—but the point is clear enough. The word-arrangement of Tran's poem is in a sense prismatic, since so many "implied sentences" exist simultaneously. By omitting all punctuation, as well as all line and stanza breaks—again: a fairly moderate constraint—Tran is able to break away from some significant literary expectations and to produce, as a result, a more startling, multidimensional poetry.

> indulge me this one time and try something new not really new but strange to the skin not really skin but language as skin

The most radical recent example of a book-length constraint, on the other hand, might be Christian Bök's *Eunoia* (2001), a book of lipograms, divided into five chapters (A, E, I, O, and U), in which every poem can contain any consonant but only its respective chapter's vowel. (Bök's constraint is, then, to exclude certain vowels.) *Eunoia* took Bök seven years to write—and people like to make a big deal about this—but seven years strikes me as not too much time at all, given that the constraint (to use only one vowel per poem) impacts every single word:

> Writing is inhibiting. Sighing, I sit, scribbling in ink this pidgin script. I sing with nihilistic witticism, disciplining signs with trifling gimmicks—impish hijinks which highlight stick sigils. Isn't it glib? Isn't it chic? I fit childish insights within rigid limits, writing shtick which might instill priggish misgivings in critics blind with hindsight. I dismiss nitpicking criticism which flirts with philistinism. I bitch; I kibitz— griping whilst criticizing dimwits, sniping whilst indicting nitwits, dismissing simplistic thinking, in which philippic wit is still illicit.

This can be, to be sure, maddening work. Like writing in a straitjacket. Nevertheless, it would be difficult to believe that such a difficult and invasive constraint would not incite—nay, necessitate—unexpected results. Indeed, in addition to creating compelling sounds ("Dutch smut churns up blushful succubus lusts"), the very intention of a lipogram is to incite strange new material. For this very reason, Bök is forced to adapt to the extreme language conditions that he himself has imposed, and he succeeds unequivocally: I can think of no stronger nor more radical example of language adaptation than Christian Bök's *Eunoia*.

Furthermore, though *Eunoia* might appear obdurately youthful, such extreme rebellion against linguistic norms is itself a form of expression, an aesthetic stance that rejects Wordsworth's claim that poetry is "the spontaneous overflow of powerful emotions recollected in tranquility." (Today, Bök's no longer writing "poems" at all, but rather encoding language into the DNA of *E. Coli*, hoping the language will be preserved for millions of years.) Poetry, for Bök, is a cryptographer's art: it's about discovering and expanding the possibilities of poetic expression. *Eunoia*'s renunciation of certain letters, which forecloses (in the act of composition) access to certain words and phrases and trains of thought, proves to be a most effective way in which to accomplish this.

***

Before moving on (*keep moving…*), I feel impelled to make two qualifying, if obvious, distinctions among constraints: all constraints are characterized by, one, their level of strictness and, two, their level of discernibility. A lipogram, an example of a very strict restraint, is what David Orr calls a "mechanical form." In his words, "A mechanical form involves a simple rule based on inclusion, exclusion, counting, or some similar procedure…. [M]echanical forms typically don't allow for the idea of degree: A lipogram that fails to obey its governing rule doesn't register as a 'loose' lipogram; it just seems like a mistake." I agree absolutely. Yet there are many poets who impose upon their writing more malleable or forgiving forms, which do indeed allow for the idea of degree. Consider, for example, the use of "dropped" lines in Charles Wright's *Sestets* (2009), a book of sixty-nine, six-line poems—his constraint being one of brevity, then—in which only left-flushed lines are counted as autonomous. That the dropped portion be considered part of the same line is, of course, a literary convention. Even so, the convention allows Wright to have his cake and eat it too: though he likely used dropped lines for a number of reasons—for emphasis, for look, for light, for air—he can nevertheless break a line and only count one of them among the six, as here:

Tomorrow

The metaphysics of the quotidian was what he was after:
A little dew on the sunrise grass,
A drop of blood in the evening trees,
      a drop of fire.

If you don't shine you are darkness.
The future is merciless,
     everyone's name inscribed
On the flyleaf of the Book of Snow.

But constraints can also be characterized by their level of discernibility. In general, the stricter the constraint, the easier it is to discern. We might compare, for instance, two poems from Harryette Mullen's *Sleeping with the Dictionary* (2002)—"Variations on a Theme Park" and "Dim Lady"—two corruptions of Shakespeare's Sonnet 130, a "Dark Lady" Sonnet. It's important to note that "Variation on a Theme Park" is an N+7, one of Oulipo's better-known creations—that is, a poem (based on an existing text) in which each substantive noun is replaced by the seventh noun following or sometimes preceding it in a dictionary. Hence, Shakespeare's original opening— "My mistress's eyes are nothing like the sun"—becomes "My Mickey Mouse ears are nothing like sonar." Because this is a procedural form, a form on auto-pilot, so to speak—the chance results of which are meant to surprise rather than provoke emotion—this is perhaps the easiest of all constraints to see: the constraint is simply not to compose, given that neither the source material nor the substitutions are the poet's choice.

Mullen's other Shakespearean corruption, "Dim Lady," on the other hand, is a bit trickier to see. This poem also replaces Shakespeare's nouns, yet the constraint is less discernible, because Mullen is simply riffing off of Shakespeare's narrative arc, so that the original—"Coral is far more red than her lips' red"—becomes "Today's special at Red Lobster is redder than her kisser." Though the perceptive reader will easily detect the Shakespearean original in both poems, particularly since the two corruptions appear in the same book, the absurdity of "Variation on a Theme Park" might suggest the imposition of a chance operation—and *Sleeping with the Dictionary* is chockfull of such language games—whereas "Dim Lady" simply uses "My mistress's eyes" as counterpoint, as a historical sparring partner. In consequence, the stricter constraint of "Variation on a Theme Park" is far more discernible.

These poems are not merely whimsical, however, as one unfamiliar with Mullen's book might assume. Indeed, the project itself—to "sleep" with the dictionary (i.e. to *sleep* or *fuck* or *make love to* or *lie dead with* one of the culture's most authoritative texts)—is thrillingly transgressive and politically profound. Like an African American quilt designer who, in Sandra McPherson's words, "reinterpret[s] standard Euro-American motifs... [so that] one design may be made to confront another," Mullen trespasses and makes known her presence, as well as the presence of "dark ladies" generally, by writing over or erasing, by word-swapping or -corrupting, canonical and therefore "untouchable" texts (like a Shakespeare sonnet). Mullen's texts declare—behind enemy lines, as it were—: "We're here, too; we, too, have a voice and stake in *this* literature."

But let us return to the principle of discernibility. My "rectangles" seemed to have found a loophole. Set in the typeface (or a closely related typeface) in which they were written, these poems appear as near-perfect rectangles. However, set in any other typeface, the uniform line-length of each poem is entirely lost: the "rectangles" will suddenly resemble typical free verse poems; from a reader's perspective, they will exhibit no discernible constraint at all.

***

For me, the combination of life and reading has provided (so far, at least) almost but not quite enough inspiration. Where inspiration fails, however, constraints can come to the rescue. In the documentary *The Miles Davis Story*, Miles says: "I can't be around a comfortable person. Nothing bounces off them. You get nothing." And I maintain a similar attitude toward my poems—or, more precisely, the act of writing my poems: I need to feel an alert, receptive, tense, even volatile engagement with the material at hand. If inspired or inventive or foreign enough, constraints can steer a writer into startling, unforeseen waters, inciting material even in the face of silence, listlessness, or (most frequent of all, in my experience) confusion.

Where shall I go next? Often this question arises from the sheer number of choices one might make in a poem at any given moment. Dean Young has defined art as "the manifestation of choices in a charged field"—an excellent definition implying that any given piece of art could have been otherwise. So how does a poet of our time, freed from the many traditional constraints of form and rhetoric, choose (or perhaps I should say *settle on*) even a single word from among so many other possible words? In light of this constant dilemma, Flaubert's dictum, "*le mot juste*"—or, "the right word"—seems to me both erroneous and arrogant. Because language is indeed a slippery fish (subjective, mutable, culture-specific, associative, nuanced, hyperbolic, suggestive—this list could go on and on), a poet can only require that his or her choices be, despite all hope for eternal grandeur, merely satisfactory in the moment of composition. This temporary, moment-to-moment satisfaction is precisely what I too require in order to progress from one component of a poem—be it a word or a sentence, a stanza-break or a line-break—to the next.

Thus constraints, even while inciting unexpected results, tend to minimize or simplify our choices, which is just to point out the obvious: constraints exclude, or necessarily include, certain elements of language. The constraint of Bök's *Eunoia* (to exclude certain vowels) limits the possibilities of his diction. Likewise, every word of Matthea Harvey's book-length erasure, *Of Lamb* (2011), has been gleaned from Lord David Cecil's *A Portrait of Charles Lamb* (1983). Or consider Joe Brainard's memoir *I Remember* (1970), an extremist's example of anaphora, in which every sentence begins "I remember…" Or Ben Lerner's "Mean Free Path" (2010) in which each stanza, except for its two opening stanzas, contains exactly nine lines. Or Dora Malech's anagrammaniacal *Stet* (2018): "Is it just a word game? / *Is a god just wartime?*" Or Marvin Bell's Dead Man poems, straddling prose and poetry (by making the sentence the poetic line) and challenging our ideas of closure (by offering two texts for each one). Or Magdalena Zurawski's *The Bruise* (2008), a novel that, barring its italicized opening pages, omits commas: 161 pages of comma-less prose. Because so many choices are, in each of these examples, predetermined, the relative constraint tends to facilitate, and therefore often accelerate, the relevant author's forward (avant-) movement.

But I am not suggesting, of course, that limitation guarantees the effectiveness of any given choice. Sometimes a constraint can be too invasive; sometimes a linguistic game of chance (an N+7, say) can produce uninspiring, even boring results. Too, what begins as a formal poem might "end," at least from the reader's perspective, very differently. Constraints may be abandoned midstream, or omitted in revision, or embedded in a larger text (as in "XLII" of David St. John's *The Face*, a free verse poem that contains, within it, a found villanelle, its lines gleaned from Novalis's *Philosophical Writings*). Well, "you can't," as William Stafford said, "be careful and responsible all the time." Things happen—the poem is often a willful child—and the poet adapts. In short, I'm not espousing some authoritative, money-back ars poetica. I am merely suggesting that a constraint can be a fruitful challenge, a temporary diversion, and—to the poet as well as to the reader—a source of comfort and delight.

Nathan McClain

BISHOP'S GLANCES

In her essay on "Image," Ellen Bryant Voigt quotes M.H. Abrams (who himself quoted John Stuart Mill) in saying, "The poetry is not in the object itself [but] in the state of mind [in which it is contemplated]." There are, of course, many poems that concern themselves with objects under a viewer's scrutiny but Mill's statement focuses upon poems primarily concerned with *how* the objects are viewed and what is revealed about the viewer as a result. Elizabeth Bishop's "The Bight" perfectly illustrates a poem primarily or foremost concerned with exploring the latter rather than the former. And the poem seems simple enough: the speaker is describing a bight. But one soon realizes that Bishop's looking is much more complicated than that.

One recognizes that Bishop doesn't simply "see" in a poem—she actively "watches"; Bishop is a poet of vantage, and vantage is always shifting in her work. "The Bight" features one of the most memorable of Bishop's endings: "All the untidy activity continues, / awful but cheerful." But what makes this ending surprising and necessary? "The Bight," with the odd but salient epigraph "On my birthday," enacts this business of actively "watching." But if the poem's ending is successful, looking back, what makes it so? Is it that the poem's ending culminates in this kind of subjective looking? Rather than focus solely upon the poem's ending, I believe it necessary to closely examine the poem's entire structure to determine what makes Bishop's ending successful.

One way Bishop creates this sense of "watching" in "The Bight" is by utilizing detail and image. Detail, to my mind, simply conveys information to the reader. Image, on the other hand, requires some additional information around or modification of a detail to transform the detail into an image. Therefore, the image gains nuance and has import. Detail can be made without image, but image cannot be made without detail. Bishop's opening sentence is a good example of detail: "At low tide like this how sheer the water is." Bishop's speaker presents information which is used both rhetorically and to contribute to the poem's tone. But what is also interesting about this particular detail is Bishop's use of syntax. I often expect to enter a poem encountering a normative arrangement of syntax (i.e., the declarative sentence—subject-verb-object) but Bishop inverts the syntax of the opening sentence—the noun or subject ("water") and verb ("is") are positioned at the end of the sentence. Therefore, the unexpected syntactical arrangement of this detail makes me curious about the emotional state of Bishop's speaker. It raises the question: why open the poem like this?

The second sentence presents the poem's first image. Notice how the sentence begins—"White, crumbling ribs of marl protrude and glare / and the boats are dry"—and how it ends—"the pilings dry as matches." Like the opening detail, "White crumbling ribs of marl" is used rhetorically, it adds credibility to the poem's speaker (presumably Bishop). The image ("the pilings dry as matches") is made through the use of simile. This early use of image in conjunction with the poem's opening detail only reinforce the implication that Bishop's speaker is not in a normal emotional state. We are forced to read on if we want to discover why. The following sentence reads: "Absorbing, rather than being absorbed, / the water in the bight doesn't wet anything, / the color of the gas flame turned as low as possible." Again Bishop utilizes image here, commenting that "the water in the bight" is "the color of the gas flame turned as low as possible." Notice the significance of structure: Bishop knows that to position the "gas flame" image directly behind "the pilings dry as matches" creates a particular effect. The "matches" and the "gas flame" are, in most cases, obviously a lethal (and rather stealthy) combination. Bishop's choice of image, therefore, seems not only to contribute to the poem's tone but also to reveal something about the speaker's psychology and emotional state. Why else would the speaker's mind reach for these specific images unless on the verge of some sort of emotional catastrophe or explosion? "Figuration," Ellen Bryant Voigt writes in her essay on "Image," "is produced by feeling, which modifies the objects within the gaze." This is to say that *how* an object is figured suggests something about the psychology and/or emotional state of its viewer; figuration grants the reader access to the viewer. Bishop is masterful at utilizing figuration in this manner, but she also controls how and when she allows the reader access to her speakers.

The poem's tone of melancholy and grief are reinforced by the next series of strange images, as "the water in the bight" is transformed in the speaker's mind first into "gas," then, "if one were Baudelaire," "marimba music" in the next several lines. The two halves of that fourth sentence set up an interesting contrast, especially when Baudelaire makes an appearance. One can either smell the water "turning to gas" or, "if one were Baudelaire," would see the water differently, could probably "hear it turning into marimba music." If one were Baudelaire, even the "little ocher dredge at work... / *plays* the dry perfectly off-beat claves" (my italics). By describing the image in terms in terms of music, Bishop makes reference to Baudelaire's synesthesia. However, the immediate suggestion is that Bishop's speaker seeks another frame of mind to enter. The poem teaches us that one's psychological or emotional state determines how the objects in one's line of vision are seen (and Bishop is most certainly a revisionist of vision).

We are quickly reminded, however, that Bishop's speaker is not Baudelaire, particular as she slowly and precisely details "the birds"—their size and seemingly brutal behavior—in the four lines that follow. The odd violence of the details—both "crash" and "unnecessarily hard"—reinforce the earlier images of "matches" and "gas flame," but notice the qualifier: "it seems to me." The speaker's psychological state colors all that she sees with a "peculiar" violence. Notice she transforms the "crashing" of the pelicans into an image (through simile), and then further modifies the image: "*like pickaxes,* / rarely coming up with anything to show for it" (my italics). None of the details or images feel completely strange or abrupt because Bishop has prepared the reader for each new image or detail through the poem's structure: the birds ("pelicans") feel like a natural progression, and the mention of the "little ocher dredge at work" prepares the reader for the "pickaxes" simile reinforcing the notion of "struggle" and "work." And for all their work, the pelicans "rarely [come] up with anything to show for it," which adds a certain frustration to the tone of the poem. This new complexity of tone creates further tension. The sentence could have easily ended at "hard" but the further right-branching syntax, particularly that odd detail—"rarely coming up with anything to show for it"—creates tension with its strangeness. Why does Bishop include this detail? What is its significance? We read on in hopes of discovering why the speaker wrestles with these feelings of melancholy and frustration. Bishop's speaker adds in the final detail, the pelicans' "humorous elbowings." There is something warm and forgiving in that image, that Bishop doesn't simply view the birds as crashing pickaxes but much more human to watch, at least from a certain vantage.

Bishop begins the next sentence with a detail—"Black-and-white man-of-war birds soar / on impalpable drafts"—and closes with an image—"and open their tails like scissors on the curves / or tense them like wishbones, till they tremble"—while the "pelicans" are still fresh in our minds. Note that the violence earlier introduced seems to persist with "man-of-war" birds and "tails like *scissors*" (my italics)—dangerous and capable of cutting. Bishop carries the image further with "or tense them like wishbones, till they tremble." "Wishbones" are an odder image, but also suggest separation and breaking. Again we are presented with various ways of seeing an object or detail; this, in conjunction with the allusion to Baudelaire, seems significant.

Bishop also creates image utilizing adjectival modification: "man-of-war birds soar / on impalpable drafts." "Impalpable" calls attention to itself as a polysyllable and takes on a more lugubrious hue when one realizes that one of its definitions is "not readily discerned by the mind." "Impalpable" recalls the "humorous elbowings" of the pelicans and also reveals that Bishop, the maker of the poem, is at play here. She addresses the seriousness of a particular melancholy and frustration, but she also addresses the work (or play) of writing itself. We suddenly hear the pun Bishop intends in "drafts" and recognize the alternate reading of both "pilings dry as matches," which could suggest a manuscript, and "rarely coming up with anything to show for it." The "Black-and-white" of the man-of-war birds also suggests the struggle of the "black" of ink and "white" of the blank page. Rather than merely serve precision or clarity, Bishop's use of adjectives, as Ellen Bryant Voigt writes in "Rethinking Adjectives," "add nuance and resonance, for evocation of emotion; in their amplifications of tone they acknowledge the poet's subjective presence in the poem." The adjectives suggest an emotive response of the speaker of the poem; more than simply decoration, they provide tonal clues for the reader to follow.

Of course many of the discoveries made discussing the poem thus far will not occur to a reader upon first reading the poem—this is why the poem's ending is so significant. Closure should lead a reader to reread the poem since there is information in the middle, the importance of which we may not fully appreciate until we finish the poem. That sort of rereading can happen a number of times and it is one of the reasons why the poet needs every detail in the poem be purposeful, to have use. If a reader rereads the poem and discovers that detail X has no real function, then the poet's credibility is placed in question. One reads a poem sequentially, moment by moment, and so the poem is something that lasts X amount of time. But if the reader is to see the whole poem all at once, as one picture, it requires a conclusion that sends the reader back into the poem.

As the poem continues, notice that Bishop's use of adjectives as modifiers of detail is very strategic. Adjectival modification is either used rhetorically, to add credibility and authority to the poem's speaker, or in the service of image, as in "The frowsy sponge boats." "Frowsy," (which means "unkempt or habitually dirty") although an odd adjective, aligns itself with "perfectly off-beat" and "impalpable" which appear earlier in the poem. This adjective reinforces the apparent sense of disarray that occupies the mind of the speaker. Primarily, the right-branching modification of "frowsy sponge boats"—"with the obliging air of retrievers, / bristling with jackstraw gaffs and hooks / and decorated with bobbles of sponges"—is used rhetorically. Consistent with earlier instances, the following sentence opens with a detail—"There is a fence of chicken wire along the dock"—then shifts and closes with an image—"glinting like little plowshares, / the blue-gray shark tails are hung up to dry / for the Chinese-restaurant trade." The images reinforce how Bishop's speaker still seems strangely preoccupied with violence or tools of violence and/or destruction throughout the poem ("plowshares" ["primary cutting blade of a plow"], "pickaxes," "scissors," "matches," "gas flame"), but why? Bishop chooses images carefully to contribute to the tone of the poem; she knows that to choose images other than those selected would create an entirely different effect.

As the poem nears its close, it makes a significant turn. Bishop's speaker revises her own vision in the next sentence: "Some of the little white boats are still piled up / against each other, or lie on their sides, stove in, / and not yet salvaged, if they ever will be, from the last bad storm." That the boats "are still piled up" recalls the "pilings dry as matches" and places in our minds, simultaneously, the world of the poem as well as the world of writing. This conflation makes the right-branching modification of the detail ("and not yet salvaged, if they ever will be, from the last bad storm") seem slightly less strange; the detail has a deceptively duplicitous reading. "The Bight" becomes both the object of Bishop's attention and the poem she's presently working through, the poem that's not yet salvaged, if it ever will be.

Bishop closes the sentence by transforming the detail into an image: "like torn-open, unanswered letters." This use of image is different than any other use of image found within the poem. The "little white boats" could have been compared to anything so Bishop's use of "letters" is significant, especially when compared to other instances of figuration in the poem. This image is close and personal. But why compare the boats to letters? The image of the "letters" as "torn-open" and "unanswered" both reinforce the speaker's preoccupation with a peculiar violence and signal a significant shift in the poem. The poem suddenly gains a deeper emotional subtext as the image suggests the speaker may possibly be involved in a one-sided relationship, her letters "torn-open" yet "unanswered." Hence "The bight is littered with old correspondences." ("Correspondences" recall also the earlier allusion to Baudelaire.) This is how Bishop's speaker sees the "little white boats"— she's transformed them into "letters" and, more importantly, what the letters themselves represent—that which is most likely unsalvageable. Note how the speaker's vision is colored by her emotional state of mind and being. That the "correspondences" are "old" suggests that the speaker, like the pelicans, worked ("like pickaxes") "unnecessarily hard" at a relationship but rarely came up with anything to show for it. Suddenly the other images of violence, and severing in particular, make better sense. The poem, this work, is all the speaker may have to show for her heartache.

To summarize thus far, notice the trajectory and movement of Bishop's poem: the poem opens on the detail of the water in the bight ("At low tide like this how sheer the water is") and moves, systematically, through numerous details and images, each colored by the speaker's unique perspective, to construct what appears to be much more than a simple physical landscape. We have to question the meaning of each detail or image and by answering those questions, we participate in creating the poem with the poet; the poet presents the materials, and the reader builds something with them.

As Bishop launches into the poem's close, notice that the dredge, absent for some time, returns. This detail is quickly transformed into an image, its sentiment reinforced, as it is juxtaposed against the poem's final lines: "All the untidy activity continues, / awful but cheerful." This final image suggests that the poem's speaker, much like the dredge and the pelicans, must continue to work despite her circumstances, despite disappointment, despite sometimes coming up with nothing to show for it. The image of the dredge, therefore, gains import and nuance. But what makes this ending both necessary and successful? For one, the ending is a surprise and, at the same time, provides the poem with a sense of counterbalance. The ending pulls against the poem's overall structure. "The Bight" is primarily constructed of details and images, and while the final two lines of the poem would still be considered detail (or description), the detail is one in which the speaker's emotional state is openly stated rather than hinted at through figurative language ("awful but cheerful"). It is also significant that Bishop ends the poem with adjectives, especially since adjectives have been used throughout the poem to both reveal the speaker's emotional state as well as the poem's underlying narrative. However, these adjectives are a surprise because the poem has taught us to expect limited access to the poem's speaker. It is this apparent shift in focus and direction that sends us back into the poem, to discover how the poem arrived at this ending, to make sense of it.

But, of course, the shift isn't sudden, we have all along been prepared for the ending by the poem's structure. "Awful but cheerful" might seem to be the only instance in which the speaker reveals her own ambivalent emotional state, but this shift is prepared for through the mention of Baudelaire—the suggestion that there are multiple ways of seeing an object, all based upon one's psychological or emotional state—as well as through the "torn-open, unanswered letters" and the "old correspondences" which further steep the poem in emotional tension. Each instance of figuration also serves as preparation for the poem's ending in that many of the images suggest struggle and work which reinforce that final "All the untidy activity continues."

Because we often read trying to anticipate where a poem is headed, counterbalancing the poem with its ending works to subvert our expectation. To end in an unexpected place is oddly satisfying and also prompts us reenter the poem if only in an effort to find out how the poet arrived there and, furthermore, why this place feels like the exactly right destination. The poem's ending shows that the poem is actually reliant upon all of its details, that none of the details are superfluous or extraneous. The poem inevitably leads its close. In the case of "The Bight," although the poem is largely structured utilizing non-discursive elements such as metaphor and simile, Bishop closes the poem rather discursively. Logically, the poem's ending feels like a natural progression from the details and images the poem presents. Any other ending for this poem may have been too predictable. Were there no sense of mystery, then what has been given is possibly too obvious; the poem risks becoming dull and uninteresting. "The Bight," however, provides clues, which are both engaging and delay the emotional reality of the poem's speaker until the end. Furthermore, the poem in its entirety actually mimics the "untidy" syntax of not only its first sentence, which delayed its subject and verb, but also its penultimate sentence ("Click. Click. Goes the dredge...") which also inverts its syntax. The poem could have easily ended after "marl" and, formally, complete itself with this syntactical repetition. But Bishop writes two additional lines. Why? Although the poem is formally complete, the life event, the cause, remains frighteningly "untidy" and "continues" indefinitely. Therefore, the poem wants to click shut and not click shut at once. There are no *formal* endings in life. Bishop understands this notion and her closure, the poem finished, as a result, serves as a kind of realization or acknowledgment of such.

Poetry Workshop

Thom Tammaro

SOME THOUGHTS ON POETRY WORKSHOPS AND THE WRITING LIFE

Early on in your writing life, you probably will be tempted—perhaps even invited—to join a poetry workshop, and I encourage you to consider doing so. But before you do, I'd like to put down a few thoughts for your consideration. If I did not believe anything could be gained by taking a poetry workshop, I would not have taught them for the past thirty-five years. But I do, so you must assume that I believe something can be gained by taking a writing workshop.

Exactly what that "something" is, is a little more difficult to pin down—like trying to pick up a bead of mercury with your fingers—perhaps "mercurial" is the word I am looking for? But let me try.

***

William Stafford, in his wonderful collection of essays titled *Writing the Australian Crawl: Views on the Writer's Vocation*, writes, "The literary world is a community in that one interchanges with others naturally and becomes an insider, not by deals or stealth, but by a natural engagement with the ongoing work of other writers, editors, and publishers." And I certainly think that poetry workshops are part of that larger community, part of "the writing life," as I like to call it.

A poetry workshop can be many things and come in a variety of configurations. For example, so much depends upon who is leading the workshop, as well as what your expectations and motivations are for taking a workshop. Ten workshop leaders may result in ten very different kinds of workshops. I know some workshop leaders who do not permit students to speak or critique manuscripts. Only the instructor is allowed to critique student manuscripts. Is that the kind of poetry workshop you want to join?

Before you sign up for a poetry workshop, you should ask yourself the following questions: "Why am I signing up for a poetry workshop?" "What do I want in a poetry workshop?" "Is this the poetry workshop I'm looking for?" And then take some time to answer those questions. Sometimes, it's only possible to answer these questions after sitting in on the first few meetings of a workshop, at which point you may choose to withdraw or continue. Poetry workshops are not for everyone. Walt Whitman never took a poetry workshop, nor did Emily Dickinson (though she did share her poems with her sister-in-law, Susan Gilbert Dickinson, who sometimes offered feedback). Maybe my poetry workshop instructional style is not what you are looking for. Maybe it is. I don't know. That would be for you to decide.

In the meantime, let me offer some general thoughts about the kind of poetry workshop that can be most helpful to a beginning writer.

- The poetry workshop instructor's job is not to make you a better writer—only you can do that for yourself. To improve as a writer, you must write. I guess I'm really talking about commitment here. Why bother if you're not committed to your writing?

- The goal of a poetry workshop should not be to make you write poems like the instructor's. (As an instructor, I can't imagine why anyone would want to write poems like mine!) Nevertheless, I know this happens. Let me be clear: success in a poetry workshop should not be measured or depend on your ability to write poems like the instructor's.

- A poetry workshop should not promote a certain form, style, trend of writing, or certain kind of poem. An instructor's bias and tastes will certainly surface occasionally—as will yours—but that's inevitable. But remember: they are just that, biases. I know a hundred people who like iced coffee and coffee-flavored ice cream. I don't. I've tried them. They're not my taste.

- The goal of a poetry workshop should not be to tell you if your poems are good or bad. Other people will surely do that for you as you venture into the public arena of the writing life. Telling you your work is good or bad will not make you a better writer; in fact, if you are told your poems are good it may encourage you to keep safe and stop you from experimenting. Likewise, if you're told your poems are bad, that may inspire you, out of revenge, to be a better writer.

- A poetry workshop instructor should read and listen to your poems and be guided by them to where they want to go, and then help you find ways of moving your poems—and you—in that direction. In fact, that should be the goal of all members of a workshop: to listen to each other's poems and find out where they want to go, *not where the instructor or the other workshop members want them to go.*

It's important to remember that when you send your poems out into the world, your name is the only name attached to your poems—not your instructor's name or another workshop participant's name. Bottom line is, you determine, in the end, how a poem grows and develops. Sometimes it may grow and develop because someone gave you good advice or feedback. It is important to listen. But in the end, it is crucial that you decide the path of your own poems.

Another bottom line: you are the final arbiter of your own work. After all the discussions, reflecting, revising, arguing, debating, revising, judging, critiquing, and more revising—you are the one who decides what your poem is or isn't going to be. Poets must learn to live with the poems they create. They have to learn to live in the world with their poems, with their names attached to them. You must claim ownership of your poems, and then say to your peers and instructors: "Thank you so much for being attentive to my work. I appreciate it. Now it's my time to decide what it is or isn't."

***

So, let me set down a few more thoughts about poetry workshops. Once again, I'm guided by Stafford's sense of creating a community of writers. A poetry workshop should provide you with the following: A time and place where you can gather with other serious, like-minded people who share some of the same values and passion for the art and craft of poetry and writing that you do. But will this make you a better poet? I don't know.

- A place where you can bring your ideas and poems for honest, careful consideration and discussion by intelligent people whose sole motivation is to make your poem—and theirs—the best poem it can be: clearer, stronger, and more effective in its communication. But will this make you a better poet? I don't know.

- An opportunity for you to learn from others and an opportunity for others to learn from you, for I firmly believe that we learn from each other, both in our successes and in our failures. But will this make you a better poet? I don't know.

- An opportunity to discover the way others perceive your work. But will this make you a better poet? I don't know.

- An opportunity to develop your writing discipline and increase your writing productivity, given the nature of the workshop and its requirements and ground rules. But will this make you a better poet? I don't know.

- To read more and read more widely—invariably you will be exposed to other poems and other writers—about the history, traditions, and current trends of poetry, and, consequently, be exposed to a variety of styles, forms, voices, techniques, theories, and poetics. When you enter the community of writing, you must remember that you are stepping into a living stream that has a long history—and an unknown destiny. When you enter the public stream, it's good to know who's gone before you and who's there now. But will this make you a better poet? I don't know.

- An opportunity to discover and reflect more about your own work—your style, your voice, your subject matter, your relationship with art and craft, your directions and inclinations—and to learn to accept, reject, alter and/or live with those discoveries if you choose to do so. But will this make you a better poet? I don't know.

The mansion of poetry is large, with many rooms on many floors. There is enough space to accommodate many. I am suspicious of those gatekeepers who would turn away potential residents. No room at the inn? For me, there is too much evidence out there that suggests otherwise. Stop by my office someday and I will show you my shelves of poetry anthologies and encourage you to browse through them to see the varieties of poetic experience.

Where you want to be in the community of writers, editors, publishers—and I would add "readers" to Stafford's list—is up to you. Why you want to become a member of this community is up to you. But wherever you want to be in the community, and for whatever reason you want to be there, I believe it is spacious enough to accommodate you. Whitman may just have well been speaking of poetry when he wrote, "I am large...I contain multitudes."

Will the above thoughts about poetry workshops and the writing life make you a better poet? I don't know. Like most things in life, there's no guarantee. You might have to join and participate in a poetry workshop to find out. And I encourage you and welcome you to do so. Consider this a personal invitation. No R.S.V.P. required.

Victoria L. Davis

REPRESENTATIVES OF ABUNDANCE

We tend to hoard the words that sustain us. Like obnoxious kids at a birthday party who claim all of the Snickers when the piñata bursts, we are quick to scoop up our mountains of poetry, guard them at all costs. But the fact is, that hoarding, that fiercely protective hiding, is the same as devouring our own words. And poetry is not a feast for one. It is a banquet, extravagant, ongoing, unweary in its welcoming. The chairs always have names on them, a place for everyone. The universal, yet intimate hospitality.

When we finally muster the guts to grace the conference table of a poetry workshop, it can sometimes feel like anything but a banquet. There's the one condescending guy who picks a fight over whether the plant referenced in a poem is native to its setting's climate (when it is). Not to mention that we are somehow strategically placed beside the award-winning poets whose starry strings of words make us feel desperately inadequate. Then there's the guy who thinks being referred to as another Walt Whitman is an insult. The girl who only gives her stamp of approval if a poem is as dark as her own. While we don't always feel quite like clinking glasses with the person across from us, to enter the business of poetry is to answer a call to generosity. We are all guests at the same banquet, some deliriously grateful, some outright shady. Nevertheless, the provision never slackens, and the plates are passed.

Everything is overflow, abundance, and we as poets are the stewards of that abundance. Dutifully, we extract fragments and parcel in them the wholeness of things. We can show you the moment that is telling of a life, the kiss telling of a love. The whisper that embodies a conversation. We seek out these representatives, however small, and become their clumsy representatives ourselves. This filling of shoes does not go untripped. There will be critique, some constructive, some of another variety. We'll be accused of cliché.

Of leaving too much mystery, of not having enough. But finding ourselves in the slimiest layer of someone else's slush pile is better than the alternative of speechlessness. If we are criticized, it won't be for the passivity of silence. Community thrives on exchange, and it is only through sharing that we are able to do the telling that our throats ache and hands cramp to accomplish.

In my own first workshop experience, I remember the slow trickling of the realization that my work was not only going to be read, but *studied.* Up to that point, when I thought of studying poetry, it had always been the work of established greats, distant and hazy figures of the past. For so long, they didn't seem like real people to me. There was a certain shock that accompanied my first time hearing a recording of Sylvia Plath. Played in one of my classes, it was a reading of her legendary poem, "Daddy." I can still hear those jarring lines, feel the weight of the images, all expressed by that rich, throaty voice. The somehow startling combination of the poet's written words with her own vocal chords, distinct. Doing justice. I had studied the words on a page, but Sylvia Plath had never seemed more real to me than in that moment. It was as if she stood in front of me. Knowable.

And I thought about her community. Who sat across from her? Who wrote the notes in her margins? Crossed out her words? I thought about the mentors, the influences that she credited. Theodore Roethke, how his work makes me stop in my tracks, just as she did when confronted by the same words. And finally, I got it. *We are part of the same community.* Roethke, Plath, the whole lot. Myself included. And yes, you, my far-off friend with this book in your hands. The table gatherings, the dimly lit readings, the smallest circles. Conduits of influence, every one of us. When we are willing to be studied, that's when we wake up the growth.

So when the day of your first poetry workshop finally arrives, you may guard that shared printer in the library, willing it to spit out the copies of your poems before you change your mind. Then, you'll feel it: a unique sense of a collective effort, a vibrant culmination of influences and inspiration that helped you come into your own, affirmed, efficient. As you feel the warmth of those pages, see your words in print, inked, voiced—for a moment, you will feel like your own little publishing house. And in the next breath, you will realize that you are exactly that. You wrote. Printed. And welcomed others to the table.

Natalie Homer

ON FINDING YOUR READERS: HOW ARTISTIC SENSIBILITY AFFECTS POETRY WORKSHOPS

Within poetry workshops, there is an important principle to keep in mind: not everyone is your reader, and, likewise, you are not everyone's. In other words, you are not going to be able to offer helpful feedback to everyone in the class/group, and not everyone will provide helpful feedback to you. The reason for this depends largely on style and sensibility. A writer who favors a clear narrative arc in a poem may not be the best reader for a language-driven, lyric poet (and vice versa). Someone who believes the purpose of poetry is to provide depth and insight may not find value in humorous poetry. A poet inclined toward the surreal may fail to see any imagination in realistic poems, and so on.

Anyone who has been part of a writing group or has taken creative writing workshops quickly finds that there are a few key people whose feedback can be trusted—these readers know what you're aiming for with your work, and their comments help you push the poem to be the best it can be. Many others may offer general help—their feedback allows you to see overall consensuses and patterns, e.g. if most people were confused by a certain line or interpreted something in a way different than intended, etc. And still others may not offer much in the way of helpful feedback at all. Sometimes this is due to external factors—perhaps the person does not want to be in the class, is unmotivated, or facing personal difficulties outside of the workshop. Sometimes, however, the factors that cause this are unavoidable, and a matter of differing artistic temperaments. This means that a reader may be able to offer insightful feedback to one writer, while simultaneously not being able to give satisfactory feedback to a different writer.

In workshops I've been a part of, whether as the instructor or student, there are some recurring patterns I've noticed:

1) **The Ideal Reader**: this person perceives the writer's intentions for the poem, makes astute observations about form and content, provides practical and helpful advice, and inspires the writer to move forward with revision.

2) **The Helpful Critic**: this person's comments sting a little—they take a blunt approach and will be completely honest—but ultimately their advice is useful and will push the poem forward.

3) **The Unhelpful Critic**: like the Helpful Critic, this person's workshop comments are blunt, but they criticize without offering advice or suggestions. (For example, scribbling "unclear" in the margin with no further explanation.)

4) **The Space Cadet**: this reader means well, but misses the mark. Often they will misinterpret the poem to be about a subject completely unrelated/unintended, and will offer advice based on that understanding. Or, if they do understand the poem, they might try to push the poem in a direction that is contrary to what the writer is working toward.

5) **The Optimist**: the Optimist only provides positive feedback. Their intentions are good, but by being overly encouraging and not suggesting any changes, they do both the poem and the writer a disservice.

6) **The Airhead**: comments from the Airhead tend to consist mainly of hearts, underlines, exclamation points, and check marks. They rarely provide negative feedback, instead opting for generalized words of encouragement such as "great job," and/or smiley faces. But unlike the Optimist, their comments have no depth and are dutiful rather than well-intentioned.

This list is, of course, reductive, but it helps to illustrate some of the recurring patterns that emerge in workshops. An important caveat is that (with the exception of the Airhead) readers don't always stay confined to one category. Often, who a person is as a reader can depend on what it is they're reading. This reinforces the main idea that as a writer, you may have different people within a workshop who will be *your* readers, and you may serve as the Ideal Reader to certain writers.

In workshops I've taken, I tend to gravitate toward poems that make narrative sense, yet are not quite linear. Poems that use language in interesting and musical ways. Poems that reward multiple readings. Poems that provide emotional resonance or insight. It is for these poems that I'm able to be an Ideal Reader—or at least a Helpful Critic.

On the other hand, there are times when I fall into less satisfactory categories. An example is when I respond to poems that privilege language over meaning. Here is an example of a few lines I composed imitating this style:

> i've made a list of every word for swan. my mother's coffee burns
> her thighs
> & in a warehouse somewhere a man is loosening his corset. surely
> by now i've
> come to realize how ocean horses hatch blue in apothecary light.

Again, this example may be reductive—but the point is to show that not all styles of poetry lend themselves well to all readers. Though I don't care for this style of verse, it certainly has a place in modern poetry and is widely published. There's nothing inherently wrong with it—yet I, as a reader, can't comment as helpfully because I don't understand its aims, and am more likely to be an Unhelpful Critic or a Space Cadet in my responses, getting too caught up in what doesn't make sense to me, rather than trying to help the poem be what the writer intends.

A kind of mutual humility is necessary when interacting with poets who aren't each other's readers. On one hand, if your poem is being workshopped, knowing that some people in the crowd just *aren't* your readers is liberating; you don't have to please everybody, and if they never "get" what you're going for, it might just be due to a stylistic difference. On the other hand, if you find yourself thinking you may not be someone's reader, know that just because you don't understand or enjoy a poem, doesn't mean it doesn't have worth. There are exceptions to both of these scenarios, of course, but the general idea is to weigh the workshop comments given and received, acknowledging that reader sensibility is a factor.

Ultimately this leads to two takeaways. The first is to understand that when receiving comments on your workshop poems, it may be helpful to identify and prioritize who is giving you the most helpful feedback—they are *your* readers and essentially, the audience you write to. The second takeaway is to recognize when you aren't someone's reader, and to do everything you can to still be as helpful as possible. This might require you to put your preferences and tastes on the back burner and examine the poem in a more analytical frame of mind, evaluating what it is and what it aims to be. The primary question should be: is it successful at accomplishing what it sets out to do?

C. Kubasta

WHEN WORKSHOP DOESN'T WORK

In high school, my creative writing teacher submitted some of my poems (unbeknownst to me) to one of those weekend college-recruitment workshops. I knew I was going to go to college, and maybe I would major in English, or Creative Writing (although the old ACT report I recently found identified Theology as my likely major). At any rate, I was thrilled to be accepted: to spend all day on a Saturday with other *serious writers* (as I already considered myself) was *very exciting*. I picked out a Writer Outfit. I may have had a Writer Binder—I know I printed my poems on fancy paper, creamy heavy stock, with a little tooth.

During that Saturday, I got some of the best feedback I've ever gotten—even as I went on to major in Creative Writing, to an MFA program, to participate in writers' groups and retreats, to find insightful readers and writers later in my career. The college professor looked at my work a long time; there was no small amount of squinting—at me, at the pages. He listened to me read and was mostly quiet throughout workshop, but at the end of the day he handed me an envelope with a small handwritten note. It said, "Your work takes risks, not all of them successful."

Likely there were also copies of my work in that envelope; probably there were notes in the margins of my poems. Perhaps he'd made suggestions about line endings, crossed out words and lines where I repeated myself, asked questions, maybe noted a strong word choice or image—the kind of incremental feedback-along-the-edges that most workshops traffic in, but all I remember is the above sentence.

Take risks, not all of them successful.

More recently, I received my favorite rejection note from a journal. It said, "One of our editors loved your work, but the other hated it, so we're going to pass."

I tell my students now, regardless of whether we're talking about writing or anything else that it's better to be interesting than pretty. I tell my niece the same thing.

It's better (I reason) to evoke a strong reaction—in art, in life, in fashion—than to be conventional & pleasing. If everyone (or most people) approve of what you're doing, you're not really doing anything.

As a beginning poet, or a mid-career poet, or maybe as anything less than a universally recognized fabulous MacArthur Genius Award-winning poet (and maybe even then), there will be many voices (subtle or not) urging you to soften the edges of your poem, to make the lines more conventional, the transitions less abrupt, the imagery more inviting or more consistent, to work within a more recognizable convention, to have a style, to stick with that style, to follow the rules, to identify your reader, to write for that reader, to think about a million things other than saying what it is you're trying to say.

Say what it is you're trying to say.

It seems strange to talk about "the market" for poetry (given the oft-talked about disappearing readership), but the concerns of that "market" do affect us. Will anyone publish this? Is it too long? Too short? Too garish? Too strange? Does it fit on a page? Does it look like a "poem"?

During an MFA workshop in grad school, I wrote a poem that was absolutely unreadable; it was the weirdest thing I'd ever written. When it came my time to read, I demurred—I said I couldn't. "Just read it," the professor said, low-voiced, all direct eye contact. He was right: its very unreadableness (its conventional unreadableness) is what made it a good poem.

It was a breakthrough. That poem went on to win an Editor's prize, the first money large enough to report on a tax return—it was an ungainly thing. Prosey & prosaic, lines littered with slashes for words that interchange but cannot replace each other fully. It was a full-throated exploration of the way gender & identity change the nature of the earliest of our sexual experiences, the spectrum of consent & power. I almost didn't even bring it to workshop because it was so different than anything my peers were doing; I thought the poem might be too fragile to withstand the workshop's polite silence and half-hearted tinkering.

The problem with workshop is that sometimes the workshop becomes its own organism, speaking with one voice, and that voice is temperance. It urges you to sand off the barbs in your work, calling them imperfections. But the problem with a too-smooth surface is that there is no friction, no purchase for anyone or anything.

In classes now, when my students say they don't know how to read something, I know they're on to something good.

If what you're writing seems too strange to be written, or to be read, you're writing exactly what you should be writing.
There are lots of kinds of risk—there are the formal risks, sure, but there's also the poem that you shouldn't write because it's too dear; it hurts to write it, to read it, to share it, to publish it. Your finger falters on the "post" button, on the "share" button. You need an obscure place, a small audience. Maybe you even have a stack of poems to read only when you know no one you know will be there. OK. Fine. But if the writing of those poems gives you the heart-pounding, sweating, blood-racing, akin-to-sex feeling, that's the poem you should be writing. But you know that—if this has happened, you know the way words have power, the way utterance makes things, like you're a real life heroine in a fairy tale, wishing things into being in the world of your creation.

Write poems that are uncanny lumpen things—the kind of poems that wait at the edges of parking lots, by the side of the road. Someone will pull their car over to get a closer look, circling the thing, giving it a wide berth, knowing teeth and claws may be half-hidden.

Write poems with teeth & claws, half-hidden.
When I was seventeen, I misread the feedback I got from Prof. X at that Saturday workshop. I thought he said, "Your work takes risks, most of them successful." I reasoned that he felt obliged to word it the other way as a kindness—he wanted to warn me about the dangers of the world, about being too bright and too talented, about trying to blow things up and tear apart the rules, about creating a non-pattern of ragged edges to talk about our lives that are all-too-often ragged edges, about thinking I was some kind of love-child of e.e. cummings and Anne Sexton. I thought I was mud-luscious, my blood running like roller skates. (We were all young once…)

Fair enough, kind sir, if kindness it was.

But my favorite students are the ones who argue with me: vociferously and un-endingly, even when I think they're dead wrong. Argue away. Do the opposite of what I suggest. Continue constructing a muscular kind of beauty out of the dross of the world, insisting in your own forms that you can make and break something new out of this language we continue to pre-wash and rinse until it comes out the other end—flattened & denuded. Words mean and matter—you make them do this.

My favorite poems are the kind that affix to my belly like a screw with T-handle for extra torque. The good poem sinks in, a quarter turn each time, roiling. You can't accomplish that if you're careful, or judicious, or worried about the effect on the reader—you have to write what matters and take the risk.

Write a poem that torques.

Kevin Pilkington

A POET'S ADVICE TO YOUNG WRITERS

Although I have been teaching writing classes for most of my adult life, I never took a writing class on the undergraduate or graduate levels or had a writing mentor. My writing teachers were on the bookshelves—I learned to write through reading. To this day, I tell students that the best teachers are the writers you read. I have always felt that writing teachers save students time by telling them who to read, and usually not what to put into their writing but what to take out. The poet Robert Lowell said, "Learning to write is learning what to leave out." Hemingway said it another way: "Every writer should have a built-in shit detector."

On a very basic level, writing workshops are time savers by showing students what not to do in their writing so they have more time to work on what will enhance whatever genre they are working in. If I knew my life was going to turn this way, I certainly would have enrolled in an MFA program. I am sure I would have matured faster as a writer and achieved more goals that much sooner. However, studying literature, mostly classical, on the undergraduate and graduate levels was invaluable to me both as a human being and as a writer. I can't imagine how my writing would have progressed without reading Sidney who tells us in his Defence of Poesy written in 1595, "The aim of poetry is to teach and delight." This is a phrase I still keep on my writing desk.

At Georgetown I first came into contact with Horace's "Art of Poetry," probably the first and best creative writing handbook, although in reality it is a letter poem. Later I was introduced to the visionary lyricism of William Butler Yeats, a poet whose poems I have read almost every week since then. Studying great literature seeps into your own writing, as I hope it did mine, through osmosis. However, I don't write poetry in traditional or given forms;

I chose to write in open or organic forms since, like many contemporary poets, I want my poems to sound closer to everyday speech and flourish in their own time and place.

I believe Sarah Lawrence College where I teach was the first or certainly one of the first to offer workshops for undergraduates taught by professional writers. There are now many fine undergraduate writing programs across the country. I would recommend to any aspiring writer who is looking to major in writing not to apply if they have stories to tell in prose or poetry. Only apply if you truly love language. Then you will succeed and thrive.

Do your research; see what writers are on the faculty and are actually teaching classes. Many high-profile writers only teach sporadically even though a given school will use their names as recruiting tools. Visit the school you are interested in and visit classes to make sure it is the right fit. Majoring or having a concentration in writing enables you to think critically and to communicate your thoughts clearly and effectively, which is beneficial across the curriculum and prepares you for a variety of careers once you graduate.

For those considering an MFA I would offer some of the same advice as above—make sure you research programs thoroughly and speak to students in the program who will offer truthful insights into its strengths or weaknesses. Remember the best programs create an atmosphere that allows you the time to explore and concentrate on your craft, taught by professional writers in the classroom who are not just names on a catalog, writers who love and are passionate about language. I can't think of time better spent than paying homage to language.

As a writing coordinator at Sarah Lawrence College, I work with undergraduate and graduate students to help them become more competent and confident writers. I work in one-on-one conferences with student writers of all levels and disciplines on a variety of assignments and projects, such as short class papers and semester or year-long research papers known as conference papers here at the College. I also work with graduate poetry students on their poems and as their thesis advisor. What I find most satisfying is helping students discover the power of language and all its possibilities, helping them discover their own voices, becoming astute critical thinkers, and observing how their writing changes and strengthens over time.

Daniel Bosch

COVER LETTER: TOWARD A NEW CREATIVE WRITING

Writers who are truly honest about art and pedagogy admit that most of the time both end in failure. At the Bauhaus this fact was bedrock, not pillow-talk: the curriculum was designed around honest play with materials.

I believe a Bauhaus-type approach might help lead to needed reform in the teaching of creative writing. So in a cover letter I submitted in application for the directorship of an MFA program, I proposed a play-based curriculum focused on fundamental "materials," mandatory cross-genre study, eschewal of contemporary readings, avoidance of cults of personality, use of the full range of grades, un-plugging of the phrase "terminal" degree, and more.

Explicit identifications of the college have been XXXXXX'd out.

November XX, 2013
Chair of Department Search Committee
Department of Creative Writing, XXXXXX

To Whom It May Concern,

I hereby submit my application for the position of Chair of the newly re-structured Department of Creative Writing at XXXXXX. A curriculum vitae and supporting materials follow this letter.

The Department of Creative Writing deserves hearty congratulations on the occasion of its rebirth. I can imagine that the process of bringing together three programs with separate if similar faculties, histories, and practices was long, difficult, and at times delicate. Yet I can also imagine that the negotiations leading to these programs' integration raised important questions about writing and pedagogy and the specific identities of the different sub-disciplines, and that the single faculty which has emerged has benefited from thorough articulation of its strengths, its weaknesses, and its visions. As I will explain, it is in part this moment that attracts my application.

Few creative writing programs have shown XXXXXX's courage in taking strong action to review and revise the way they do things. (Some of your faculty may soon write the stories that trace and shape your recent history.) Yet whatever particular historical causes led XXXXXX to undertake a restructuring of its Department of Creative Writing, I do not think it can be fully explained as a local phenomenon. Literary artists have been teaching writing in American colleges and universities for over a century—a period of great and accelerating technological and social (if not artistic) change. The expansion of PhD-granting (as opposed to MFA-granting) programs; the preference among undergraduates to enroll in Creative Writing courses rather than in English Literature courses (and the shifting budgetary terrains these preferences may prefigure); the breaking of color bars at many institutions that had kept so many faculties relatively homogeneous; the explosion of non-print publishing opportunities (some good, some not so good); the emergence of networks of writers that span continents and oceans rather than towns; among other factors, these have encouraged writers connected to the academy to rethink the roles a program in creative writing can and ought to play in sustaining literary arts and artists. Many of these writers believe, as I do, that the education of literary artists can be more rigorously artistic and less-inflected by academic scholarship, and that it can make more sense with regard to the stakes at play in authentic artistic endeavors—that the education of writers should be both more artistic and more literary.

So, though my application for the position of Chair begins as a celebration of the steps XXXXXX has already taken, I want here above all to encourage the Department of Creative Writing to seize this moment to embrace further and even more radical change, in keeping with a long-range goal of establishing the soundest, most exciting, and most effective Department of Creative Writing in history, a community of literary artists and students of literary art which is committed not only to its own reformulation, but to discovery and implementation of powerful pedagogies and policies that will lead to the reform of the entire discipline. I want to encourage the Department of

Creative Writing at XXXXXX to refuse to recreate itself in the image of past programs in creative writing.

What alternative vision might I propose for the Department? Part of the joy of working together with a group of self-conscious artists to discover the means by which future generations of artists might best be trained has to do with the fact that such work is co-discovery, and no such curriculum can be described in advance of the pedagogical experiments which will produce it. Nonetheless, certain principles have been articulated upon which such an experimental approach might be founded, and we all know from our own experiences how various creative writing pedagogies in wide use for the past sixty years succeed and fail. Have you seen the diagram (designed by Johannes Itten in 1922) which is a visual inscription of the shape of the Bauhaus curriculum (in German and in English translation, below)? It achieves a greater clarity and wholeness than could be achieved in twenty pages of prose, and it can guide those who would think forward toward a profoundly new and engaging pedagogy for literary artists.

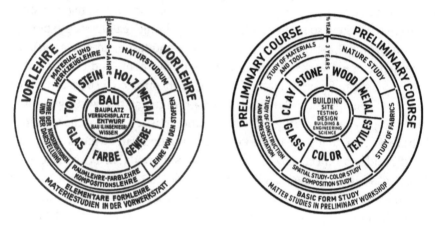

(Johannes Itten, in Gropius, 1922)

Time in the Bauhaus diagram moves from the perimeter to the center, from fundamental studies to informed artistic practices. The outer ring is a ½ *Jahr* (or six-month) Preliminary Course in Materials, a student's initiation into fundamental practices regarding the most basic "stuff" of art—in the case of literature, sound, word, syntax, image, narrative, character, song, time, and silence—without which initiation no strong conversations can be had, and little substantial progress toward mastery is likely to be made.

Next the Bauhaus curriculum demanded three years of intense coursework under different artist-teachers in such areas as presentation and design; color, composition, and space; and "nature study," (in literary training, these might be courses in Book & E-Book; Space on Stage and in Story; Prologues; Lines; Low Comedy; Images; and Writing from Life) each segment of which was conceived as necessary preliminary training and thus the basis for later workshop courses in the distinct practices associated with materials such as Glass, Metal, Wood, Stone, etc. (In a literary curriculum on this model, the penultimate inner ring might consist of seminars or workshops in specific sub-genres such as Personal Essay, Three-Act Play, Realistic Prose Narrative, Verse Monologue.) At the heart and center of this diagram, as in a literary curriculum modeled upon it, is one or two years of focused execution of minor and major projects, a hard-earned chance for the artist-in-training to use their skills and to "Build" with the full support of the arrayed cohort of instructors and fellow "journeymen." In a literary training program, I would hope, this final and most-demanding portion of the curriculum would lead to something distinct from what is currently called a "thesis." A better term might be borrowed from medieval and renaissance guilds—in German, *"Meisterstuck"*—with the understanding that any built object which satisfied the requirement for a "masterpiece" admitted its maker to an adult role in the family of makers. Certification following completion of such a curriculum should not be called a "terminal" degree, because everybody in the family of makers knows that to be an artist is to be humbled nearly every day with regard to one's skill and lack of skill and the recalcitrance of one's materials. To have built a masterpiece means only that one's years as an apprentice and a journeyman are behind one. Horace said it: *"ars longa, vita brevis."* Chaucer translated it, "the life so short, the art so long to learn." No good comes from promulgating or participating in arts training programs that pretend otherwise.

Though individual students will vary in talent, substantial achievement in *ars* takes so damn *longa* because it involves the acquisition of skills which are hard to learn. To pursue art is to confront (hourly, weekly, monthly, for decades at a stretch) failure. The everyday experience of working artists is that they routinely fail to hit their mark, to draw the best line, to choose the stronger word, to sound the right note, and these are the stakes that make success in art so satisfying. The admission of this fact can and should liberate the artist-in-training to play the harder and thus learn the more in an atmosphere of passionate experimentation. Imagine, with me, how it would feel to teach as part of a curriculum that offers students neither a fanciful vision of immediate literary (as opposed to popular) success nor a quasi-psychological journey toward some sort of self-revelation (like that described years ago as central to Professor Graham's pedagogy at the Iowa Writers Workshop), but a reality principle: a literary artist's joys must be found in serious play with words, sentences, images, characters, stories, etc. Imagine, with me, building a curriculum which frames students' play in direct assessment of their perfectly normal and very much expected failure to demonstrate that they have acquired necessary skills, a curriculum which is honest about the long road ahead and has no truck with false currencies like inflated grades that jolly students along. Implicit in the Itten diagram is the notion that there are many specific materials, tools, operations, and vocabularies which must be conveyed to apprentices by experts in as comprehensive a manner as possible, and that students will as a matter of course fail to demonstrate substantial proficiency in techniques which are crucial to further achievement. Advancement through such a curriculum could not be earned by mere accrual of credits.

The specificity of the Bauhaus curriculum is obvious when compared to the vague curricula posted by almost all American creative writing programs, for example the program stipulated by the course catalog from XXXXXX (traced out in part below), which is typical. The sketchiness of such descriptions suggests, contrary to fact, that there is little known about how writers have constructed great literary works, or that if such knowledge exists, it is best not to discuss the building blocks of poems, plays, and stories, and how artists handle them, in too much detail:

Poetry Workshop: Intermediate

Through in-class writing exercises, the reading of model poems, and discussion of student work, students are encouraged to produce poetry of greater sophistication. Familiarity with work of notable poets is strongly encouraged.

Craft Seminar

Rotating topics craft class. Students read literature of specific periods and movements in order to generate poetry (and hybrid writing forms) based on these reading assignments. Craft Seminars that have been offered in past semesters include Poetry Translation, Hybrid Poetics, and Literary College (*sic*).

Craft Seminar

Rotating topics craft class. Students read literature of specific periods and movements in order to generate poetry (and hybrid writing forms) based on these reading assignments.

Graduate Thesis Work

One-on-one intensive revision of the book-length thesis manuscript and/or critical essay required for graduation with an MFA in Poetry. Repeatable once.

(XXXXXX Creative Writing Program Website, 2013)

Vagueness like this serves programs in creative writing that are built around the development and exploitation of cults of personality in "popular" professors and in "star" students (the ones who have "it" when they walk in the door). In such programs students sign up for courses "*with* Professor (name)," not courses "*in* (technique)". Such programs consider it inappropriate to require Professor (name) to address any particular subject matter; they also typically abstain from requiring students to acquire any particular skill or fluency. Might such policies stem from the lack of criticality suggested by the wording above, where at a relatively early stage of their coursework (e.g. "intermediate"), students are expected to be producing "poetry"? A more realistic view of writing must allow that the very best literary artists mainly fail to write anything remotely so good as "poetry."

How many of us who teach creative writing are so good at either writing or teaching, or work among faculties that are so supremely accomplished, that our professing of what is in fact a craft ought to be given such a free range? I love Housman for declaring he "could no more define poetry than a terrier can define a rat." But Housman's wit does not imply that we ought not try to say clearly what we think we are trying to do in a course of study. And if associate and full professors, with all our faultiness, are allowed and encouraged to deliver vaguely defined courses which are not integrated into an understanding of how they function in the education of artists, should we not find it concerning that such ill or loosely defined courses are the bases upon which graduate student teaching fellows build courses in creative writing for the non-majors? Look at how Josef Albers described the effective but modest work done in a Bauhaus preliminary course:

> First we seek contact with material.... Instead of pasting it, we will put paper together by sewing, buttoning, riveting, typing, and pinning it; it other words, we fasten it in a multitude of ways. We will test the possibilities of its tensile and compression-resistant strength. In doing so, we do not always create "works of art," but rather experiments; it is not our ambition to fill museums; we are gathering experience. (Albers)

Why should teachers of writing too not aspire to such humble, clear, and useful foci for coursework? And to such an owning up to what we really accomplish? Ask your colleagues around the country: a year in a typical program's history is recalled by the names of the students who were reputedly the most promising, not by reference to any particularly interesting approach or work which was developed in a program's courses. Then imagine, with me, working in a Department of Creative Writing which will conscientiously admit that its students may fail to produce excellent writing, but that *never* fails to articulate, with the greatest specificity and precision possible, its highest goals and standards—a program which tells time by the excitement generated by the work of learning to write. Imagine, with me, working in a community of artists committed to striving, aided by continual co-observation and collaboration, to occasionally reaching its highest goals and standards, even if only with the tips of our fingernails.

The lack of clearly articulated technique-, skill-, and material-based curriculum like that of the Bauhaus has contributed to at least one further unfortunate tendency among creative writing programs: a kind of amblyopia regarding the work that ought to be used as examples of excellence. When students study "with a professor" rather than "in a craft," when creative writing courses by design do not focus on conveyance of knowledge about materials and testing of specific and well-defined techniques, the reading lists for courses end up emphasizing contemporary authors' work, especially writing produced in the past 20 or 30 years, and especially work by friends or acquaintances of the professors, who return the favor by assigning acquaintances' books in their own courses. Professors tenured on the basis of their own books, which are not very strong, tend to "teach" contemporary work, in no small part because it is so humbling to continually confront the strongest work from the past, and even though this confrontation is thrilling. Yet students of literary art thrive best when they are constantly immersed in the very best poems, plays, essays, novels, folk tales, libretti, short stories, etc. In Spain there are pigs that eat only chestnuts; the taste of their roasted flesh is fabled. Fifteen years following *any given now*, however, critics no longer sing the praises of contemporary writers whose work tastes like the not very strong work that was fashionable in *any given then*. Let our students read literature if they would write it! Let them engage Dickinson before Dickman. (Pick one!) Let them interrogate Lessing (pick one!) before Lasky! Let them cry over *The Sorrows of Young Werther* before the letters of Wenderoth! And while we're at it, won't students learn how to do really interesting work all the faster when they are liberated from programs that require them to take workshops which focus entirely on forced drafts by writers who have not yet acquired strong skills?

Today's academy talks a lot about how it values "interdisciplinary work," perhaps especially with regard to the arts. But most connective and genre-crossing "work" in the academy is allowed only after an individual practitioner has been induced to shut out for six to ten years any noise coming from other departments. A strong training program in the literary arts must avoid siloing its most experienced students: this deep generic specialization expresses a relatively recent and fundamental misunderstanding of the history of literary composition, which has always been most alive when it is inflected by multiple approaches. The Itten diagram bodies forth the inescapably interdisciplinary nature of the Bauhaus curriculum, which is perhaps the single characteristic most responsible for the incredibly innovative work of its artist-teachers and students. Gropius and Kandinsky and Feininger and Albers and Albers and Itten and the rest understood that to struggle with any particular medium is likely to yield lessons useful in preparing to struggle with another medium, that artists who have been trained to work with and to imagine in glass will make more interesting and compelling art in wood, plaster, and steel.

The same wisdom is applicable to training in the literary arts. Imagine, with me, a department that set its student writers immediately at the confluence of the three major literary forms, Verse, Prose, and Playwriting, so that each young artist faces the challenge of each form armed with the best practices of the other forms. No matter how certain a young artist is that she was born to be a novelist, she will become a stronger literary artist if she grasps the fundamental dynamics of composition in verse, in prose, and for the stage (or screen).

The literary arts, inextricably tied to the word, to time, and to silence, share perhaps even more than the various plastic and visual arts. Plato wrote the world's most powerful philosophy in dialogue form. (He wrote lyric poems, too.) Emerson's work in verse nurtured his work in the prose essay. *Faust* is a stronger play because Goethe wrote novels and lyrics. Chekhov wasn't diddling around with short fiction; his mastery of story-writing is inextricable from his mastery of playwriting. Soyinka's work in poetry and memoir has explicated and undergirded his theatrical vision. Hughes' "Simple" stories are not simpler-minded because of his work on an *avant-garde* "Weary Blues." Beckett's prose plays and novels reverse the sonic density that animates some of his poems. Hardy's architectural fiction was the charrette of his success as a lyric poet. Borges' and Bishop's incredibly powerful prose fictions are not the products of minds which have been temporarily distracted from poetry in verse, they are the products of minds and hearts that enter into fundamental productive dialogue with and have learned to exploit one form when they write in another. As the short list of artists above demonstrates, there is no sound basis whatsoever for the idea that isolated training in a single genre leads to literary excellence; in my opinion, training in one genre at the expense of others is a partial cause of some of the weaker tendencies in 20th-century American literature.

When artists-in-training begin with foundations in many media and are consistently asked to work in several genres at the same time, as they were at

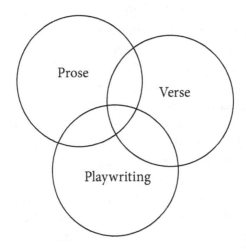

the Bauhaus, they become, through actual need, synthesizers and translators. In such literary training novelists would explain to poets how their narratives work or don't work; a playwright's account of a character's development would become the basis for a short story writer's radical reconception of her protagonist; inspired by a monologue by a poet-colleague, an essayist would turn, in his sixth paragraph, to a passage in verse. Translation and creative mis-translation have been, for millennia, the intensest workshops of literary autodidacts. This fact ought to be put at or near the center of the pedagogical apparatus through a required course in (assisted) translation. But such experimentation has been discouraged by American creative writing programs, usually via an argument that the translations produced by students in creative writing programs wouldn't be any good! Here again a lack of criticality forces a missed opportunity, and provides further evidence, if it were needed, of the strangeness of American creative writing program design. (As if students' "own" apprentice writing was generally any good!) Such an argument misses the point of work in translation, through which even fumbling hands can begin to take apart and re-assemble a superbly constructed object.

I have held here that most writing fails, so I embrace the likely failure of this letter—and my application. Yet I hope that I have succeeded in interesting you in something better and more important than my chutzpah. XXXXXX need not let set and harden the floor it has poured for its new Department. The discipline of Creative Writing needn't proceed as it has proceeded so far, and lots of practitioners—I daresay at least some members of your Department—know this from lived experience. The discipline doesn't yet try hard enough to foster the production of truly excellent literary artistry. Yet a truly ambitious Department of Creative Writing can look forward not only to a good faith relation to fundamental truths of artistic creation, but to leadership by example. Such an audacious program would earn its leadership by the production of a significant portion of the excellent literary artists of the late 21st century. And in the much nearer future it would begin to attract, on the basis of its principles and its honest and demanding programs, the most discerning and desirable would-be literary artists.

I have used the Bauhaus curriculum as a prompt to help me put forth some principles that I believe should be on the table in any strong training program in the literary arts. Let me close with an outline of policies which I would argue for if I were appointed Chair of the Department of Creative Writing:

- Development of skill- and material-based curriculum with detailed course descriptions and explicitly stated required outcomes
- Mandatory cross-genre study with no "major" decision until late in second year
- Required coursework in Playwriting and Literary Translation
- All artist-teachers use the full range of grades from A to F
- Artist-teachers agree to discourage students from embracing the idea that literary composition is a form of self-discovery or therapy
- All artist-teachers and graduate students observe other artist-teachers' and graduate students' courses on rotating basis
- Tenure-track artist-teachers teach all undergraduate courses with graduate students assisting
- No courses should be *based on* student works (though they may include student work); individual feedback should be given through individual communication (email and conferences)
- No more than one in ten courses should be *based on* writing produced in the last twenty years (though courses may include such recently produced work)

- The four journals at XXXXXX ought to be combined into one ambitious professional-level literary arts journal aimed at a public readership and an active role in literary life, to be staffed by faculty and students
- The city of XXXXXX, its neighborhoods, newspapers, museums, magazines, libraries, schools and universities, ought to be engaged as a working laboratory for literary artists in training

Won't such a list of policies provide a lot to talk about? I promise that in person I am not nearly so long-winded as I have been in this letter—indeed, I am a careful, critical listener. I appreciate your taking the time to read what I've put down here. I would be delighted to hear from you regarding any questions you have about my application.

Good luck with your search for a new Chair! I am

Sincerely yours,

WORKS CITED

Itten, Johannes. Diagram of the Bauhaus curriculum first published by Walter Gropius, 1922. Lithograph. 20.2 x 29.3 cm. From Walter Gropius, *Satzungen Staatliches Bauhaus in Weimar* (Statutes of the State Bauhaus in Weimar), July 1922. Bauhaus Typography Collection, 1919–1937. The Getty Research Institute, 850513. © 2019 Artists Rights Society (ARS), New York / VG Bild-Kunst, Bonn.

Quoted Material from the XXXXXX Creative Writing Program website. Accessed on November XX, 2013 and presented verbatim.

Albers, Josef. As quoted in "Creative Education," in *The Bauhaus: Weimar, Dessau, Berlin, Chicago*, edited by Hans Maria Wingler, published by The MIT Press, Cambridge, Massachusetts, 1969, 142.

James B. Nicola

BLOOD, SWEAT AND GENIUS: ALTERNATE PATHS TO POETRY

Poets are born from persons in all sorts of ways, and at any time of life. Whether you are 21, 51, or 81, if you feel you want to be, or *have* to be, or even *are* a poet, you might feel daunted by the time and tuition of the seemingly requisite graduate degree in creative writing. For you, I have good news: William Shakespeare never got one. Nor did Tennyson, Byron, Keats, Shelly, or either of the Brownings. They were all English, of course.

What about American poets? Of Emily Dickinson, Walt Whitman, and Robert Frost, the one who got a graduate degree in creative writing was— why, none of them. None of them even graduated from college.

An MFA, while a worthy credential for teaching at the college level, does not guarantee that you'll be a writer. Telling an Irishman to get one would be like telling a bird to study aerodynamics.

Writing as career or pastime will demand certain aptitudes and attitudes, but there are many paths outside of academia where you, like the poets mentioned above, might acquire and develop them.

***

In his Lifetime Achievement Oscar video presentation (2003), Peter O'Toole said:

> Any good actor will tell you that the common denominator is private study, for months if necessary, so every nuance, every phrase, is considered and thought out well in advance.

Who might serve as such a coach for the writer? Once upon a time, it might have been the editor.

The movie *Genius* (2016) focuses on the relationship between *wunderkind* novelist Thomas Wolfe *(Look Homeward, Angel)* and editor Maxwell Perkins. After his first success, Wolfe (Jude Law) brings in three crates of scrawled-on pages with a sequel. Perkins (Colin Firth), committed to "putting good books in readers' hands," has faith that this unwieldy trove warrants a few months of evenings working together on it.

As they get to the end of chapter 4, Perkins reads aloud the section that introduces the female character. Firth delivers Wolfe's prose with such clarity and reverence that you are impressed by its sheer beauty and creativity. You might even feel like applauding. I know I did.

The passage starts with the room full of smoke, "the haze of the cigarettes and cigars swirling miasma-like." Wolfe tells us not only the brands of cigarettes people are smoking, but also the personality associated with each brand. His protagonist Eugene, once "accustomed to the haze," finally sees the woman. She is wearing gloves that creep "like living tendrils" over arms "normally ivory" but which now are "sun-kissed as a blush"—that is, "the incarnadine discovery inside a conch shell seen for the first time by a bewildered zoologist as he is undone by its rosy, promising pinkness." Wolfe then tells us that the woman's eyes are "blue beyond blue," a phrase so mellifluous that he repeats it before clarifying the inscrutability of that hue with "like the ocean." That ocean is one which "he could swim into forever and never miss a fire-engine red or a cornstalk yellow." What is more, "that blue, those eyes, devoured him and looked past him and never saw him and never would, of that he was sure." The notion of eyes devouring anything, much less what they don't see, belongs to the province of poetry—surely Wolfe's intended goal, for Eugene now understands "what the poets had been writing about these many years" in such a way as to feel a brotherhood for such "lost, wandering, lonely souls." Next, Wolfe introduces a paradox of soundless sounds, lending another poetic aspect to that moment of falling instantly, hopelessly in love. But then he recasts the "clatter of his broken heart" as a moment of "sure silence." Lest we misconstrue from that silence that Eugene is fine, Wolfe informs us outright that, in fact, "his life was shattered."

Perkins recognized that opulent language could become overblown, digressive rather than descriptive, effusive rather than effective. So he asks Wolfe to consider "every nuance, every phrase" from the reader's point of view. His questions can largely be summed up as variations on "But what's the point here?" And the point of this passage of Wolfe's has nothing to do with the smoky miasma that filled the room or the cigarette brands that caused it; nor with zoologist, poet, tendrils, ivory, conch shell, fire engine, cornstalk, or ocean, which were not even in the room; nor with how many creative ways one might describe the blue of someone's eyes when a soul is suddenly smitten at the sight of them.

Wolfe manages to see what Perkins sees, or rather, to hear with his ears, and, in a final flurry of inspiration, reduces the description to say that (1) Eugene saw her; then (2) noticed the color of her eyes: blue. One more sentence describes falling so quickly in perhaps the only way possible, as something *im*-possible, magical, in poetic terms that are right on point: "no one in the room even heard the sound."

At my screening of *Genius*, there were audible gasps in the room at this point. One was from me.

Well may we wonder whether "the sound" was merely metaphorical, or Eugene letting out an audible gasp, groan, whisper, or wail. And in making us wonder, the twenty-five words Wolfe chose, replacing 232, have the impact of many more. The difference is, to quote Mark Twain, "the difference between lightning and the lightning bug."

With Perkins' guidance, Wolfe eventually reduces his 5000 pages to a manageable heft and another successful novel.

Their teamwork demonstrates the two components of genius: *idea fluency*—having a lot of ideas—plus *discrimination*—the ability to select which ones are worth developing and, in the end, keeping. You might have heard Thomas Edison's maxim that "Genius is 1% inspiration and 99% perspiration." Think of discrimination, then, as *perspiration properly applied*.

The *Genius* suggested by the movie's title, therefore, might not be Wolfe—or Perkins—but rather what transpired when they were in the same room working together.

***

Wolfe certainly had talent, passion, drive, and a tale he just had to tell. But he brought a few other things with him when he walked into Perkins' office with those crates. First: a *working knowledge* of both grammar and literary style.

In this Age of Self-Expression, however, many students, from primary school to post-grads, never realize how important this knowledge is, not just for a writer, but for a leader of any kind. (What is creative writing, after all, but an attempt to *lead* others on a journey to your soul?)

Winston Churchill, as a youngster, used to practice exercises in grammar and rhetoric the way a piano student might practice scales. By the time he was called on, he was not only willing but also ready and able to put his skill to use with a radio broadcast that countered "the odious apparatus of Nazi rule" so effectively that the speech has gone down in history—and in the film *Darkest Hour* (2017). (The appendix of *Whose Grammar Book Is This, Anyway?* includes the text of the speech.)

Notwithstanding that the very vowels and consonants of "odious apparatus" make the Nazis sound like an ogre to be vanquished, the remainder of the speech might represent the most effective use of rhetorical technique ever known. Churchill's heightened language succeeded in lifting his listeners to those heights. How? Through two motifs, "we shall" and "we shall fight," which charge the speech through repetition (rather than through figurative speech, the wont of poetry). Churchill starts out by telling his countrymen, first, what "we shall not" do: "flag or fail." Then what we *shall* do: "go on to the end." Then *where* "we shall fight": "in France," "on the seas and oceans," "in the air," "on the beaches," "on the landing grounds," "in the fields and in the streets," and "in the hills." He repeats "we shall fight" in each clause until we cannot help but believe it will be so. He laces the sequence with *how* "we shall fight" as well: "with growing confidence and growing strength," and "whatever the cost may be." Two other essential things "we shall" do: "defend our island," and, last and most important: "never surrender."

My father often told me Churchill's story to illustrate how important grammar and style are. They might even be enlisted to save the free world.

What about stateside? Think of Lincoln's stirring speech at Gettysburg in 1863: "that a government of the people, by the people, and for the people, shall not perish from this earth." Consider the alternative devoid of rhetorical repetition: "that a government of, by, and for the people shall not perish from this earth." Though more concise, this version is so prosaic as to be lackluster compared to what he chose. Lincoln's diction appealed to the blood and guts as well as the mind and, like Churchill's, not only rallied a nation at a time of crisis, but has been inspiring mankind ever since.

Rhetorical devices such as the above types of repetition were identified and named as far back as ancient Greece, if not earlier. They are the tools and techniques of any writer which, if mastered, can transform, as if by magic, into the very structure and substance of poetry or prose. Some of these devices involve repetition with variation: repeating a word but in a different form; rephrasing an adversary's argument in such a way that you can disprove your version rather than what he actually said (a tactic still prevalent in politics and academia); and the repetition not of words, but of sounds, which you know as assonance, alliteration, and rhyme. To these devices add parallel structure, such as antithesis—comparison and contrast (e.g., Alexander Pope's "Man proposes./God disposes")—plus overstatement and understatement, symbolism and simile, and a slew of others, and you, like Churchill, will start to become a literary stylist.

Grammar and style are to the writer's words what nails and hammer are to the carpenter's wood. You cannot construct an effective essay, novel, speech, play, or poem without them; for all these types of writing are descendants of classical Rhetoric.

If you feel you could use a brush-up or a self-directed introductory course, there are plenty of books available. For grammar, C. Edward Good's *Whose Grammar Book Is This Anyway?* (Barnes & Nobles Books, 2002) is a good place to start. For style, two essential texts are Strunk & White's *The Elements of Style*, and William Zinsser's *On Writing Well*. Having a Chicago *Manual of Style* on hand should prove helpful to any professional writer; I also frequently refer to Evans & Evans' *A Dictionary of American Usage* for reviewing issues like split infinitives and dangling modifiers.

***

A second gift Wolfe brought to the table in his sessions with Perkins was the *attitude* of a writer. Of course he loved what he had written, as writers must: How else could they share their work? But more importantly, he was willing to fall out of love with what he had written in order that future readers might fall in love with what he had not yet written. And that made him eventually hear his words through the ears of another, which, in turn, inspired him to revise.

The art of writing is the art of rewriting.

Absent a Maxwell Perkins at your side, though, how can you develop the ability to distinguish the journey from the digression, the lightning bolt from the lightning bug? Here's a hint: You can't be a better editor, or rewriter, of your own work than you are a reader. This will mean acquiring an ear that can hear your own material as if for the first time and then respond as your potential readership might.

An ear that is *experienced* and *open* at the same time seems like a paradox: But it is the essential foundation for productive revision, notwithstanding the sweat, blood, and possibly tears that might be involved.

Dorothy Parker said, "I can't change five words but that I change seven"— but what astonishing perfection in her poems and prose. Parker also worked in Hollywood. Eliminating a carefully nurtured line of dialogue was like "killing your babies," she said, a trope still used in the movie industry.

In drama, however, as in poetry and fiction, the author is the supreme authority on the final draft. All the producer or publisher can do is make strong suggestions (and then decide not to produce or publish, perhaps). Staged readings and workshops provide opportunities to see a play on its feet; but acting guru Lee Strasberg said that even then there is nothing more difficult than for a playwright to "see what is there." So it made sense when I heard playwright Michael Weller recommend, once you got your play absolutely perfect, that you put the manuscript in a drawer for six months and forget it so that you could take it out again and look at it fresh. Only then might you be able to revise it and make it truly perfect, at which point your best move was to put it back in the drawer for six months. Then repeat the cycle. Again and again.

When does the cycle come to an end? That's up to you. Sam Shepherd revamped his play *Buried Child* decades after it won the Pulitzer Prize. Many plays have several published versions, as does Marianne Moore's famous poem "Poetry," which first appeared as an untitled poem. You might know that Walt Whitman kept revising, augmenting, and republishing his masterful collection *Leaves of Grass* every few years from 1855 to its final edition in 1892, the year of his death.

Several literary journals' editors suggest that a poet not submit a piece until at least six months after it is written: coincidentally, the same span of six months that Michael Weller recommended for playwrights. Time, then, is the author's ally when it comes to falling out of love with what you have written and seeing *what is there.*

For help in figuring out what to do with a poem when you do take it out of the drawer, you might begin with Ted Kooser's *The Poetry Home Repair Manual: Practical Advice for Beginning Poets*.

***

An MFA program might be particularly valuable if it includes reading— a lot. Particularly close reading. But an alternative path might be—to read. Closely. A lot. Playwright August Wilson *(Fences)* left high school at age fifteen to pursue his education independently at the Carnegie Library of Pittsburgh. Moss Hart got a night job so that he could spend his daytime hours in the New York Public Library reading plays. By the time a Broadway producer teamed him up with George S. Kaufman, the preeminent comic playwright in America, Hart was ready for him and collaborated as an equal, not a subordinate. Check out Hart's winning memoir, *Act One*, for the story.

Along the way, you might even get paid to study great art if you write about it, too. George Bernard Shaw and William Inge worked as drama critics before they started writing plays. Frank Nugent wrote movie reviews for the *New York Times* for years before he started writing his own screenplays. His credits include one of the greatest films of all time, *The Searchers* (1956).

***

Each of these authors developed an *experienced* ear. What about its *openness*?

Wolfe was incredibly fortunate to have Maxwell Perkins show him the way and then keep him on track—as literary compass, so to speak. Still, it took years, not months, and the process was excruciating. And the world hasn't known the likes of Perkins for decades. So you are probably going to have to serve as your own literary compass. But you don't have to go it entirely alone.

I have grown to cherish the generosity of friends and colleagues with literary leanings who give honest responses to my work. A circle of such trustworthy "eyes and ears" might be essential for every writer today. Some have been kind enough to pore over manuscripts of full-length poetry collections of mine: they read the whole thing aloud with me over several meetings or send me notes. Inspired revision always ensued.

Joining a poetry or writers' workshop at your local library or community center—or forming one—would give you opportunities to hear others read your material, and vice versa. Oftentimes the feedback will be spot-on, too; over time you will be able to determine which feedback is usable. Do write down *everything* that is said, though, because the comment you disregard one day will be just the thing you'll want to remember six months later when you take that poem out of the drawer for another round of "repairs."

Writing everything down at a workshop also encourages colleagues to give you *more* feedback, for it suggests that you are taking all comments seriously for subsequent mulling over. How much mulling is up to you, of course.

Another useful strategy: have specific questions, like: *Is the title evocative and appropriate? Does the length of the lines seem right for this poem? Is the movement, from beginning to middle to end, effective? Does the punctuation, or lack of it, make sense? Did I overlook a dangling modifier?* and so forth.

When a comment seems to have broader applications than the present poem, write it down. Start to keep a running list of questions you can later ask yourself, when alone, to help you consider "every nuance, every phrase" of future writing as your readers will. This will increase the chances of your perspiration being properly applied, absent a Maxwell Perkins at your side.

Density of diction is, of course, one of the defining characteristics of poetry. Philip Levine said it might take him ten readings of a poem to start to "get" it, and he was one of our greatest poets. So you will have to judge whether a colleague (or editor) has invested enough time and focus to warrant your agonizing over what they said about your poem.

A poem might, for example, establish its own syntax in an arrangement of sentence fragments, word clusters, lists, or the like that require the reader to do most of the "work," similar to what minimalist or conceptual art asks of a viewer. Other poems might seem clear the first time one reads or hears them, but additional layers of meaning start to become evident on subsequent readings. Ideally, the process of parsing such a poem will be satisfying, invigorating, or even delicious. Casual comments of others after only one read might be, for the most part, premature.

In other words, some poems-in-progress may benefit greatly from the in-depth consideration of a single set of eyes-and-ears, but not so much from the cursory considerations of several. T. S. Eliot incorporated Ezra Pound's feedback on *The Waste Land*. Once it was published, academics and poets all over the world started writing about it—and getting it wrong, as far as Eliot was concerned. But did he revise the poem? No: he republished it with copious footnotes!

Emily Dickinson likewise might have deferred to the editor who said, "This poem doesn't really rhyme." But she knew how to enlist slant rhyme expressly to establish a conversational tone and intimate rapport with generations of readers long after she and that editor would be gone. Thank goodness she was her own literary compass.

***

Another thing that Thomas Wolfe had was a sense of the sublime: the ability to recognize when something is not just good, but *right*; when all parts contribute, with appropriate proportion and emphasis, to the whole; and when the whole, then, is perfect.

When this sense of the sublime is accompanied by the yearning to attain it, you have a writer in the making.

The sublime seems like part and parcel of the practice of poetry. For when a poet decides (or realizes) that a poem is finished, that moment is tantamount to deciding (or realizing) that the poem is now impossible to be improved upon: that no punctuation, word choice, line ending, etc., can be altered without diminishing the poem.

I remember coming across the term *perfect pitch* to describe poet Robert Hayden on the back of his *Collected Poems*. I was puzzled as to what that could mean for a poet, as opposed to a musician, particularly one who wrote in unrhymed verse. Then I came across his poem "Monet's 'Waterlilies'":

> Today as the news from Selma and Saigon
> poisons the air like fallout,
>   I come again to see
> the serene great picture that I love.
>
> Here space and time exist in light
> the eye like the eye of faith believes.
>   The seen, the known
> dissolve in iridescence, become
> illusive flesh of light
>   that was not, was, forever is.

O light beheld as through refracting tears.
Here is the aura of that world
    each of us has lost.
Here is the shadow of its joy.

Part of the point of the poem, I believe, is never explicitly stated, but achieved *between* the lines through the juxtaposition of Selma (civil rights activities in Alabama) and Saigon (the Vietnam war), against an implied elsewhere: New York, Paris, or anywhere the narrator might have taken delight in one of Monet's water lily paintings, but decidedly not Saigon or Selma. *What am I doing here—and not there?!* the poet *seems* to shout, silently, between the lines (though he doesn't). This particularly resonates with me, for I have time and again considered the question of art versus activism. Even though Hayden never met me, his lines evoke an exhilarating ounce of anguish every time I read them aloud to a friend. How? It might be in the poem's movement: from the *specific* fallout of the day's news to the *universal* observations on light, love, space, time, and faith (evoked by the painting) to a *universal specific* about the world—the *joy* each of us has largely lost simply by living conscientiously. It might be something as technical as his choice of end words (*light* being used twice, please note). But the truth is: how Hayden moves me—I can't say. This inscrutable ability, I would suggest, is the *perfect pitch* of a poet.

Many Shakespeare fans have identified a similarly unexplainable sublimity in two particular lines from *Richard II:* "For God's sake, let us sit upon the ground/And tell sad stories of the death of kings" (III. 2).

Think of a piano, guitar, or violin being adjusted as it is tuned. In a similar way, you keep adjusting your poem-in-progress until the moment its "vibration" is in tune: you feel a tingle in your spine, and you know—that's it. When your listener does too, your suspicion is confirmed, and you know your poem is in tune, or nearly. Unlike that of a musician, though, the perfect pitch of a poet is probably acquired over time.

Dickinson said she knew poetry was poetry "if I feel physically as if the top of my head were taken off." Whether you feel a poem in your head or your toes, your stomach or your spine, feel a wetness in the eyes or a frog in your throat, feel your heart skip a beat or your lungs miss a breath—that's poetry.

When I come across a new poem that does one of these things to me, I write it down so that I can go back to it—even memorize it and perform it, personalizing the poetic choices the way an actor would a passage of dialogue. Sometimes only through "learning by heart" do I begin to understand *in my heart* how in heaven's name a poem works. I highly recommend this practice to help develop your sense of pitch and passion for perfection.

By the time I started reading essays about poetry—yes, *literary criticism*—I was on a mission of trying to unlock the secrets of the great poets. *Poets on Poetry: Sixteen Famous Poets Consider Their Art*, edited by Charles Norman, is a great place to start. So in some strange way I understood Poe when he was talking about the "effect" on the reader he was going for with his long lines; and T. S. Eliot, when he said that there is no such thing as free verse—from the poet's point of view.

Free verse isn't free? How can that be, thought I. Eventually, though, it made sense. After all, there is only one combination of words in one order, set on a page in only one way that is right for the poem. When yet unfinished, it holds the poet in its thrall to keep working on it. Like a sculptor, the poet is obsessed and possessed by what no one else can understand, chiseling away all the marble that is not the statue. And only the artist has a sense of what to chisel away, and what to leave for subsequent polishing.

***

There was one more component to the writer's attitude that Thomas Wolfe brought to Maxwell Perkins' table: his eagerness. He was nothing short of indomitable. Nothing would stop him, nor any of the other writers mentioned above, from writing. Why is this?

I think it is because they cared. Caring is what makes you both interesting as an artist and resilient. Tony Barr suggests in *Acting for the Camera* that caring is the secret to energy in acting on film. I think it applies to all the arts and all artists.

Yet at festivals and in workshops, I run into many students who confess to me that they don't write outside of assignments for classes. One bemoaned the financial straits that required her to take a year off. I asked her, *What's stopping you from writing?* She said, *I have to work.* I asked, *Can't you write before work?* She said, *I guess so, sure.*

Then why don't you, I said. She said, *I miss the prompts we get in writing class.* I said, *You need prompts to write?* She said, *Well, no, I guess not.* I shared some of my own experiences, and eventually suggested, *Maybe what you need to do is to get yourself to the point where you can't not write.*

How do I do that?

Don't you look at the world and see that it needs your help? Don't you know that there are soup kitchens right here in town? That there are more homeless and displaced people today than there have been in all the other ages of humanity combined? Have you ever thought about joining the Peace Corps, or even just taking a backpack across Europe, or Africa, or Asia, or South America, or working for AmeriCorps VISTA, or, if you need to stay closer to home, volunteering to help some non-profit or political candidate you believe in, or . . . .

As the list went on, her eyes widened. *Wow!* she said, struck by the notion that the world quite possibly needed—her. Her face lit up with joy—and a plan.

I'm here to tell you that the world needs you, too. First, to learn about those who try to counter despair and suffering with hope and resilience, combat ignorance and myopia with wisdom and wonder, or confront injustice and cruelty with bravery and action—and are in sore need of a voice like yours to help them. Your words can be their champion as well as your own: When you witness enough stories of plight and pluck and it dawns on you that you might be of service, you won't need prompts, writing exercises, or a class. You'll write every day. Even with a full-time job. You'll wake up early or write during your lunch hour. You'll find the time somehow, because you must.

Work on the person you are, in other words, and how you care about the world, from the miracle of each bee to the divinity of each blade of grass, from the inhumanity of man against man to the plight of the meek and maltreated against the mean and mighty. Then, if you must shout, you'll shout; if you must write, you'll write.

***

Succeeding in a writing career might be another story, but there are many paths to success, too. Philosopher Lao Tzu, in prison, dictated his poems, the *Tao Te Ching*, to his jailer. Likewise Milton, having gone blind, enlisted scribes when he "wrote" *Paradise Lost*.

Early in her career, Pulitzer Prize winner Eudora Welty couldn't get published for the life of her, but then found small presses that started to take her short stories. Little by little, more people—and publishers—started to take notice.

Frank Herbert couldn't get his futuristic novel *Dune* published (other than serialized in a magazine), but an unlikely publisher, known more for automobile manuals and magazines than for books, finally took it on: It became the best-selling sci-fi novel of its time.

Robert Frost moved to England for three years and had two poetry collections published there before returning to the United States where he would eventually win four Pulitzer prizes.

And the list goes on. Each found a way for their work to break through, and so can you.

***

A graduate program, then, could be a wonderful way to help you immerse in creative writing, as well as guide you through a lot of close reading. But that is no reason to let either the program or the lack of one stop you.

Above all, don't enroll in one *instead of doing* but rather *in order to do* what you need to do to become a writer, which you now know includes:

- Making a study of grammar and style.

- Making it a regular habit to read and study great writing, to develop the experienced ear. No, not so you end up writing like your favorite poets, magnificent as they may be, but so that you, too, might recognize the sublime and ache to achieve it yourself.

- Writing, rewriting, and perfecting all you can, but then putting your work in a drawer for a while so you can take it out later to revise with open eyes and ears.

- Above all: Caring. At least as much as Winston Churchill and Abraham Lincoln cared.

Archibald MacLeish not only won three Pulitzers (two for poetry, one for drama), he also served as assistant secretary of state during WW II. Because he cared. Even if, like Thomas Wolfe (perhaps), all you really care about is writing, that could be enough—if you care in such a way that nothing can stop you.

But the world does need our help today as much as it ever did. When you care to the very core of your soul, the inspiration, the perspiration, the dedication, and the discipline will come. So will the words.

Everyone's path is different. Whether or not yours includes a degree—in poetry or political science, creative writing or comparative literature, journalism or jurisprudence—I wish you Godspeed.

Even more, I wish for you a career that brings you to a place, personally and professionally, where you can't help but take us on a journey to your soul, via your words, because you know it will be a trip well worth the taking.

Publishing and
the Literary Community

Robbie Gamble

POEMS AS PILGRIMS

I recently evolved into one of those increasingly common creatures, the Emerging Poet. (I sometimes wonder what it is we are emerging from: some warm and comfortable womb of creative ectoplasm? Or some deep dark crevasse of naiveté that has shielded us from harsh daylight of the literary business? Or both?) As an Emerging Poet, I now possess two things: a sheaf of poems that I am deeply invested in, and a desire to share these poems with the wider world.

Oh, these poems! They have progressed from little "Ahas!" of inspiration into clunky drafts and then less-clunky re-drafts, and then re-re-drafts that start to flow. The duller ones have been shoved into desk drawers for weeks or months at a time, in order to ferment and "find their voice," emerging wiser and ripe with new strategies for presenting themselves authentically on the page. Others have been picked apart and reassembled in workshops, or had drastic surgeries performed on them by revered mentors, and some of these have healed and realigned and grown into healthier beings. There comes a point when the survivors feel more or less complete. And my desire emerges to prop them up and send them out for all to see.

I have had a number of conversations recently with fellow Emergers about the Submission Process, the emotional rollercoaster of exposing our precious poems to the whims and judgement of that other lofty species, the Editors, in the hopes of convincing them to make a prominent place for our pieces in their prestigious journals. We all have stories to share, from the occasional high of an enthusiastic acceptance letter to the all-too-frequent low of those impersonal form rejections. Some of my friends bear rejection stoically. "When a rejection comes in, I just send that packet right out again," they say. Others have been devastated when that perfectly honed group of poems they just knew in their gut was a perfect aesthetic fit for *The Nonpareil Quarterly* gets bounced back to the inbox in less than a week with a curt "Sorry, this just isn't for us." I have been submitting in earnest over the past year, and I have experienced my own broad spectrum of feelings in response to the inevitable stream of rejections. And I still have this swelling sheaf of work, and a desire to share.

Kathleen Spivak was a student of Robert Lowell, and apparently was present, Forrest Gump-like, for just about every significant Boston literary event in the nineteen-sixties and seventies. In her excellent memoir *With Robert Lowell and His Circle*, she describes being invited out for coffee one time with Lowell and Anne Sexton, and listening in as the two great poets kvetched about the publishing business and the pitfalls of rejection. They both agreed that a three percent acceptance rate was about the best they could expect. Three percent! These Pulitzer Prize-winning literary icons were accustomed to the idea that only three out of a hundred of their submissions would find their way into print. And this was long before the exponential proliferation of MFA programs and online writing workshops and the legions of all of us earnestly Emerging Poets. I find great consolation in this anecdote.

Once, after a discouraging cluster of rejections (they do seem to come in waves) I went for a long walk in the Maine woods to clear my head. I picked my way along an undulating, moss-carpeted trail as sunlight shafted through gaps in the spruce canopy overhead, and I found that I was happy just to be in motion, detached from time or destination. My thoughts wandered, as they do on long walks, and at some point they came around to my poems, and my efforts to find a fixed place for them in the world. I realized that the poems were on a journey too, from conception to revision to the ups and downs of the Submission Process. What if I thought of them as pilgrims?

In many spiritual traditions, people take a period of time out from their ordinary lives to travel somewhere, on foot or by other means, often at great hardship, in order to achieve a deeper understanding of who they are and how they relate to the broader world. There may be a destination involved, say Lourdes or Mecca, but much of the spiritual growth occurs along the way. And even if the journey is hard, there are moments of joy in it.

I now imagine preparing my poems as pilgrims by placing a little staff in their hands and a pack of provisions on their back before sending them out into the world with a click of the Submittable button or (much less frequently now) stuffing them into an envelope with a SASE and dropping them in a mailbox. And I know a few of them will find new homes. Many more of them will return to me, a little wiser, perhaps bearing a note of encouragement or advice from a kind editor. Some will cycle in and out, travelling long and hard, and eventually I will see that they need a different flourish, or some deeper nourishment, in order to have the strength to go on. And some will flounder, eventually recognizing that their path is to end in obscurity, and that will be okay, for they journeyed as well as they could. My hope is that all these poems will grow into who they are meant to be while on pilgrimage, and that I might vicariously grow along with them, and perhaps other readers, too.

Whitney Sweet

COVER IT! COVER LETTERS FOR MAGAZINE SUBMISSIONS

Having to write a cover letter for anything is a particularly awful task. Just like a cover letter that would accompany your resume when you are applying for a job, a cover letter to a literary magazine is introducing you and your work to the editor or readers who might choose your piece for publication. As the editor of a literary magazine, I can tell you that I have seen a wide variety of cover letters, some good, and some not so good. There are a few important things you need to include in your letter, such as a salutation, information about why you have chosen the piece you are submitting to that magazine, a perfunctory knowledge of said magazine, and a sign off, which can include some basic biographical information about you, the author. Below, I will go into detail regarding these cover letter building blocks.

The Salutation

Any good writer who is taking their career seriously should do some research about the publication to which they are submitting. Firstly, when you see a call for submissions, be it an annual call that lasts only a few days, or a rolling call for submissions that is open all year long, you as the writer should be looking into the publication. When you find the name of the person who will be reading work, use it in the greeting of your letter. You can go with the traditional route of Dear Ms. Name, or Mr. Name, or you can be contemporary with a more gender-neutral approach of Dear First Name Last Name. If you do not find a name for the editor or reader of the submissions, address it to Dear Magazine Title.

Knowledge of the Magazine

Now that you have established your hellos, there is something that you MUST ALWAYS DO. I cannot stress this more strongly. You must, under all circumstances, read the submissions guidelines. You must follow these guidelines. This illustrates to whomever will be reading your work that you have researched (at least a bit) the magazine. As a professional, you should be going to the magazine website, looking at all the tabs, reading about the editor, even following them on social media if you want to be thorough. If you have some cash to spare, purchase a copy or two of the magazine. If you're broke, head to the library to see if they have a copy you can read to get a feel for what the editors like. Now, before you send in a piece, ask yourself an important question. Does my piece fit into what the magazine has previously published?

Because you are smart and have done your research, you can now follow those submission guidelines to the letter. This means format, document type, number of pieces in a submission, and that you have curated your own work. As an editor of a magazine, I can tell you, I appreciate when the person submitting says why they feel their piece would fit into the mandate of my publication. This is helpful because I can know what to expect when I move forward into reading their work. If you cannot find a reason why your work fits into the scope of a magazine, perhaps it is best to move on and try somewhere else.

I have had several occasions where someone has submitted everything they have ever created, expecting me to review it all and cherry-pick the pieces that fit in to my magazine's mandate. In one case, I even had someone say they didn't know how their work fit into the magazine, but that I could choose something from the twenty-plus pieces they had submitted. Um... no. Most editors would just delete this email, along with all your work without even looking at it. There are submissions guidelines for a reason. Editors are busy people and are possibly working for free on the publication to which you are submitting. It shows professionalism and respect for other people's time when you take the time to know your stuff and follow the rules.

A Bit About Your Work

When you have found a magazine where you think your work belongs, you should write a short blurb about the pieces you are sending. Consider what people will care to know about the work. One person who submitted a piece to me said the work was based on an event that happened in their life, but that it was important the piece remained a work of fiction, without saying anything about the actual piece. This, dear friends, doesn't matter to your reader. The work will be what it is when the editor reads it. They will not be considering how you fictionalized or created poetry out of a true event. A cover letter is not the place to work out your angst against your ex. If you have written a poem about a breakup, perhaps something more effective to include in the cover letter would be a short statement about how the poem is intended to capture the difficulties of heartbreak, or the emotions surrounding the ending of something. You want to put a direction of interpretation into the editor's head without revealing too much about the piece. After all, once a piece is published, it no longer belongs to you. You cannot tell every reader how to interpret your work.

Your Bio

As a new writer, it's okay that you don't have a lot of credentials or publications under your belt. Don't fabricate anything to make it seem like you are more important and successful than you are. Everyone had to start somewhere, and an editor will appreciate that you are diving into the crazy world of literary magazines. You can write something simple like a background of your education, or what type of work you do. You can say you are a new writer looking to break into the writing world. All those things are good. If you have managed to publish a few pieces, great! Include that as well. If you have won prizes, or have been asked to write a poem for your cousin's wedding, tack that on. The bio is a place for the editor to get to know you as a writer. Some editors might be impressed and dazzled by experienced people who have lots of publications and degrees, others might not. Either way, lack of experience shouldn't impact whether an editor will read your work. Never be ashamed to be at the beginning. Keep your bio short and sweet. Somewhere around 100 words or less is great. If you are feeling uncomfortable about your lack of experience, it's also okay to not include a bio. Most publications will ask you for one later if they are interested in publishing your work. You can tackle that hurdle when it comes along if you prefer.

The Ending

When you are signing off, be respectful. Tell the editor that you appreciate their time and effort in reviewing your work, and that you hope to hear from them in the future. That's it.

A Good Example

I include here an example of the type of cover letters I like to receive. You can use this as a template if you like.

> *Dear Whitney Sweet: Please consider "Title" for possible publication. I love the mission of TROU and I believe my poem about two queer people finding love in difficult circumstances will capture the attention of your readers.*
>
> *Thank you for your consideration.*
>
> *Best,*
>
> *Author Name*

That's it, short, and to the point. It illustrates that the person submitting has researched the magazine and has considered why their work might fit into the mission of the publication. It is polite and professional, and makes me want to get to the important part, which is the poetry itself. You will also notice that this does not include a bio. This is fine by me. Sometimes a little mystery into who wrote a piece is a good thing.

As you can see, writing cover letters seems hard at first, but it doesn't have to be. You just need to keep in mind that to be taken seriously as a writer, you must take the submissions process seriously. If you follow these tips and tricks, it will make you look like the professional writer that you are, even if you've never published anything before.

Helen Ruggieri

REJECTION

Some of us so love rejection that we put ourselves in the way of it. We are used to it, we want it, we need it, we take up occupations where we can be assured of getting it. It's our cocaine, our crack.

I was born when my mother was just beginning menopause. We are euphemistically referred to as "change of life babies." I'm sure the last thing in the world she wanted was a baby. My sister was recovering from rheumatic fever and required constant care, and two male cousins had moved in with us because of the Depression.

My mother's baby brother (32) lived with us between trips as a steward on the Cunard Line's Bermuda run, and he was so fussy if a shirt wasn't ironed right, he'd throw it back in the wash. She let him get away with it. Me, I was the one who was rejected. I was the one she didn't have the time for, have the heart for. I know she was busy. I'm sorry. But early on, I learned what life had in store for me. Those early lessons are the ones we learn best.

I grew up a nomad. My parents moved every other year. This inures you to being the outsider, the one who doesn't fit in, the one on the edge, the rejected one. My parents paid little attention to me, busy packing and unpacking, planning the next move.

When I got into high school I selected boys to like who never liked me back. That way I could be sure of a constant supply of my narcotic. When I applied for jobs I always applied for the one I was least likely to get. Ditto.

One of my best job rejections was at a manufacturing company in a small upstate city. I was collecting unemployment benefits and the counselor at the State Employment Office sent me out to interview for a job in the personnel department. They made the appointment and gave me a little card with the time and place. When I arrived the woman in the office handed me an application to fill out before she would talk to me. Fill this out first, she insisted. The application wanted to know if I was allergic to any chemicals, what size smock I wore, if I had any relatives employed at the company. It sounded like an application for working in the manufacturing facility itself, not the office.

I tried to mention it to her, but she was seething about some previous life which I became the focus for. The woman behind the desk snatched the application out of my hands. I said that I'd been sent about the opening in personnel. She told me there was no opening in personnel. And in response to my open mouth, she turned her back on me and began shuffling papers on her desk.

When I got to the parking lot someone had parked behind my car, blocking me in. I went over to the employee entrance and talked to the guard who called the owner of the car. As the owner stormed across the lot toward me, I assumed the position of the sorry one. I mentioned that the slots hadn't been marked in any way and I was sorry if I'd parked in his place. He said nothing, got in his car and peeled out spraying me with gravel.

When the unemployment counselor asked me how the interview went, I told him there was no job. He didn't believe me and called up to make sure I'd been there. They couldn't find my application. I think I convinced him that I'd been there because he didn't turn me in for whatever they turn you in for—missing an arranged interview while collecting unemployment benefits? But this experience serves as an example of total rejection. There aren't many days in your life that will provide you with such perfection.

As if my daily life couldn't provide me with enough rejection I elected to fancy myself a writer so I could provide myself with additional rejection on a daily basis. I was about 22 when I sent out my first poem. I sent it to *The New Yorker*. Why not start at the top? Better to be rejected by *The New Yorker* than some lesser rejecter. When the poem came back with the printed rejection card I was so embarrassed I tore it up into little pieces and fed them to my wastepaper basket a few flutters at a time so no one would tape the pieces together and discover what it was. I was humiliated by the fact that I' been rejected. I was so young I hadn't yet recognized my destiny.

Over the years, however, I've become a connoisseur of rejection. Most magazines don't have the resources and imagination available to compete with manufacturing companies. They are left with only a little note to do their work for them. They put you in your ordinary place: "Sorry, we have decided against including your work in our magazine"; or, "we are sorry that the material you submitted is not suitable for our magazine." Ordinary rejection. Not much imagination. The tone is not arrogant enough to make you angry. You just stick it in your drawer after having stabbed it with a pair of scissors several times and forget it.

Some magazines send reverse rejections. They don't want you to reject them just because they rejected you. They begin with sad tales about the millions of envelopes pouring in to their tiny office, their unpaid staff who do this for the love of literature, rising printing costs, the times, the state of the art, etc. Bad timing. You're not likely to feel sympathy for a magazine who has just told you, "We cannot use the enclosed material."

Some magazines try to combine rejection with a sales pitch: "Perhaps a sample issue will help you to decide which poems to send." I like that one a great deal. I used it myself during a brief stint as an editor (rejecter). Of course I was rejected by the rejectees (the potential audience/purchaser). So be it.

My favorite flattering rejection letter begins: "Your manuscript has been rejected, but we liked your style and insist on your sending us more." Several paragraphs further down is the hook, "submissions must be accompanied with a ten-dollar reading fee." No seasoned rejectee will fall for that one. We'll take our rejection straight up, thanks.

My favorite rejection notes are perfectly insulting. This takes daring and imagination and such a head full of conceit there's no room for additional opinions. These rejecters are at the top of the class. They write letters you can revel in. You have been put firmly in your place by a master. These are the rejection notes which become collector's items. "Thank you for your submission, but the judges feel you are not making a contribution to American letters." Now that's a rejection. It's hard to maintain standards these days.

Many rejecters of late are so neutral it's hard to find anything worth getting riled up about. However, many editors scribble little notes at the bottom for you to savor. My personal favorite came from a magazine asking for new and interesting work: "nothing new or interesting here…" handwritten on the bottom of the note does wonders for your blood pressure. Yes. Good stuff.

Lately, however, I've noticed an alarming trend in rejection letters: excessive sorryness. These notes are so sorry you feel sorry you made them feel sorry by sending them material. Don't fall for that. I want to reassure them—hey, don't be sorry. I send out regularly, alphabetically, systematically. You're one magazine on a long list. This doesn't mean you are not making a contribution to American Letters. Relax.

However, replying gets into the dangerous area. Never respond. Don't bother. Go out and get another rejection, a better one.

With the advent of emails you are lucky if you get a rejection at all. You just never hear. At the end of the year you can delete those past their expiration date. My favorite email rejection came with the email addresses and names of all the rejectees in the TO: line. That's pretty poor. I was almost tempted to go online and check to see how bad their mag was.

As a serious collector, I have sent to places for no other reason than they have particularly gruesome, nasty, illiterate, or exciting notes: for example *Mad* magazine: a full-page drawing of Alfred E. Newman giving you the finger. Hard to beat that.

A little magazine from the 70s called *Vile* sent rejection notes that said: "not vile enough." I got one. *Kayak* had a picture of a man with his head in a vise. Good stuff if a rejection note can provoke a smile from the rejectee.

In the course of a twenty-year period of sending out I've collected over a pound of rejection notes, some printed squares, full-page letters, scribbled "sorry" on a scrap of paper with indecipherable initials. I've lamented the fact that online submissions give you online rejections if you're lucky. However, I've managed to get my share of what I needed. Along the way I've often thought of not sending out. That would solve the problem of rejection notes entirely, but it's like rejecting your mother. You can't do it. Nothing in the world will change the fact that she's your mother, your biology, if not your destiny.

My advice to beginners—reject rejection. Find better things to worry about—global warming, quantum entanglement, ISIS—anything you can't do anything about.

Whitney Sweet

REJECTING REJECTION: KNOWING WHAT YOUR WORK IS ABOUT

When you are just starting out as a poet, it is sometimes hard to know how to handle rejection. One of the biggest lessons I have learned thus far in my career is how to reject rejection. This might sound standoffish, but what I mean by rejecting rejection is that as a poet and an artist, you must learn how to stand your ground and know that sometimes, the criticisms and rejections you receive are just plain wrong. You must learn to take your lumps and move foreword gracefully, while always being mindful of the core of your work, your message, and your poetry.

I was lucky enough to seriously begin work as a poet during my time at university. I took several creative writing workshop classes. In those classes, we shared our work, printing out enough copies for everyone in attendance. Everyone had the opportunity to express their thoughts on each piece we read. Most times, we discussed line breaks, changing words, fixing rhyme and rhythm. Other times, we argued over punctuation or imagery. These classes were a valuable learning experience for me. Firstly, I learned how to let go of my work; learned how to give it away. Once a poem is published, it is for public consumption and interpretation. You no longer have control over the piece. You can't tell every reader what it was you meant. These classes taught me to be clear and concise with my imagery and meanings.

Secondly, the workshop environment taught me how to have a thick skin. If you receive a critique on your work, it is not a critique about *you*. Though you might feel you have written the poem in your own blood, remember, it is created by you, not of you. Lastly, the workshop environment taught me how to understand my own work better, my mission in writing it, and what messages I wanted to keep, and those the piece could do without.

When I first started out sharing my work with others, I would try to incorporate every piece of suggested criticism into my poetry. This made the poems muddled and unclear. I quickly learned that my work will never please everyone, and that's okay. Was the message of the piece clear? Had I managed to present interesting rhythm, rhyme, and imagery? Does the form of my poem properly suit its function? If I could answer yes to these questions, then I knew I was secure in believing the poem to be whole and complete.

In the workshop environment, you get to know the other people well. You benefit from an understanding of their likes and dislikes and can judge if their criticism is biased or something that is truly a fault in your piece. For those who have come to writing poetry on a different path, I suggest trying out a workshop to learn more about yourself as a writer and learn more about the heart of your work.

Unfortunately, when you enter the world of submitting work to literary magazines and contests, you have no way of knowing what the editors or panel of readers like or want in a poem, though you do have the opportunity to introduce your poetry with a cover letter. You read the submission guidelines, choose your pieces to submit, give it a sales pitch in your cover letter, and you hope for the best. Often (very often) your work will be rejected. Mostly, you will not get a response and you will be left to assume after six to twelve weeks that your work was not selected. Sometimes, you will get a form rejection letter, thanking you for sending your work in for consideration, but the piece "was not a good fit" or "not what they are looking for at this time." And rarely, you will get personalized feedback. It is in this instance that you need to know yourself and your work. I will share with you now two situations in which I had to know myself and my work when I received personalized feedback.

The first instance was during a time when I had a poetry mentor. The mentorship was the prize I had won in a contest. It was an invaluable resource and I am so thankful to have experienced one-on-one coaching. While my mentor and I normally saw eye to eye on any changes that could improve my work, there was one instance in which I heartily disagreed with the guidance my mentor offered. My mentor suggested that I perform major surgery on a poem. The poem was raw and purposefully didactic in nature. My mentor did not like the didactic tone of the poem and encouraged me to remove this element from the work, also suggesting I rearrange the stanzas while I was at it. I tried to do what was suggested. I spent days arranging and rearranging the lines and stanzas. I removed the teaching elements of the poem. What was left was all wrong. I found myself crying at the thought I was "supposed" to change this poem so dramatically. After days of struggling with the piece, I wrote to my mentor and said I would not change it; the poem was exactly as I had intended. My mentor disagreed, wanting it to be "the best it could be". I knew it already was. That poem was ultimately published in an anthology.

My second example of rejecting rejection was when I sent a chapbook to a publisher. Two months went by, the time that was stated on their submissions page that I had to wait to receive a response. When I received no response, I assumed the chapbook had been rejected. Weeks later, I received a lengthy letter from the publisher, apologizing for taking so long to respond, but that they like to give extensive feedback for each submission, so it took longer than anticipated. I thought to myself, "too bad this work was turned down, but at least I get to have some valuable feedback." Unfortunately, what awaited inside the letter was not very helpful.

While I read over the comments, it became immediately evident that the publisher had not read my cover letter, which disclosed information about the areas in which they had found fault. They had suggested I cut a large portion out of a poem that had previously won an award and had been published elsewhere. The publisher also failed to see the connection of theme throughout the chapbook and had not understood the viewpoint I had presented. Returning to my point about not being able to point out each nuance of your work to a reader once a piece is published, it is important that your work can stand without a cover letter. However, in the case of sending work to publishers, a cover letter serves as the first glimpse of the work and must reveal the intended heart of your writing. I don't know why the information I provided in my cover letter was ignored, but the evidence I found in the rejection letter made it plain that the person reading my work and I were not on the same page.

I thought deeply about these flaws the publisher had uncovered. Had I been unclear in my theme? Had I been wishy-washy about my viewpoint? After reading through every suggested slice and dice of my work the publisher included, I was met with a strange final thought at the end of the letter. The publisher wrote that because they had taken so long to respond to my submission, they wouldn't be surprised if I had found a publisher elsewhere for the chapbook.

I was flummoxed. Why, if this work was as faulty as they suggested, would I be able to find a publisher elsewhere? And if it was worth publishing, why didn't this publisher take the opportunity to do so when it was presented?

Let's put aside for a moment the fact that I was left feeling hurt, angry, and confused by this letter of rejection. This letter was poor in its purpose and execution. I could have spiraled out of control, trying to rectify these faults, ripping apart my work, leaving it unrecognizable. But instead, I chose to hit the delete button, secure in the knowledge of my own creativity and poetry; choosing only to accept the final sentence of the letter, knowing the chapbook was good and worthy of (eventual) publication. I also thanked my lucky stars that my poetry had not been accepted by a publisher who didn't "get" my work.

The lessons I offer you from these experiences are lessons that taught me to consider criticism carefully. Sometimes it is worth trying out the suggested changes to a poem, just to see if they fit. Often, you will come out the other side with something better, but sometimes you already have the perfect form for your poem.

Listen to your gut feeling about your work. When push came to shove, my tears and heartache regarding making proposed changes told me that I was going the wrong direction with my work. I learned too, that sometimes, people are just plain wrong about your writing.

You can reject rejection. Not every piece of advice, criticism, and suggested edit will be right for you or your work. Over time, you will learn what the heart is in your poetry, what your style and message are. This knowledge can only be learned and earned through trial and error, failure and success. Share your work widely when possible, this way you will learn how to gauge criticism to see if it rings true for you. Then, when you do succeed, the success will be even sweeter because you will know you have been true to your craft.

Linda Simone

THE STUBBORN POEM: TACKLE OR TRASH?

We've all been face-to-face with at least one—the poem that refuses to show up on the page. In my case, it was a persona poem, not something I'd written much of before. How difficult could it be? You find someone you're interested in, pretend to be that person, and write what could be their thoughts. Piece of cake, right? Well, here's my story. Judge for yourself and hopefully, take away a shred of hard-earned wisdom.

While touring San Antonio's Japanese Tea Garden, I learned about a woman who, in the early 20th Century, migrated with her family from Japan to California to the Alamo City. She had once run the garden's Bamboo Tea Room. As a recent San Antonio transplant myself, I wondered if she, too, found it hard to understand a new culture, make friends, and feel a part of the community. I was inspired to explore her life in a poem in her voice. I let the idea simmer until I saw a call for submissions for an anthology of southwestern persona poems. Ah, the perfect home, I thought, for the poem I had yet to start. Beginning was the first hurdle.

The next barrier: getting to know my subject, Miyoshi Alice Jingu. I did online research and asked for help from the San Antonio Library's Texana and Genealogy reference desk. I read books about the city during that era, photocopied articles, printed out website pages, and highlighted so many facts that the pages appeared to be stained in egg yolk. I learned that in 1926 the City of San Antonio invited Miyoshi and her artist-husband Kimi to call the Japanese Garden their home and run the tea house. Within 15 years, the family, once called a "unique asset" of the city by the *San Antonio Express*, was deemed "enemy aliens" and forced out of their beloved home.

Now that I had the facts in hand, the drafts began. With so many intriguing details, the poem was quickly shaping up to be an epic. In early revisions,

I moved lines, shortened phrases, added and deleted details. What looked back from the page was not a poem at all, but a seemingly endless list that read more like an historical essay broken into lines. My husband Joe said it didn't sound like poetry. I read it to three dear friends at our annual writing retreat. Their initial silence told me I had much work to do. My friend Terry said to focus on a seminal moment in Miyoshi's life rather than trying to tell her whole story. Ann suggested internalizing Miyoshi's struggle: how would I feel if I were evicted from the home I loved? I knew everything they said was right. But how to fix? That was a hurdle yet to clear.

After my friend Sarah raved about a master class she had just taken, I thought maybe a poetry workshop might help. The local writing venue, Gemini Ink, was serendipitously offering a persona poem workshop. Was this luck or karma? My friends wisely advised not to bring the current draft along, but rather to go and simply absorb what the class had to offer.

Poet Khadijah Queen provided a range of persona poems for the group to discuss, and gave exercises so that we could experiment with various approaches. At first I was disappointed that she did not critique what we wrote, but I quickly saw how freeing this was. I asked her advice on getting unstuck when working on a poem. She echoed my friends' counsel: don't tell too much and find a moment when your subject is faced with a pivotal decision. Okay. I had a plan.

Several versions later, still unsure the poem was improving, I grew discouraged. Meantime, the anthology deadline inched closer. I had hit a wall—this poem simply refused to get in line. Maybe if I allowed some distance, I might be able to see it with fresh eyes. So, after a few weeks busy with life, I reluctantly re-opened the doc. I hated it. Every change I made just further muddied the waters. I was about to abandon the whole idea, chalking it up to an exercise in self-flagellation when I learned that the U.S. Poet Laureate, Juan Filipe Herrera, was speaking at a local college.

In the packed room of 200 people, Juan was authentic, funny, and encouraging. He stressed the importance of believing in your own voice—a message I really needed to hear at this point. When I approached him for his autograph on his newest book, I asked what he did when he got stuck on a poem. "Put it away, try writing about anything else—a leaf, a pencil—just write," he said. "Ditch the beginning and end; you'll be left with the 'pineapple.' And if all else fails, write it backwards." The pineapple? Now that was a new one on me.

So I followed Juan's tips. The poem looked better, then didn't. I incorporated new language from internet searches on the poem's key images. It was beginning to look like progress. At this point, whether or not the anthology accepted the poem was moot. It had become my personal challenge…was this poem going to win or was I?

Twice more I shared it with Ann, who responded with more questions: *Can you visually show what Miyoshi is letting go? What one image carries the reader through the poem's terrible events? Has the moon abandoned Miyoshi?* Each time, I sighed aloud, considered her comments, and got back to work. Finally, a full 25 revisions from where I started, I liked where the poem had landed—and I respected the journey. Two weeks before deadline, I screwed my courage to the sticking place and hit submit. It felt amazing to have worked through barriers of crafting and self-doubt to meet the challenges of an idea that wouldn't give up on me, aided by people who *never* give up on me. Miyoshi Jingu, the woman I wrote about, was strong. Even after her husband's untimely death, she ran the successful tea house while rearing her eight children. She responded to prejudice with dignity and forgiveness and, in the end, triumphed. Writing in what I imagined to be her voice made me stronger, too.

The following month, Dos Gatos Press accepted "Tea House of the Texas Moon." I was beyond ecstatic, partly because the acceptance validated hard lessons learned through six months of revisions, but mostly because Miyoshi Jingu's story deserved to be told.

The anthology, *Bearing the Mask*, sits prominently on my bookshelf as a reminder that an idea that wriggles itself into your brain provides an invaluable opportunity to work and grow, create and polish, and make something you're proud of.

Laura M Kaminski

WOW! NOW WHAT?

Let me tell you a secret: these are my favorite emails to receive, the ones that come from poets who have just received their first acceptance letter from a journal. I remember my "Wow!" moment, my first acceptance email for a submitted poem. It came on December 31st, 2012, after I'd been actively engaged in a daily personal practice of poetry for four and a half months. And 2013 opened with a newfound sense of validation, credibility... and then my own "Now what?"

Every few months since then, I've taken time to record in my journal why I write, and what I hope to accomplish or gain from it. Whenever I receive a "Wow! Now what?" email from a poet, I relive my own "Wow!" moment vicariously, and then respond with some excerpts from that journal. If I know you, poet, and you emailed me about your first acceptance, you've seen at least some of these notes. If I don't know you yet, and you're still floating with the exhilaration of your first acceptance, congratulations! As for "Now what?" you may want to consider the following from my own lessons learned (so far) along the way.

- Don't take rejections to mean that the poems you submitted don't have value... they may need revision, they may not be a good aesthetic fit for that particular journal, they may not quite meet criteria stated in the journal's guidelines.

- If you don't understand the guidelines, email the editors and ask for clarification.

- Research—and I really do mean research. Study journals you enjoy reading and try to get a sense of their aesthetics and demographics.

Read the poems, read the bio statements, look for sub-themes in accepted poems that tend to appear in multiple issues. Read at least 50 poems and their accompanying bio statements for each poem you submit.

- Keep your own bio statement short and unassuming, in keeping with what they usually publish. With didactic, faith-based, long, or rhyming poems, be sure you've seen those kinds of poems in a particular journal on several occasions before you submit them. If you're going to preach, do it to the choir, so to speak. A faith-based first-person experience poem stands a chance at most journals, as long as you don't imply other people should believe or practice the same way you do. (Since my own poetry has become progressively faith-based as I've continued writing, these were both important discoveries for me.)

- Keep very close track of your submissions, particularly if you decide to do simultaneous submissions. I usually avoid submitting the same piece to two journals at the same time, after going through the mortifying embarrassment of having the same poem accepted in two places on the same day, and having to apologize to the editors of one of the journals for messing up their issue plans and work and reading time they'd invested by withdrawing the poem.

- Keep close track of what poems were published where and when... it may seem silly at first, when there's only a few, but that list will grow, and you'll be glad to have it when you need it.

- If you are on social media, share poems you like from the journals you like... even if your own work doesn't appear in those issues. It will help you connect with other poets from those issues, and contribute to the literary community as a reader. Also, now that I'm an editor, I've learned: editors as well as poets love to see their work visibly appreciated.

- When you run across a contemporary poet whose work you really enjoy, search out more of it. The process will often lead you to discover new journals that you enjoy and where you might submit your own work.

- When you read a poem that inspires you to write one, use an epigraph or an acknowledgment at the beginning of the poem clearly indicating the source of inspiration. (There are rather a large number of good reasons to do this, and no good reasons not to.)

- "Poets reach out to poets"—that's a quotation from poet, editor, and educator José Angel Araguz. I first "met" José because I researched his work and found contact information for him after reading two poems of his that really stunned me in an issue of *Right Hand Pointing*. If there's someone whose work really resonates with you, explore it, and reach out to them.

- Take advantage of free opportunities to explore ways of reading a poem. There are a number of free online workshop communities, and some literary journals occasionally include articles from an editor exploring why a particular poem works. José's blog, *The Friday Influence*, is an excellent place to "watch" someone else read a poem; it's free, and he posts every Friday.

- If you read several issues of a journal and don't feel like it resonates with you, move on. Also move on if you read a specific poem several times and feel cross-threaded all the way through. There are thousands of other venues, and other poems. It's a buffet with a wide range of choices; give yourself permission to indulge your own tastes and choose how you spend your reading time.

- Also: if you don't like a poem by someone else, please do move on. It serves no purpose to offer negative, unsolicited criticism. Be open to the possibility that the poet will discover the issues with the poem all on their own. Also be open to the possibility that the only issue is that you have stumbled upon a poem for which you are not among the intended readership. It's okay not to like a poem. But do be kind, and stay kind...you're far less likely in any case to regret making a kind comment than the other sort.

- Determine a budget for reading and writing, and stick to it. If you have enough money, it's easy to buy books of poems and subscribe to journals on impulse, but if you set a small budget—a book a week or a book a year doesn't matter as long as it is within your means—then you are both supporting the literary community in the same way you are asking them to support you, and you are also forcing yourself to really focus on what appeals most to you. There's never enough time to read everything, so concentrating on a few carefully selected things can help keep burnout and over-reaching and disappointment from setting in.

- Think about your own philosophy regarding published vs. unpublished poetry. Some journals require a poem never have appeared (i.e. been visible to a reader) anywhere in order to consider it unpublished, so it can't have been posted on social media (Facebook, blog, whatever). Other journals consider a poem to be unpublished as long as it has not yet been accepted by an edited journal.

- Who are your readers? How important are the formal publication credits? Is it more important to have the subscribers of a print journal have access to your work (exclusivity and reputation and recognition), or are you trying to say something in your poems to anyone who wants to hear it, and so are more interested in establishing a readership?

- Be patient with editors who take a long time to respond. If you are not already aware of it, do know that most are volunteers, and life gets in the way often enough.

- If you have a poem that you really want to get right, and it doesn't quite seem to be falling into place... or one you're not sure is working... ask friends (poets or editors who have become friends), if they have time to take a look. Be really clear when you send the request that it is perfectly okay if they don't have time, but if they do, you'd value their opinions on a poem. If they agree to let you send it, do, and thank them profusely for their time and input.

- When you've received request input from someone on a poem, honor their time and effort by taking that input into consideration, even if you don't think much of it, and really do try to revise the poem. You may hate how it turns out, you may love it. You may eventually scrap all revision attempts and return to your original version. Either way, the input is of value, because it gives you an opportunity to re-engage with the poem and find out what really feels right to you.

- This is the single most frequently repeated note-to-self in my own poetry journal: don't be afraid to revise. You can always return to the original version, and none of the effort you invest in revision is ever wasted. Don't be afraid to revise. Try switching narrative viewpoints. Try moving from given forms to free verse and back. Try not looking at the poem for a week, then rewriting it from memory; any lines you can't remember are... well, by definition, not so memorable, and still need work.

- Once every few months, write a note to yourself about why you write, what you're getting out of it personally, what need it is fulfilling for you, why you keep doing it. Take the time to ask yourself questions, and answer them honestly, then consider those answers. If you find yourself in a poetry slump when nothing seems to be working well on the page, it may be because your own perceptions and aspirations have changed, and your poetry practice may need a course adjustment, a realignment with your own ideals.

So... take what's useful, blissfully release the rest... of this essay, of any critique you receive, of lines in your own poems when revising, of any of your own perspectives and opinions you may have outgrown without really noticing along your journey. And, because it bears repeating, don't be afraid to revise. None of the effort you invest in revision is ever wasted.

Joan Leotta

EXCELSIOR

Staying encouraged in the face of rejection is hard, and many (including myself!) have written on ways to keep one's spirits creative and upbeat in the face of a wall of editors who say "NO!" to our work. However, success can be tricky too. Success can cause us to sit back and relax—which is also "death" to creativity. We need to constantly challenge ourselves as artists to improve, to try new things and to reach for higher (more difficult) outlets for our work. Much of this essay appeared on Trish Hopkinson's blog in July 2017. Her blog is one that is worth mentioning—she regularly posts places to submit and often interviews editors of poetry magazines. The interviews are great reading. Her questions expose what editors are looking for in submissions, which is vital information for any writer.

Using Success as a Motivator

When I am fortunate enough to receive an acceptance or even win a prize, I have adopted the habit or repeating the mantra, "onward and upward." The three words relate to a Longfellow poem and the struggle of a mountain climber. Although I don't recall the entire Longfellow poem, "Excelsior," I do know it deals with a young man, who in face of bad weather continues onward and upward into the Alps with a flag emblazoned with the word, "Excelsior!" The Italian Alpine society was so impressed with this 19th-century poem that the young man's banner word became part of their motto.

For me, the call to keep moving onward and upward has been and is still a way to keep myself moving in my chosen field of writing. Writing is a calling which, like mountain climbing, has a lot of ups and downs. (Bad pun intended.) The call to keep moving onward and upward, to improve one's work is a positive stress, an encouragement to work.

As I noted above, writers often hear about moving onward through rejection, using rejection as building blocks to success, learning from rejection. The many aspects of overcoming rejection in a positive way include persistence, (sending the work out again), revision to make the work better, reviewing markets to select ones more suited to particular works. I agree with this approach and indeed, persistence has a hallowed place in my reserve of tools to keep myself going when I get a Dear Author letter.

However, I have come to realize that success also benefits from the advice in that motto, "Excelsior!"

Yes, receiving an acceptance letter from a magazine or press is a time for joy, for celebrating. An acceptance validates that piece of work as being worthy to be read by the public at large. The danger of acceptance, however, is that we might receive this "attaboy" as a message that we have *arrived*, that we are in the place we need to be and now need only to keep producing work at this level. Instead, I believe we should take each acceptance as a challenge to move higher. We should not rest on the plateau. Instead, we should move onward and upward, challenging ourselves to write even better poetry, break into even more difficult markets, and try new literary forms.

I love all of the poems I have sent out—that's why I send them out. I want to find readers who will also enjoy them, maybe even love them. However, I also love the *craft* of writing. So, while I allow each acceptance to validate me as a writer, I also consider it a challenge to improve myself. The mountain of writing "perfection" has no summit—it's a moving target. We can always improve.

Fueled by the hope generated by acceptances, there are five ways I work to continually improve my writing. I have found these to bring success to me and hope they will do the same for you.

1) Seek out journals of a "higher" level (with regard to acceptance/ rejection rates) and or journals that publish people you admire, but that you have not yet "cracked." Read the poetry they have accepted. Study that poetry as you studied poems in school. What makes them work? Are they interested in poems in a particular form? Free verse with attention to meter? Edgy topics?

2) Look at forms of poetry you have not yet tried and strive to write in those forms and find publication homes for your work. Read those

forms. Over the past year, I tried villanelle, ghazal, and haiku. I succeeded in villanelle and ghazal, but those tiny little haiku proved elusive until this year. Last fall I attended a workshop on haiku. Just this past week I read an essay on writing haiku (by a poet I admire) and it added further insights which led to a group of haiku and acceptance of one of that group by a literary magazine specializing in haiku.

3) Challenge yourself by taking a poem you have already written and transforming it into new shapes and forms.

4) Challenge yourself with a contest—a topic you have not thought of before and write it out.

5) Challenge yourself with timed writings, or writing in a particular form or number of words each day. You might not get much that is worth publishing out of this, but it will lubricate the wheels of your creative engines.

Above all, avoid the temptation to regard success with complacency. Acceptances are a call to move on, climb higher, and to reach deeper into our creative selves to craft poems that come before more sets of eyes (and ears for audio poems), and touch more hearts.

Katie Manning

HOW TO NETWORK AS A POET

I used to think that "networking" was just a scummy thing that business majors did. I thought it meant feigning interest in people because they might be able to help you somehow in the future. I was shocked to discover that networking doesn't have to be scummy and that I'd been accidentally networking as a poet all along.

Writers always advise other writers to read a lot and write a lot, but I would add that poets need to connect with other people who read, write, edit, and publish poetry, not because those people might help them, but for the sheer joy of connecting with others who enjoy the same weird and wonderful thing. When you make these connections, a side effect will inevitably be that you will come across more opportunities as well.

Here are a few ways to network as a poet:

1. Contact people whose work you admire.

One of my favorite things about being in the world of poetry is that our rock stars are often accessible. We can find them online and send them messages, and they will often write back. Of course some of them won't, but in my experience, most do, and they're happy to hear that their work has reached someone.

When I was a graduate student in Louisiana, I came across a poem in *The Pedestal Magazine* that took off the top of my head. I read it again. Then I read it again. Then I thought, "I have to find this poet and tell her how much I love this poem!"

I had never tracked down a poet like this before, but I searched online for "Nicelle Davis" and found her blog. I left a comment telling her that I loved that poem. She replied that my comment made her day. I invited her to send work to my school's literary journal, and she did. Then she tracked me down in the book fair at the next AWP conference just to say hello and thank me again for my encouragement. Then I moved to California, not too far from her, and I started teaching her book in my poetry classes. She came to talk to my students. She came again, and she and her son spent the night at my house. Then she taught my chapbook in her class, and I drove my very pregnant body through the mountains to meet with her students. Then she planned a wonderful event in Los Angeles—The Poetry Circus—and invited me to be a performer. Then I solicited one of Nicelle's poems that I'd heard and loved for the first issue of my newly created literary journal, *Whale Road Review*. Then I performed in another Poetry Circus; I have met so many poets and publishers in Southern California because of this event. Then I moved down to San Diego and invited Nicelle to be the featured poet at my university's annual Poetry Day…

I could go on, but you can see that what began with a blog comment has grown wildly over the last several years into admiration for each other's work, shared opportunities, and friendship. I couldn't have known that all of this would follow my comment, and I didn't contact her because I wanted anything from her at all; I was just a reader who loved a poem and wanted the poet to know.

2. Write reviews.

One of the most challenging acts of literary citizenship is reviewing newly published poetry books, chapbooks, and albums. Reviews are hard to do well. They need not be dry; a good review can be an engaging essay on its own.

The best way to get into reviewing is to read several reviews in a variety of publications and see what most appeals to you. It's also important to read the guidelines for review submissions. Some journals have review copies to send to potential reviewers. (Free books!) Some want reviewers to send a finished review for consideration. Others require a query or even samples of previous reviews first. Some only consider reviews of full-length poetry books, and others are open to reviews of chapbooks, albums, or other forms as well.

Ultimately, if you want to review for a specific magazine, then pay attention to their written submission guidelines and also to their unwritten aesthetic preferences based on the other reviews they've published. If you want to review a collection of poetry and don't have a venue in mind, consider looking into the magazines that have previously published pieces from that collection or that have previously published your own poems.

People in the poetry world don't agree on the purpose of reviews. Some reviews offer an overview of the strong and weak points of the work and conclude with a final assessment of its value. Other reviews provide a strategically detailed glimpse into the work that allows readers to choose whether or not the poetry is for them. I tend to follow the advice of one of my mentors: if you don't love something, why would you spend so much time and energy reviewing it? Why publicize it at all? I prefer to spend my efforts on work that I love and want others to know about as well.

Note: this does not mean that poetry and poets should never be criticized, but rather that we should be careful with our own limited resources, especially when we're newer to the poetry scene. This also doesn't mean that we should write positive reviews of work we don't love. If you've received a review copy from a journal, it is okay to tell the editor, "I read the book you sent, and I'm not the right person to write this review." You might offer to return the book or to review another book for them instead.

When you review poetry, you make connections with the poet, with their publisher, with the magazine editor who publishes the review, and with people who read the review. I recently had a non-poet friend tell me that she had read my review of Luci Shaw's *Sea Glass* in *The Cresset* via social media and had purchased the book as a gift for a dear friend as a result. This sort of networking extends its branches far beyond my ability to track.

3. Edit or read for a journal.

From the oldest print magazines to the newest online literary journals, most publications rely on teams of people to read submissions. If you find a venue whose work you love, consider volunteering for them or even applying for an editor position. If they say no, then you've let an editor know that you love their work, and you've lost nothing. If you do become a reader, assistant editor, or genre editor, then you will get to see the behind-the-scenes world of publishing, which will inevitably make you a better submitter of your own work and connect you to the writers whose work you publish.

I've also found that connecting with literary journals, editors, and poets on social media allows me to see a pretty constant stream of calls for submission, which means I don't have to go searching for places to submit my own work. Editing literary journals has connected me more widely to other people in the poetry world than anything else I've done.

Since I started my own online literary journal, I have connected with so many of our authors on social media. Initially, we make this digital connection so I can tag them and promote their piece that we've published, but beyond that, I also promote their future publications and clever posts. I end up seeing or hearing about kids, jobs, trips, and more. Then I get to meet many of our contributors in person at conferences and workshops. As if it weren't rewarding enough to read and share such wonderful writing, sometimes this act of networking also results in dear friendships.

4. Attend readings, conferences, and workshops.

Not all of us can afford to attend major conferences and out-of-town workshops, but if you're able, it's a wonderful thing to gather with fellow writers. Whether or not you do the large events, try to get to your nearest reading series or open mic. Again, this is not so much about promoting yourself or selling your books, but those things will likely happen if you're engaged with poetry communities.

As I type these words, I'm in Santa Fe at the Glen Workshop, which is put on by *Image* journal. When I first came two years ago, I walked into the dining hall for the first meal and felt like everyone else knew each other. The next morning, I went to my poetry workshop, which was led by Carolyn Forché. I was thrilled to meet one of my favorite living poets, but I was also terrified to be in her presence and in the company of the incredible workshop participants. This workshop turned out to be the most ideal combination of rigor and warmth. Carolyn made us work with daily assignments on top of the pieces we'd prepared before we gathered, and we read each other's work closely and critically, but we also managed to avoid condescension and competition in our conversations. We showed each other some genuine care, and many of us have stayed in touch since then. I also wound up meeting other writers and artists at meals, in afternoon writing sessions, evening events, and after-hours gatherings. When I came back to the workshop this summer, again to participate in Carolyn's class, I knew I was signing up for hard work, but I also knew that I would enjoy reconnecting with friends and making new ones. I knew that I'd get suggestions on my poems in the workshop, but I'd also get affirmation and encouragement. When I'm here, I feel like I've found my people.

***

I certainly don't want to suggest that the world of poetry is idyllic. As with any field, there are some hyper-competitive and selfish people. There are some writers, editors, publishers, and organizations that seem to thrive on conflict and chaos. There are workshops and events that feel more cut-throat than supportive. There are also people who only want to self-promote and don't care at all about connecting with others. As just one example, some people perform at events or read at conferences and then leave without watching anyone else. We don't have to be those people. We can be good readers and listeners. We can celebrate each other's achievements. We can be kind and connect with each other for the pleasure of camaraderie. When you network like this, you might find, as I have, that the relationships are the best part of this poetry world, and any opportunities that come your way as a result of those connections are a nice bonus.

Tasha Cotter

FINDING (AND SERVING) YOUR LITERARY COMMUNITY

Creative writers are often hesitant to share their work—and who can blame them? Being a creative writer is all about self-exposure: we often share our darkest journeys, our irresistible questions, and the stories of our lives on the page. Good writing is *brave* writing, and so the hesitation to share that work with the public is often strong.

After I earned an MFA in Creative Writing in 2010, I felt more comfortable sharing my work, having gone through many creative writing workshops where my work was critiqued. When my first full-length collection of poetry, *Some Churches*, was released in 2013 with Gold Wake Press, I understood that part of being an author would be to share my work with others. But how does one go about that, I wondered?

Whether you're just getting started on your creative writing journey, or going through the publication process for the first time (congratulations!) these five tips will help you step outside the creative journey and start thinking about how to make connections locally—and regionally—to share your work with others. Promoting your work and reading in front of others is one of those skills that gets easier over time, so let's get started:

1. Connect with your state poetry society.
Getting involved with your state poetry society has lots of advantages. There's the possibility to meet other writers from around the state, and many host annual conferences where members can come together to share their work or hear a lecture. (And maybe *you* could even teach a workshop.) This is not just a great way to network, but it's a chance for you to share your work with your peers. Connections are *highly* valuable as a working artist.

2. Participate or volunteer with a local reading series.

You can find a reading series in many cities around the U.S. Advantages include: the ability to share your work with an audience, sell your books, and (hopefully!) make a positive impression with the host—who may invite you back! (Side note: it's also a good idea to attend these whenever you can to support local artists.) So how do you locate a reading series? The simplest way is to look online. For example, *Poets & Writers* magazine's website offers a quick search for reading venues. Their database allows you to narrow down by city. You can also simply google "your city + reading series" for a quick run-down on reading series and events happening near you. Here are four worth checking out:

- Writers Can Read—Huntington, WV
- Flying Out Loud—Louisville, KY
- RiverTown Reading Series—Paducah, KY
- InKY Reading Series—Louisville, KY

3. Consider leading a community workshop.

You may think you're not qualified to teach a creative writing workshop, or that you don't have anything to offer aspiring artists, but if you've published a book or earned an MFA in Creative Writing, it's likely a local library or community center would be delighted if you pitched a class to them. It's OK to think small at first: only want to teach a single class on a Saturday in the summer for an hour? Try it and see how it goes. The more organized you are in your pitch and the more professional you are, the better your chances.

4. Offer to help. (Think summer programs for young adults.)

Many states offer summer programs for high school students that are geared toward the arts. Often these summer positions are paid, and it's a great way to build connections with the staff and promote yourself as an artist and educator.

5. Get involved.

Have you noticed a trend here? The best way to start getting "out there" as an artist and getting comfortable sharing your work with the public is looking for opportunities to be of service and ways to establish and build relationships. These relationships and networks of people will be there to support you as a future author—and they may very likely buy your book when the time comes.

Nancy Reddy

PUBLISHING AND THE LITERARY COMMUNITY

In the opening weeks of the MFA, my classmates and I were tasked with screening manuscripts for our university's poetry book prize. All of the manuscripts were submitted on paper via the mail, and so each of us was assigned three boxes of forty manuscripts each. They were sturdy cardboard boxes, the kind you might select for packing books when moving between apartments and then regret, because they were too heavy to comfortably lift. We sat in our shared office, surrounded by the reading posters and abandoned student portfolios and other detritus of all the poets who'd passed through that space before us, and attempted to sort through our piles of manuscripts.

Although there were some manuscripts you could easily toss to the side—God entered the contest yearly for a while, and his cover letters grew increasingly snippy as his divine poetic insights went unrecognized by publication—being a first-round screener showed me just how hard it is to rise up against the odds of the slush pile. All of the manuscripts were clearly the result of hard work. Someone had labored, in the case of each manuscript, to write and revise and order and rewrite and rewrite and reorder the manuscript. They'd researched book prizes. They'd printed clean copies of their best work, written out a check for the reading fee, and taken that earnest hard work to the post office in a manila envelope. And the odds were nearly impossibly against them. We were only allowed to promote for consideration in the next round of screening three or four manuscripts from each box—less than 10 percent of what we read.

As I read through manuscript after manuscript, overwhelmed sometimes with the material heft of other poets' labor, I thought about my own poems, which I was first beginning to send out in a serious way. I imagined them fighting their way through—or not—piles of other people's poems, trying to muscle out all the other poems in editors' inboxes and stacks of printed poems. I imagined them sharpening their elbows and rising above the fray, victorious. Or not—as I received rejection after rejection, as is the way with literary publication.

This is a remarkably dispiriting way of thinking about publishing creative work. I do not recommend it. I'd like instead to suggest another way of thinking about literary publishing. I'd like to suggest that we think about seeking publication as one way of being in community with other writers.

Later that same year, when my classmates and I founded the literary magazine *Devil's Lake*, I was able to think about publishing in a less hostile way. I took on the role of Founding Reviews and Interviews Editor, and in that capacity I had the privilege of reaching out to poets whose work I had loved to ask them questions about their work and their process or, in the case of reviews, of being able to say, *here is a book I loved, and here is why. I think you should read it, too.* And when I was reading through the slush pile, I was able to see how much really good work there was, and to appreciate how amazing it is to live in a time when so many people are working hard at the almost always unpaid and unrecognized labor of writing poetry. We were able, when we accepted poems, to begin to build relationships and community around us. Some of the poets were local, and we became in-person friends, sharing poems over brunch and poetry groups at each others' apartments, and others we loved and supported from afar, meeting for off-site readings at AWP. We hosted events at our town's Book Fest each year, and they became a space for local writers to talk about their craft and share that expertise with a broad audience.

As a result of that experience, my general thought about publishing is this: if you want to take up space—if you want your poems to earn inches in print magazines and screen space in online publications—you should work to make space for other writers, too. This can happen in lots of ways: buying books, attending readings, sharing new writing you love on your social media feeds. If you don't have the funds to buy all the books you'd like to read and share (who does?) you can request that your local public library or university library buy the book. You can write reviews on Amazon and Goodreads. You can write to poets whose work you love and tell them why. (I'd guess the number of poets in this country who are too famous and too widely read to appreciate a note from someone who's actually read their work is in the single digits.)

These practices are often gathered together under the rubric of Literary Citizenship, which generally speaks to ways that writers can participate in literary communities. Extending this metaphor of community a bit farther, I like to think about literary magazines and literary publishing as a kind of neighborhood. So when you're considering which magazines to submit to, it might help to think not about how to sharpen your elbows and push down all the other poems in the slush pile—but to think instead about which neighbors you'd like to meet. Which journals are publishing new writing you love? Who do you want to be talking to? If you're not sure where to get started, a few ideas: CRWROPPS (run by the poet Allison Joseph) sends daily emails with all kinds of poetry news, including calls for submissions, jobs, fellowships, and other interesting tidbits. *New Pages* and *The Review Review* (both online) publish reviews of literary magazines, which can be helpful to get your footing in the landscape of poetry publication. And when you find writers that you love, follow them on social media and watch where they're publishing. Then get out there and meet your neighbors.

The Poet's Journey

Marina Blitshteyn

POETRY HAS VALUE

poetry has value, but i'm reluctant to say how much money that is, as reluctant as i am to admit how much money i spent on reading fees and application fees and just "hey notice me" fees this year. my credit card statement keeps my secrets. on a good month, which is a month i feel pretty good about submitting, it rockets to roughly $400. on a bad month, which is a month i don't feel good about the poems or the business or a soup of both, it could be a measly $30. that's how much it costs for a press to consider my manuscript.

in my heart i know it's a scam on par with the housing market, but i'm not business-minded enough to understand how money is manipulated in this country to stay in the few hands who've had it all along. some barely even get to touch it, but they know they have it, and knowing is the prize. or knowing you have it means knowing you can lose it just as quickly, which is the poison. for those for whom money is abstraction, i bet poetry makes intuitive sense. there can exist this art, this form, that comes from nothing and amounts to very little still. money isn't the object here, and many of us "working" poets or "emerging" poets believe that. some say fame or prestige or maybe validation, but that comes and goes even faster than money. it's a faulty fix, a temporary salve on a larger wound of general worthlessness.

because when we write poems, or rather when we can't resist that urge anymore, very few of us write for a normative purpose—to appease an editor, to profile a current or popular event, to sell pharmaceuticals. the closest we come is in the infamous mfa, where poets sit around drinking cheap box wine and feeling like inheritors of the world together. such is the case, but the crushing burden of having to write on cue or to a weekly assignment is just another way we learn what value poetry holds.

when we graduate we sometimes say we "hold" an mfa in creative writing from suchandsuch university. some have said they "attained" it. in good company we laugh about its uselessness, where it isn't hanging in our offices, how far it got us creatively or professionally. it's tough to talk about it in terms of investment because the door is pointing towards the crisis of higher education in general. and that door is marked exit. but to sidestep that call for a little longer, my primary allegiance has always been to poetry, so it's hard to do the math on that. it's dividing everything by zero. it's multiplying everything by zero. if this is a zero-sum game i'm probably in the right field. it's always felt like my game because i've done a lot to make sure the writing is first in my heart, money a distant third.

arrogant, self-involved, delusional, privileged. i take them all because they're true in many ways. it's easy to think poetry is a luxury in america and i once believed it. but the kids i taught (too briefly) in what they called an "underserved" school knew all the lyrics to things, kept a certain reserve of energy for reciting them at bus stops and lunch breaks or halls. in peak grief my friends turn to me for some poems to read at funerals or just to feel wiser about their loss for a bit. in moments of glory, a line or two. at weddings a kind of sermon from our priests of the invisible, as wallace stevens said. left and right a touch of poetry, if we dare call it that, has touched the rich and poor alike. and how can we forget the blessing that was claudia rankine's *citizen*. how it allowed my students to think about racism in america through many faces of "you," even their own.

all this is to say i'm still resistant to calling poetry writing labor, as resistant as i am to the idea of "work" in general. poetry for me has always been the fun part, an escape from capitalist expectations. even when it's hard i think at least i'm not working. at least i respond to the needs of something more permanent than the latest gadget or a finicky administration. i still believe in my spirits—they've stayed with me through sickness and health, for richer or poorer, through an mfa in nyc to an adjunct labor battle i witness firsthand. that's the work i'm much more comfortable tacking a price-tag to. and expect to make a living wage of. and demand some benefits with. the rest, as i say, is poetry.

Leonard Franzén

BEING A POET

I am at my own release party in Copenhagen, Denmark. I'm nervous because I'm supposed to read my poems in front of an audience. Before I read, I pour gin and tonic in a plastic mug and drink. I have stage fright.
I step up. Look at the audience. At all the Danish people. I don't think they understand Swedish. I for sure have a hard time understanding Danish.
I read, and it's over. I'm glad it's over.
I guess I'm a real writer now?

During my BFA there was an ongoing discussion about when you are a writer. This question may seem weird to English-speaking people. You're a writer when you write, right? The thing is that it's impossible to translate "writer" to Swedish. The word doesn't exist in my language. The word "author" exists, but not writer. You can't be a Swedish writer. You can be a Swedish author, but that is after you've been published. You can definitely be a Swedish poet. But when are you a real poet?
Here are some possible answers:
1. When you write poetry.
2. When your work has been published in an online journal.
3. When your work has been published in a physical journal.
3. When your first chapbook is released.
4. When your first "real" book is released.
5. When you're famous because of your poetry.

Pick one or all of the above.

I never call myself a poet. My friends call me a poet sometimes, when they are joking with me. They think poetry is dorky. I guess I think so too sometimes. I mean, some poetry is really bad. Being a poet is not always the same thing as being an excellent poet.

I thought things would change after my first poem was published in a Swedish online journal.
I thought I would feel different after my first poem was published in a Swedish paper journal.
And after my first poem was published in an American paper journal.
And after my chapbook was published by a real publisher.
But I didn't.
I don't know why I don't feel like a real poet.
And why some people call themselves poets even though they haven't been published.
Maybe they define themselves by the first definition. They write poetry hence they are poets.

I guess some people want to call themselves poets because it gives meaning to their writing. In the same way as a person performing surgery needs to be called a doctor.
It's a role and an activity and they are interlinked.
I would call myself a poet if all I did was write poetry. But I spend more time sleeping, eating and watching TV.

People who call themselves poets have an image of poets. People who don't also have an image of poets. The word is filled with connotations. Some think of a slam poet, others think of the Nobel Prize winner Thomas Tranströmer. Others think of Sappho.
The poet is an outsider in this society. He or she gazes upon the world from a distance.
Some people like to think that.

Do people really call themselves poets? I'm starting to doubt it. I don't know what it's like in the U.S. but here in Sweden there are only freaks that call themselves poets:

Young men with kooky facial hair and top hats.
Middle-aged New-Age women.
I wish someone could inform me on the situation in the U.S.

Here is my conclusion.
It is your choice if you want to call yourself a poet. Nobody is going to say you're not.
If they say you're not, then they are wrong.
They can't prove you're not a poet.
They will think you're pretentious. Especially if you haven't published anything.
That's their problem.
It's okay if you write poetry and don't want to be associated with so-called "poets".
It's your choice.
If people want to call you a poet anyway, they are wrong.

Being a poet doesn't make you a good poet.
Being a published poet doesn't make you a good poet.
Being unpublished doesn't make you a bad poet.

So I guess anything goes.

J.G. McClure

THE MISEDUCATION OF THE POET: HIGH SCHOOL AND THE FEAR OF POETRY

When I was an undergraduate taking one of my first poetry workshops, my poet-professor joked that "high school is where poetry goes to die." I chuckled, thinking he was simply making fun of the melodramatic effusions of teenage writers.

I've since come to realize that what he was getting at is a much more systemic problem: that the way we're taught about poetry in high school (the last time that many people will likely ever read a poem) bleeds the living energy from poetry and teaches students that the art is nothing but the dusty stuff of a museum of antiquities.

Some years ago, it was my good fortune to be able to teach four introductory poetry workshops at a major university. In addition to being the gateway course into the Creative Writing Emphasis, the course also allows the students to bypass taking a supremely unpopular research course. The result is a mix of students from all disciplines, some of whom want to become writers, and many of whom want to avoid, at all costs, writing a policy research paper. I discovered that nearly all of the students simultaneously held two mutually exclusive notions about poetry. One, that poetry is easy—you just write whatever you feel! And two, that poetry is impossibly arcane—all thees and thous and Grecian Urns and anapests. Among all these students—intelligent, well-educated students drawn from the top of their high school classes—I had only two or three who had read a contemporary poem. Most of the students vaguely recollected some of Shakespeare's sonnets, a few remembered Keats by name. After that, all bets were off.

I was disappointed, but not exactly surprised. My high school had excellent teachers of literature, including a PhD. I was lucky. It was there that I began to discover how powerful literature could be, and I can't thank those teachers enough. We read everything from *Gilgamesh* and *Beowulf* to Keats and Coleridge to Williams and Eliot. And yet, not once did we venture past the Modernists. There were no Creative Writing classes offered.

Still, one of the teachers, Mr. Moore—a balding hippie who would bring his Telecaster to class and shred some riffs before talking passionately about variation of sentence structure—took it upon himself to teach his AP English Language class about writing more than just the essays the national exam would require of us. He took us into the woods to walk through nature and write poems about it. He sent us off to roam the campus and write poems about it. We didn't workshop the poems, and he didn't critique them.

And to be honest, I doubt I could have handled it if he had—I was a nervous kid and didn't think I had a creative bone in my body. Though I understand his reasons for encouraging our efforts and avoiding criticism, the approach had the unintended effect of implying that poems were the spontaneous outpouring of emotion—not pieces of craft to be revised, torn apart, and rebuilt in order to make them better. The poem as it was written was the poem as it would remain.

But it was obvious to me that my efforts were nothing in comparison to those of the great dead we were reading, and I had no sense of how to improve them. Nor did I understand *why* I did the things I did. I sat at a picnic table under a tree and wrote about some falling leaves and trampled acorns. Most likely we had been reading Wordsworth, and I had intuited that poetry meant writing about transience and death and how great trees are. I had no sense that poetry had moved beyond those tropes, that contemporary poetry had been trying for decades to escape from the Romantic tradition that still forms so much of its foundation.

In "The Education of the Poet," Louise Glück describes her discovery of poetry: "I read early and wanted, from a very early age, to speak in return. When, as a child, I read Shakespeare's songs, or later, Blake and Yeats and Keats and Eliot, I did not feel exiled, marginal. I felt, rather, that this was the tradition of my language: *my* tradition." Crucially, Glück sees herself here in *conversation* with the great dead, not merely a passive recipient of their brilliance. And yet, think of your high school poetry courses: you'd read the poems, maybe recite them, learn the Greek names for metrical feet, talk perhaps about imagery—you'd study the poem as an alien object, something complicated from the past to be reluctantly understood.

The idea that you could speak *back* never entered the discussion, at least not in my experience. Even when Mr. Moore attempted to put us in conversation with the canon, we were cast less as writers-in-dialogue-with-other-writers and more as clever parrots: we had to write an imitation of Whitman, using the stories and scenes of our own lives. Though we were making something, the goal was simply to fit our stories into the structure Whitman had already established. It was an exercise in mimicry, and a good grade meant being a good mimic. Though there was certainly a value in learning about Whitman's music through imitation, the idea that we could speak back to Whitman, speak *against* Whitman, never appeared.

Setting aside the lack of dialogue with the poets of the past, consider how the poems themselves are discussed. "What is the poet trying to say?" the teacher asks—as if the poet had tried and failed to say something very simple. When Keats wrote "Bold Lover, never, never canst though kiss, / Though winning near the goal yet, do not grieve; / She cannot fade, though thou hast not thy bliss," what he meant to say was, "Urns are pretty cool. But maybe they're not always cool. Because, you know, etchings don't get old, but they can't move either, and that's kind of a bummer." In high school, every poem has to have a tidy message, and you have to be able to name it.

What I mean is this: poems are taught as *messages to be decoded,* not as *irreducible experiences.* No wonder students are impatient with poetry! If the goal is simply to pick out the moral of the poem, then students are absolutely right that poetry is dull and overly complicated—platitudes can be stated much more concisely in prose. This type of message-hunting fails to convey that the way something is said is inextricable from what it means. It fails to convey that a poem is an experience the reader undertakes. It fails, in other words, to convey that there's any difference between the experience of reading, say, *Hamlet*—really feeling his indecision, his false starts and worries and paralysis and rage as they all unfold—and the experience of reading the SparkNotes summary of the play.

Fast-forward to college, to these students sitting in my Intro to Poetry Writing class. They feel like their poems have to have a message, but that that message needs to be obscured by plenty of Poetry-with-a-capital-P. The models that they have to work from are some faintly remembered Shakespeare, maybe some Keats, and a lot of Hallmark cards.

The result is highly overwritten language, a lot of purple greeting-card speak used to dress up an otherwise simple moral axiom. Inevitably, most of the submissions rhyme and attempt meter. (But since they've only studied meter as a set of abstract rules, never in practice, the meter is always garbled.) The syntax is forced through all kinds of painfully Yoda-esque contortions to make it fit the rhyme scheme. (Again, not surprising since that was fine in the Renaissance and nobody has informed them that things have changed.) Some students know that poems don't have to rhyme anymore, but they don't really have a sense of *why* a poet might use free verse in one situation and *why* a poet might use a sonnet in another. The idea that you *don't* just write whatever you feel—that the poem is a carefully made thing, that it is an ordered series of narrative/imaginative/sonic/moral experiences that the reader undergoes—is new.

At first, students will ask how to know where they're *supposed* to break their lines—they want a formula. (Poetry is, after all, just a bunch of rules—remember all that stuff about iambic pentameter?) When I tell them that it's all a question of what *effects* they want to create with their line breaks, that anything they do in the poem has myriad ramifications and precludes everything else they could have done in that moment instead, they're at once frustrated and relieved. Typically someone will say, with a mix of complaint and awe, "I never knew writing poems was so *hard*."

Around that point in the course, a funny thing happens: the students, nearly all of them, start to really *care* about their poems. They come to my office and spend half an hour talking about a few lines. They bring me revisions and more revisions. They discuss their work with their classmates, arguing aesthetic points and comparing their techniques to what they've seen in Glück or Larkin or Stafford or Siken or Lux. The poems improve immeasurably, and the students move from talking about what a poem *means* to talking about what a poem *does*.

At the time of writing, I've been teaching Introduction to Literary Journalism, and I've been surprised by the differences I've seen. From the beginning, the students' writing is far stronger. Sure, there's a bit of overwriting—any beginning writer deals with that—but it's to a far lesser degree than the overwriting I would see at the start of my poetry courses. Nor do they feel the need to overcomplicate their pieces, or to throw in some thees and thous to make sure it's literary enough. Moreover, the students are more passionate from the first day, and they're much more comfortable engaging critically with the articles. If they hate an article, they'll tell me—and they'll tell me articulately *why* they hate it.

But when I show my Lit J students a poem, they turn suddenly quieter; only the bravest will say anything. Even in my poetry classes, it took several weeks for the students to overcome their fear of criticizing poetry. I suspect this is because in high school, they *didn't* criticize poetry—the great poems were great, no question about it, now go try to decipher them.

Since Literary Journalism didn't fully emerge as a recognizable genre until the last few decades, essentially *all* of the pieces that my Lit J students have read have been contemporary, free from the stifling aura of reverence and from the old-fashioned language of the poetry they've grown up having to read. They've seen the Lit J writers as writers, not quasi-mythological voices from the past. They've learned, in other words, to *read* Lit J, rather than to fear it.

Of course, I'm not suggesting that we should stop teaching high-schoolers Shakespeare, Keats, or any of the other foundational poets. If it weren't for reading *Hamlet* and "Prufrock" and "Ode on a Grecian Urn" in high school, I doubt I would have become a writer. These works moved me deeply, though they did not make me feel that I could speak back.

That feeling didn't come until later, when I sat as a sophomore in my first poetry writing class, reading Larkin's "This Be the Verse." The poem works so well because Larkin knows the tropes of children's rhymes, and because he is self-consciously speaking within and against that tradition. His comically-exaggerated-but-not-exactly-insincere argument—go kill yourself, and after you've killed yourself make sure not to have any children—interacts with the bouncy tetrameter of the nursery rhyme to produce an experience that couldn't exist in any other way. It's the result of a poet writing in dialogue with the past in order to create something wonderfully new.

"And you can say *fuck* in a poem?" someone asked.

"Of course you can. Say what the poem needs you to say."

What does the poem need us to say? To know that, we need to know the poems of the past and the poems of the present. We need to learn the language poems speak, and how and when and why that language has changed. And if we're going to get anywhere, we've got to learn how to talk back too.

Abayomi Animashaun

WRITING AGAINST CERTAINTY

After 20 years of writing poetry, I find it's becoming ever more difficult to find the necessary language that appropriately encapsulates my notions of its *what* and its *how*. By this, I mean what poetry is supposed to be about and how I'm supposed to approach it.

Gone are the certainties of my MFA years, when I got into rows with teachers who tried in vain to help me understand that there are infinite entry points to the poetic landscape and that the more approaches I come to understand, the more planes of metaphor I might have at my disposal to give shape to the vibrations of my own imagination. But in my bull-headedness, I was convinced that the only poetry worthwhile had to be accessible and representational.

Back then, poems were self-contained constructs with palpable terminal points, and they often had little to do with each other. Each poem had a reason and a lengthy treatise rehearsed and defended at the slight drop of a hat. I was always working on poems ABC for reasons XYZ. Moreover, I preferred hearing myself talk about the ideas rather than actually being in my study, quietly writing the poems.

And when one *big* poem was done, I would return to my "Book of Certainties," pull out another big subject and set about justifying it and finding words for it. On the surface, I was pronounced and sure. But when I was by myself, outside the lights of performing for friends, I had this nagging idea that my poems (the beginnings, middles and endings of which I knew and could articulate before even writing them) were overly determined and, to be honest, boring.

Besides, I came to find the notion of arguing each reader into accepting the validity of my work a tiring proposition. How long was I to do this? And to how many people? How could I be sure that what I was writing was precisely what each person needed? I grew weary of my own bombast. And while there are many poets in whose hands certainty of how each poem should be *and* what each poem should be about (before they start writing said poem) is a worthwhile tool, I've come to realize it is not for me.

The more I've read and pushed further into the poetic landscape, the lower I have brought those standards—with their loud and colorful positions—with which I adorned myself when I first started. Now, I willingly reach for the same books I denied and find myself teaching poets I railed against to my own students, who, in a few cases, have reacted with the same sure vehemence as I once did. And my pleas of "don't be like I was" have, in a case or two, fallen on deaf ears.

Since certainty (with a big "c") is no longer a compass I use in navigating that wild and engaging frontier of poem making, I find myself more open to possibilities. I'm eager to re-learn and re-see. And I've come to have a particular faith in the creative impulse that sometimes leaves me awake at night and has me reading authors with whom I'm enamored without guilt and others I might have rejected based on borrowed poetics. Most times, I don't even know where I'm going before I begin writing. In the best way possible, this approach leaves me riven. It's a beautiful thing to feel the *knowing* with which my old poetry was informed brought into near stillness and, essentially, silenced.

This way, I am better able to feel each hue and undulation of my imagination come together and take on words, phrases and paragraphs that fill pages and, in time, take on tone, affect emotion and arouse mood. At its best, this approach has allowed me to grow in ways I couldn't have conceived almost 20 years ago. Poems are no longer clearly defined constructs with precise terminal points for me. Instead, they've become, if I may, a long conversation, an expansive dialogue that stretches from my contemporaries all the way back to Adam and Eve.

Now when I sit down to write, it's not with set homilies and locked brows, but with a childlike wonder that allows me to see beyond myself and the little I think I know. I wish I could explain it. I wish I could provide some neat language for it. But something inside of me becomes more generous and humane when I approach poetry this way. When I'm done, I find myself with a surprised understanding of whatever subject I gently engage. Within this understanding, I experience a renewal of sorts that often lifts me beyond the drudgery of the everyday.

Aaron Brown

ON MEDIATION

A few weeks ago, I came out of a classroom building and noticed a bird perched on the hood of my car. It was a small gray bird, with obsidian eyes that contained a simultaneous depth and *joie de vivre*. Of course, after smiling at it, greeting it with a few words—the bird staring back at me the whole time—my first impulse was to take a picture of it with my phone. I tapped the screen, focusing on the bird, its expression still curious, wary, humored. The screen flashed, the image saved, I sat down in my vehicle.

The bird wouldn't go away. I turned the engine on. I started the windshield wipers. I even motioned my hand toward it, hoping it would fly away. I had less than an hour to get home, grab lunch, let out my dog before my next class, so I was beginning to get nervous. I started to pull away out of the parking spot, but then seeing the bird remain there, a breeze ruffling its feathers as it stared serenely at the road, determined to cruise along clutching the hood of my car, I found it humorous enough to want to take a little video. Again, I paused, got out my phone, and started filming.

As my car slowed to the first stop sign, there was a sudden gust of wind. The bird opened up its wings, fluttered upward for a second—before quickly the wings downturned and it flew straight to the asphalt below, disappearing from my sight. I stopped my car, shocked. Thinking I had just run over the poor thing, I looked out and saw the bird lying on the pavement, its wings fluttering before growing still. I convinced myself that because there was no blood, no exposed inner organs, that the bird had avoided my tires. I convinced myself that the bird was ill, was dying of some terminal bird illness, and that it was on its way out even before I got there. Surely, it wasn't my fault, or was it?

I decided to drive away. Later, I tried to eat my lunch and thought about the bird. What was this odd innate desire I felt to record the bird's presence, its flight, its descent? What does it say about me, that my first action was to take a picture—as proof to myself, to others—that there was a bird wanting a joyride that turned into a trip of death? Perhaps if I had been more interested in the bird's safety rather than my own mediation of the experience, could I have saved the bird, figured out a way to help it take flight and find shelter in the nearby trees?

***

I recently attended a talk by Alan Noble, author of *Disruptive Witness*, in which he describes this worrisome, twenty-first-century desire we have to record experiences as they are happening, to share them with the world, and to wait to see what kind of response we get. "What is lost in this whole transaction?" he asked. The *experience itself*, the feeling of appreciating something for what it is, rather than for what one can get out of it. In my rush to record the bird, something was lost—some beauty that I had missed, so concerned about the frame of representation.

***

I am reminded of a memory I have from graduate school when I entered a mentor's office, carrying a fresh poem in for feedback. The poem attempted, miserably, to observe the look on a boy's face as he walked with his father out of a Maryland taqueria and looked up at the full moon. The poem (I've since thrust it to some dark corner of my computer where I can't find it) even acknowledges the speaker's own failure to get the experience right, to reflect this memory truthfully, accurately.

My mentor, in her wise, measured way, showed me how weak the poem was, how intrusive my own voice was to the actual subject matter of the poem. I was writing a poem trying to stand in for the experience itself. I didn't know how to write the experience any other way. I left the meeting with a poem I knew I couldn't save, no matter how hard I tried to revise it.

I haven't written a good poem in six months. Whatever writing a good poem means. If that means a poem you can sit back after finishing its final line, realizing that there is real "felt experience" (to quote Mary Oliver) within it, then I probably haven't written a good poem in a year. All too often, I try to encroach upon the poem, to make of it what I want—to turn it into the Poem rather than the poem. (And here I nod to Ben Learner who discusses in *The Hatred of Poetry* our need to get away from what we think of as THE poem and become comfortable with just writing poetry in its mundaneness and its beauty.) Is my trespassing into the poem a trespassing into the sacred? Or are poems the same as afternoon runs: you go on them when you can and sometimes your body hums in pleasure, other times the first mile is the experience of hell itself? Whatever this pursuit is, my poems keep coming out flat, drained of any real feeling.

In my writing life, I'm beginning to realize that not every experience, not every memory, not every thought can be made into a poem. And that's okay. Mediating experience into poetry is not something that can be forced. Nor is mediation always beneficial. There are other forms—the lyric essay, the short story—that are perhaps more suited for a certain experience, a certain thought, and I find myself writing in these forms more and more. I feel guilty acknowledging poetry's own failure to express everything, a failure that is probably rooted in my own inability. Still, perhaps it is poetry's own failure to mediate every experience that makes it what it is. If poetry is a consecration of experience, there must be something outside of that consecration to provide contrast. Is it heresy for me to say that genres other than poetry are not as sacred, that they exist to elevate, or at the very least differentiate, poetry as such? And while poetry consecrates, surely it cannot consecrate *everything*. If it could, poetry wouldn't have the same distinctive power. It wouldn't be poetry.

***

After lunch that day, I drove by the parking lot where the bird had fallen. I slowed my car and looked through the passenger window expecting to see the small bundle of wings. I took in my breath when I realized it wasn't there— the bird was gone. This time, I had no phone out to capture the experience.

I haven't tried to turn it into a poem. (And here again, I'm guilty of lan- guage—*turn it into*—implying utility, something to be benefitted from an experience.) This time, I simply saw the bird's absence, wondered to myself, and continued on my drive.

Tanis MacDonald

ROWING AWAY FROM THE DESERT ISLAND OF GENIUS

Many of us come to poetry fragile or apprehensive or incredulous, but we hang around and stick our toe in the water, and finally, somehow, are emboldened to try writing a poem despite its oddness and despite the fact that we have very little context for how art is supposed to work or how we are supposed to make it. The fresh start that writing poetry can represent can be a true mental refuge, and it should come as no real surprise that many of us equate such a refuge with making a break for it, geographically. While leaving one place and going to another (presumably) better place might mean dragging all your problems with you, it can also mean, especially when you are young, a potent new beginning. Most of us—even those of us raised in environments that were not arts-friendly—invest a certain amount of faith in what writing will do for us; sometimes it's a ticket to move us away from where we are, sometimes it's a way to stay in one place but make our worlds larger. We may have ties to our community from which we want respite, even though we may not be interested in cutting ourselves off completely from the homeplace. In that case, we may refashion our living spaces into working spaces and do our best to mimic the isolated genius in a private space, even when—especially when—our own spaces are anything but.

The image of the poet sequestered in their office—or better yet, a garret—is an enduring image in which people invest even now, when with a tablet and a WiFi connection, any coffee shop, library, or waiting room can be your garret. The sequestered writer is still a powerful image at least in part because it feeds the fantasy of independence, self-reliance, and isolated genius that seems to define the creative life. But the term "isolated genius" is an oxymoron. Even when we work without anyone else in the room, we work in tandem with our peers, with the cultural conceptions of what good poetry consists of, with our present and former teachers and the texts from which we learned, and with writers we've admired and never met, spiritual or intellectual mentors, or maybe alongside people whose writing drives you crazy and whose example you are striving to defy or push back against the status quo.

Writers are often shy or introverted people, so the myth of the isolated genius can feel attractive because it makes our (sometimes devoutly desired) isolation appear as though it is solely a function of our superior brains rather than a stark manifestation of our loneliness or social awkwardness. Who wants to admit to those? It's so socially awkward to admit to social awkwardness. The benefit of remaining isolated as an artist is that you never have to pay attention to anyone else's art, or even acknowledge that anyone else makes art. Put too many owls in a small cage and they will each gaze out of the bars, affecting serenity and independence, narrowing their eyes as though to assert, "There are no other owls. No other owls." There will be times when you need to do this, to meet a deadline, to start a project, to work on something challenging, but it's no way to live for much longer than a week. There are, inevitably, other owls.

I still laugh remembering the time that I read about a famous novelist's process, including his rigorous routine of writing from 10:00 to 5:00 every day in complete isolation, except for lunch at noon sharp, prepared by his wife, and his 3:00 break, when his wife would knock on the closed door to his office to bring him coffee and cookies. The Great Man was "isolated" and rigorous for exactly two hours at a time. Nice work if you can get it. The truth is that the myth of the isolated genius benefits very few artists, and women and BIPOC artists almost never. It's a romanticized image, made popular by the media via the boasts of a handful of writers who assert their individualism as being beyond the need for peers. Of course, decades of literary criticism invested heavily in "Great Man Theory": the assertion that genius requires no explanation and no context, that some writers are just transcendent and anyone who is anyone thinks so.

Believe me, I understand the appeal of this claim. It's a heady idea that writers can tap into an idea beyond the ken of the great unwashed reader. If I thought it would get me coffee and cookies delivered to my office every day at 3:00, I might subscribe to such a theory of unquestionable natural-born genius myself. The truth is more realistic. All artists are a product of their culture, including beginning artists. The truth is also a good deal less romantic, and quite frankly, a relief to admit. There may be a good deal of mystery in how an idea makes it to the page, but you don't need a direct pipeline to the gods. Even Thoreau had neighbours at Walden Pond.

Ashton Kamburoff

CLEANING HOUSE: POETRY & REVISION

I recently moved to a beautiful home in the quiet town of Smithville, Texas, to start a year-long writing residency. A whole year in the largest house I have ever lived in, left to nothing but my own devices. When I started this writing journey, I did not know such opportunities existed: I had never heard of a "writing residency" (and I actively encourage you to research them). When I found out I was accepted into this position I began to ponder all of the wonders that solitude in a town far removed from major cities might offer. I envisioned long nights on my porch, reading and writing, listening to nothing but the sounds of cicadas clash against the hard siding of my new home. It was to be a year of observation and amazement at the simplicity around me.

The house came fully furnished. Couches, chairs, a bed. Kitchen utensils and bath towels. I was instructed that I needed to bring "nothing," so I sold everything. I kept my books, my records, and my clothes, but I ditched the old furniture and few appliances that were standing on their last legs after three years of grad school and four years of undergraduate studies. I was amazed at my sentimentality, how hard it was to sell an old green leather chair on Craigslist for $15.

The first few days in the house were difficult. I wasn't lonely but I was cognizant of how *quiet* my surroundings were. Smithville is a town of 2,000 people and everything effectively shuts down by eight in the evening (minus the bar and the 7-Eleven). I grew up in Cleveland, Ohio, in a noisy suburb that was speckled with streetlights and turn signals shining through my bedroom window. Neighbors argued, planes flew overhead, ambulances announced themselves nightly. This was a departure. This was some "Sound of Silence" type scenario that I knew was coming for me but maybe I had not fully prepared for.

But I am convinced that the difficulties acclimating were due to my own peculiar nature. I couldn't locate anything in my new house. I would open a drawer looking for a spoon to find the curvature of emptiness. I sat down on the couch and noticed all of the awkward angles that existed between my view and that of the built-in bookshelf. Chairs held no symmetry. Things weren't dirty, but the house was well-worn, and all the hard-to-reach places needed a little sprucing up. The place was mine, but I needed to make it "my own".

I spent an entire day cleaning. Reorganizing. I ripped the furniture out of each room to mop and polish the hardwood floors and I gave each windowsill a proper washing. This affair was something that needed to be done before the process of writing poems could begin. One thing I have noticed about myself as an artist and as a writer is that I must be totally in sync with my environment before I can begin to produce quality work. I don't do well on vacations and I am never able to write when visitors stop by for a few days. Like all writers, I need a degree of solitude, time, and space, to be able to write, but I think that I am a bit more, let's say, *funny*, when it comes to my immediate surroundings. Oftentimes, when people say "now you have something to write about" due to a life experience that involves commotion, I find myself resisting their assertion. If I want to write, then I need *nothing* to happen, and I need that to happen for days at a time.

But if we believe that everything that happens to us is part of the "Writer's Journey" then cleaning house is indeed an element that must be noticed and praised. When we write a poem, we are builders. Poems are creations and they are habitats for our thoughts, fears, desires, and countless other emotions that would take pages to fill. Like any habitat, they must be maintained. If they go on unaccounted for they begin to grow stagnant with dust and the surprises that were once so pleasant to experience become crusted shut, like an old window that needs to be coaxed open. We might be contracted to write the poem, but we must also be custodians of our work and our attention to the intricate details of our habitats, our poems, are essential.

Perhaps cleaning the ledge behind the washer/dryer is unnecessary because no one will see that it is dirty, but if you live in your house, you'll *know*. And that *knowing* is enough of a motivation to wrestle the hulking units away from the wall, dab your cloth in bleach, and meticulously wipe away the dust and lint of many, many months. And within the house of a poem, maybe that ledge is a line break? The dust? A tired ending or a weak transition that we know exists because we are the inhabitants.

Writing poems, like cleaning a house, can never be perfect. There is always some nagging reminder of a flaw. But I truly do believe that best presentations are worth something. If we are going to clean house, let us clean deep.

I don't believe it is any coincidence that *stanza* in Italian means "little room." Our stanzas are the rooms within the home of the poem. Just like you wouldn't cook breakfast in your bathroom or shower in your living room, stanzas must carry utility and practicality. They cannot be arbitrary. In a way, they must instruct our audiences how to live within our home. Here's an exercise that will highlight the necessity (and excitement) of the stanza. Take any poem you have written and rewrite the poem in three different ways. Instead of focusing on language or punctuation, offer three variations of stanzas. If a poem is one stanza, break it up into couplets, tercets, and quatrains. Doing this will allow us a greater understanding of how line is functioning within the poem. It will force us to make decisions regarding where we will break a line and where a stanza meets its conclusion. It will announce language and show us the associative leaps made in the poetic process. Once you have offered three variations regarding the stanza, you may then begin to approach the individual words within the line and edit as you see fit.

Christine Beck

HEARING VOICES

It was 2003 and I was in a barn—Robert Frost's barn in Franconia, New Hampshire, with fifty would-be poets perched on metal chairs, swatting mosquitoes in the heat and transfixed by a man who promised to teach us to be poets, although he was not himself a poet. Donald Sheehan was a classics professor from Dartmouth who had created an annual conference for poets called The Frost Place.

Don presented an imposing figure. He had a white flowing beard reaching to his belt buckle and eerily blue eyes. His French blue, tailored shirt told me he knew it would mirror his eyes. But his most arresting feature was his voice. He spoke slowly and kindly, as if he were speaking to children. There was the hint of world-weariness. An undercurrent of suffering. But also an expansiveness of spirit, as if we were prodigals finally home and he had cooked the fatted calf.

Notebook at the ready, poised to write ten tips to make the world love my words, I was not prepared for his advice: abandon any hope of being special, release my desire to be heard, and fall in love with the work of the person sitting next to me.

> Fantasy
>> let go
> Your task
>> envy
> Read sharper, clearer
>> forgive
> gently

failed attempts

incarnate in the heart
     root is joy
as a small child
     fall in love

I recalled my first writing workshop a couple of years before in which we had weekly assignments to write a nonfiction piece and also read a novel. I was baffled as to how reading Nadine Gordimer's fiction could help my writing. The instructor replied, "each week, I can see a bit of the writer you have been reading creep into your work." I wondered if this was Don's idea—that we pick up something another writer had already mastered. But no. It was more fundamental—the idea exhorted by St. Francis to seek more to understand than to be understood. Don was preaching a radical theology—that our work would improve if we stopped dwelling on it and put our attention elsewhere. In a way, he was offering the same advice as Emily Dickinson, who advised writers to come at poetry "slant," not barging in through the front door, but perhaps finding the warped door at the back of the garden, to slip in without knocking, bell-ringing, or announcement.

Don knew we were all obsessed with being published, with being admired, secretly hoping that at workshop, the instructor would say, "Nothing much to comment on here. This is a fine poem. Send it out!" Don asked us to "let go of the fantasy of being discovered."

No name tags, said Don. We were to learn to recognize each other, pay attention, use no memory crutches. I wasn't good at memorizing names and worse, once someone introduced himself, I was too embarrassed to ask him to repeat his name. But sometimes, I had to make a connection, name tags or not. I was standing in line for lunch on the grass when I stepped on a bee. A sudden surge of pain shot from my foot up my leg. I hadn't been stung since I was a kid. And I realized that if I keeled over from anaphylactic shock, no one would have any idea what had happened to me. I turned to the woman behind me and said, "Sorry, but would you mind just watching me for a few minutes? I was just stung by a bee and I want someone to know that in case I have a reaction." "Of course," she said, and began to watch me intently. After about five minutes, I said "Ok, guess I'm fine. By the way, I'm Christine."

"Patrice," she said. But she was not done watching. "Stop, please, I'm ok." I finally got her to stop watching by starting to talk.

Patrice was a teacher at a private high school. She taught at a Waldorf School. The only Waldorfs I had heard of were a hotel and a salad. Her course was called Eurythmy, a kind of movement between tai chi and modern dance that she said had an educational purpose, although I couldn't imagine what it was. So I asked her to show me. Wearing a diaphanous long-sleeved blouse, long curls blowing in the wind, Patrice stood on a grassy slope, the White Mountains at her back, and as unself-consciously as if she were reaching for a napkin at the dinner table began a flowing series of movements in which she raised and lowered her outstretched arms, while bending forward and back. She looked a bit like an elegant crane.

> The crane, the light against its angles
> in dark water, otherworldly in elegance,
> and still, so still,
>
> and its breast beating so hard, I could almost
> see its heart just there below the sheen of feathers
> that I wanted to reach, but could not reach,
>
> You asked me what I wanted, what I wanted,
> and I thought of the crane, its long resilient
> neck, so thin compared with my desire.
>
> and I didn't know how to say it, that I wanted
> to rest on the bench, silent and serene, like the crane,
> secure in knowing that no one could hurt a crane,
>
> no one would hurt something so close to innocence,
> like water falling a thousand feet down a cliff,
> sprinkling rainbows over stone.
>
> I want the knowledge of the crane,
> the certainty that I am of both sea and shore
> and yet not either sea or shore.

I am here and it is there,
and all the traveling I want to do
is from here to there.

***

I guess you could say I fell in love with Patrice, with her style, her grace, her totally different way of getting into the work—slant you could say. By the evening we were to perform our poems, we were a team. I stood up and read Patrice's poem about the statues of Buddha being destroyed by the Taliban while Patrice acted out the words of the poem in Eurythmy. Voice and body, we traveled from here to there.

At the end of the week, Don shared a prayer. (In the following years of poetry conferences, lectures, workshops, and readings, I have never, ever, found anyone bold enough to pray.)

"Grant that I may deal straightforwardly and wisely with each person, neither saddening or embarrassing anyone."

I later learned that Don came by this prayer, the beard, and his firm belief in the value of being fully present and extending oneself to others through a series of events that touched me profoundly. After the conference, I researched on the internet one of his lectures on *The Brothers Karamazov*. And that's when I discovered why Don Sheehan and I shared such a bond. He disclosed how he had been raised by a violent alcoholic father, as I had been. At the age of nine, Don said his father's bouts of rage had become intolerable, leading to the break-up of the family:

> [O]n this particular evening in late June, the bouts of raging had grown longer, and the calm spells meant only that he was re-gathering his will for the next round of violence. The second round that evening had been about twenty minutes of raging at all of us in the kitchen - and breaking some dishes - and then he stormed out of the kitchen and through the dining room and into the living room: and all was suddenly quiet. Making my way on tiptoe across the dining room, I peeked around the living room door. He was sitting on the couch, staring at his hands.
>
> Then I did something that still takes my breath away. I walked across the living room and sat down on the couch right

next to him. I picked up a magazine from the coffee table and opened to the first pictures I came to, and I pointed to one. "Look, Dad, isn't that interesting?" I didn't dare look at him.

No answer. After a moment, I looked up at him, and I found that he was looking down at me. Over fifty years later I can still see my father's eyes. They were sad eyes, yet peaceful, warm, and profoundly *young*, with all the wildness gone out and, in place of it, something like *stillness*. And I felt all at once peaceful...
He looked at me for a long, long minute, and then he spoke. "You're the only one not afraid of me."
I was just old enough to know what gratitude sounded like in my father's voice. And so to this day and hour, I know what *the person my father* is sounds like when he speaks.[1]

Years later, Sheehan visited his father's grave and read aloud a letter in which he told his father he was okay and forgave him. It ended: "I love you. You love me. Do not forget this."

Shortly after his long drive home, Sheehan began to hear voices. They said: "*Lord Jesus Christ, Son of God, have mercy on me, a sinner.*" The voices continued day after day, tormenting him. Believing he might be going insane, Sheehan ultimately discovered that the words came from an Eastern Orthodox prayer. He began to study. Eventually, he converted.

I converted religions too, not as willingly as Don. In 1958, my mother was baptized as a Witness in the East River of Manhattan during a huge convention at Yankee Stadium. One day I was a Presbyterian, patent leather pumps and velvet pews. The next, I was on a street corner selling *The Watchtower* and *Awake* magazines. God didn't tell me to convert. My mother did.

Jehovah's Witnesses believe that there will be 144,000 people resurrected from the dead after the war of Armageddon to rule in heaven with Christ.

---

1. This quote originally appeared in an article entitled "Dostoevsky and Memory Eternal," by Donald Sheehan, published on August 24, 2006 on the Dartmouth College website. It has since been removed. An introduction to the article appeared on a website of the Eastern Orthodox Church. www.orthodoxytoday.org/articles6/SheehanDostoevsky.php but does not contain the quoted material. More recently, the quote appeared in *The Grace of Incorruption: The Selected Essays of Donald Sheehan on Orthodox Faith and Poetics* by Donald Sheehan, published by Paraclete Pressin 2015.

Each year at the Memorial of the last supper, Witnesses who have heard God tell them they are among the 144,000 stand up to show the congregation they are in the special group. Apparently, they've been told by God.

Here's Lucy, 4 foot 8, and 82,
her hump a harbinger of what's ahead
if Armageddon doesn't hurry.

Patient and implacable, Lucy blues her hair,
applies pale pancake, rose pink blush,
ready for ascension.

I doubt I'd vote for Lucy to represent me up in heaven,
but Theocracy is not a voting matter.
She says her name is in the book.

Lucy stands, tucks her eyelet hankie in her purse,
peeks to see if anybody new is on their feet this year,

wonders what she'll do if Brother Grimes stands up,
Brother Grimes who's been doing Sister Smithers,
which should disqualify him in anybody's book.

The Brothers Karamazov was my favorite novel in college. I loved the outlandish love affairs, the internecine squabbling, the philosophical debates about God and the meaning of life. Today it strikes me that the confusion, drunkenness, and brokenness of the son Dimitri mirrored my father's misery as a hopeless alcoholic. My dad died broken, destitute, and alone. He wanted to be a writer, but alcohol was more powerful than the pen. The last photo I have of us is standing in front of the Rescue Mission where he lived, not as dramatic or colorful as the Brothers K, but equally memorable:

A snapshot from 1968. My face faded,
long blonde curls cascade to frizzles
like wings of hummingbirds.

His hat, a shapeless cotton, top squared,
narrow brim above his awkward grin.
His too-short pants, mis-matched socks.

I'm in a shiny purple maxi-coat,
fashion next to no-fashion, me
next to not-me.

Bring him back: the father who was not-father,
standing with a daughter who's fading,
who for that moment was willing to pretend,

arms entwined in an inner-city parking lot,
that he might someday take her arm
and walk into another picture.

I continued to come to The Frost Place every year until Don retired in 2008. The conference hired new management. It's still there. I continued going for a year or two. But without Don, it became interchangeable with other conferences closer to me. I drifted away. Patrice and I still meet up every year or so.

The last time I saw Don was in 2008. He had retired from directing The Frost Place, after leading it for twenty-seven years. He came to give a guest lecture about translating the Psalms, and spoke with enthusiasm and quiet conviction about his desire to capture their original cadence by translating from the Septuagint Greek. This quiet man who survived the trauma of a violent childhood, who heard voices, who each year embraced a group of ego-driven writers as if we were the child who won the spelling bee, was alight, finding melody in ancient Greek, comfort in its cadence. By 2010, he was dead of a stroke, his master project unfinished.

I may never hear the voice of God. But I still hear the voice of Don.

Jessamine Price

CRAZY THINGS WE DO FOR LOVE: LEARNING POEMS BY HEART

My parents were uncool. When other families were getting an 8-track and listening to Stevie Wonder, we were playing Puccini and Mahler on an old turntable. But because they were uncool, they gave me one of the best gifts a poet could have. They taught me how to own a poem completely and learn everything from it: they memorized poems. My first step in becoming a poet was listening to them repeat beloved poems from memory while tucking me into bed each night as a child. Decades later, I still replay poems in my head when I can't sleep. These poems have taught me much of what I know about poetry.

Memorization seems archaic in the era of Google and smartphones. It also seemed pretty archaic in the nineteen-sixties, when my parents registered for a college class in the art of reciting poetry. We do crazy things for love. It was the only class they took together before my father's scholarship program was discontinued and he had to transfer to the state university. When I was born a few years later, they still remembered a dozen poems between them. My mother went for shorter, lyrical poems like Robert Frost's "Stopping by Woods on a Snowy Evening." My father was more ambitious. He knew a few shorter poems—"Sea Fever," by John Masefield, was a favorite—but the tour de force was his rendition of Robert Service's 68-line Yukon tall tale, "The Cremation of Sam McGee."

> There are strange things done in the midnight sun,
> By the men who moil for gold;
> The Arctic trails have their secret tales
> That would make your blood run cold.

That poem made the hairs on the back of my neck stand up. He was so convincing that I was six or seven years old before I realized my father never really prospected for gold.

That was the nineteen-seventies, the era of black-and-white TV and big, clunky rotary-dial telephones. Hasn't the world changed now that we have video games and smartphones, social media and streaming video? Are there any reasons to memorize poetry in the twenty-first century? For poets—whether beginner or experienced—the answer is yes. Some poets may succeed in writing great lines without ever committing to memory a single line. But for me, remembering has been my road into writing and publishing poems I'm proud of. Just as importantly, memorization is how I express my love for poems—and like many of the things we do for love, it might look useless and crazy to people with cooler heads.

I began to memorize poetry before I could read, thanks to my parents and the power of repetition. A child's brain thirsts for language, and it soaks up rhythm and rhyme. (Hence the popularity of nursery rhymes and children's songs.) When I entered junior high school and got my own paperback copy of *Immortal Poems of the English Language*, I found myself unintentionally remembering my favorite lines. Poetry offers ear-worms as catchy as any Rick Astley song, though poems use cadence instead of melody to infiltrate your brain. Earworms like these:

> In Xanadu did Kubla Khan...
> The world is too much with us...
> I will arise and go now, and go to Innisfree...

A few of the catchiest lines of poetry embed themselves in our culture so deeply that even people who "don't like poetry" know them. Ask a few Americans to fill in the blanks in these lines:

> "Quoth the raven, 'Never _____'"
> "O Romeo, Romeo, wherefore art thou _____?"

You'll get plenty of headshakes—not all Americans grow up speaking English or cheering the Baltimore football team—but a few people will know the answers: Nevermore! Romeo! And dollars to donuts, not all of them are poets. So the first reason to memorize poetry is simply because you can't help it. Canny poets for centuries have engineered poems to stick in our heads. Don't fight it.

But if you love poetry, you'll find yourself wanting to remember more than one or two lines. You'll want to know one or two of your favorite poems all the way through. And here is the second reason to memorize poetry: to find out what you really love. Our ancestors in the days before movable type committed entire books to memory. We don't have to do this anymore. We can be choosy about what we'll memorize. But how to choose? With just a Twitter feed or an internet search we can be inundated with new poetry all the time. The immediacy of all this poetry on the web is a treasure and burden, like everything else on social media—the constant news, the never-ending commentary. We have access to more poetry than anyone before in history. But we also have more opportunities to be distracted. On the internet, I sometimes find myself reading a poem once, noting the author's name, and then quickly moving on to the next poem. Sometimes I don't even read an entire poem. Too many verses in the middle? I feel rushed, I skip to the end. I want to keep going, keep looking for the next new thing.

When I experience poetry in this distracted frame of mind, I'm disrespecting the author's hard work. Worse, I'm denying myself the pleasure of relaxing into the poem and taking a journey with it.

In junior high school, my two best friends discovered Coleridge's poem "Kubla Khan." They loved its eccentric images and incantatory quality so much that they started to memorize it. I was jealous when they recited it together, so I made myself memorize it too. The three of us learned the whole thing and when we got together for slumber parties, we would recite it together. We were weird twelve-year-olds. But we got as much enjoyment out of that poem as anyone ever did. "Kubla Khan" isn't a poem I would set out to memorize now, but I still remember every line. We recited it in the car on the way to my best friend's wedding.

Memorizing a poem is the ultimate in slow, deliberate poetry appreciation. And since memorizing is a slow, deliberate process, so is choosing a poem to memorize. You need to find a poem where you respect every line, where every line has something interesting and memorable to say to you. A poem where you're not tempted to skip to the end.

Finding these poems is hard—or will be if you have developed your own poetic likes and dislikes. If you love every poem you read—if you can't choose—try memorizing a bunch of them. Which ones can you remember a week later? Perhaps those are the poems you really love, not the ones you want to love because your professor likes them or they won an award, but the ones you really love.

This is important, because poets need to know what they really think and feel, not what they're supposed to feel. A confession: I like Shakespeare, but I've never been able to remember any of the sonnets. There are passages from the plays that stick in my mind something fierce: "Perchance to dream, aye, there's the rub," "And all our yesterdays have guided fools the way to dusty death." Hamlet, MacBeth, I just can't quit you. But it's never worked out for me with the sonnets, not yet. I know this because of which lines my mysterious brain holds fast and dear. Someday, sonnets, perhaps someday I'll be ready for you. For now, I prefer the expansive free verse of the dramatic monologues.

I hear someone asking, can't you memorize any poem through sheer will-power? What does love have to do with it? My answer: certainly you can force yourself to memorize, the way medical students learn the names of the bones and tendons before the big test, the way Jeopardy contestants master the American presidents and constitutional amendments before their reckoning with Alex Trebek. But if you're a poet, there's no high-stakes testing. No one pays us big bucks to read or write poetry. We do this out of a fascination with language, out of a desire to let loose our barbaric yawp across the roofs of the world. If poetry requires an act of sheer willpower, perhaps you've picked the wrong art form. Would you prefer to write stories? Paint portraits? Writing poetry presents challenges, but they should be exhilarating challenges. Poetry shouldn't cause you pain.

Memorizing good poems by other writers will make your own poems better. This is the third reason to learn poetry by heart. When I sit down to write, I hear in the back of my head the rhythms, words, and syntax that I love. The building blocks are there—the lines and poems I remember from John Donne, John Keats, Alfred Lord Tennyson, Robert Frost, Sara Teasdale, and the anonymous authors of "Beowulf" and "The Wanderer." Often as I'm writing, I hear a kind of rhythm in my head, telling me I'm looking for a certain pattern of words and stresses. I sense the grammar of a sentence before I know what words to put in it. It's like all the poems I've ever memorized form a series of molds. I pour my poems into structures that already preexist somewhere in my brain. A great poem takes more than a great mold, of course. But the mold gives me a starting point, a sense of possibility.

Having these building blocks and drawing inspiration from them isn't the same as imitating the poems you've memorized. It's true that imitation can be a good way to start. When I was first writing poetry in junior high school, I loved John Keats and Samuel Taylor Coleridge—so I wrote Romantic sonnets and trippy fantasy epics. But as I memorized more poems over the years, my own voice developed. My style of writing is now a combination of all the poets I love—a unique combination, as my DNA is a unique combination of the thousands of ancestors who came before me.

The poems I love to memorize usually have regular rhythms such as iambic pentameter or tetrameter. As a result, the poems I write have a touch of formality, though I rarely set out to write formal poetry per se. But if the poems you love are by Gertrude Stein, you will write poems that reflect her patterns and influence. If you love the poems of Adonis or Yusef Komunyakaa or Claudia Rankine, you will write poems where a few rays of their light shines, refracted through the stained glass mirror of your own words and images. Memorization—or "learning by heart" as our ancestors called it—is an act of love and devotion. The poems you love will return that love by inspiring your own work.

Some types of poetry are easier to remember than others. It's generally easier to remember poems that use literary devices like alliteration, rhyme, rhythm, anaphora, and compression, poems often labeled "formalist" today, though many writers who are not "formalist" make use of them. But if you don't like this kind of poetry, don't set out to memorize it just because it's easier. Focus on poems you love.

If you find that the poems you love are hard to remember, that, too, is an interesting lesson. Perhaps you're looking for freedom from all the established patterns of language, including the oral literatures of the past. Perhaps you dislike rhythm and rhyme because they appear so often these days in advertising slogans and political cant. Perhaps you love the loose, rambling rhythms of a late twentieth-century poet like John Ashbery, or like the language poets of the nineteen-seventies, you love poems full of disjuncture. These styles of poetry might be hard to learn by heart. If you can't memorize poetry, ask yourself why not. The answer will help you understand more about yourself and the poems you want to write. There are schools of thought today that say memorization and recitation are bad for poetry, that poems should be slippery, ambiguous, hard to remember. I don't get much pleasure from this style of poetry, but I understand why other people do, and I think the poetry they love is "real poetry" as much as the poetry I love.

"There are a thousand ways to love a poem," Donald Hall wrote, "The best poets make up new ways, and the new ways mostly take getting used to." Are you trying to invent new ways to love poetry, ways that have nothing to do with the ancient tradition of oral verse? That's cool, too. The twenty-first century is ready for your innovations. But first, memorize a poem or two. Look at verses and words with the up-close care that memorization requires. Let these other poets' rhythms and images into your heart and remember the writers who came before you. Take a few steps in their company as you set out on your journey.

TIPS ON HOW TO MEMORIZE POETRY

If you're ready to give it a try, here are some tips for how to memorize a poem:

1. Copy it out longhand (with pen and paper!) a few times.
2. Repeat it aloud again and again.
3. When you think you remember a line or verse, try writing it out from memory.
4. Use gestures, if the poem lends itself to them. Remembering gestures can help you remember the associated words. The more dramatic the gestures, the easier it will be to remember. Later, when you remember the whole poem, you can recite it without the gestures, and the memory of the movements will help you remember the words.
5. Other people find that walking or swimming is a helpful way to remember. Repeat a new line to yourself each lap, or memorize a new verse each time you go for a hike. The repeated rhythmic beat in an English poem is called a "foot" for a reason.
6. Think about the emotions in the poem. If the poem moves from happy to sad or from funny to serious, use that to help you remember the order of the words and lines.
7. Visualize the images in the poems. For some people, this is more helpful than thinking about emotions.

8. Sometimes you have to go slowly, one line at a time. If you can memorize just one line per day, you can learn a whole poem in a few weeks.

9. Like any kind of deep thinking, memorization works best when you turn off your computer and phone and give yourself some quiet.

10. To take it to the next level, try to write it from memory with the correct punctuation. This will teach you a lot about how poets have used commas and dashes.

11. If you repeat your poem aloud to other people (to your kids at bedtime, perhaps!), don't forget the meaning of the poem. The meaning—and the emotions behind it—are more important than the rhythm. Over-emphasizing the beat can make a serious poem sound like a Mother Goose rhyme or Dr. Seuss.

12. Remembering the meaning is particularly important if a poem uses enjambment. With enjambment, a thought may continue smoothly from one line to the next. For example

> We are such stuff
> As dreams are made on, and our little life
> Is rounded with a sleep.

It would be unnatural to take a big pause at the end of each line. Instead, save the major pauses for the periods.

You can discover more advanced memorization techniques with a quick internet search. But I've memorized hundreds of lines of poetry using the simple methods here, including poems in French, Arabic, Chaucer's Middle English, and a little bit of the original Dante's *Inferno*. Perhaps it helps to have an anxious disposition; memorization helps me calm my brain when my thoughts are going in circles.

NOTES ON THE POEMS QUOTED HERE

"There are strange things done in the midnight sun / By the men who moil for gold" is the start of Robert Service's "The Cremation of Sam McGee."
"In Xanadu did Kubla Khan" is the opening of Samuel Taylor Coleridge's "Kubla Khan."
"The world is too much with us," is the beginning of William Wordsworth's most famous sonnet.

"I will arise and go now, and go to Innisfree" is Yeats' "Lake Isle of Innisfree."
"Quoth the raven, 'Nevermore'" is Edgar Allen Poe's "The Raven."
"O Romeo, Romeo, wherefore art thou Romeo?" is from Shakespeare's "Romeo and Juliet."
"We are such stuff as dreams are made on" is from "The Tempest."

The poems I memorized growing up were mostly by British men, but there are many "catchy" poems by women and people of color. Looking back to the Harlem Renaissance, we have the powerful verse of Gwendolyn Brooks, Langston Hughes and Paul Lawrence Dunbar. Among Latino and Latina poets, we have formalist writing from Rafael Campo, C. Dale Young, Julia Alvarez, and Rhina P. Espaillat. And today, I particularly like the lively, rhythmical poems of Jericho Brown and Allison Joseph.

J.S. Watts

THE POET'S JOURNEY

Whenever you start writing poetry, whether as a child, teenager, or at whatever stage of adulthood (you really are never too old to begin writing), you have embarked on a multi-layered journey. The length and nature of the journey are down to you. If you and poetry don't take to one another, it could be a very short one. If you become serious about the poems you are creating, the journey could easily last for the rest of your life.

If you are expecting this essay to describe the journey in intricate detail, you are about to be disappointed. I do not believe it is possible because each poet's journey is unique and personal to them.

Take four successful and internationally acclaimed poets: Walt Whitman, Sylvia Plath, Ted Hughes, and Sharon Olds. Their poetry is different. The style and subject matter of their poetry is different. Their personal life stories are different, even in the case of Plath and Hughes where the poetry and the lives overlapped for an intense and formative period. The journeys taken to create their poems are incredibly diverse.

According to my mother, my poetic journey started at the age of four. (I would have dated it as later.) That must have been almost as soon as I could write, but who am I to doubt my own mother? Moreover, she claims to have physical proof: a copy of my first ever poem, which is tantamount to black-mail material.

Other poets I know and rate did not write their first poems until well into adulthood. Their journeys have followed different paths from my own, but have produced poetry as good and probably better than mine.

Journeys start at different times and for diverse reasons. Some people write for the uncomplicated love of it. Others may regard it as communication, self-expression, therapy and healing, a way to make sense of their world, a route to getting published or an itch they just have to scratch, or, indeed, any combination of the above.

With a range of starting times and reasons for travelling, any map I could draw of the journey(s) is already complicated.

You may by now be asking, if each poet's journey is so unique, what is the point of writing a piece that attempts to define it? It's a fair question.

The answer could be that I am a glutton for punishment. More positively, I would argue the very fact that creating poems is a journey, rather than a finite event, is the important thing, not the detail of the journey. I would, however, also comment that whilst each journey is different, there are milestones along the way that most poets are likely to come across at some stage.

So why am I stressing the importance of the journey?

Basically, poetry is like any art or craft, you need to work at it repeatedly to make it good. You don't believe me? Well, would you expect to pick up a trumpet and play a decent tune on it that others want to listen to without practicing first?

Assuming you're not a literary genius whose poems emerge fully formed and absolutely perfect from the get-go, your poems are going to develop and improve over time. The more you write (or practice) the more likely your poems are to get better. That applies equally to the writing and editing process for individual poems and any wider poetic career development across multiple poems. Even the greatest poets have taken time to achieve their greatness and have left behind them (in more ways than one) early poems and juvenilia that are not at the highest standard of their later work, but which are, in effect, the roots of their oeuvre.

Most poets I know would say their aim is to write the best poem they possibly can. It requires hard work, trial and error to achieve the best. It's called honing and polishing your craft and it takes time. In journey terms, it's the route travelled from the weakest poem to the strongest one because, if you are committed to your poetry, you and your writing cannot stand still.

The journey forward (and occasionally back) that you take is unique to you and your poetry, but there are aspects to it that will be familiar to many poets.

For starters, your journey is unlikely to be a straight-line trajectory upwards. Life inevitably has its ups and downs and writing poetry is part of a poet's life. It goes without saying, therefore, that your poetic journey will have its ups and downs. It may not be that the quality of your writing fluctuates, but your response to it is more than likely to. You'll write a new poem that you think is wonderful. Give it a little time and you will wonder what you ever saw in it. Give it more time and you may decide it was an okay poem after all. We've all been there. The poem doesn't change, but your feelings towards it do. It's part of the journey.

To help your writing be the best it can be you will need to read a considerable amount of poetry, hopefully much of it contemporary. Sounding like Wordsworth or Shakespeare was great for Wordsworth and Shakespeare, but not so great for a twenty-first century poet. Sticking thee or thou in a poem doesn't make the poem sound literary. It just makes it sound false and like a copy of an old-fashioned poem. As a poet, you're trying to find your own voice, not mimic those of dead poets, however good. To find your own voice, though, it really does help to read the poetry of others, hear how they sound and work out how the poets achieved it. Also, if you don't love poetry and want to read it, why are you trying to write it?

The writing of poems inevitably entails editing and re-writing. These are likely to be an integral part of the ups and downs referenced earlier. Editing is a vital task if your poems are going to develop and improve. I only stop editing my poems when they are published, and sometimes not even then.

Ah yes, the getting published thing. If you are writing purely for your own pleasure with no intention of having even the smallest poem published, then this is part of the journey you can skip. If, however, you are hoping to get at least some of your poems published at some stage by someone other than yourself (self-publishing has introduced a whole new and alternative path to the poet's journey) then you will experience the joy of submitting and being rejected—over and over again. And, guess what? Rejection hurts.

Whether it is a single poem, a chapbook or an entire collection, and potentially regardless of the quality of your writing, you are going to receive a huge number of rejections. Even successful, big name poets have had them. I can remember being told this when I started submitting my poems for publication in literary magazines. Fine, I thought. Forewarned is forearmed: I'm prepared. Except I wasn't. However many rejections you think you'll get, you'll receive more. The sheer volume of rejections is soul-crushing, but if you're a poet wanting to be published, unless you choose to go straight into self-publishing, you are going to have to deal with the rejections.

Editors and publishers receive many more submissions than they need. They have to be selective. It's not personal for them, but it will seem so to you.

You are the one who will have to work through the rejection and come out on the other side, stronger and still fresh for the fight. Traditionally published poets are published because, in addition to the quality of their writing, they persevere.

Rejections come in all shapes and sizes. They can be impersonal, overly personal, dismissive, supportive, rude, helpful, and sometimes they do not even appear to relate to the work you've submitted. The art is to ignore them and learn from them simultaneously and move on. The journey isn't going to stop for a bucketful of rejections (however big the bucket).

Having hauled yourself over the mountain of rejections, what else might you expect to come across on the poet's journey? Well...

- You are unlikely to find riches. You are never going to be wealthy (or even earn a living wage) from writing poetry alone. Poets who make their living from poetry don't just write it. They perform it, teach it, write articles about it, judge competitions, run workshops on the subject, and so on.

- Whilst few people think they could be brain surgeons, an amazing number will think they can write better poetry than you and may offer you unsolicited advice. Poetry is frequently subjective and they are entitled to their views. Some of them may even be right.

- A sad number of people do not like or even read poetry. You are going to meet some of them and they will not be the slightest bit interested in your poems. Move on.

- On a similar note, poetry *is* subjective. Not everyone is going to like your poems, even if they like and value poetry. It may have something to do with the quality of your poems or it may have everything to do with the people concerned. If you don't think it's to do with the quality of your work, move on.

- The feeling of completing a poem that, for the moment at least, you are totally satisfied with is rewarding. (If you are not totally satisfied with your poem, why aren't you still editing it?)

- The feeling of reaching out and touching someone with a poem you have written is rewarding and amazing.

- Sometimes your poetry may take you down a path that you hadn't envisaged. Give in to it. Sometimes poems know better where they are headed then their poet does.

- If you are motivated by an inner need to write poetry, the only way to scratch the itch is to write poetry. Give in to it.

I'm sure there are alternative milestones that other poets will have rested on, but the above are the ones that come to my mind when I consider the likely similarities and overlaps in a poet's journey when compared to others. As I said at the beginning, though, there are many poets and many journeys. They begin in different places, for different reasons and end at different destinations and those destinations may not necessarily be the ones originally intended by the poets themselves.

Along the way there may be milestones or stop-offs that other poets have visited, but the poet's journey remains just that—the journey of each individual poet. It is a journey to be treasured, nourished, and worked on, for a lifetime if need be.

Diana Rosen

PAVING THE PATH TO A POET'S LIFE

I didn't even know I was on a journey when I first began to write poems, in my late forties no less. I was working in a bookstore alongside some stellar poets who introduced me to a whole new world of contemporary men and women poets who astonished, energized, bedazzled me with what they wrote about, and how.

Two of those poet-booksellers conducted freewrite workshops, and they invited me to join in. What an adventure! I was relieved of rhyme, comforted by stanza length choices, introduced to the music of enjambments or end stops, and most of all, excited to leap off the edge into a prompt.

As a journalist writing nonfiction books, articles, and website posts, I was used to space constrictions and a short poem can definitely be constricting. I also pursued facts, not fiction, so the poet's journey both freed and challenged me. A poetry prompt is different from an editor's assignment to "get the story." It is something totally opposite. It is an invitation to release imagination, leap into experimentation, conjure images with no other purpose than to put pen to page and see what flows.

While I never gave up the storytelling element of journalism, I was no longer attached to the precision of factual reportage that is necessary for genuine news stories while writing my poems. Technically, I was free to drop articles, eschew subject-verb-object, play with metaphor and simile, embrace music within my poems from inner rhymes to cadence within lines.

Still, how to segue from the brutality of *facts* to the world of imaginative fiction that didn't rely, much less need facts? If I witnessed something that was blue, but aqua worked better in the poem, could I pursue what works vs. what is correct? The answer, after many attempts, was absolutely. I was able to transfer my ideas into the whimsy of fantasy, the softness of dreams, and to leave objectivity behind as I dove into where no journalist is supposed to go: emotions.

Emotions! What a fraught word. Good. Bad. Ugly. Hurtful. Blissful. At first, writing about them was a release of almost immeasurable comfort. Then came the conundrum of writing about experiences best discussed with wise counsel. Are these dives into despair self-indulgent? How could they possibly engage a reader? Is the personal ever truly universal? What IS the role of a poet?

Still struggling with those answers, I was invited to share my poems at readings and loved the experience. Listening to other poets at readings taught me so much about presentation, speech, theater, and honoring words. More than anything, reading my poems aloud to a live audience was concrete evidence of what worked and didn't quite.

Many classes, workshops, how-to books, and one-on-one counsel with poets have all been fantastic resources to make this journey ever fascinating and make my poems stronger. As for my continuing work in journalism, poetry helped me. I thought more about word choices, considered the shape of the story in depth, became more creative with my poetry techniques when exercising the principles of my nonfiction craft.

My poetry still contains shreds of my journalism experience. The who, what, where, why, when, and how of Journalism 101 provide as good a blueprint as any to show the poet what's missing, what needs to be deleted, especially if you enjoy writing narrative poems like I do.

Writing poetry, like novels and short stories, is, in a way, like being an actor. You can enter different worlds, become different people, and make the endings of stories you know so well just the way you want them to be, not as they were or are.

Poetry, too, is a lot like tea, a drink that can relax the body as it clears the mind. Poetry invites both the calming meditative experience of being lost in telling a tale while challenging the mind to tell the story plainly straight, or so crooked it meanders in places you've never even conjured before.

I am still learning how to write poems, and love that there is still much to master. Advice? Of course, I have suggestions. They are to:

- go at your own speed

- seek good counsel

- pay attention to what works and what doesn't and learn to

understand why
- challenge yourself with consistent practice to the point of expertise
- share what you learn with others
- have fun

Traveling on the poet's journey is like mastering a musical instrument, it's all about the practice. In a letter to reporter Maurice Eisenberg, written after the Germans were driven out of France in 1944, the celebrated cellist Pablo Casals wrote, "Now that the enemy has been forced to leave, I have resumed my practicing and you will be pleased to know that I feel that *I am making daily progress.*" Whether you have been forced into silence or have abandoned the practice of your art, I urge you to resume the practice. You will find solace, excitement, sorrow, satisfaction, and much joy.

Amy Miller

A STATE OF BLUNDER: MY FIRST READING

Oh, readings. When we're young, unpublished poets, we dream about the readings we'll do, all spotlights and podiums and influential editors in the audience. And then we finally get to do one—and let's just say we have to revise our dreams.

My first foray into the world of poetry readings was back in 2001, when I was fairly new to the writing business. I'd just had three poems accepted by a good literary journal based in Texas, and then I got more good news: the journal's editor emailed, asking if I'd like to read at their issue-release party in Austin. This was a huge deal, since I lived near San Francisco, 1,700 miles away. *Whoa*, I thought, *this good journal is actually inviting me, a barely published poet, all the way to Austin to read. This could be my big break!*

Now, dear reader, what I didn't realize—and what I will clue you in to now, so you can experience the full ridiculousness of this story—was that the editor had sent this invitation not just to me, but to *all* the poets published in the new issue, roughly 50 people. Experienced writers know this drill: the editor wanted a good crowd at the launch party and was casting out a net, hoping a few poets within driving distance would show up to read.

I did not know this drill.

What I did know was that I really, really wanted to do this reading. Flying to Texas! To read poetry! It seemed sort of nutty, but I had a good-paying job and vacation time coming, so I quickly replied to the editor and accepted the invitation. She answered back with a masterful mix of graciousness and incredulity: "Oh...how nice that you're willing to come so far. I'm afraid we can't help you with travel expenses." *OK*, I thought, *this is one of those poetry gigs that doesn't pay. Maybe they're all like that.*

No matter; I booked my flight and arranged for lodging in Austin, with a side trip to my grandmother's hometown of nearby Shiner. And the editor had said to bring books to sell at the book table, so I hastily got to work assembling and hand-stapling 20 copies of a chapbook, my first ever, which I packed carefully into my suitcase. *Do not forget the chapbooks!*

About a week before I was scheduled to fly out, my manager at work called me into his office. He had news of a different sort: I was fired. The company that had employed me for 14 years, that had often told me I was so special that they could never replace me, was laying me off. It was two months after the 9/11 attacks, and whole industries in the San Francisco area, including mine—magazine publishing—were convulsing and laying off thousands of workers. So many people were out of work that vastly overqualified PhDs were applying for entry-level jobs like editorial assistants and receptionists. Clearly there wouldn't be enough jobs for all of us. I had no idea how I was going to pay the rent.

And there I was, sitting on plane tickets and hotel reservations for a harebrained trip to Texas—hundreds of dollars about to drain out of my now-critical bank account. And from the emails flying around about the reading, I was starting to realize that the invitation wasn't, in fact, an honor individually aimed at me. Other poets would be reading there as well, all from the Austin area—pretty much anyone who could drive there on a Saturday night. So this was another way in which I was not as special as I'd thought.

But the tickets were bought, the rooms were reserved. And in the crapstorm that had become my life, I felt like I needed something good, something fun and impractical that didn't involve moping around the house, eating Pop-Tarts and circling listings for menial jobs. I wanted something that made me feel like a writer, not a loser. So I decided to go to Texas.

By the time I flew out on a Friday morning, I'd come down with a painful head cold—a sign, I felt, of a really mean universe—and had to pop aspirin and cold medicine on the plane all the way to Houston. There I picked up a rental car and meandered west across central Texas, drifting through towns like Sublime and Yoakum. I spent a nostalgic day in Shiner, eating fried chicken with white gravy and hot peppers, gulping down cough syrup, and marveling at the grand old houses that my great-grandfather, a German carpenter, probably helped build. By the time I arrived in Austin for the reading, I was nervous as hell, my hands actually shaking as I walked in the door of the little bookstore. To my astonishment, the place was packed—all seats taken, people standing three deep at the back and sitting in the aisles on whatever patch of floor they could find. I quickly counted heads; there were about 100 people crammed in there. *Whoa*, I thought, stepping over legs and backpacks on my way to the podium, *this is a thing.*

I sat down with the five other poets up front and settled in, trying to calm my nerves while I listened to the first few readers. When my turn came, I stood up and gave a decent delivery of my handful of poems, only making one gaffe when I lost my place in the middle of a poem and had to pause for about 200 years while I figured out which line I was on. Afterward I sat down, enjoyed the other readers, and then the reading was over—*poof*—and everyone stood up and starting milling around in a sort of giant cocktail party.

And now I was in a situation way more frightening than a reading—now it was a roomful of people who all knew each other, gravitating into little clutches of conversation. I stood there alone, putting my poems back in my purse and taking a few deep breaths, trying not to think of all the times I'd stood in a room like that before, feeling awkward as hell while a crippling shyness—a phobia that had plagued me my whole life—tightened around me like a giant hand. No, no, no—I was not going to crumble with social phobia this time. I'd flown all this way! To star in this show! I needed to just loosen up and be normal, like all these other people. I found the makeshift bar and poured myself a plastic cup of wine. Sometimes booze helped.

A saw a friendly-looking group and sidled up to them. But they soon disbanded, leaving me alone again. Tried another group—same thing. I sought out the hosts and other poets, but they were deep in talk with friends. I studied the artwork on the walls. I nursed my drink. I tried to look happy and inviting. And slowly, like a hiker slipping backward down a steep trail, I could feel myself falling into a full-on panic attack. I stood there, in something approaching physical pain, for about another twenty minutes and then gave up, set down my drink, and walked out the door. I got into my rental car and sat there in the parking lot for a long time, shaking with frustration. Was I really this messed up? Had I come all this way, just to be derailed by a whopping attack of shyness? Maybe if I calmed down, I could go back in...

But it was too late. People were starting to stream out of the store; the party was breaking up. Half-relieved, I thought, *Well, at least I'll go back in there and get my chapbooks from the book table.* But then it dawned on me:

in my nervousness, I'd completely forgotten my chapbooks and had never put them on the table. In fact, I'd never even pulled them out of my suitcase. They were still in the trunk of the car. I was officially a loser.

I drove back to my hotel, the saddest sad sack in all of Texas. The next day I drove back to Houston on rural roads that seemed a lot gloomier than they had two days earlier. I caught the evening flight home. Back in my house, I left the chapbooks in the suitcase for about a month, unable to look at them.

But honestly, in spite of all that, this is a happy memory. Yes, *ruefully* happy, but now it makes me laugh. It was one of those learning experiences your mother tells you you've just had, right after you've smacked your head on the sidewalk. This experience taught me a lot of things. First—really, don't forget the books. And even though that was one of my all-time worst attacks of social phobia, I did survive it, and I did learn from it, if only as an example of something I never wanted to happen again.

But the main thing I learned was that it's good to just show up. Yes, it was crazy to fly all that way to do that reading. And yes, I've done a few other readings since then that probably didn't justify the travel and hotel costs. But readings are unpredictable; even at the tiniest ones, you often meet great people in the audience. Sometimes you meet other authors who hook you up with other readings or publishers or who knows what. It's all a crapshoot, the chaotic mathematics of personal encounters. But you keep coming back to the common denominator: you, standing up in front of people and reading your work because someone invited you to do it. And maybe there's no hotshot editor out there in the crowd, but you have to admit—it is, actually, a little bit of a dream. And a story you can tell your writer friends for years to come. And a notch in your resume that says, yeah, I did that nutty thing. Because I'm a writer, and that's what we do.

Darby Price

A MICHAEL BAY BRAIN: ENCOURAGING WORDS FOR THE WORKING POET

One night, during my first year of graduate school, I was killing time in the kitchen of The Auld Shebeen, an Irish pub where I worked as a server. I wasn't supposed to be working there, technically—the contract for my Teaching Assistantship stipulated that I couldn't hold additional employment during my three years in the MFA program—but, like everyone else, I ignored that part of the contract in favor of eating regularly. Working outside of the program did make my life harder; on top of Writing Center hours, graduate-level course work, and the ostensible reason that I was there in the first place—to write a lot of poems in a supportive, engaging environment—hauling plates of bangers and mash took up time, physical energy, and brain space that I really would have preferred to give to my poetry. Some days, I worried that I was sabotaging my dreams just to pay the rent. But I persisted in both writing and working, and as I was reminded on this particular night, poetry can and does happen under duress and in all corners of the human experience.

It was getting late, and the dinner rush had long since passed, so the pub was pretty quiet. A few groups lingered in the bar area, but that was the bartender's responsibility, so I was holed up in the kitchen playing on my phone when suddenly, I heard an uprising of voices—men's voices, which always sound angry to me when they're loud. Then, without warning, someone entered the kitchen with such gusto that the door smacked into the wall with a *BANG!* It startled me. My brain put the yells, the bang, and the motion of the door together, and I had a clear, split-second vision of a violent altercation. A boozy quarrel that ended with one man pulling from his waistband the kind of high-powered pistol that I always feared in this concealed-carry state. The door kicking open was the reaction of metal meeting metal traveling at high velocity: a gunshot. The bar, quiet again, was a grave.

Of course, this was just a vision. The gunshot hadn't really happened, and I realized a second later that the raised voices belonged to men ribbing each other, laughing loudly, just people being people with a pint of Guinness in front of them and a pint already working through their bloodstreams. But I was still a little shaken. I've always been possessed of what my husband and I call my *Michael Bay Brain*. It's not uncommon for me to have visions of the worst, most violent possible outcomes while I'm doing ordinary things, like running on the beach (a sudden tsunami rips across the sand and sweeps me away with hundreds of other beachgoers), driving down the interstate (the 18-wheeler in front of me jackknifes, splintering, and the cars around me plow forward in a fiery pile-up), or even clipping my nails (the spring-loaded clipper digs not into nail but flesh, shearing off a chunk of my fingertip). It's highly possible that this is a function of some as-yet-undiagnosed anxiety disorder, and I'll admit that it isn't pleasant to go about the world imagining mundane scenes devolving into horror, but on the flipside, my Michael Bay Brain is a huge asset to me as a poet. In the case of the Irish pub, that proved especially true.

I stood there, elbows propped on the counter next to the soda dispenser, thinking about what would happen if an argument really did turn violent in that space. My first thought was that I'd be in deep trouble financially. I was dependent on tips for my livelihood—what if the restaurant turned into a crime scene and I couldn't work for weeks? I'd be skating on very thin ice in terms of my ability to pay rent and buy groceries. My next thought was even more grim: *What if I'd been standing on the other side of the room, rolling silverware or something, and that* had *been a gunshot? What if I had been shot through the door?* My reaction to this question was both very surprising and very telling: I didn't think about pain, death, or the inconvenience of being hobbled by a gunshot wound. I thought again about the money. It occurred to me that, although I wouldn't be able to work, I *would* be entitled to worker's comp and/or some pain-and-suffering money. The vision again ballooned, and I found myself daydreaming about getting shot in the leg—a clean wound through the meat of the thigh, maybe, away from major arteries and bone—and being free from the burden of outside work for the rest of my grad school days. The daydream became a fantasy, an elated sort of realization that *I would never have to work in the service industry again.*

This was, of course, a completely insane thought. I knew it even as I mulled it over. And as with all of my best insane thoughts, I wrote it down. I started scribbling notes and images on my server's order pad, flipping the small pages breathlessly as I filled them with the lush, specialized language of sidework: *Marrying ketchup. Ramekins. The expo.* As I wrote, I returned to my first thought—the larger impact of restaurant-as-crime-scene—and I thought about the elderly couple who came in every Friday night and sat near the band, and how disappointed they'd be if their evergreen date night establishment was shuttered. I jotted that down, too. I got so engrossed in the scene in my head, from the yellow caution tape to the blood all over the highly polished steel of the expo, where plates are passed from chef to server (a clear desecration of all that American culture holds dear in food safety), that I didn't clock out right away when I finally could. I stayed for ten, fifteen, twenty minutes longer, writing and writing, and nobody bothered me.

Those scribbled notes torn out of a server's order pad became a long prose poem that was eventually accepted for publication by *Cimarron Review*—the first major publication I had to my name. I was incredibly proud of this, of course, and I still am. But it isn't just the poem itself, which I like to think captures something of the sheer desperation of my entire generation, which has become the overworked bedrock of the so-called "gig" economy. It's also about the circumstances surrounding that publication. I was severely overworked that whole academic year, but particularly that semester; I felt that I barely had time for writing poetry, which was the whole reason that I'd moved clear across the country and left behind a life that I'd built in California. I was going to a therapist on campus once a week to help me process being so overwhelmed, and between that, my classes, my job, and the writing I had to do for workshop, the only time that I really got to relax was between the hours of 11pm and 12am, when I let myself sit down with a glass of wine and watch The Daily Show. It was a rough time emotionally, financially, and spiritually. I found myself in crisis: *What am I doing?* I asked myself often. *Am I even accomplishing anything?*

Thankfully, things did turn out all right eventually. When that first academic year ended, I gritted my teeth and took out some loans, which allowed me to quit the outside jobs and focus solely on writing, reading, and teaching. With new breathing room in my life, I poured myself into my graduate community. I became the Poetry Editor for *Phoebe*, which allowed me to work with some of the country's most talented poets. I made great friends with whom I remain close today (including my husband), and I enjoyed the feedback and guidance of one of the best mentors I could have hoped for. And I knew, even as I capitalized on these gifts for the last two years of my MFA, that this protected time and space was fleeting.

My point is this: all beginning poets have lives around them already, and if you're reading this, you're no exception. You might be considering grad school, or you might be in high school, wondering how to get started in this world; you might have a young family already, or you might be retiring, or you might be single and awed by your own possibility; but whatever your situation, you are almost certainly dreaming of having more space and more time to write. This is the constant, ephemeral goal of the poet: the residency, the scholarship, the children at grandma's for the weekend—whatever our version of space and time looks like, we all wish for more of it. Wherever we are on the journey, life continues to press in on all sides, and the only thing that we can do is take advantage of opportunities when we have them and carve out space for ourselves when we don't. Because let's be real: the image of a poet sitting in a quiet, light-filled study—maybe one that looks out on the pepper garden, or on the dark edge of a beckoning forest—and hammering away at a trusty Underwood while a Cuban cigar wafts fragrant smoke from its forgotten place in the ashtray is, to put it mildly, bullshit. It's the image primarily of white male academic poethood, and it does not even reflect the reality of most white male poets. Wallace Stevens, a giant of American poetry, worked for most of his life as an insurance executive. Donald Hall spent years as a sports reporter, covering baseball in particular (he even appears in *No No: A Dockumentary*, about the extraordinary Dock Ellis). Phillip Levine famously spent some of his most formative years in automobile factories. There are as many of these stories as there are poets in the world, and though each life is different and shaped by different forces, the commonality remains: for almost all of us, poetry will not be our only trade. And even if it were, the rest of the world would continue to demand something from us. In other words, we all have to fight to create space for poetry at every step of the way. The fight can look different at different stages, so no matter how little you think you're giving to your art, please believe me when I say that it is still a gift you are giving yourself, and it is still worthwhile.

This has certainly proved true for me. The MFA was not my golden ticket to an uninterrupted writing life on some idyllic farm in upstate New York.

Instead, I went through a long period of difficulty post-grad school: I was stymied at first by a long cross-country move, a stressful job search, an even more stressful apartment hunt, and the inevitable financial ship-righting that my husband and I had to undertake after all of that. Because solid academic jobs are really hard to land just out of grad school (part-time adjuncts comprise about 50% of all university-level instructors), I spent the first two years working two or three jobs at a time, trying to get more experience and help make ends meet. I was what academics in Southern California call a "freeway flier": there were days when I ate my lunch with one hand as I drove down the ill-famed 405, shuttling from my morning classes on one campus to my afternoon classes at a campus an hour away. On "off" days, I tutored high school kids who were prepping for college entrance exams. It was a very busy life, and it turned out to be a little too busy for my creative mind to thrive. I went through long stretches where I didn't write anything new. Still, I kept myself in the game by reading over and revising old work and sending out poems when I didn't know what else to do with them. This turned out to be a good approach: several of the poems from my thesis got picked up, including one that was published in *Beloit Poetry Journal*. These victories were exactly that: not just a nice validation of my voice and vision as a poet, but an actual triumph over the challenges that I was facing at the time. Like any good victory, they flooded me with a sense of confidence that was vital to my ability to move forward and fight another day for the time and space to write, revise, or compile a packet for submission.

Now, though the academic life continues to be an unpredictable ride (when I first wrote this essay, I celebrated the fact that I was employed full-time at *just one university!*; since then, that one university cut a whole roster of its full-time Lecturers, and I spent my summer scrambling to find another part-time teaching position), things are better in many ways, and I'm filled with gratitude for that. I've had poems published in well-regarded journals, and one of those journals has been kind enough to publish me twice. I've made wonderful friends in the poetry world, and I have a supportive, vibrant community of writers around me. In that gauzy cocoon of time that was my just-one-job period, I completed a manuscript of prose poems of which I'm incredibly proud. I feel more stable in my purpose now than ever, even if it hasn't been easy (it took several hours of journaling one recent night to remind me that, no, I didn't want to suddenly scrap everything and become a corporate darling just to get the bills paid). My time, my efforts, and, yes, my money (you may have noticed that submission fees are *de rigeur* these days) are precious resources, and the wisest investment of those resources—for me, at least—is in the craft of writing. And the thing that I've had to realize is that, no matter what else I feel that I haven't yet accomplished, my persistence has already paid off. Even when the writing didn't go well, or it was only once a week or so, I *did* write during even the leanest years. When I wasn't writing, I was sending older work out. So the work continued, in one fashion or another, and like the tortoise lumbering down the raceway, I kept pushing forward at my own pace, obstinate in my conviction that if I didn't win, I'd at least reach some kind of finish line.

All of that is to say that we can only live the lives that we have in front of us, and there are days when we have to choose between writing a poem and having clean underwear, or writing a poem and feeding the kids, or writing a poem and caring for our aging parents. Poetry is work, real work, and as such it requires a place where focus and discipline can happen. That's why there are so many prizes dedicated to giving poets time, space, and the financial resources to keep their lives together while they dedicate their energies to writing. If you don't have those resources, you might not have easy access to space and time, and that doesn't make you a bad poet. It doesn't mean you will never have the space you want, nor that you've failed in some way to achieve True Poet-ness. It just means that your life is ongoing and dynamic, and that you—and I—we are struggling to find the balance.

No matter how tiny, unsatisfying, or spare your writing time and space might feel, then, keep creating it wherever and however you can. Keep faith with yourself; deny the voices in your head that would tell you that you're being selfish or frivolous for taking half an hour for yourself. Read others' work with a pencil in hand. Don't feel inauthentic if you don't have a sexy Moleskine: jot lines on a crumpled up receipt, a paper plate, a server's order pad. Assemble your ideas on the page. Send it out when it's ready, even if you're not. Grow a thick skin for rejection: unless you got drunk and socked the editor at a party, it's almost certainly not personal. And even as you try to share your work with the world, know that publication is not the best measure for success, even though we all want our words to be read by another (and it is true that being published never, ever gets old, if you're anything like me; when I finally do get a book published, I imagine my head will explode).

Rather, your growing skills—your sharpening sense of rhythm and sound-play, your feel for a good line break, the *aha!* moments when you finally find *exactly the right word* to show the reader what the world looks like through your weird, warped, Michael Bay-brain eyes—these are the small joys and triumphs that will propel you forward and make you feel more fortified. These are the moments that will keep you coming back to that sacred space in your office chair, at the dining table, on the bus, or next to the soda machine in the kitchen of an old Irish pub.

Reclaiming Artistic Space

Megan Merchant

HOW TO CONTAIN THE WHOLE FRACTURED WORLD

It is the blue hour, my children are nearing sleep, and a dozy quiet has settled into the bones of this house. I am writing this essay unprepared, and a bit frightened that I might not succeed in scrapping it all together. But, I am no stranger to this tactic—the *let's just see what happens* magic of not having a recipe, or enough time. If I waited until I knew what I was going to say, I might never sit down and tend to the page. There are too many other tasks to complete.

I just finished taking a knife to the dryer's lint trap—my attempt at unclogging the potentially flammable fuzz that has clotted in that net. This could become an image in a poem, or it could fall into the blurry tasks that fill my days as a stay-at-home-mother of two.

I have grown so familiar with this chaotic life that I am actually afraid of the silence. I have taught my brain how to compose inside of the flurry of our daily agendas, loud joy, bleeping video games, and crying children. Out of necessity, I have taught my brain how to carry a poem until it is ready enough to find the page and not worry about catching it at the moment of inspiration, or committing to it before it is gone. It is, after all, just a poem. It is not my son's daily seizure medication. It is not my children's safety, or happiness. I have learned to release the assumed importance of creating, which in turn, has bloomed a great appreciation when the poem tumbles into being. I have learned to treat it like spirit, one that I absolutely trust will show up once I can find the time to tend to it properly, even if that takes seasons.

This past spring, we had two hummingbird eggs appear in a low-branch nest. I visited the mother every day until she grew comfortable with my presence. I could have extended my hand to feel her bright feathers, but chose not to. Instead, I spoke to her about my day, the weather, and motherhood. When her babies hatched, she allowed me to linger breaths away from the nest. She showed great trust. When I spoke with her, it was no different than speaking to the poems-in-wait, or honoring the creative process.

That process is not mystical in the sense that it is wholly shrouded in mystery. Yet, I will be the first to admit that I do not fully understand how the poems come into being. I have learned, over time, this is actually of little importance. I see it much like I see the difference between religion and spirituality. One is a container for the other. The poem is a container for the spirit. I was a container for my two children, who share my genetic makeup, but are not my creations. They came from somewhere else. And if I spent too much time trying to logically puzzle it out, I would miss too many moments of laughter and joy. I would miss the beauty that is their lives. I would miss the lines, hymns, images, and sounds as they are unfolding.

There are hundreds of sources that teach writers how to shape a container, or poem. There are exercises, handbooks, gurus, mentors, and websites that outline form and technique, but little exists that risks insight into how to catch the humanity and heart to fill it. Or, how to thread the pulse. I have learned—that comes with living mindfully. If/when I am moving mindfully through this world, I am paying attention to the bright language of nature, joy, sorrow, and motherhood. I am taking it all in without grasping, or closing around it too tightly. I am like the dryer net catching lint—only in this case, hoping that when the time is ready, it will spark.

There are other sparks too. For instance, when I first began submitting poems, one editor replied to my work almost immediately. He rejected them in under an hour with the reasoning, "We don't publish mommy poems in our journal." I was, of course, furious for his instant devaluation of my work, but then realized that his negation of my role in this world was more of a challenge than a rejection. If he did not want to hear my voice simply because it was rooted in motherhood, then I would project it louder. I would figure out what unique perspective I had to offer, then find the most beautiful container to hold it. This degree of commitment, however, comes with some heartache. Anything that you invest your spirit into does.

There was a day when I appeared alongside that hummingbird nest to find only one of the baby hums nestled inside, still weeks shy of being flight-ready. The nest itself had cinched tighter around that singular pulsing body, erasing the room where the second baby slept. Although temporary, that container shifted to fit the spirit that occupied it. It shaped itself around loss.

I thought, at first, that its death was my fault. That a raven had seen my footfalls and followed them to the nest. That my need to be that close to something beautiful had caused damage.

But this is not true. It is not even close to a truth. The hummingbird baby did not disappear because I saw it as an image, or a metaphor. Poetry is not a separate thing. Our presence in this world is a direct engagement with it. It does not excuse itself from daily life, from the chaos, struggles, and noise. There are poems waiting in every dark and light corner, every nest and house, and every aspect of the roles we assume as human beings. They sink into our blood and bones, and without rush, wait while we carry them for as long as is needed. And whether it is raw courage, or a mindful practice—when the poet shows up without an agenda or endpoint in mind, the spirit is given a chance to speak.

Claudia F. Savage

LEAVE THE DISHES: HOW WE CAN BEGIN WRITING AGAIN AFTER CHILDREN

Making art takes dreaming as well as time. But when I turned thirty-eight and had my daughter, River, all writing methods fell away. I was frantic and exhausted. I owed it to myself, and to River, to find a way to continue my artistic life despite the challenge of raising her. She needed a mother who was her fullest self—and that woman had to figure out how to write. I've tried many methods, but these six worked best.

Deep Attention—in Quick Bursts

The poet Li-Young Lee once told me he came back to poetry after bathing his boys before bed, watching the light come through the trees in a window above them. He felt this attention, this noticing, was more important than any other work he was doing at the time. Sometimes, it is not about making work as a mother-artist, but just allowing yourself to experience unhurried sensation. Stopping the constant rush for just a moment. I often feel a poem begin when I look at my two-year-old's sunlit hair. Encourage your child to touch the petals of a daisy on walks. Touch them with her. Point out the birds rising from a neighbor's rooftop. Watch how their dark wings contrast with the sky. And, to capture those thoughts...

Notebooks, Notebooks Everywhere

Don't just carry a notebook with you, place notebooks everywhere you are during the day—in the stroller, the diaper bag, your purse, next to your bed, the car, and in the kitchen. Being a mother means that artistic ideas are quickly replaced by crying children. Don't worry about the topic, just get it down. One day I wrote the following lines after nursing my daughter:

I thought your eyes would be blue.
Sliced sky over the breakfast table.

This reminds me of the most important shift that happened to me when I started to...

Work Smaller

You know you're not going to write a 700-page novel or fill a gallery when you have an infant. But, maybe you were once prolific and your inability to write even one poem a month makes you feel like an utter failure. For me, I decided that I had to work smaller since the best time I could work was during my daughter's naps. At the end of the day I was so tired I could hardly eat dinner. Nikki McClure's beautiful book, *Awake to Nap*, was done specifically during her son's naps. Many artists talk about this tactic. At first, River's naps were so short I only got out one or two lines every other day. A poem took weeks for a first draft. Then, I realized that I could work smaller on multiple pieces at once, coming back to each one as I felt inspired. This was a departure for me, but it felt easier, especially once I started to...

Exile the Editor to Fiji

Sleep deprivation and stress can make the internal editor huge. It's a good idea to exile her until confidence in your new art-making ways returns. I'm not talking about no longer critiquing your work. I'm talking about exiling that voice that doesn't allow you to create in the first place. The one who tells you everything you make is terrible. For the first year of River's life I made the decision to just focus on generating. I filled notebooks with two-line pieces, sketches, and non-fiction rants. Sometimes, the work was a reminder that I was having a hard time. Once I wrote:

> I write in secret on the couch. Pretending to remember the garlic on the grocery list. *Got that? Yeah. Milk? Yup.* I am bloodless. A husk.

Once River started sleeping a bit more at night, I began to trust myself to edit some of the pieces I'd made. But, before that happens for you, let the editor have her piña coladas far, far away. And focus instead on a way to...

Develop Routine or Ritual

So, what do you do with all those jotted-down sketches and lines from a given week? Try to develop some routine or ritual around some kind of completion. For me, my time was one hour on a Saturday morning. Often I was so exhausted I just stared at my notebooks, but, eventually, I started to crave that time when I could compile my disparate things from the previous week's notebooks into something. It was a good time to assess how I was doing as a writer. What things were working (that notebook in the bathroom got soaked from the duck toy) and what things were surprising. (Did I actually write a line after a 3 a.m. feeding?) And, finally...

Forgiveness and More Forgiveness

If nothing gets done that week or that month, you will be fine. Forgive yourself. You will come back to it if you just focus on making space for yourself. Remember that whatever you make during this time of childrearing should be celebrated. There is nothing more powerful than rediscovering yourself on the page, for yourself and your children. However you make it work is good.

David S. Maduli

SHOREBREAKS

ocean of home

> i could always hold my breath underwater
> a long long time, even as
> a little girl. back then i could read
> the same book over and over for hours
> i could also go for days
> without eating

In the vast ocean there are endless, continuous waves. At times they build in frequency or amplitude, but they are always coming. The vast ocean is also many oceans, and there are many shores the waves reach. There are waves approaching the Farallon Islands, and at the same time there are waves barreling toward the southern Philippines, the Cape of Good Hope, the Caribbean, and so on and therefore and such and such. Imagine the ocean is the great pool of consciousness of the universe. The waves are the forces that carry those thoughts, ideas, memories, bodies, spirits, colors, sounds, words, breaths. They are always present, and they are always whirling, reacting, colliding, mixing, submerging and surfacing.

Having barely made it through the first semester and just starting a new one in an MFA program with a one-year-old and three-year-old in tow, tough news came in the form of a thin white piece of plastic: my wife was pregnant again. Not knowing how to respond, I dropped the take-out lunch on the table, mouthed "oh," and then headed out for my writing time that had been previously agreed-upon and Google-calendared. I didn't write. I parked at the library and leaned back the car seat, drifting in and out of sleep. A few days later when she asked me what we should do and eventually said, "We can't keep it," I responded, "If that's what's best for you..." knowing damn well only she had the guts to decide for both of us, for all of us.

green gold

vein shoulder blade gold
knot hangnail gold
broke ankle gold
lost larynx gold

The artist, or any human being for that matter, can go to where the waves are. There are many maps and markers and documents from those before that point the way. There are also living masters who can take us to secret or secluded reef breaks and shorebreaks, places that have been passed down through the ages. We might also find a special place unintentionally, while out for a nice stroll or row through an area we've never been. There are things we need to do to prepare ourselves for the journey and for when we get there. Muscles we need to build, tools we need to learn how to use—some tools may be gifted to us, some we might have to earn, others might require that we fashion them ourselves. We will have to prepare our bodies and minds: learn how to hike, swim, breathe. Learn how to navigate paths, read the weather and the currents. Learn how to speak to the people and the flora and fauna. At some point we will reach the water, set off into the water, and encounter the waves.

At the moment of encounter we will need all of our training and muscle memory and knowledge of tradition to both recognize the movement of the wave and to catch the wave. Then what we need is courage and confidence to stand up and ride it. To ride that wave, for that instant or moment in time—and some definitely last longer than others—is to be immersed in the consciousness of the universe. The artist's hand, tongue, body, mind and soul are moving in unison with the universe. What the artist creates is both reflection of the ancient and projection of the futuristic. It actually doesn't matter, both old and new are the same. What the artist creates is evidence of that ride on that wave at that moment in time.

Over a year later I finished my thesis and my program, my wife was finally up for a full-time position after years of the adjunct grind, and my two children growing fast. For two years I'd written diligently about my 99-year-old grandma's house in the Outer Mission of San Francisco, a home that has held four generations of family and immigrants from the Philippines. I'd written about my experiences as a 14-year veteran of public school middle and high school teaching. I'd written about life through the lens of music, through the ears and fingers of a DJ. But it was in this last semester that I began to understand and attempt to investigate the confluence between fatherhood and writing. I created a private blog and enacted a daily practice of audio recording my children's voices, snapping photos, and jotting down things they say. At two and four they were discovering language, testing it out, playing with it, experiencing the joys and frustrations of expression. Every night I would review the media on my phone and write a response: prose, a poem, a fragment, whatever came. I would tell my classmates I learned to steal my kids' best lines! More importantly, I learned to be more present in my time with them and do my best to give them their dad at his best.

At the same time it is only a small sliver of that wave that the artist catches. There may be others riding that same wave miles away. There are definitely others catching other waves in other places. The waves keep coming, they are constant. If the artist misses the wave, there are infinite more waves. An artist may cultivate a favorite path and place to go to catch the waves, and it may become easier and faster to get to over time. If the path to one break becomes overgrown and impossible to reach, there are infinite more paths and beaches and reefs and shores. No matter what the path looks like, or where it is located: on a guarded country estate, through a treacherous jungle, down steep cliffs, or right beyond the backyard gate, the waves are the same because they are the force of the same vast ocean.

> To de-compartmentalize these important parts of my life has enabled my writing to come with less resistance, my work to flow better. I'm also coming to the realization of what all of this is for: I am called to write with the wildness and gentleness of our son, to wield the strength and silliness of his big sister. I must approach the word with the fierceness of their mother who kept on when there was no hope her husband would return from his own abyss. I am honored to write around and into the negative space that is the child we left behind, in part to let me be a writer. In all of this I am reminded about my silence that I must reach through, burn through, every time I face the page.

No one owns the waves or controls them or directs them just as no one can own or control the ocean. Nor do we own anything of our journeys in the waves. We can only bring a seashell, a handful of sand, seaweed in our hair, salt drying on our skin—even gashes on our legs from coral—to share with others and to remind ourselves what is out there, and where we have to go to find it.

—|—

family is a shore

the trucks stammering up and down the block
waves. water clear
but will not slake thirst. Undertow
violent, changing its mind
constantly
sand gets in everything. some might call sea
meeting land
abuse. others may describe it
as embrace

Claudia F. Savage

RECLAIM ARTISTIC SPACE THROUGH MEMORIZATION

Writers are often a quiet, introspective group. We mull. We ponder. We say things like, "I can't come over; I need time to gather my energy." When you have children, though, especially when they are young, constant need can take over quiet introspection. Nothing like two hours of "water, water, blanket, blanket, mama, mama, mama" for making your child's nap time become a mama necessity, too.

Getting your own artistic thoughts to arise in this din is ridiculously difficult. Even if you somehow, magically, still have a regular time you write, writing is not just about sitting down at the page. You need all the steps leading up to that moment—reading books, observing, thinking about your characters, engaging the backyard dogwood starting to bloom.

So, how do you preserve mental space for your work? For me, since the birth of my daughter, it has been about memorization. Memorization helps me hold onto my own language for more than a minute. It has become the only way I can quiet the two-year-old's burgeoning vocabulary lodging in my head. It is easier than you think. Here is what I recommend:

Pick Some Short Pieces That Have Strong Meter

I can still remember some of the poetry I memorized as a child, partially because of its strong meter, like this familiar Yeats, from "The Wild Swans at Coole":

> *The trees are in their autumn beauty,*
> *The woodland paths are dry,*
> *Under the October twilight the water*
> *Mirrors a still sky…*

In your own work, it helps to start memorizing poetic pieces that have strong meter to cut through the exhaustion of parenthood. A piece that is only two or three stanzas long works well and will feel more manageable than a piece you adore that is several pages. Of course, if all you write are longer pieces (or if you are a fiction writer) pick a small section of the piece to commit to memory. It helps if you feel really proud of the piece. This is no time for humility. Memorize work that you will like thinking about during the weeks to come. These lines, as you lie in bed, sleep-deprived and cranky, will help you remember why you make art.

Devote Time Each Week to Memorizing

Even in high school, I remember theater kids running around reciting their lines. I have found the easiest way to memorize is to pick a stanza and repeat it to yourself. Maybe it has been years since you think you memorized anything, but I guarantee that you do it all the time. I'm sure there is a favorite recipe you put together without looking at a cookbook because you've done it dozens of times. Or somehow you remember that new extra-long password for your computer at work. Memorizing your work requires the same skills of repetition and practice. The added joy is that you are internalizing *your* work into your body. Take ten minutes at the beginning of each weekday writing session and pick a piece you feel strongly about. Each day, read the same six lines out loud to yourself. That weekend, try to say those lines to yourself while brushing your teeth or once you get into bed. Then, the next week, pick the next stanza to work on and add to the memorized one, reciting the lines you know and reading the ones you do not. Build a house of words in your mind, week by week, foundation to roof.

Recite to Your Child

The best part of memorizing your work might be this last step. Recite the pieces you have memorized to your children. Remember that they have no way of knowing if you memorized all of it or if you recite it correctly. They only know that the tone of your voice has changed from daily corrections and affirmations to something entirely different. It is something that is not about them, but comes only from you. For a few minutes, they get to share in your language, your creation. You don't have to make it into a formal mama concert requiring your children to sit on the couch while you stand and recite in front of them. (Although, a poet friend of mine has a regular "poetry reciting night" once a month at her house where all the members of the family participate.) You can just start reciting something while your children are walking through the park with you. Recite a piece to them while you are in the car together going to the store. Recite something during bath time. Have a poem sneak up on them while they are eating a snack. Have their favorite doll "recite" it.

Hearing memorized poems has become a favorite activity for my girl. She regularly says, "Poems! Poems!" when we are doing the dishes. I often have to stop scrubbing and ask, "You want mama to recite some poems?" "Yes, mama poems!" Maybe it is the fact that my voice softens as I slowly remember the words or their rhythm, but, for now, I have a very small, very enthusiastic fan of my work. She's two. Her name is River.

Tanis MacDonald

THE DEAD GIRL'S BOOKS

When I was thirteen, the young adult daughter of my parents' friends' died; she committed suicide. I was never told why. It's possible that neither my parents nor hers knew why. She was twenty and so much older than me; she lived in a different world, the way it is at that age, when seven years might as well be seven light-years. I didn't know her, though I may have met her when I was too young to remember. I heard about her death long after it happened, when her parents were at our house for dinner and I could tell from the odd lull in the adults' conversation that something was not right. I could see that Mrs. K____was tearing up, and because I grew up in that buckled-down era in a stoic family, I had never seen an adult cry, certainly not Mrs. K____who I had known all my life as a woman who was neither conciliatory nor sunny, but wry and sharp-tongued, unafraid of disagreement when talk turned to politics at those dinners, as it always did. The sight of her face hitching and eyes reddening at our dinner table was so alarming when I asked about it later, my mother couldn't dissemble. She said H____, the K____s' daughter, had died by suicide. I don't remember what I thought. I didn't get very far when I tried to think of why someone might kill themselves. I didn't know enough about her, or about anything.

Sometime later I inherited H____'s poetry books—Leonard Cohen's *Selected Poems* and *Flowers For Hitler*—and it seemed then that the mystery might be solvable. My mother stood at my bedroom door with the books, offering them to me like the strange gifts they were. To be clear, it wasn't unusual for me to get second-hand items from the daughters of my parents' friends. My girl cousins all lived far away, and so while my brother and my in-town boy cousins conducted a brisk trade between themselves in used toys, my sources always came from farther afield.

I still have these books. They are in my office, with the other girl's name written on the fly-leaves, some poems marked with a large X beside them ("The Failure of a Secular Life," "Leviathan," and "Heirloom") in *Flowers for Hitler*, which also bears a stamp on page 33 from a Winnipeg high school library. The first page, where the pocket for the lending card would have been glued, has been torn out, and the tape that fastened the call number to the spine still sticks to the front cover. Both books were dog-eared and knocked about when I inherited them; they were demonstrably much-read, important to the young woman who owned them. The ex-library book status of this copy of *Flowers for Hitler*—a fifth imprint that was released in 1968—suggests that she may have stolen the book from the school library because she liked it so much, and that she was inspired by this first book to purchase Cohen's *Selected Poems* (a fourth printing from March 1969) a year or two later. The publisher's release of these two books so close together speaks to Cohen's immense popularity at the time, in those post-Centennial Pierre Trudeau-era years. McClelland and Stewart clearly knew a hot commodity when they saw one, and published accordingly.

What does it mean to inherit a dead girl's books? In M. Scott Peck's *People of the Lie*, the psychiatrist retells an infamous story of parents who, after their elder son committed suicide by shotgun, "gifted" their younger surviving son with the older boy's weapon. According to Peck, the message is implicit and horrible: you're next, go now and do likewise. Pecks reports that the parents protested that they were not well off and that the shotgun was an expensive item, that they did not wish to say anything with the gift but rather logically redistribute the dead boy's worldly goods to someone else who could use the gun for hunting, and cited the younger boy's now-inherited responsibilities to help furnish food for the rural family. When I first read this, I was aghast at the apparent murderous callousness, especially since the friend with whom I was discussing it had an older brother who had died by suicide and the cruelty of those parents seemed to be in the room with us as we talked. But I wonder about it now, not that I especially wish to absolve anyone, or could even if I wanted to. Peck was speaking of a context outside of his social class, and he was swift and sure in his judgement as only a certain kind of medical professional can be.

Now, decades later, I know too well that when people die, their stuff doesn't dissolve into thin air. It has to go somewhere: to the attic or basement, to friends, to charity, to the dump. I know that imprudent decisions are made all the time by families who are grieving and sleep-deprived and occupy a completely different world from people who can still see all their loved ones in one room. I think of Cohen's moody books, full of poems of despair and lust and suicide and torture and Holocaust-survivor guilt, and now that I am older than my mother was when she stood in the doorway with the books in her hands, I admit that it seems odd to give another child a dead girl's books that were so scored by violence, both personal and historical.

But we were a starving-class family undergoing a shift into being striving-class. My parents were rural children during the Great Depression and I lived in their world where "waste not, want not" was an unbreakable law. I understood that we didn't have money the way some of my friends' families did, and to refuse "perfectly good" items when they were offered to me was not really an option. This was known as "turning up your nose" and it was a very particular Protestant sin. It meant you thought you were too good for things; at best you were a snob, and at worst you were deluded. If I didn't like a thing that was offered me, I knew there would be dozens of chances to pass it on to someone else later. (Except if a family member gave it to me as a birthday gift and then there was no getting rid of it. Ever.)

It would be easy to draw a line from Cohen's poems, chronicling his own well-known struggles with depression and the frequent appearance of the word *suicide* in his early work, and claim that reading these books contributed to the young woman's death. But I don't think people live—or die—like that. It seems to me, looking at the poems she marked, that the books were helpful to her mental state rather than hurtful, that they provided solace when little else could until, finally, nothing helped. This very well may be a case of me projecting my reading experience on to the books, or me resisting the reading that books are murderous.

As my mother stood in the doorway, I could see that the books were clear evidence of a sophisticated world; the covers showed Cohen's profile gazing off to the right, wistful, handsome. The books had belonged to an older girl, after all, and pretty much screamed contraband: books that I would not be allowed to read if my parents had read them first. My best friend had a copy of the underground classic *Go Ask Alice*, with its drug use and sexual freedom, and we knew that such books were designed to be hidden from parents. This was a world in which I was usually sent out of the room if there was sex on television. But here my mother was handing these books over like she was the most permissive parent in the world. When I opened *Flowers for Hitler*, I could see the first poem had the word *nymphomaniac* in it. Chalk one up for the intimidation factor of poetry because I don't think my parents even cracked the covers.

It was obvious the books were cool; Montreal cool, big city cool, sexy cool, a gajillion miles away from me-on-the-prairies cool. They were also my first indication that poetry could be political. Poems were titled "All There is to Know About Adolph Eichmann" and "Goebbels Abandons His Novel and Joins the Party" and there were lines about mushroom clouds and the bleakness of running out of opium. There were poems in which Cohen tossed around words like *torture* and *cuckold*, and *Flowers for Hitler* contains a play script, "The New Step: A Ballet-Drama in One Act," which openly defies standards of beauty and ends with a fat girl dancing in her apartment and telling her beautiful roommate that she'll dance any way she wants. I had no idea what to think, and I would no more ask someone about it than I would cut off my own arm. And whom could I ask? My friends? My teachers? My minister? I just read and reread and reread again. It was, in some ways, an excellent introduction to the basic tasks of being a poet. I spent a long time puzzling over a book that was both accessible and baffling: one that I could read, but that I couldn't quite understand.

And who was my benefactor, the girl who bought and stole these books, who wrote in them and marked her favourites? It was a *Great Expectations* moment, with H_____ as my Magwitch, transported to another world. But Magwitch returns, transformed and seeking revenge, and H_____ has not. My parents are both dead and so are hers and there's no one left to ask about her or about her love of Leonard Cohen's work. I can only make of her what I can from the books themselves, in literary forensic fashion, as markers on a map of someone's life. So many years later, I am looking not for why she killed herself but rather how she lived and what she loved and I know that as I do so, every answer I get will be at best a trace, absence scratched onto absence. For instance, when I read H_____'s books as an adult, I wondered what the S written beside some poems in the Table of Contents could stand for. I checked *suicide* first, partly because Cohen mentions it several times in the poems, and partly because, however salacious or unfair, I was working with one of the few concrete pieces of information I had about H_____. But suicide didn't turn up in any poem marked with an S. Other words don't quite fit all of them: *Sex? Scars? Sleep? Songs?* "Suzanne Takes You Down," arguably Cohen's best-known poem and song, is not marked with an S, but instead with a tiny slanted pencil mark beside it in the Table of Contents: neither a checkmark nor a comma. "Pagans" and "Story," both from *Let Us Compare Mythologies*, also have that small slanted mark in the *Selected*'s Table of Contents. "The Music Crept by Us" and "What I'm Doing Here" are dog-eared; other poems' page numbers are circled in the *Selected*'s index of first lines at the back of the book. If it was a code, I could not crack it.

I returned to the largest marks in *Flowers for Hitler*, three bold Xs marked beside the poems in the body of the text. All three poems were about torture and pain and the unbearable atmosphere of modern industrial capitalism that can offer no solace. It is up to the poem to see and to say what it sees, repeating whenever the reader returns to the pages. The context, for all three poems, suggests Cohen's work with Theodor Adorno's admonition in 1949 that "to write poetry after Auschwitz is barbaric" and that if " critical intelligence" is to survive, it must move away from what Adorno calls "self-satisfied contemplation." Later, in 1966, Adorno retracted part of this statement to say that "perennial suffering has as much right to expression as a tortured man has to scream," but also that "the drastic guilt" of those who survived the Holocaust finds a purchase in "coldness, the basic principle of bourgeois subjectivity." This may seem like heady stuff for a young Jewish man from Montreal to be writing about in the 1960s, but critics are pretty firm that Cohen's work spoke from this legacy for much of his life; if it seems heady for two young Christian women from the prairies to be thinking about poetry and barbarism and how to write pain, then and now, I can only speak for myself. I was sexually assaulted by an older boy when I was twelve, and while there was much in Cohen's poems that I did not understand when I first read them, I could dizzily discern the shape of the pain in Cohen's "Heirloom": "The torture scene developed under the glass bell/ such as might protect an expensive clock." I need to be clear that my assault was in no way comparable to the torture and deaths of six million Jewish people in the Holocaust. But the poem saw me: my relief was in finding this stark language that spoke about cruelty as I had been introduced to it. This is sometimes how we learn to read: through empathy, through finding that someone else's pain and the history that accompanies it illuminates the unnameable in our own minds.

Equivalence is not usual, nor is it necessary for good writing and passionate reading; I still don't know how Cohen made our realities overlap for several lines at a time. And I don't know what H___was thinking when she read "Heirloom"; she marked these poems for reasons of her own. As advances, even provisional ones, are made in the diagnosis and treatment of depression, I've thought of her often, and how much what might have been beyond medical intervention or assistance then would have been treatable only a decade later. Or not. This too is just a guess, and most days it seems wrong to think that I know her or to presume to understand her reasons.

Whenever you read a used book that has been lovingly marked by its previous owner, you are reading two texts simultaneously: the version printed on the page, and the other, hovering slightly above it, marked and circled by the previous owner. At thirteen, I needed all the help I could get. I absorbed Cohen's words and H___'s reading practices. When I posted a photo of these two books on my Facebook page in 2017 as part of a series I was curating on vintage Canadian poetry books, the books received a deluge of testimonies from writer friends, calling these the first poetry books they ever bought, or owned, or smuggled home from the library. I don't know their reasons, either.

When I studied Cohen's poems in university, my professor called Cohen "creepy" and I had to admit that this is sometimes true and is even noted (though not attributed) on the back cover of the *Selected* in a blurb that calls Cohen "a beautiful creep." Such early influences can have long-term effects, especially when they are accidental. Like families, we can't choose them, simply because we don't yet know how. Sometimes, they come walking in your door, borne on the back of grief and happenstance and guilt. The two Cohen books on my shelf travelled from H___'s apartment in Toronto, packed and brought to Winnipeg by her devastated parents who didn't know what they should do or could do with their beloved daughter's prized possessions. I don't know why or how they thought of me for the books, but my guess is that they didn't want to throw them away, yet they couldn't bear to have them in the house. Somehow, my mother agreed to take the books and give them to her voracious reader kid, either against her better judgement or just because she too did not know the right thing to do. The four adults, the K___s and my parents, would be friends for the rest of their lives. Time passed and I grew older than H___was when she died. I moved to Toronto as she had. I took the Cohen books with me and lived through university degrees and boring jobs and bad boyfriends and a few more cities and an aggressive tumor that landed me in hospital and recovery and adulthood.

Life is long and it is shockingly short. Sometimes you collide with the ephemera of someone else's history, and sometimes it sticks, no matter what you know or what you don't, its heat and coldness flying at you out of a dark cumulus of pain you still can't see through. You are young, you reach up to catch it from the cloud, and then it's yours. It doesn't have to mean anything until it does.

John Guzlowski

LANGUAGE AND LOSS

My friend the writer Christina Sanantonio and I have been having a conversation about writing about loss. It's a conversation fueled in part by the suicide of the novelist David Foster Wallace back in 2008. She wrote me a long letter about how we use or don't use language to talk about loss, and about how hard it is to write about loss.

One of the things in her letter that really resonated with me was something she said about one of my favorite writers, Primo Levi, the Holocaust survivor and author of *Survival in Auschwitz*, who, like Wallace, apparently took his own life. Primo Levi frequently talked about the frustration of trying to write about loss and suffering, especially the loss and suffering he and so many others experienced in the Nazi concentration camps. He felt we needed a new kind of language to talk about what happened there. Christina wrote that we ache for a language that doesn't exist.

As a poet, I've spent the last 39 years trying to find words to describe what happened to my Polish-Catholic parents in the German concentration and slave labor camps and what those experiences make me feel. I write about this event or that image; and no matter how powerful the original event described by my mother or father I can't really describe it, explain it, bring it out of the past. I can't bring it out of memory into this life. Instead, I'm left pushing around some words, trying to make myself feel what I felt the first time I heard that story when I was a child. Sometimes I think I almost succeed, but most of the time I know I'm not even close.

For me the poems that work best are the ones with my parents' actual words in them. Those words are the real thing. In my poem "Here's What My Mother Won't Talk About," my mother refuses to tell me anything about the murder of her mother and her sister and her sister's baby and her own rape.

All she will say to me is, "If they give you bread, you eat it. If they beat you, you run." Likewise, in my poem "The Work My Father Did in Germany," my dad tells me what he said to the German guards who tormented and beat him and blinded him, "Please, sirs, don't ever tell your children what you've done to me today." There are bits and pieces of my parents' words scattered throughout my poems, and when I read these words out loud my parents are there with me. I'm again a kid listening to my dad tell me about the day he saw a German soldier cut off a woman's breast or listening to my mom tell me about the perfect house she lived in in the perfect woods in eastern Poland before the Germans came. My parents' words are a kind of magic for me.

But how do I convey this magic to other people?

I think sometimes that all I can do is read my poems out loud and show people how the poems affect me. I guess what happens then is that my words become like my parents' words. I become my father and mother for that moment in the poem.

Sometimes, I think, this touches people, conveys the magic to them.

I've seen this happen at some of the poetry readings I've given. A person stands up at the end of the reading when I invite questions, and he doesn't say anything. He just stands there. I don't know if the person even has a question. Maybe he just wants to show how much he feels my parents' lives; or maybe the loss I talk about somehow reminds him of a loss he experienced and couldn't talk about and still can't talk about.

For me one of the central images of the Bible is the image of the Tower of Babel. It represents in my eyes the moment when humanity became trapped in language that would not communicate what we needed to communicate. It was a second fall from grace. Our lives became chained to a language that doesn't convey what we feel or what we mean. Although we have this deep need to say what we feel, we often can't explain it to ourselves or to other people. Sometimes our words fail us and sometimes other people fail us. They can't bring themselves to listen to our stories of loss. It's hard to take on that burden.

When my father was dying, he told me a story about a Lithuanian friend of his in Buchenwald Concentration Camp who had made love to a German woman and contracted VD. He came to my father and asked him what should he do. My father said, "Go to the river and drown yourself." His friend thought my dad was joking, and he went to another friend who told him, "Tell the Germans what you did." My father's friend did that, and the soldiers killed the woman; and then they beat my father's friend, castrated him, and killed him.

Fifty years after his friend's death, when my father was telling me this story, he still didn't know what he could have said to his friend to save him from what happened.

No matter how hard it is to tell someone something, no matter how hard it is to get beyond the Babel we're caught up in, I think we need to try.

Will it change the world? Make anything different? Better?

We can only hope.

Duane L. Herrmann

AWAKENING POET

When very young I had this desire, this fantasy, this vague yearning to make stories. I didn't know the difference between poetry and prose then. I was only two or three. I liked stories. I liked the characters in them. I liked what happened in stories. I liked the time with my mother that a story could engender. Stories were magical things that appeared mysteriously and magically in books, magazines and newspapers. I didn't know how they got there, but I wanted to make them.

I supposed stories were made by people, but a special sort of people far distant from the normal people in my family or that I saw in normal places. None of them made stories, I never saw them do it. I eventually learned that an aunt of mine had written two poems—about me! That was amazing!

I made stories myself. The first one started with a dream. I had been looking at a comic book. The characters in the comic were bugs who lived in upside down, broken tea cups and similar human castoffs. I had a dream about them one day. When I woke up I wanted the dream story to continue and, since I was the only one interested in that comic, and had had the dream, I was the only one who could make the story. So I did.

I don't remember any of it now, and I certainly didn't write it down. I didn't know my letters.

This and similar stories went on for several years. Then one day I was in a place far from home and I was told that two writers were also there. Real, honest to goodness writers! Did they look anything at all like the normal people I knew? I had to find out, but no one could know. I was told to stay away from them, so I could not be obvious.

I found out where they were located. I figured out a way to get there unobtrusively. I determined the best time for sighting them, then set my plan in motion.

I crept silently, carefully and slowly. I could not give myself away. I didn't want to be disobedient.

As I crept closer to them, I began to hear a sound that I'd never heard before. It sounded much like rain. The sky was sunny and there were no clouds, so I knew it could not be rain. Whatever it was, was music to my ears. It was an enchanting sound.

The closer I became, the louder and more distinct the sound. There were pauses in the sound, but not many. It was continual, rising and falling—dancing.

Finally I was close enough, I knew they would be directly in sight when I simply looked around the corner. I still had to be careful not to be seen. I could not "bother" them.

I quickly peeked.

There sat two young men, veritable gods, typing on their typewriters! I was spellbound. They looked just like normal people, but SO different!

Before I could get caught, I withdrew and hurried away so that I could not be found near them. Still, I was in heaven! I had seen two actual writers, actually writing, I floated away. They looked as normal as anyone else. But they were WRITERS!

If such normal-looking people as they were could be writers, there was no reason why a normal-looking person such as myself could not also be a writer. I did not know then about my aunt, but she did not write more than those two poems until much later when she began writing family history.

Today, decades later, I am a writer. I have poems, stories, history, and more published in several languages in countries in four continents. I am a Writer. Writing gives a reason and purpose to my life. All because of my desire and awakened awareness that I also could be a Writer.

I saw these writers when I was five years old, the summer before I started school. Writing was not easy though. Unknown to everyone until I was a grown man with children, I am dyslexic. I was only able to learn to really read after second grade. That summer I walked a hot lonely country road a mile for special tutoring from a retired school teacher who lived at the end of our road.

Once I could read, I still had obstacles. The major one was that I was expected to take care of the cooking, housework. and childcare which overwhelmed my mother. I was the oldest, three more followed me. I was put to work when I was two. By the time I was thirteen I was able to manage the house, alone, while our mother was gone to a distant summer school. She came home on weekends, creating chaos. While she was gone the house was quiet and clean, meals were on time, the garden was cared for, and my little brothers, for the only time in their childhoods, did not fight and bicker. It was the most wonderful summer of my life.

When the summer session was over, I was put on a tractor to begin farming. Though I tried, I found it difficult to write while driving a tractor in a field. I could not write in the house either, so I taught myself to write in the total, absolute darkness in bed at night. At least I was writing. Writing without looking at the paper is a skill that has come in handy while I travel empty country highways. I've written some of my best poems that way!

In the eighth grade I wrote a story which was the first one I showed anyone. I gave it to my teacher. I expected it back, but that never happened. As a senior in high school I wrote a play which the drama teacher wanted to produce, but I had no confidence to do that. I wasn't able to get that back either. The only thing I have left from my childhood writing is a story I wrote in fifth grade on pages of a very tiny notebook.

I also have some poems from high school. Two were published my senior year in the newly created high school literary journal. I don't know how long it continued, but I have the poems. In college more of my poems were published, and my first news articles. I was ecstatic.

Because I am dyslexic, with cyclothymia, an anxiety disorder, and PTSD, I have difficulty remembering what I've written so I've tried to keep a list. It is now eighteen pages long, single spaced.

Don't even ask me about spelling!

What do I write about? Mostly my life. I learned that saving and reusing was the only way to survive. I've carried that over to my writing. I write about my life and experiences, either as straight memoir, or combined in new ways to make other stories and poems. Even when I've written stories set on other, imaginary planets, the experiences there with people are based on my own life. Even when I've written about possibilities after this life, I have used knowledge and experience gained in my life.

My childhood had been so miserable, my mother's constant screaming and my inability to anticipate her whims, that any life other than my own was preferable. Every night, going to sleep, I would make up another part of long continuing stories. Some of these I told to my younger sister when we slept in the same room, but even then, after she had gone to sleep, I would resume my own, private story.

To make these stories truly separate and better than my life, the very first action killed all the rest of my family. I couldn't think of any other way to avoid having to take care of them in the story. I was feeding my baby sister when I was two and a half. My next job was to help my mother dress herself. When the next babies came, I was pressed into changing their diapers. Soon, I was also having to wash dishes, cook meals, clean house, and do laundry. The latter would take all of a Saturday. It was done in the dank basement, sometimes with a resident frog for company, always with spiders and crickets.

The washing machine was older than I was. The sides were so high, and I was so short, I could not reach over the edge to get the clothes out—not even when I used the stick! When I was first ordered to run clothes through the wringer (and don't dare let the buttons stand up or they will pop off!) it was well above my head. I could barely feed the clothes into it. One time, after I'd grown taller, I wondered what the wringer would feel like, so stuck my fingers in. It quickly pulled my arm up to my elbow. I just managed to remember I could turn it to "reverse" before it pulled my arm off. Not every child remembered that, or could reach the control. I've now written a poem about that!

There were three rinse tubs which all the clothes had to circulate and be stirred through. And, each time, they all had to go through the wringer. With a family of six, this job would take all day. When the motor finally burned out, I was the happiest little ten-year-old boy on the planet!

When I could not stomach the food I was forced to eat, and expelled it—I was forced to swallow my vomit. And I have a poem about that! To my surprised it is published.

Once when I could not wash dishes fast enough, I was whacked over the head with a heavy serving platter and given a concussion. I had to hold on to the counter to stand upright.

When I tried to play with my little brothers, either I bumped them too hard or I was yelled at to do some work.

At two I was suicidal when I realized, through the intensity of her screaming at my defectiveness, that I had ruined my mother's life. But I had no idea how to cease to exist. By the time I was eleven, I was suicidal again, but this time I knew several ways to accomplish it. I wanted a way that was guaranteed to be successful, and not cause me more pain. I had had enough pain. I did not have the money to buy the sleeping pills I wanted, so I lived.

Reading my poetry and short stories you will find bits of all this in them. In using my life I have touched other lives which were not so very different, giving them courage to continue, because they know now they are not alone. There is power in poetry! Many of these childhood poems are now gathered together for the first time in a collection entitled: *Remnants of a Life*. A few had appeared earlier in *Ichnographical: 173*.

Over the decades my poetry has been published in several countries, from Canada to Cameroon, and on the internet. My poems have won awards and accolades that amaze me. A short video was produced by one publisher to announce some of my poems they published. A small collection of my poems have been set to music by a composer in South Africa. I have even been nominated and considered for being Poet Laureate of the State of Kansas. That in itself is an honor!

Most importantly, writing the poems has helped me heal. Poetry is empowering! In writing about experiences one could not control, one gains control. Writing is empowering. I control what I write. When I write about my childhood, I gain control over it. Poetry is Power!

I have also written histories, memoirs, short stories, children's stories and a science fiction novel.

It has been said that writing is a sign of a person's existence. I write, therefore, I exist.

I guess that's a good enough reason to have stayed alive.

A Way of Seeing the World

Stephen Page

POETRY IS ABOUT PLACE

When we talk about Poetry and Place, most of us immediately think about nature poets writing poems in a pastoral setting: John Haines chopping wood next to his shanty in the Alaskan frontier, Gary Snyder striding up and down mountains hunting deer to keep himself involved in the food chain, Walt Whitman looking up at the clouds while lying in the grass next to a river. But Place in Poetry does not have to be the frozen tundra, the Rocky-Mountain trails, the riverbank—there is the urbanscape and the land of the imagination. Wherever you as a writer choose to live, whichever space you choose to occupy, you have to write about Place. Place is Poetry. Poetry is Place.

Haines believed he had to go to the wilderness extreme to find Place. He needed somewhere beyond the peripheries of civilization, somewhere without electricity, somewhere without combustible engines, somewhere in the *natural* order of things. Haines said, in his collection of essays, *Living Off the Country*, that:

> It has been obvious to me that for some time that contemporary poets lack the force and conviction of ideas... I learned that it is land, *place*, that makes people, provides for them the possibilities they will have of becoming something other than mere lumps of sucking matter.... As D.H. Lawrence has told us, there is a "spirit of place"... William Carlos Williams, in his book, *In the American Grain*, attempted to find what he felt had gone wrong with America from the start—the inability or refusal to recognize what was actually under our feet, or in the air, and to live by that... I think there is a spirit of place, a presence asking to be expressed; and sometimes when we

are lucky as writers, and quiet in a way few of us want to be anymore, a voice enters our own, becomes mingled with it, and we speak with a force and clarity not otherwise heard.

Haines goes on later in his book of essays to say, yes, we cannot all live in the wilderness, some of us need to stay in our cities and work. I think what Haines is saying is that your place once found and written about gets you and your writing closer to the truth of things, closer to the workings of the universe. It does not matter where Place is, it is only through Place that it happens.

Gary Snyder needs nature also for Place. Nature is where he finds poetry, and his poetry is nature—in other words, his poems become the things he writes about. In his book, *Left Out in the Rain*, he says that: "This complicated gathering of poems, tight and loose together, is like an understory ecosystem of the Old Growth. It needs rain. Some are plain and some are highly adorned." An example of his poetry reflects how his poems are nature themselves:

Elk Trails

Ancient, world-old Elk paths
Narrow, dusty Elk paths
Wide-trampled, muddy,
Aimless... wandering...
Everchanging Elk paths.

I have walked you, ancient trails,
Along the narrow rocking ridges
High above the mountains that
Make up your world:
Looking down on giant trees, silent
In the purple shadows of ravines
Along the spire-like alpine fir
Above the high, steep-slanting meadows
Where sun-softened snowfields share the earth
With flowers.

I have followed narrow twisting ridges,
Sharp-topped and jagged as a broken crosscut saw
Across the roof of all the Elk-world
On one ancient wandering trail,
Cutting crazily over rocks and dust and snow—
Gently slanting through high meadows,
Rich with scent of Lupine,
Rich with smell of Elk-dung,
Rich with scent of short-lived
Dainty Alpine flowers.
And from the ridgetops I have followed you
Down through the heather fields, through timber,
Downward winding to the hoof-churned shore of
One tiny blue-green mountain lake
Untouched by the lips of men.

Ancient, wandering trials
Cut and edged by centuries of cloven hooves
Passing from one pasture to another—
Route and destination seeming aimless, but
Charted by the sharp-tempered guardian of creatures,
Instinct. A God coarse-haired, steel-muscled,
Thin-flanked and musky. Used to sleeping lonely
In the snow, or napping in the mountain grasses
On warm summer afternoons, high in the meadows.
And their God laughs low and often
At the man-made trails,
Precise-cut babies of the mountains
Ignorant of the fine, high-soaring ridges
And the slanting grassy meadows
Hanging over space—
Trails that follows streams and valleys
In well-marked switchbacks through the trees,
Newcomers to the Elk world.

(High above, the Elk walk in the evening
From one pasture to another
Scrambling on the rock and snow
While their ancient, wandering,
Aimless trails
And their ancient, coarse-haired,
Thin-flanked God
Laughs in silent wind-like chuckles
At man, and all his trails.)

The poem is one with the two subjects, that is, the elk and the narrator walking down the trails. The meter, assonance, alliteration, and word choice become the subjects in action. The lines move effortlessly from trochaic to iambic, occasionally anapestic, as one would occasionally miss a step while walking upon a snowy ridge, but it is never forced, never unnatural. The consonant sibilance adds a slipping and sliding effect to the step. The poem becomes the subjects moving in Place.

Walt Whitman wanted to represent the land in his philosophy and his writing. He wrote about Place, his place, America, and he became Place (or so in his ego) by writing about it. The first poem of *Leaves of Grass* starts:

I CELEBRATE myself,
And what I assume you shall assume;
For every atom belonging to me, as good belongs to you.

I loaf and invite my Soul;
I lean and loaf at my ease, observing a spear of summer grass.

Houses and rooms are full of perfumes—the shelves are
          crowded with perfumes;
I breathe the fragrance myself, and know it and like it;
The distillation would intoxicate me also, but I shall not let it.

The atmosphere is not a perfume—it has no taste of the
          distillation—it is odorless;
It is for my mouth forever—I am in love with it;

I will go to the bank by the wood, and become undisguised and
     naked;
I am mad for it to be in contact with me.

In other poems of the collection Whitman becomes the growing trees by writing about stretching his arms. He becomes Manifest Destiny by writing about expanding himself. He uses language to become one with Place. Louise Glück, in her book *Proofs and Theories*, talks of finding her place—Place where she could write. She describes moving to Vermont and accepting a teaching job on short notice. Glück describes colleagues finding her "a place to live, a bedroom in a rooming house, a wonderful room with orange paisley wall paper and a huge four poster bed, a cross between old New England farmhouse and bordello." She also "reads" the first poem she wrote in the room.

In the poem, titled "All Hallows", readers will notice Glück is speaking about where she is. She has found Place and put Place in her poem. (And a wonderful poem it is.) She goes on, talking not only about finding Place geographically, but finding Place in life and Place in the world—which includes her second occupation, that *thing* most writers need to support themselves financially.

What she is leading into is, and she goes on to explain this, that after she began teaching she was not writing as well as she should have been, but it was not teaching that was distracting her, it was her fear of losing her writing ability to the distractions of teaching that made her go through a period of block. She later got over it and realized it was not her life that was getting in her way of writing, it was her mind. In the book she talks about Place in another way, in the manner that when a reader reads a poem about a certain place, the reader occupies that place: "I think of those poems the reader co-authors as places occupied, and, therefore, as points of departure."

I am sure you know a writer or two who keep saying to you, "Oh, I never have time to write what I want to write because life keeps getting in the way." My answer to that is, flumbug. Write about what is getting in the way—write about that place. Take every interruption and write about it, take every fear you have and write about it. Sharon Olds, at least for most of her writing career, never let life get in her way. She wrote about her family, which most people use as an excuse for not writing. Olds did not let life get in her way, she did not let the fact that she had children stop her from writing, she did not let her subway transits to and from teaching get in her way of writing. Her poetry was about her life. Her poetry was about her place.

Place does not always take place where one is living. The writer may have a vivid imagination and be able to write about Place from a source as simple as a newspaper article, a book, or a story told. Numerous writers have written credible books about wars they have never fought in, of lands they have never visited. Emily Dickinson is a fine example of a writer who wrote of countries she had not travelled to. She went there instead using her education, her library, her dinner conversations with people that came to visit her family. Here is an example:

> YOUR riches taught me poverty.
> Myself a millionaire
> In little wealths,—as girls could boast,—
> Till broad as Buenos Ayre,
>
> You drifted your dominions
> A different Peru;
> And I esteemed all poverty,
> For life's estate with you.
>
> Of mines I little know, myself,
> But just the names of gems,—
> The colors of the commonest;
> And scarce of diadems
>
> So much that, did I meet the queen,
> Her glory I should know:
> But this must be a different wealth,
> To miss it beggars so.
>
> I'm sure 'tis India all day
> To those who look on you
> Without a stint, without a blame,—
> Might I but be the Jew!

I'm sure it is Golconda,
Beyond my power to deem,—
To have a smile for mine each day,
How better than a gem!

At least, it solaces to know
That there exists a gold,
Although I prove it just in time
Its distance to behold!

It's far, far treasure to surmise,
And estimate the pearl
That slipped my simple fingers through
While just a girl at school!

If you ever get stuck writing about your place, write about another place. Listen, read, borrow.

Richard Hugo wrote a book entitled *The Triggering Town*, which has as a major theme, Place. For Hugo, Place is the "triggering object" of poetry, the starting switch (what some might believe is caused by the muse). The "triggering object" is the now, the where he is at the moment. It could be anything, a car starting, a conversation in a bar, a fish flipping out of the water—then the poem starts. The poem might not stay on the matter of the subject that triggered the poem, but is nonetheless the triggering factor—and it comes from Place.

Basho and many of his followers of haiku believed in a thing that Bruce Ross calls "the haiku moment." What that essences to is that we humans are a part of nature and are spiritually one with everything in the natural world, but we have lost or forgotten how to be with the spiritual oneness—we are outside it; it is only through trying to keep ourselves inside the oneness that we find haiku—it takes conscious effort at first, but then, like meditation, it just happens—it happens in many ways; one example might be: while on an early morning walk in late autumn you are looking at the ground, noticing the dead leaves and you sense only stillness, quiet, sadness—then, the flap of wings of a cardinal leaving a branch startles you, the sound reverberating through you, the scarlet feathers a sharp contrast to the ochre branches—all giving you a second or a "moment" of being one with it all (and an arbitrary awareness of season). The hard part is getting that feeling written to make the moment eternal, or at least written well enough that the moment can be lived over and over again for readers—the main point here being, getting Place vivid. A good haiku is not an easy thing to master. Jorge Luis Borges said, a haiku is or a haiku isn't.

It is nearly impossible to talk about Place in Poetry without talking about Poetry in Place. To become one with the land, one with the wood, one with the sea—and write about it—that is the goal of many writers. Haines took off to the last frontier and found Place. Snyder jumped on a barge and went to the Orient to get his head together and then he returned to the United States and lived in the mountains in order to find Place. Whitman rolled in the grass and became the land to find Place. Of course not all writers can sell their houses, leave their families, quit their jobs, and go to the Klondike, to Mount Saint Helens, to the Potomac and lie naked on its bank (and many writers would not even want to); but all writers can write about their place. Poetry must have Place. Place is the root of the poem, the grounding force. Just like all language needs a speaker to validate language as we know it, all literature needs a somewhere. It needs a setting, a place where the action happens, a place where the speaker is speaking from. Where and when Place is depends on you, the writer. You must decide—is it your now, where you live, your present; is it elegiac, your past, a place you have been; or is it in your imagination, from your education, what you have heard. You need to be aware of Place. Poetry comes from Place. Poetry is Place.

Kari Treese

ON FINDING POETRY AND PLACE

Driving on interstate 5 North, the Nisqually river valley opens like a flower below the crest of a hill just past exit 114; the highway cuts straight through the marsh. There is the river mouth opening into the wildlife refuge on the left and the tree line sitting on the horizon. Below, the sky bearing baby tufts of cotton clouds with Mount Rainier rising in the distance covered in bright white snow, crisp and clear and clean.

In the valley all along the highway on either side, scotch broom blooms in golden flowers. I look in awe at the magnificence of that color—that violent yellow—against the spring day and I am overwhelmed with sorrow. Sorrow because I am leaving.

I didn't grow up in Washington, but I spent three years in this place. Not a true resident, yet I am attached in a way that is difficult to fully comprehend. I feel like this place has latched onto me, and the parting is like a tearing. When I go, I'll be leaving a part of my soul here to soak in the rain in the winter, to eat up the sun in the summer. I hope I can find my way back to collect the pieces of myself that are left bereft of body and breath. They lie dormant, waiting.

I found Cytisus Scoparius (also known as scotch broom, scot's broom) flowering in spring in the empty field near my home. Known for its distinctive golden flowers, it was originally a native of Europe and North Africa but was imported into California in the 1850s as a decorative shrub. It is not hard to see why.

The crabgrass and weeds nip at my ankles and I see a garter snake dart through the twigs while my feet crunch a narrow path. The yellow buds smell like honey and the warmth of white sheets dried on a line in the middle of summer. Rough, spindly branches birth pods of silky petals soaking color from the sun.

Scotch broom had a practical use, too, as a sand stabilizer and a deterrent to erosion. It was meant to keep the earth from sliding away under the force of water and wind. But scotch broom is now classified as an invasive species. The virulent shrub often outcompetes native plants forming short dense forests that inhibit the growth of other life.

Its seeds come in pods that litter the surrounding area. Unlike other shrubs, the seeds of a scotch broom can remain viable for 30 years, though I've read estimates as high as 80. One plant can produce as many as 12,000 seeds per year. Over the maximum life span, one broom can produce 240,000 seeds.

Imagine holding 240,000 seeds. Some context: the average adult native English speaker's vocabulary is composed of about 20,000 words. Imagine what we could do—what you could write!—with 220,000 more words. Each word a seed of meaning and life waiting, hibernating until the right composition helps it bloom.

***

Homesickness depends entirely upon one having a home. With the use of an article, *home* refers to the place where a person or animal dwells. Even a dwelling is easy. A cardboard box, tent, single room, studio apartment, cave on a hillside—all of these could be home then. But without an article or possessive, *home* becomes "the place where one lives or was brought up, with reference to the feelings of belonging, comfort, etc., associated with it" [OED].

Bringing up, being brought up: the language reminds me of my childhood dwelling. It was a small house, not fancy. The first memory—the first memory I can recall—takes place in this house. There was a blue tarp over the floor. The addition in the back wasn't finished. I can hear the crinkling of the tarp and I can feel the smell of paint drying in my nose. Skip to when I was older—how much I can't say—and I pierced my knee on an old wooden fence decrepit in the front yard, graying with age and infested with decay. Skip to when I was nineteen, when I left with a husband and a baby the size of green olive, no pit, in my belly.

I left home—that dwelling where I was brought up—and set out to find another place to bring up, to be brought up, to be. Leaving California—once home and comfort—for other states was easier than I thought it would be. Now, going back, returning as some sort of prodigal Cali girl, feels antithetical to who is emerging, being pulled out piece by piece.

***

Poetry entered my life late. I have friends, writing friends, who have always written things. Paper poems on scraps of tissue or bad poems—really atrocious poetry—that hide in their old notebooks or journals. I didn't do those things. I have no old notebooks or journals or diaries from teenage years. No angsty writing will be discovered and published posthumously. Every poem I've ever written can be dated no earlier than 2012. Every poem, every essay I have written was composed in Washington.

***

Three years is barely enough time to be considered a resident. I have hardly even begun to understand the rain.

I have only just begun to see how the moss creeps, year after year, up the underside of the bridge. I have only begun to feel the way the mist collects on faces and in hair when the clouds aren't crying, but emanating sorrow in water from the sky. It isn't enough time to appreciate the way the cold seeps into extremities. Or the way the constant gray is comforting because the openness of the blue sky is oppressive in its vastness. To see the sky always— to be ever aware of one's smallness is overwhelming. So you grow to welcome the clouds like a cold blanket when it's too warm.

The poet lives to see, to feel, to witness life. To do this, we must be open, ever open and aware. This awareness is exhausting. It feels like driving over the crest of a hill smiling only to cry at the yellow flowers of an invasive species that is ruining the natural landscape.

Poetry is invasive. It takes over. When we are swept up in life, our voices pour out onto pages and into microphones and through form and verse we are relieved of our overwhelming awareness, if only for a few moments. And to get back to that feeling of release and relief, we write again and again pouring, gushing like geysers jettisoning hot water into the atmosphere.

Staring at the yellow swaths of scotch broom lining the highway, I realize why I am attached to Washington, to the clouds and the rain, to the pervasive cold. This is where I became a poet. Rather, this is where the poet inside me who has always been there awakened.

Awakened by: the gentle drum of the rain on the roof, brilliant sunshine that is so much brighter because I haven't seen it in months, the traveling, driving, moving I have accomplished in this place. Constantly on my way toward knowledge, toward being, toward discovery of self, others, and world.

I see now that this place helped me become who I have always been, who was only sleeping, dormant like seeds peppered through the soil waiting for the perfect moment to sprout and invade the landscape.

A poet, a feminist, a woman, a writer unencumbered by the labels and roles I fill. I am not mother or wife, though I act as both mother and wife. I am not daughter or friend though I act as both daughter and friend. Rather, I am. I have found that which has been hidden inside my body, folded in seventeen layers of being that society has wrapped around me, and moment by mile driving on this road, experiencing place and home and knowing, I am unraveling layers. I have pulled the proverbial sweater thread and I am naked.

***

Donald Hall writes, in his collection *Essays After Eighty*, "Poetry abandoned me." For my sake, I hope he isn't right. I hope that poetry and language don't abandon any of us who have dedicated our lives to its forms and treasures. I hope it only changes.

Gillian Parrish

POET IN THE WORLD: BETWEEN WORLDS

We hear a word—a word bearing bad news, bearing good news—and the world stirs in our stomachs, swirls in our chests. The world presses on us, presses outside in, pulls us inside out: the world seems designed to widen us. We can be taught to fight a wider mind, to fear the great open meadow of it. And so, we find our many ways to close down, to align ourselves with this and not that, closing the flow between inside and outside, closing the flow between body and mind, world and word, closing the flow between us. Poetry lives in the in-between space, indeed, collapses the between spaces through words—which are themselves made of betweenness—spun of flesh and breath, spun of things and thoughts of the world.

This piece was to be written in the scarce between-times this busy week, was to be talked into my trusty recorder as I walk in the morning, drive to work, or take a bath, for I've learned over the years that writing flows from a body in motion. And the writing is also a body in motion, a mind in motion through the bodies of words. We see this movement in the transitions where the thought or feeling shines in the spaces between—in the turns, in the leaps, in the gaps between words.

And this talk of leaps and gaps makes me think of that consummate form of transition: the haiku. When teaching about this old form of "thinking through things," I always seem to use my single sports metaphor, for haiku shares with basketball the feel of one foot planted, the other free to pivot, to connect in any direction.

For a healthy society, writing cannot be only for people with free time to spare. In these too-busy times, these bottom-line times, times when most of us are working longer hours, we learn to do our deeper work more and more in the margins. We must find ways to live deeply in the gaps of our days. And we may find that this writing in the gaps makes for honest lines, because we are writing in the midst of the moving world, not writing apart from it.

This piece is written late. The gaps of the days this week were filled suddenly with unscheduled tasks: a sudden presentation for incoming students, a day spent in phone calls for another student in crisis. Yes, the world presses in on us. But whose world is it? The dog who needs a walk? A friend who needs comfort after a loss? The student needing legal help? The girl in the front row asking how a thesis is made?

This was not to be written in the voice of a teacher, but I'm home now writing here in the 11th hour (yes, 11 p.m.), after three hours of talking with students about writing. So this offering is made with that world still spinning in me. I reflect that when I teach poetry, I introduce it as "making," as "world-making," which also makes it a place to see how we make our world together. I introduce poem-making as a connection-making mode of mind, in which things are brought to the space of the page to be seen freshly. We explore how this fresh seeing might mean deft movement between lenses, seeing a thing in close focus and then shifting to a wide-angle view that allows us to see the thing within the greater contextual web.

Connections happen here in this magic space of the page, things come together, perhaps dovetailing, perhaps refracting—giving us a new vision of a thing. I might talk about poem-making as a practice of listening inside and out, as a path of perception, as a place to come to clarity through a quality of attention that itself is a kind of love. I might (and this is harder to do on paper, as here it may sound high fallutin') mention that poetry is something like re*lig*ion, with its root "lig" shared with "ligature," a root that means "binding back," binding back what is fragmented, reconnecting things that we think of as separate into their natural wholes, returning our world to itself—always innately holy.

Poetry does this; it is a ligature between mind and body, words riding the breath, finding shapes of things in the world, bringing them back inside where they live in us. Poem-making can be a practice of listening, of hearing lines that rise from voices inside and out. It can be a school of silence; it can help us hear under the words, help us come close to things again through our hands and hearts, our throats and guts, after living so long in our heads. And no, it's not that that head logic is bad logic, but it's not the only logic, and our downfall is that we've allowed it to take over, we've allowed a very narrow way of seeing to swell into a terrible habit of abstraction that is decimating the forests for the trees.

Orwell spoke of this in a much-quoted yet much-needed passage from "Politics and the English Language," which has sadly remained relevant every year since he wrote it. He shows us how our abstraction works: "Defenceless villages are bombarded from the air, the inhabitants driven out into the countryside, the cattle machine-gunned, the huts set on fire with incendiary bullets: this is called *pacification*." And then: "People are imprisoned for years without trial or shot in the back of the neck or sent to die of scurvy in Arctic lumber camps: this is called *elimination of unreliable elements*."

We're in a moment as a species of unprecedented speed and strategy. It's a numbers-driven time, cut loose from both flesh and spirit and the voices/words that live between—an anesthetic mode of mind required for the brutalities of colonial world-making. Taking poetics as world-making, and aesthetics as a way to wake up, poem-making can be a radically natural act—a contemplative space that includes body logic, heart logic. In his book *Poetry and the Body* John Vernon notes that "we are both divorced from our bodies and driven too deeply into them." And it's partly this strange estrangement that makes the exploitation of nature and other beings possible.

Here by "body" I mean a deeper intelligence that drops below our ordinary habitual thinking *about* situations, and moves into a more immersive, sensing mode. We can feel this intelligence when our stomach churns, when we feel a fluttering in our chest. We come to know "body" as a field of awareness wider and deeper than our skin. Poems tend to speak from that preverbal space as much as they speak from our usual quick grids of words. And as such, words in poems often carry a deeper sense of life in them, life which stirs the deeper life in us, wakes us up to even the surfaces of our lives again.

Against the grain of our current cultural training, this space of poem-making—in our day and on the page—is more receptive than acquisitive, agile and open to coincidence and change, a space of listening, of loving attention, of a nimble, moving, yet deeply rooted mind. The poet George Oppen writes of coming to know ourselves by clearly seeing the things "we live among." Poems are a zone of reflection, of pulling the stuff of the world, the stuff that is us, out of the flow of time, out of the speed of our times, so we can see, feel, turn these things over in our minds, in our hearts, in our guts—by way of words formed in our throats that run between them.

It is the 11th hour. The world presses in on us as we press harder on it. Suddenly we must prepare for this and that. Suddenly the unforeseen (and foreseen) happens, is happening as glaciers melt and corals crumble. Suddenly we spend the day running to the doctor for a friend, rushing to meetings, calling organizations to help a student seek political asylum. He cannot go home now, this kind school-teacher, this speaker of five languages, this devotee of Hikmet and Rumi and Fużūlī. He has come here on fire to refine his writing. He wants to offer words that speak as and with and for his people, our people, Syrians, Turks, Kurds. He learns while he is here reading, writing, working, dreaming, that his friends are being imprisoned. He's known that people at home are jailed, that state-sponsored torture and murder are happening, and now it has come closer to him, closer to us. His final presentation is on ghazals; he tells us that their form, their return of rhyme and refrain, perfectly reflects the semazen, the dervish dance—turning as the world does, one foot planted, one foot moving, one arm towards the earth, the other towards the skies. Between mind and heart and word and world, between each of us, the poem lives.

Kathryn Hummel

বশ্বি দেখেবার আমার উপায় | BIŚBA DĒKHABĀRA ĀMĀRA UPĀẎA | MY WAY OF SEEING THE WORLD

I never studied poetry composition, though the subjects I took at university sometimes veered up on; circled around *reading* poetry. Novels, nonfiction, and critical theory I found much more compelling—despite various starts and stops to allow for wage-earning, travelling, scholarship application, and finding (a temporary) direction, I ended up with a PhD in Social Science. A few years later, I also ended up with a collection of poetry. The two are not unrelated. My PhD research was focused on ethnography in Bangladesh, where I'd lived for over a year before starting my degree; because it involved Bangladesh, my project also involved poetry. Since the strength of the connection between this country and my journey as a poet surprises me, even now, to set down, it is, I feel, a story worth telling.

I started to write poetry to entertain my friends.
Now I continue to stop them learning the whole and shocking truth.

These lines, taken from my PhD thesis, were written while looking back on my arrival in Bangladesh as a development program volunteer. At the time of leaving Australia, I was also a columnist and, during my first year in Bangladesh, explored the country through regular prose dispatches to my editor. These columns show me up, accurately enough, as young, diffident, and inexperienced. I had never spent a significant deal of time away from home, had never lived in a so-called developing country; was not deeply conversant with Bangladesh's history or post-colonial, post-liberation struggles. Yet I knew enough to distinguish Dhaka from Dakar and despite being thoroughly frightened, was ready for every kind of exploration you might name.

I began with walking and reading. The first book I bought in Bangladesh was Kaiser Haq's *Published in the Streets of Dhaka: Collected Poems 1966–2006*. With a determination that transformed rapidly into fascination, I rifled my way through this volume—I, who hadn't read a full collection of poetry for years, perhaps never. Through the beautiful, brutal, damning, exultant, sharp, and whimsical pitches of Kaiser's voice, I saw my observations of Dhaka city distilled. It was a voice belonging to a country I was merely visiting and throbbed with feelings I couldn't articulate yet—and many I never would, or could, as a *bideshi*/foreigner.

Kaiser writes of a modern Dhaka composed of distant "oblongs of light" ("Windows"), as high-rise apartment blocks peer into each another. From another perspective, the speaker's Dhaka is motley, humming with energy:

> The sun goes down, a luckless balloon,
> Leaving a spray of gold in the air.
> Patches of city sward,
> Houses, new and old,
> Even slums, even the crow jerking homeward
> Wear a robe of gold
> As it explodes over the horizon's brink.
> ("Sunset Song")

Far from being detached, the speaker is deeply involved in the arterial life of Dhaka. He wittily defies those who condescendingly regard the city as an uncivilised tropical outpost while asserting his attachment, even to the harshest of its realities:

> ... Here I'll stay, plumb in the centre
> Of monsoon-mad Bengal, watching
> Jackfruit leaves drift earthward
> In the early morning breeze
> Like a famous predecessor used to
>
> And take note too
> Of flashing knives, whirling sticks, bursting bombs,
> And accompanying gutturals and fricatives of hate,

And evil that requires no axis
To turn on, being everywhere—
("Published in the Streets of Dhaka")

More than that, the speaker's *flânerie* is conveyed with enough lucidness to make anyone, new or old to the city, sympathetic:

When I walk the moon-spangled street
to the labyrinth of slums and sewers
through which is my straightest homeward route
the night deals a hammer first
("Homecoming")

A combination of my role as columnist and my burgeoning fandom led me to meet and interview Professor Kaiser Haq. My determination wasn't hampered by thoughts of how exactly I might bring this meeting about: in the way things often flow in Bangladesh, it was as easy as writing an email; making a phone call. Recorded when I was new to Dhaka in March 2007, the interview wasn't published until after the devastation of Cyclone Sidr[1] and aptly examines the role of a writer at times when escapism and reflection through creativity are equally vital.

What I did not expect after this interview was the friendship Kaiser offered; his interest in my writing and his support of my work during—and beyond—my time in Bangladesh. To this day, I proudly refer to Kaiser as my mentor, though I'm conscious it's not how he sees himself. Deservedly respected across the creative and scholarly spheres he inhabits, Kaiser makes the qualities of generosity, erudition, and humanity appear simple to foster and practice.

If Kaiser's poetry encouraged me to read more, Kaiser himself encouraged me to write. Luckily, I wasn't overburdened with work at the non-government organisation to which I'd been assigned—I was also looking for a way to commune with Bangladesh beyond the genteel, middle-class confines of my office. The first poem I tentatively wrote in Bangladesh twangs with Kaiser's influence:

---

1. Category 5 cyclone Sidr caused extensive damage to natural resources, infrastructure, water supplies, and sanitation in Bangladesh when it struck the south-west coast on 15 November 2007. Up to 10,000 deaths have been estimated following the disaster.

Actually,
I've noticed something, living in Dhaka.
Actually,
There's a sub-conscious sub-continental influence
like wailing wallahs in the alleyways of my mind
I just can't find the word,
Actually.

The poem has never been published, though I did email it to a small group of friends, fellow volunteers undergoing their own rites of discovery in Bangladesh. Their warm reception of this and other poems made me consider the possibility that what I was writing wasn't entirely idiosyncratic: perhaps I was seeing what others were seeing; maybe what I wrote allowed them to feel what and how I did. Every poet, I think, dreams of being so understood. Little did I know then how fortunate I was in my audience.

Bangladesh contains a unique poetry culture. Except in the opinion of my friend Firoz, who thinks all poets make too much noise and only write to persuade objects of desire into bed à la Robert Herrick, identifying as a poet in Bangladesh is respectable, even admirable. Writing poetry is a popular hobby for many; you will often hear rickshawalas intoning the lyrics of Rabindranath Tagore as they cycle the streets. The feelings Rabindranath relates, my friend Hasna once told me, casually, are the ones his readers recognise within themselves. Like a great gardener, he digs them out from deep inside. Lalon Shah, the Baul poet and musician, is generally revered in Bangladesh—not only for his creative works, but his lifestyle and philosophies that espouse a vision of a world free from caste, class, and racial discrimination. In Bangladesh, it's common to refer to celebrated poets by their first names, an informality borne of intimacy rather than disrespect.

To me, poetry seems well mixed into the lifeblood of Bangladesh's culture—hardly surprising, since it is composed and recited in a language that Bangladeshis fought for the right to speak freely.[2] In post-colonial Bangla-

---

2. "Bangladesh" literally translates to "land of Bangla (language)," in recognition of the nation's struggle to speak its native language over Urdu, which was proclaimed the national language of Bangladesh (East Pakistan) by Pakistan (West Pakistan) in 1948. The Bangla Language Movement was political as well as ethno-linguistic, with a large-scale uprising against the Pakistani government occurring at the University of Dhaka on 21 February 1952. The protestors killed during the demonstration are considered martyrs and commemorated annually on the Language Movement public holiday.

desh, this history is muddled by the elitist associations attached to learning, speaking, and writing in English. Yet even when I was just beginning to study the Bangla language, I was able to feel through hearing it. As my social circle in Dhaka increased, the time I passed with friends involved, quite naturally, having poems dedicated to me, written about me and read to me in friendship, fits of passion, or simply writer to writer.

This culture is quite at odds with the one I later encountered and became involved with in Australia, where poets are considered rather twee and occupy the bottom tier of the literary scene. This opinion is, understandably, not shared by many poets themselves, since they—that is to say, *we*—often seem quite incapable of self-deprecation. Aware that being a poet in Australia is nothing like being a poet in Bangladesh, I've been reluctant to seize that particular handle, declaring to the poets that I am an ethnographer and to the anthropologists that I am a writer. In my local circle, a particularly pushy colleague insists on labelling me as a poet, no matter how much I resist my identity being so dictated. (Yet why not be poet/ethnographer/writer at the same time, or some at the same time, or none? It's no bad thing to explore the boundaries of writing and self, separately and together.)

For all the ubiquitousness of poetry in Bangladesh, I clearly remember it was Ranju, an unassuming NGO co-worker of mine, who introduced me to the work of Jibanananda Das (1899-1954), a pre-modernist poet who was born in Bangladesh, died in Calcutta (Kolkata), and wrote across the borders of East and West Bengal. Thanks to Fakrul Alam's thoughtful translation of Jibanananda's selected poems into English, this introduction deepened into an understanding. My favourite poem from Professor Alam's assemblage is Jibanananda's satirical, autobiographical '*Kabi*/The Poet', which contains a set of lines never far from my consciousness:

> Never mind—
> Let's read his poems
> Countless optimistic poems
> Each like a goldflake cigarette
> Popping out of the loaded slotmachine of his life.

The poetry of Jibanananda has inspired and continues to inspire my own poetry. In 2012 I went on a post-PhD holiday to India and spent Christmas in the city of Alappuzha, Kerala. Despite the self-imposed edict that I was there to relax, not write, I couldn't stop myself:

> My Christmas communion
> was with the green air
> & Jibanananda,
> smoke & fire on a night of song.
> A Goldflake cigarette
> offered an opportunity.
> I dared to put my hand
> in the slot
> and feel the countless
> vibrations within: thought of
> that poet of another green,
> of train tracks &
> the unknown end.
> ("Christmas Communion")

"Christmas Communion" was included in my first collection, *Poems from Here*, which contains some of my earliest work. Bangladesh and its effects are imprinted on almost every page: Kaiser, who wrote a blurb for the back cover, understates that "[Kathryn] has a particular fondness for Bangladesh, whose physical and social landscape has inspired/provoked much of her poetic output." In some ways, *Poems from Here* is a favorite among my books because it traces my attempt to discover the world, or a part of the world; certainly it articulates my re-discovery of poetry, the connections I made through it and the uncovering of a certain ability within myself. Each of my subsequent books continues to limn some of these journeys, but not all. Next month, I will return to Bangladesh after an absence of three years and hope to find new and different paths to walk—just as I hope, one day, to pay fitting tribute to a country and people that have had such great impact on my writing, education, and personal development.

If anyone was to ask me, the reluctant poet, for guidance in writing, my first suggestion would be to visit Bangladesh—figuratively, if not literally. These journeys should include extensive reading, so as not to be hemmed in by the parochial concerns of one "scene." There are infinite ways of writing poetry and distributing it, just as there are ways of living. If you have the privilege, travel—not necessarily far. If you have the capacity, learn languages beyond your own in order to read the poetry of different cultures. In it, you will probably find some strands of universality. Locate a group of people who respond sincerely to your work, whose criticism is just and clear, as well as supportive. These people need not be poets, or even writers. I wouldn't dream of advising anyone to write for themselves or others—but I nevertheless see the beauty in writing as an act of fellowship. Write from a strange place, if not a foreign one. Write with empathy and with attention to the finest detail. Write with more self-awareness; less self-criticism. Start a page and don't re-read the starts; likewise, don't discard them. Nothing is wasted in a journey. Follow Jibanananda, unlike the glittering, fashionable flocks Shamsur Rahman writes about. Better yet, follow no one: find your own way (or ways) of walking.

Our paths may cross. I look forward to the possibility.

REFERENCES

Das, Jibanananda. "The Poet/Kabi." *Jibanananda Das: Selected Poems with an Introduction, Chronology, and Glossary.* Translated by Fakrul Alam. Dhaka: The University Prtess Limited, 1999.

Haq, Kaiser. "Homecoming."*Published in the Streets of Dhaka: Collected Poems 1966–2006.* Dhaka: The University Press Limited, 2017.

Haq, Kaiser. "Published in the Streets of Dhaka."*Published in the Streets of Dhaka: Collected Poems 1966–2006.* Dhaka: The University Press Limited, 2017.

Haq, Kaiser. "Sunset Song."*Published in the Streets of Dhaka: Collected Poems 1966–2006.* Dhaka: The University Press Limited, 2017.

Hummel, Kathryn. "Christmas Communion." *Poems from Here.* Hobart: Walleah Press, 2014.

José Angel Araguz

KEEPING THE CONVERSATION GOING, OR SOME STORIES I CAN'T TELL WITHOUT ROLLING MY R'S: A MEDITATION ON LATINIDAD, DISIDENTIFICATION & SOME POEMS

Identifying as Latinx is not the end of a conversation but the continuation of one.

This conversation began when I was a high schooler in Corpus Christi, Texas, afraid to speak Spanish among my friends, but necessarily speaking only Spanish at home. Back then, calling me Hispanic or Mexican-American would get you an ugly look from me. Later, in college, when I found myself criticized for not being "Chicano enough" at a poetry slam, I felt like something was taken from me that I hadn't known was mine to claim. It is important to note how in these two times in my life the terms that were problematic for me came from the *outside*. Nobody was teaching me these terms; long before I studied cultural theory, cultural theory was studying me. ¿A poco, no? Like such studying, being able to identify as anything is a privilege. It is the privilege of knowing the terms, and the privilege of being able to choose or dismiss the terms for yourself.

As a poet, I identify via words. Being a poet means identifying moments of evocation. The term Latinx evokes some of me, as does Hispanic, as does Chicano, as does Mexican-American, as does heritage speaker. But only some. My own personal list of terms that I feel evoke more of me include *punk* and *cursi*. Each of these terms is a meeting of my personal experiences and the outside world; they are how I am perceived as well as how I can navigate those perceptions back to myself.

So now the outside world presents *Latinx*: my understanding is that the "x" allows for the gender binary of "o/a" and "@" to be disrupted. Pues, I like that. That's punk to me. It's punk when language changes, and having people find and use their voices to establish community is also punk. My identifying as Latinx is not intended to take anything away from anyone else, but rather to keep the conversation going, on the inside as well as the outside.

Identifying as Latinx forces me to think on the nature of the word *identify*, and how much nuanced action is implied in the term. When you identify something, you recognize it. In police investigations, witnesses are asked to identify people in a line-up. Identifying also means claiming. When someone dies in public, next of kin is asked to identify the body. When you identify *as* something, this something has lined up in a way that you identify yourself within it. When I identify as Latinx, it is because I have read up on what this word means and compared it with myself, and seen that enough lines up between this meaning and the source of meanings in my life that I see myself in it. When a friend is going through a struggle you can relate to, you tell them *I identify with you*. What you mean is that what they are going through lines up with something inside you, an experience, a memory; you recognize in their struggle something of your own. You feel compelled to reach out to them to spare them, to empathize, to carry some of their burden.

Identifying, in this light, becomes a narrative act; you are choosing to have your identity mingle with words, claiming those words for yourself. And yet, when we claim a word, the word also claims a little of our identity, blurs it in relation. And we hate to feel blurred. Case in point: high school me giving an ugly look at someone calling me Hispanic; college me labeled as not "Chicano enough," feeling called out and abandoned by a culture I didn't realize I needed until another person took it away from me. Again, long before I studied cultural theory, cultural theory was studying me. Similarly, long before I identified as anything, I was counteridentifying against everything.

Pues, esa bronca es para los chavalos. Older now, I get to read the story of my life up until now and do a little reidentifying, a little recognizing, un poco de reclaiming. Reuse, reduce, recycle, no? Y también revise!

So far, I have been speaking in terms of binaries: of outside terms and inner struggle; of identifying versus counteridentifying. José Esteban Muñoz's concept of *disidentification* goes against this binary of identifying and counteridentifying, and identifies another option, one that takes the materials with which one would identify or counteridentify with and creates a new expression, a disidentification that is new, unique, and *in motion*. This idea of motion is key: to identify or counteridentify is to settle, to choose a side;

to disidentify means to enter a space where one can glimpse what it means to be a choosing entity, and where one can interrogate what it means to choose.

This space is crucial in the writing of poetry. The reading act is an aesthetic act; that is, it is an act of motion. As Jorge Luis Borges notes:

> Un volumen, en si, no es un hecho estético, es un objeto físico entre otros; el hecho estético sólo puede ocurrir cuando lo escriben o lo leen. [A book is not an aesthetic experience, it is a physical object among others; the aesthetic experience can only occur when the book is written or read].[1]

I come back to these words often in my own writing because of how clearly they isolate what the poetic craft puts one in touch with. That this poetry thing isn't about the book publication, that poetry doesn't exist physically in the book or the writer (or reader) but rather is made up of the intangible air moved by reading and writing. An air that is personal and which blurs the personal, troubles it, expands it.

This is what I mean by motion. When Muñoz describes "a representational contract [being] broken" by means of disidentification, through which "the social order receives a jolt that may reverberate loudly and widely, or in less dramatic, yet locally indispensable ways," I can't help but read it as a similar description of the aesthetic act, of motion. For a writer, who works in solitude, this "jolt" occurs inwardly, the artist themselves jolted away from one idea of themselves and into another sense of identity, a furthered identity. This jolt happens word by word, line by line, always in motion.

When I speak of "stories I can't tell without rolling my R's" I am also speaking in terms of motion. There is the poem that gets written, and then there's the poem that exists around it in terms of stories or memories that are revised out of the poem. In writing a poem, we move away from "how it happened" and focus on leaving on the page or declaring on the air a new happening. Below is a sequence of four poems presented in terms of what is in the poem and what is left out, with the goal being that what is left unsaid between these two sides will ring through and represent the motion I exist in as a poet. I choose this approach rather than to perform a critical analysis of my own work because I feel that whatever raw material comes up in this writing will be more manageable and more interesting to listen to than my

---

1. The translations of Borges here and above are my own.

using big words. Ultimately, these are simply some notes and reflections about what moved inside me as both a writer and as a human being who also identifies as Latinx.

There's that word again: identify. Writing and reading poetry can help us identify ourselves, confirm our experiences and what we know, but it can also disturb that identity, trouble it, complicate it, and expand it. This latter quality implies disidentification, that is, the creation of a new, unique, and *in motion* expression. Muñoz's term captures some of the air in which real change happens, the air in which one can "... disidentify with ... [one] world and perform a new one" (xi).

To new poets: I share the poems and stories below to encourage you to embrace the identity of poet alongside the other identities you embrace and/or wrestle against. Let all facets of your being disturb, trouble, complicate, expand, and illuminate what ends up on the page. The poet's journey is your own to travel; the reader only gets the souvenirs. Track the miles of who you are, and know that you are always in motion. Only by staying in motion, and being true to that motion, can we keep the conversation going.

*****

Joe

Back in Texas, I was Joe, not José,
my buddies too afraid of the accent
that stood out like a sweat drop
on the brow of a spooked é.
You'd be spooked too if sound
could make an umbrella of your throat

with just one word. With English, the throat
grinds gravel in its shadows. Say *José*
and feel the billow and bloom of sound,
a scissors' snip as the tongue slides, that accent
now a curl on a shaggy haired é,
jet black and waiting to drop.

My friends were ready to drop
classes or pick up teachers by the throat
in Spanish class and fill the room with their gasping 'e-e-e!'
All to avoid saying words like *Porque* or *José*,
as in—*Por qué José no tiene* accent?
But that's exactly what I mean! That sound,

that Tex-Mex, Spanglish, barefoot in the mud sound.
It was enough to make me want the sun to drop
from the sky; in the dark, my skin would accent
nothing. I could live in that black where the throat
swallows tears, drown the José
in me, reclaim and silence that é

that stares back from the page, that é
questioning me with its cocked eyebrow. No sound
sleep in that house where even my mom didn't know José
It's Joe, Mom, not José! and I wouldn't let it drop
until the bird of her voice died in her throat,
all for Joe, dark syllable without accent –

Joe, who went to the land without accent –
college—Joe, who never dropped *E*
but swallowed oceans down his brown throat
straight from brown bottles, who bobbed, blinked at the sound
of glass thudding—Joe, who let his mother's call drop
with her crackling voice asking for not-quite-José –

when *Joe* leaves her throat now, I am lost to the sound.
Each accent is the sound of force, that é
would take flight, not drop. *It's me, Mom, José.*

What's in the poem: A sense of Corpus Christi and the way it taught me and others how to deny and hide ourselves. How my friends and I squirmed in Spanish classes, afraid to roll our R's in public but talking only in Spanish with our abuelitas at home. How going to college created distance between me and where I came from, a distance that could have divided were I not an ambitious reader. How I was able to read my way back into *José* from the denial that was *Joe*. How the formal structure of a sestina with its repetition that feels like chewing on six words helped me take on material I didn't know needed facing. How a youth's yawps of identity and counteridentity are humbled in the face (and phone calls) of familia.

What's left out: How when one of our white history teachers told us some solid Corpus truth about how our high school was built as an answer to desegregation, namely to "keep the Mexicans out of one side of town," none of us knew what to do with it. How this was also a high school that one city official deemed unfit for anything other than training auto mechanics and nurses.

***

The Name

for Pedro Araguz Aldape

Asked where the name comes from, I grow quiet,
and in another voice begin to tell
how those ending in *Z* are from the Moors
who ruled Spain 800 years. Some agree,
read into my black hair and dark skin
what they wish to. I let the disguise of story
take over, let it pass across the feeling
in my chest that tells me I've lied, even
when I haven't. A name is wind and ink,
a name is memory. What does it matter?

*

What does it matter my mother didn't want
my father in my life, even in name,
and reached out to her father for his?
Who remembers that, and who can clearly

tell it, when Mexicans stack up last names
like a trail of crumbs behind a person,
syllables broken off a whole to meet
and make another whole, a map of breath
drawn over so one can't get lost. Eventually,
everything gets lost. What does it matter?

*

What does it matter letters and sounds hold,
become a space where the lost young man I am
can look and catch a part of the old man
my grandfather became? What does it matter,
except that I remain and have to face
the name, have to explain it, give it meaning:
the name, the house at the edge of a landfill,
the hat held in his hands as we talked, the wind
leaving behind a faceless and fleeting sound.
Asked where the name comes from, I grow quiet.

What's in the poem: How much I know about my grandfather and the name
I inherited. How little I know about my grandfather and the name I inher-
ited. How much form can hold, and how much repetition can expose.

What's left out: How I hadn't questioned my name too much until I was
invited to spend the night with a friend's family in Abiquiú, NM. How my
friend's father ran the local mosque and was the one to begin conjecturing
about the 'z' in my last name. How I spent years after wondering about ori-
gins, and how little I knew about origins. How when my grandfather died,
I was in Oregon. How I had come in from the rain carrying groceries and
listened to the message my mother left, her voice breaking through static.
How I felt the cold from the rain seep into my bones. How I put down the
phone, turned, and put away the groceries. How this poem moved from
tightly rhymed terza rima to a looser argument in three ten-line stanzas.

***

Don't Look Now I Might be Mexican

That was the title of the book in my dream. I was on the cover, black hair slicked back into grooves, like a record with sunlight needling off. The Mexican flag laid across my chest in a slant, slung over my shoulder like I had won a contest. I had on a blue blazer, khaki slacks, and yellow shoes. I hear the Colombian girl I work with say: *You look dressed to ask for a loan. Ready to get that taco truck?* No, I am here to tell people about eighteen wheelers, families as cargo, caught, stunned to have to go back. *¿Que te crees?* I want to tell about La Llorona by the side of a river so distraught from losing her child she became a myth. *Why the banana shoes then?* Not banana: my feet are the color between stop and go. *Is that why you're not smiling?* I look back at the photo, see my head hanging over the green, white and red. Is it shame or defeat that radiates like sunlight at my feet? I could be La Malinche. I could be my father with a son he threw into the ocean. I could be my mother with a son of postcards and phone calls. Did I say it right or are those shoes made of straw, am I to be heretic in this crusade of borders and kin? *Your ghosts are women crying over dead children? Isn't that everyone?* I tell her there is no river deep enough to slake the thirst of a land too dry for neighbors. She laughs. *It's raining, it's always raining. When rain hits a river, all it does is disappear.*

What's in the poem: How living and working beside other Latinx in NYC changed me. How learning about La Malinche and La Llorona felt like learning about myself.

What's left out: How I see this poem as one of two poems that are a key into my poetic obsessions. How many other poems I have with the imagery of rain hitting a river. How red my ears turned at the question: *Ready to get that taco truck?* How this poem evolved from another poem about La Llorona, the narratives splitting between something I wanted to say and something I had to say. How the evolution of the poem was from free verse to prose poem, and how the prose paragraph keeps the voices in the same room. How some part of me is always asking of my work: *¿Que te crees?*

A Poco

for Ramon

This piece of paper is work? A poco?
I won't believe that, ni un poco.

It's work for me with this good eye,
one bad eye from broke glass, pero a poco

tu with two don't struggle here?
And with books and school? A poco

you all talk about it, in class, I mean,
about what it means? That's work. A poco,

I'm not here, you don't write about me,
right? My bad eye? I bet you do. A poco,

no? You have nothing else? You have nothing else.
Don't say it looks like a bruise gone white. A poco,

no? But don't say it. Say it's a marble, or
like my granddaughter says: *A poco,*

you can't see out of that fish eye, abuelo?
Can you see me? Nope. Ni un poco.

What's in the poem: How my fascination with ghazals and my fascination with South Texas Spanglish work together. How my co-worker Ramon had a clouded eye.

What's left out: How Ramon's clouded eye wasn't glass because taking it out would have caused more overall damage. How Ramon's thumbs were permanently purple from hammering and missing and hitting his hand. How when we worked side by side at Billy Pugh Co. making equipment for oil rigs I felt both honored and intimidated. How the more I wrote into this poem the more I left Ramon's voice behind. How the biggest breakthrough in writing the poem was having this meta-Ramon ask the question "You have nothing else?" then declare flat out "You have nothing else." How this meta-Ramon is really me still guilty years later worried I don't do enough on the page or in my life to honor the people who have helped me survive. How this species of interrogation is never done with, because it is how I honor those who have helped me survive.

WORKS CITED

Borges, Jorge Luis. *Obra Poética*. Emecé Editores, 1960. Print.
Muñoz, José Esteban. *Disidentifications: Queers of Color and the Performance of Politics*. University of Minnesota Press, 1999. Print.

Jon Hoel

COMMUNALITY: MARY RUEFLE AND A POETICS OF GROWTH

> *I suppose, as a poet, among my fears can be counted the*
> *deep-seated uneasiness that one day it will be revealed that I*
> *consecrated my life to an imbecility. Part of what I mean—what*
> *I think I mean—by "imbecility" is something intrinsically*
> *unnecessary and superfluous and thereby unintentionally cruel.*
> —Mary Ruefle "On Fear," June 2012

***

The distinct feeling—often inevitably—of being fully wed to poetry in your life can be a treacherous thing. Anyone who has even a modest amount of familiarity with the job prospects for teaching English—tenure-track or otherwise—can probably attest to the notion. There's an old joke about pursuing an MFA in creative writing because it's such a *lucrative* degree. But: it's pretty much all been said before. This cruelty of dedication has an irritating constant banality and people have devoted entirely too much time to pontificating about it already. It should stand without saying by now, but to sling some fixated weight I'll attach Marie Howe, who at a lecture, proclaimed: "Poets should write to save the world. We cannot be defined or hindered by something like finances."[1] Writing poetry in this way might appear daunting, especially to a young person in the contemporary political, socio-economic moment, but it doesn't have to be. Perhaps it's more of an inevitable end than a discernible objective. The poet can deteriorate with words, the poet can also

---

1. Marie Howe was divulging on some theory after discussing *The Uprising: On Poetry and Finance,* a manifesto by Franco 'Bifo' Berardi.

mend with them. They can do what they will, and, maybe it does function as prelude to the whole saving-the-world thing, but it's more of an affectation on a reckoning than a reckoning itself.

It makes me think about Mary Ruefle and the end of her poem "From Here to Eternity":

> It means you are more interested
> in the shadows of objects than objects
> themselves, and if asked to draw anything
> you would only need charcoal
> to convince the world
> it is waiting, in the shadows
> of things, and you will wait back.

In that sublime tradition of perspectivists in poetry—Stevens particularly— there is an individualistic importance to *the shadows*, and there is definitely interest in them for Mary Ruefle, who has an overarching shadow of subtext veiling the importance of her work, sometimes with such a veil that any reader cannot access it. Negation—the overwhelming absence of thing-ness can be frustrating to pursue as topic—in terms of its subjective angles, it can be difficult and at times, incomprehensible to decipher in other people's poems. What becomes clear with Ruefle's relationship to poetry is its immenseness, its rapid depths. You feel it in her collections, the polychromatic quality of staring at a Matisse; your eyes move with the brush strokes, you first feel the warmth of the medium, then begin to ascertain more.

Ruefle, who teaches in the MFA program at Vermont College of Fine Arts in Montpelier, also infamously resides in the woods of Vermont, where she is difficult to reach, except via cryptic communications with her publicists, and then subsequently, only through traditional post. Anyone who has read Ruefle's work will agree: her poetry speaks for itself. The quality of both her poetry and prose writing—Ruefle herself does not spend much energy differentiating between genres beyond simple lineation—is of such a heightened caliber that even if she suddenly and uncharacteristically jumped in with an abundant Twitter presence, it would not ruin her writing, atmospherically or otherwise. The mystique is desirable but at the end of the day, more aftereffect or aesthetic than necessity, as perfectly summated in a *Chicago Tribune* review of her 2013 collection *Trances of the Blast*, by poet Michael Robbins, who said of the reputational dilemma: "...When I try to describe her work, [it] makes me throw up my hands and say, 'Oh, what's the use?' She lives in the side of a hill and eats children, OK? Get reading."

Importantly, we distinguish between the physical *act* of writing itself and the *process*. The act demands solitude. Ruefle discusses a lot about invisibility on a multitude of levels in her 2016 *Paris Review* interview. She felt the inconspicuousness, the invisibility of writing poetry. It's escapism but also a landscape for creation, because of its indiscernibility.

For me, this recalls Rimbaud: "In the morning I had a look so lost, a face so dead, that perhaps those whom I met *did not see me.*" Mary Ruefle's poetry is often immersed in a thick mist of contradiction. Her poems are somehow both elegiac and whimsical, deeply meaningful, and somehow, unutterably meaningless.

The first time I met Ruefle was at a reading at a tiny gallery in the Berkshires, Gallery 51, a handful of years ago. It was a small reading and at the end, she took questions from the audience. A then-colleague and dear friend of mine, Devin Snell, posed a prevarication-laden but ultimately lecture-defining question to her, in the context of people encountering her prose writing more often not as writing *about something* or *writing about writing* but *writing about nothing.*

"What would you say you write about? It doesn't seem like your poems are about anything. If this isn't writing about nothing, what is it you would say you write about?"

Of all the questions of that evening, this was the one that seemed to excite Ruefle. Her eyes lit up and she smiled widely and nodded, glad that somebody in the audience had *got it*. She confirmed to Devin and the rest of us that her poetry was not about a deciphering or offering up some catharsis, at least, not in any traditional sense—that it was a translation of her inner life. The full response is labored, but Ruefle has also noted that her poems don't have an *intent* necessarily and that this is difficult to explain. It was certainly perplexing to hear at the time and has taken me up until the present moment to grasp even slightly. I'd like to believe I'm starting to understand through reading her poetry and prose. Maybe more importantly, I am starting to understand my own writing in this way.

Understandably, the experience of profound and elongated solitude is super romanticized—*fetishized* by poets. It's no surprise, it's a long-been-brewed idealization. *Walden* was published in 1854, that's 160-plus years of reverence, theses, and emulations. More recently there's been solitary poetic expositions like *For Emma Forever Ago*, or *Dawn* by folk musicians like Justin Vernon and Phil Elverum alongside reclusive writers like Salinger and McCarthy, who have done a fine job of modernizing the tradition. Great twentieth-century filmmakers like Tarkovsky and Bergman both seemed to insist that great writing must only come from solitude—Bergman famously found solitude on Fårö Island (population 572) off the coast of Sweden—and that perhaps their writing themselves was conducted in such a fashion.

And Mary Ruefle.

I think intense solitude is worth incorporating into your craft, its ethos. But I want to dismiss the idea of reclusion in the *process* of writing. It can be tremendously rewarding while maneuvered through with even a vaguely constructed community of writers. To be engrossed in the study of interpreting poetry while absorbed in dialogue and conversation with other poets, themselves equally enthusiastic and dedicated to craft, challenges you as a writer to constantly up the stakes for yourself and to deepen your commitment to your own craft. I do not think Thoreau or Ruefle would disagree— Thoreau in his *Walden* years would often visit friends in town for dinner— and I think what probably matters most at the end of the day is growth. Personal fulfillment, etc. but most of all, growth. To see how these choices and changes affect the quality of the poetry you create. Learning the amalgamation of the personal and the objective, the solitude and the collective.

Todd Davis

PRESENT TO THE WORLD, PRESENT TO THE POEM

This afternoon, driving to the bicycle shop to have a tire repaired, I noticed every person on the street was looking down at their hands. A man walking out of a deli. A woman smoking a cigarette on the corner. A girl sitting on a bench, drinking a Mountain Dew. Passengers riding in cars. Even a few of the drivers of those cars trying to navigate the narrow, crowded streets while glancing at their phones.

The sky was that rich October blue. Orange maples brightening, yellow birch fluttering. The sassafras and black gum trees still holding a few leaves, and the tamaracks busy preparing their needles to turn that otherworldly gold in early November.

I live on an ancient migratory flyway in Pennsylvania, and at this time of year, if your head isn't cast downward, you can spy all manner of raptors riding updrafts, slowly flapping their wings, moving on toward wintering grounds.

Technology, in particular our addiction to smart phones, poses a problem for those of us who hope to make poems. All of the people I passed on my errand were transfixed, beguiled by the siren song of some dreamed-for news or message, something of import that only metal and electricity might deliver.

I don't want this to be a luddite rant. Ned Ludd's protest in the 18th century wasn't very effective in slowing the progress of machinery and industrialization. But I do hope to counsel any new writer that while technology can be a helpful tool in the writing process, it can just as easily become a distraction, or, worse.

Emily Dickinson reminds us that writing poems is about telling the truth slant. I can say with a rare degree of certainty that our smart phones do not offer the best way to learn to tell it slant. In fact, I'm convinced they're a method of diverting us from the world that sprawls before us, a world that beckons us with ten thousand things, as Buddhists claim.

So the question is: how best can we be *in* the world, present to the sacred and desecrated, witness to grace and suffering, which, of course, is at the root of poetry?

Naming represents one of the oldest human acts, and it creates the possibility for intimacy, for moving into relationship with a particular tree or flower, with another person's past and the ways that past informs who she is in the present tense.

I think one of the best ways to work at writing is to name what our eyes pass over, to seek out appellations for things we don't know.

On a bookshelf next to my writing desk, I have many reference books and field guides which I consult frequently. Even when I'm not looking for a specific word, I take these books and page through them, often discovering something that leads to a poem I didn't know was locked away.

And learning to name the world isn't enough. Imagining the stories behind what we name—both human and other-than-human stories—is an integral part of the writing process.

What happened to the person who hit the deer now dead by the side of the road, and what did the other deer who crossed do once one of their numbers was dying? What of the person who works for the highway department and must collect the dead bodies of animals hit by cars? Each day as we see life pass around us there are myriad questions we could ask, questions that can lead us to poems.

Most of us have a difficult time sticking to New Year's resolutions—an exercise plan, a commitment to eating healthier, the promise to get more sleep. Simply saying that we need to pay more attention to the world, that we need to name it, to imagine the stories behind what we see, likely won't lead to the writing of poems.

To make the task a bit more concrete, set a modest goal. Keep a list—in a journal, on your smart phone (yes, they can have practical uses in writing sometimes!), wherever you jot things down. One of my poet friends always has index cards in his pocket for exactly this purpose.

The list should be comprised of two things you notice each day. At the end of the week, take one of the things you noticed, that you named, and imagine a story behind that thing. Don't demand the story be elaborate. Pretend you're a painter. Frame one moment in the story. Write it down. Play with perspective. Play with the language of description. Try to make music from that language. This can serve as the skeleton of a poem.

If you do this 50 weeks out of the year—(Everyone needs two-weeks of vacation!)—you'll have 50 possible poems and over 700 things that you've noticed.

You'll also have lived a life more present to what's going on beyond your own concerns, alive to the burgeoning life that surrounds us, that helps to make the best of our poems.

Noah Davis

SUBSISTENCE POETRY

My students told me that they didn't have anything to write about.

I smiled and shook my head as I walked around the room collecting their first poems of the semester.

"These are going to be great, and we're going to make them even better," I said, trying to hide the sweat stains under my arms. I had not fully prepared for August in Bloomington, Indiana, the southernmost locale I'd ever lived. The move from central Pennsylvania, stresses of the first semester of graduate school, and the fact that the senior sitting in the far-left corner of the circle was my age had me hoping that I *could* make things better.

For many of the students, this was the first collegiate assignment they'd completed. An assignment that didn't have an answer key or a set of guidelines except the fifteen-line minimum. Several stayed after class to ask how much the poem was worth, afraid that a B in a humanities course would keep them out of the Kelly School of Business.

That weekend, I saw that my students were telling me the truth: they didn't have anything to write about. Except for two poems, the topics of the beach and fraternity parties threaded the drafts.

I went into the MFA directly from undergrad. My fall workshop with Adrian Matejka was the first formal creative writing class I ever took. Up to that point, I participated in an atelier relationship with my father, a full professor who teaches creative writing at Penn State. While we fished the small streams in the mountains above our home for brook trout, he'd talk about the intricate uses of line breaks and form, but what was most important to the poem was its substance. He mused to me that no matter how attractive your cast might be, and no matter how expensive your rod is, the fish will not eat unless it believes the fly will give it sustenance. That is what a good poem is: sustenance.

But where is that sustenance in the world of my students? The world of universal food from McDonald's and Chipotle, universal dress from H&M and Victoria's Secret, universal entertainment from Netflix and YouTube, universal self-assurance from likes and favorites, and universal escape from the present through Androids and iPhones.

I started class on Wednesday with an explanation of the most common comment I left on their poems.

"When I write 'Hallmark nice' on your papers, I'm talking about the language on throw pillows at our grandma's house. We look at them and it's what we expect to see on the couch. Nothing interesting, but nice. And when we read the words, we have the same level of excitement as when we open the Hallmark card and see that our aunt couldn't write 'Happy Birthday' by herself."

One or two students smiled and shook their heads, while others blinked and flipped through the pages of their notebooks. A young woman with a blonde ponytail raised her hand.

"So you just want us to write about bad stuff? You don't want us to write about feeling happy?"

"I want you to write something with any feeling."

For the rest of the class, and the class on Friday, and the following Wednesday, we discussed, wrote, and read what it meant to have substance in our work.

The culture of consumerism tells us that what we buy is ours to throw away. So many of the experiences my students have had are casually dismissed because they are banal and unfulfilling.

Each day I asked them to write about the experiences that lingered.

What clung to their insides when they saw someone feed a child for the first time. When water got stuck between their nose and mouth. When the moose tracks ice cream was melting in the hot van and dripping into the cracks of their fingers while Mom was yelling at something on the radio they didn't understand. In these enduring memories and occurrences, we find the substance that we can write about and feed ourselves with.

Although some students remained in the mindset of generalities, the church wafers of the poetry world, others gave me images of eating cereal out of wine glasses, a grandfather coughing through their entire bat mitzvah, and turtles swimming beneath rice paddies.

None of my students said they would continue to take creative writing classes at Indiana. In one of my final meetings, a student told me he was sorry and only wanted to take courses towards his major. "As long as it lingers, it's going to help you," I said zipping up my backpack, trying to judge how fast I had to walk to make it to the bus on time.

He paused as I held the door for him. "How do writers see all those little things?"

"They usually only talk to paper, but even paper wants a good story."

Kari Wergeland

ROCKS ARE NOT ETERNAL

I once helped a student at Cuyamaca College think about what keywords she might use to do some searching in a library database. She was after at least five sources for a college comp paper. The topic: "Getting into nature alleviates stress." I thought we might have to try a few different search terms before she got what she needed, but my first idea (nature AND stress) worked beautifully. It was clear other approaches would have taken her further.

People are writing about the benefits of spending time in the great outdoors, which can only be a positive thing. It's no secret limited resources in our government coffers continue to spark fights over what should be funded, not to mention how our public lands should be used. In the face of serious problems with education, impending wars, and infrastructure projects, our national and state parks may not always fare well. We need to be reminded why they matter—how they keep us healthy and sane.

I've been working on that—staying healthy and sane—since I took an early retirement from my library career in 2017. I actually began working as a professional librarian in 1989 (and I've worked in libraries in some capacity or another since 1979). I could have plugged away as a full-timer for another decade, but in 2016 breast cancer took a pitchfork to me.

Throughout some eight months of cancer treatment, I had plenty of time to meditate on what I would do when I was all finished with medical appointments and given a clean bill of health. Once that first tumor shows up, the danger of recurrence becomes something a cancer survivor must live with. Though this reality might seem obvious, I never understood what it meant in an instinctive sense until I found myself on the big C roller coaster. I doubt I'll ever have the same confidence in my health again.

During chemo I lost my appetite for most pleasures. The one real treat—on days when I was feeling a bit better—was a walk along the shore, particularly on Torrey Pines State Beach. If happiness was to be found during that period of my life, it was there.

As my strength began to return, trips to the Anza Borrego Desert State Park helped me come to the deep realization I probably got lucky. I might be a little stiffer than I used to be—my earlier stamina didn't fully materialize—but I can still enjoy everything. That was the point of all those months of treatment. Perhaps the consolation prize is this: what matters to me now is significant in a heightened way.

I developed a taste for the outdoors early. My parents began packing the car, tossing my brother and me in with the gear when we were preschoolers. These trips remain high on my list of childhood highlights. When I'm out in backcountry, I can still feel a younger version of myself perking up to experience the sound of an owl hooting at night or wild turkeys gobbling in the morning. This child likes to walk the beach with me—or spend time in the forest. She still loves views in the round. Indeed, volcanoes became inextricably tied to my early forays into the natural world.

When I was very young—seven or eight—Lassen Volcanic National Park was my favorite camping trip destination. I loved the trail running alongside boiling mud pots and steam vents—the earth seemed alive and foreboding. The smell of sulphur still emerges with those memories. Yet I was sorely disappointed when I finally summited Lassen. I didn't find a crater filled with hot lava up there. I'll have to head to Hawaii for that, I guess.

What I did discover were rocks born of volcanic activity—pumice and dacite. Some of these rocks were pretty new. This captivated me, because I felt rocks in all of their "rockness" had been around for an eternity. I got a clearer picture after my father informed me Lassen was an active volcano. He told me a series of eruptions (the biggest blast occurred on May 22, 1915) had created a bunch of new rocks. Of course, this made me wonder if Mount Lassen could erupt while I was on it—if any of the volcanoes around me could go off. I thought about how the ground moves, how it slowly changes like a living, breathing creature. A mountain lets go, and a different landscape is born.

My rock collection had already been discarded by the time I visited a mysterious lake in Oregon. As I took in Crater Lake for the first time, I found myself thinking about volcanoes all over again. Crater Lake came into being after the eruption of Mount Mazama, which was actually a cluster of overlapping volcanoes. The initial eruption occurred some 7,700 years ago. The blast formed a caldera—a volcanic bowl or crater. After the collapse of the Mazama summit, water filled up this caldera, turning it into the deepest lake in the country. The lake, which could serve as a backdrop for any fantasy novel, is not fed by river or stream, thus it remains unusually pure. Walk along the crater's rim, and you will be rewarded by crystal-clear hues of spectacular blue. This shifting blue isn't its only outstanding feature. As Crater Lake took shape, one ancient cinder cone situated inside the caldera managed to keep its head above water to give us Wizard Island. (Since I was a fantasy-reading teenager in those days, the little island appealed to me.)

My volcano dreams were finally realized during my senior year in high school. Mount Saint Helens erupted! While hot red lava did not spout into the sky, the huge clouds of ash that did were a good enough representation of my imaginings. I didn't actually catch the eruption in real time, but ash drifted as far south as Southern, Oregon, where I resided in those days.

It was strange to receive sand from another land. The grit flipped into a metaphor: sudden change—a new reality—times demanding a sharp survival instinct. A child's fantasy about a crater filled with bubbling lava became something that could be visualized, documentary style. And the stories of devastation that appeared in the news—the old man who refused to leave his home near Spirit Lake—brought brushstrokes of reality to what had once been an exciting show in my mind. My family had visited Spirit Lake the year before, and what I loved about the recreation area ceased to exist after the eruption.

Many years later, I returned to the site of Spirit Lake to check out the new park designed around the flattened mountain (now Mount Saint Helens National Volcanic Monument). I found the story of the land skirting this famous volcano nothing short of reassuring. The earth was regenerating into viable ecosystems before everyone's eyes. Though the park's vistas revealed an entirely new outline, evidence of healing was everywhere.

It feels like my own recovery is going well. The initial post-treatment screen came with good news: no evidence of cancer. Subsequent screens have come out the same. My energy level has rekindled to almost what it was. I've been getting some backpacking in—more camping and hiking. I hope more journeys rest in my future. These trips don't have to be about volcanoes. I could hike in Sequoia National Park or Point Reyes National

Seashore. There's some great backpacking in Eastern Oregon. I've always wanted to make my way over to the Wilderness Coast in Olympic National Park—or *around* Mount Rainier on the Wonderland Trail. I do continue to meditate on volcanoes, their role in the worlds that have mattered to me. You can't miss them, really.

Now that I've retired, I've ratcheted up my writing schedule. I did this once before—left a good library job to write. It proved to be an adventure with ups and downs, not to mention regular communion with the nature. And I finished a novel—it took me a year. Or so I thought. Many drafts (and many years) later, this novel is finally done (this time for real). The task at hand remains firm, selling the darn thing. From a publishing standpoint, I'm doing better with my poetry.

I'd hoped to bring out some fiction in the nineties. The book publishing world was still recognizable back then—the literary stars, cool and widely known. In Seattle, where I was working as a librarian, authors would roll in to face robust audiences, people who actually asked questions and bought signed copies for relatives and friends. Sherman Alexie—three years my junior—was living in town, telling stories about how he aimed to publish his first novel before he turned 30. I believe he managed to achieve this goal. Meanwhile, we librarians in the Seattle Public Library had trouble keeping up with the demand for certain books. The media would promote a title, and then we'd have to acquire multiple copies so our patrons could elbow their way onto the holds list.

I figured it was only a matter of time before I joined this compelling scene of readings and signings—bookfests. Like many writers, I liked to take comfort in nattering on about the few editors who handwrote encouraging words on their form rejection letters. Then when *The Seattle Times* offered me a monthly column for the express purpose of reviewing children's books, I thought I had it made. My novel was for young adults. It was making its rounds through the U.S. Postal Service. Surely this would all come together.

I still think about the agent who asked for a rewrite on my first book and then ultimately rejected it. I considered this a huge failure. It paralyzed me, setting me back for a number of years. And then in the 2000s, the same thing happened—this time with a different book and a different agent. If only someone could have held my hand and told me how lucky I was to have gotten that far. My glass was half-empty for the longest time.

I came pretty close to throwing in the towel on my writing in the mid-2000s. I set it all down and celebrated what was going well—a career in a community college library. I was tenured and part of a lively faculty. The constantly changing library field kept me hopping. New technologies would surface at regular intervals, leaning into my learning curve. I spent time teaching online—and face-to-face. And though I still got to buy books, e-books began to eat into the book budget. Along the way, I became a loyal fan of California Community Colleges, the largest system of higher education in the country.

But even as I tried not to write, I couldn't help myself. There were times when I just needed to get something down. What I managed to write felt like poetry. This made me think, why not? Why not learn to write poetry? I liked the fact that poems generally have little commercial value—that I could write them without becoming stressed out over the publishing industry. I was desperate to remember why I ever decided to write in the first place. I needed to embrace the joy of playing with language all over again—for the sake of loving words, well-crafted lines, and meaningful pieces. At some point, I started taking workshops. I hired a mentor, poet Jim Moore, through the Split Rock Arts Program. In 2012, I completed that ubiquitous MFA through Pacific University. Around that same time, I took a spin with Createspace and self-published two books of poetry.

After this, I made myself—absolutely forced myself—to face *Writer's Market*. I quickly learned I was out of touch with the publication process, which had pretty much moved online. I already knew about *Poets and Writers*, which does offer plenty of updates on all of this. My MFA writing community clued me in on resources like Duotrope, Submittable, *AWP Writer's Chronicle*, and NewPages, not to mention the necessity of using social media. I sorted through all of these possibilities and decided how I would employ them to develop my new submission strategy. After that, I began to submit poetry to journals around the country—and even a few markets overseas.

When the acceptances began to appear, hope seeped and then finally flooded into my being. I was seeing some success in a different genre, so maybe I could stop calling my fiction a pipe dream. I mustered the courage to peek at my novels, one at a time, and I made a vow to exhaust all of my avenues before I left those pages to languish in a drawer for good.

I started with the revision process. Then I stumbled onto a long prose workshop taught by David Ulin, former book editor of *The Los Angeles Times*.

I took it twice. I was happy with my progress, but those manuscripts seemed to be stranded in the nineties. To get a handle on what I had to say right now, I started writing short stories.

Yet those dreaded submissions!

I knew I was procrastinating over agent queries for the novel that was ready to sell. I would think about getting to it, and then I'd experience major resistance and find something else to do. The reality of cancer treatment finally woke me up. While I was still dealing with chemo brain, I took little steps toward trying to sell one novel—and later, the other.

I still haven't published any books of fiction, though two novel manuscripts continue to circulate, along with a handful of short stories. All I can say is, agent nibbles on the longer works have come in here and there, though progress remains slow.

All is not lost. I've had 84 poems and one poetry chapbook accepted. The chapbook is a long narrative poem about breast cancer. While this wasn't the outcome I imagined when I was a young writer dreaming of my first novel sale, I know I should be happy. I've worked with MFA instructors who were quick to boast they only wrote poems. Poetry in their eyes is the superior genre—they see no reason to be bogged down by prose. I'm not quite ready to make such a claim. But would it be the end of the world? Besides, in 2019 I finally saw two short stories come into print.

I have carried my writing life into retirement!

I'll admit, I was nervous about starting over again after more than 16 years in higher education. The last time I holed up to write and spend time in nature—in 1999—I was surprised to discover I was much happier when I added part-time librarian to my weekly schedule. I liked the combination of writing and some librarian time better than full-time writing. Now that I'm actually a retiree, I have a third novel in-progress, what Anne Lamott has dubbed "the shitty first draft." It's an unwieldy project—I've still got a lot of research to do.

Retirement has been busy. If everything continues to feel so amplified due to my new status—Breast Cancer Survivor—I refuse to waste another moment. I need to get on the trail and sleep under the stars. I've got to contribute in some way. I want to keep up with the news. I plan to spend time with loved ones. I must submit, submit, submit. I keep thinking these intentions will bring on anticipation and peaceful fantasies, but as I continue to go over everything I want to do, the pressure builds. I have to pinch myself to remember why working on healing—well-being—is paramount right now. I don't want to be dead before I'm dead, but maybe...

Occasionally, I ponder the efficacy of my writing life. Memories of the literary 90s stand in contrast to what I'm observing these days—so many eyes glued to smart phones. Younger people have different priorities, and who am I to judge? Yet I can't help but feel sad. It seems like I belong to an older culture, one that is dying out as a newer technological—global—world emerges.

I'm not completely out of the loop—I am working as a librarian again, part-time for the Los Rios Community College District. If truth be told, many of our students don't seem to have the patience or inclination to truly absorb the books I buy for the library. This has led me to speculate whether literary audiences are even out there. Students will use books if instructors dictate they have to have one book and two articles for their most recent paper, but few browse the stacks—as I once did—for passionate reasons. Their passion lies with the Internet.

I'm not exactly a dinosaur—I've kept up with many new technologies, particularly in the library field, but also in my private life. I'm not afraid of new software—new apps—new ways of doing things with computer, tablet, and phone. I've even pondered how I might fare in one of today's computer science programs. (I have a minor in it—1985.) Yet I'm also not a junkie trying to memorize every little shortcut. I don't need to complete things as fast as possible. I work out what I need to know for my purposes and leave the rest of all that code for others to enjoy.

Before I was diagnosed with breast cancer, I was already learning to slow down, breathe, and listen. Listening to the birds—listening to the waves—got me through chemo. I'm not worried about having a lot of money in retirement, because I know I can make do with simple pleasures. A walk on the beach—a hike through the forest—a stroll in the desert—is most of what I need. Real talks with real friends and family as we sit down to eat real meals pretty much rounds out most of the rest. OK.... Travel. Romance. A good book.

I have wondered if post-millennial people will eventually come back to the quieter, slower joy of sinking into long-form writings, A.K.A. books. Will they have the courage to feel stupid for a while in order to develop some mental muscle, instead of going after the instant gratification they receive from their phones? Will they find a reason to ruminate on complexity, deeper meanings? Will they be willing to do what it takes to train their minds to be supple, strong, multidimensional, and wise, as opposed to reactive and simplistic? The Internet is bringing so many resources—so much information—to our fingertips. Yet people don't apply the sort zeal to reading they often manage to conjure when they find the need to train their bodies. Instead, they race from one new human-made sensation to the next, making do with sound bites and websites—summaries.

And now I'm hearing YA books have to have their sexy on. I guess this is even becoming true for middle grade novels. I've never been a prude about sexual elements in juvenile books. In fact, I count myself a member of Judy Blume's first young audience. Her work mattered to me. But now it feels like sex is required. What happened to the story about love and wisdom—the story about characters transforming their lives, not to mention the world? Do we always have to have loud—pounding—sexy-cool action, like a rattle hanging over a crib, to hold people's attention? I've had this same question about movies. Whenever I watch a series of upcoming attractions, I often think, "Has anyone heard of breathing?" It's like we can't be trusted to have a quiet moment.

Every so often I consider the possibility of disconnecting and becoming a luddite in the backcountry. Gentler scenes appeal to me right now. I remember a world younger people can't completely fathom. My novels (1993, 1999, 2002) are already historical fiction! And what I have to say about the 60s, 70s, 80s, and 90s—in other words, my pre-Internet life—may never be of use to the culture superseding those decades. I have faced this. That said, I plan to stick with the vow I first made when I was a teen. Try as I might, I can't unweave writer from my identity. If rocks are not eternal, neither are stories or poems. Another volcano might go off—or maybe there's a lake to enjoy. Any of this could make its way onto the page.

Guillermo Cancio-Bello

CRAFTING A POEM, DEFINING A SELF

Craft is, at its root, process. Behind the combining of textual elements such as rhyme, meter, strophe, metaphor, etc., exists the process of creation, those unique authorial choices that signify some deeper exchange. It is that deeper exchange, where the poet engages himself in relation to others and the larger world, that is the core of a poet's craft. Relationship becoming the key to understanding the crafting of the poem and the poet.

Dr. Murray Bowen, who pioneered a theory of family psychotherapy based on his research and observation of other natural systems, understood the basic emotional unit to be the family, and not the individual. He saw the family as existing in an emotional field which can be compared to gravity, *where each planet and the sun, by virtue of their mass, contribute to the field and are, in turn, regulated by the field they each help create.*

People develop and learn to function within their system. They are constantly reacting to shifts in the emotional field. With every shift, each individual affects every other individual as they interact in reciprocal relationships that are governed by and create the emotional field to which they respond.

Dr. Bowen described two forces that exist in this field: togetherness and individuality. Togetherness drives us toward others, for affiliation, for approval, etc., while individuality is the drive to be autonomous. The level of functioning in any system and any individual depends on the ability to balance these two forces. Both the chameleon and the rebel can be seen as reacting emotionally due to an anxious focus on others. The pull of togetherness generates anxiety, and we often attempt to relieve that anxiety in an automatic way, i.e. rebellion or blending in, which then produces more anxiety, and creates a negative pattern, or cycle.

Dr. Bowen defined the goal of any individual as the ability to differentiate, and define a self, within the emotional field of the systems of which they are a part. One's ability to differentiate is determined by their capacity to distinguish between thinking that is governed by emotionality versus thinking that is based on principle and an assessment of the facts of any situation. One's ability to be flexible and adaptable requires a thoughtful and firm stance, not blind reactions to emotional shifts from others. It is within these currents and relationship pressures, both positive and negative, that people develop. No one develops in isolation.

Poems, too, do not happen solely within an individual; rather they are emergent phenomena from within the systems of which the individual poet operates. They are a product of the psychological, biological, social, ecological, and spiritual factors acting on and within the poet. From the emotional impulse that is the spark of a poem to the discovery or insight that can result from a poem, the process of craft is synonymous with the process of differentiation.

Robert Hass, in his *Little Book on Form*, wrote, "The sentence imitates insight. It is the mode of individuation, the thought that separates us from others and gives us a self." In that light, the poet's thought, and its subsequent expression, become an attempt to differentiate within the emotional field in which they exist.

One cannot not exist in relationship. Symbiosis is a fact of nature. And the fact that the self cannot exist outside of relationship makes any form of expression a statement on one's position to themselves and to the external world. An individual's expression, and especially the thinking behind it, can be driven by either their emotional reaction to the pull of togetherness, that anxious focus on others, or it can be driven by their thought-out and reasoned principles. It is the poet's work to understand themselves as invariably connected to every part of their system, to be observant of the reciprocity of all life, and to simultaneously continue to remain thoughtful in the face of stress, threat, or any form the pressure of togetherness takes. It is the poet's work to differentiate. Poems become evidence of that process, and artifacts of that struggle.

One of the first poems that comes to mind as I write this is Emily Dickinson's poem that begins:

There's a certain Slant of light,
Winter Afternoons -
The oppresses, like the Heft
Of Cathedral Tunes -

Dickinson is responding emotionally to a seen object in the world. The minute she becomes aware of what the object is, that "certain slant of light," she begins to think about the feeling that is generated by the emotional impulse. The entrance of the thinking mind is the birth of the poem, as well as the signal that the self is attempting to differentiate amidst the pressures of the emotional field and the pull to simply react to alleviate anxiety in whatever form it takes, whether that be loneliness, hopelessness, anger, etc. Dickinson sits with the discomfort of thinking through her emotion rather than trying to relieve it.

Discomfort implies growth. A poet's craft is no different. Craft requires the ability to sit with discomfort, to not attempt to resolve the situation in a reactionary way when anxieties rise. Part of craft is waiting, and wading, in uncertain currents, struggling to distinguish between feeling and intellect, discovering what you truly believe, and traversing toward insight.

Heavenly Hurt, it gives us -
We can find no scar,
But internal difference -
Where the Meanings, are -

None may teach it—Any -
'Tis the Seal Despair -
An imperial affliction
Sent us of the Air -

When it comes, the Landscape listens -
Shadows - hold their breath -
When it goes, 'tis like the Distance
On the look of Death -

Poetry is powered by the life-forces of both togetherness and individuality, by the drive to be heard and understood, to be one with others, to be accepted and loved, as well as the drive to be separate and define an autonomous perspective free from the mandates of others. Where poetry is an act and evidence of the process of differentiation from the pressures of togetherness, it is also proof of our connectedness and the mutuality inherent in all relationship systems. Without the reality of our interconnectedness and interdependence there would be no need for self-expression.

The act of differentiating, of separating one's intellectual response from one's emotional response, is a poetic act. The ability to think about one's feelings rather than be governed by them grants perspective, space, and opens up possibilities in the way one can think. And the ability to think in new ways opens the door for discovery and insight. The process of differentiating leads the poet toward a lightness of mind in which the poet can think about the gravity and pull of the world, or togetherness, with its endless variables, rather than reacting blindly to it. Crafting a poem, at its best, is crafting a self. And the poetry made carries the music of our steps as we attempt to understand and balance the forces that govern all of life.

Sophia Terazawa

FOR IN EXILE, WE SPEAK OUR BODIES INTO BEING: NOTES ON WRITING WHILE WORKING/FAILING TO DECOLONIZE DESIRE

Sister-poet, you must now protect your heart. Withdraw from that which hurts simply because you've known the way it hurt before: to fling your love into the darkness of a country who will never know your strength and never have the spine to love you back. Sister, know the color of your skin. Know exactly where it stops under the white touch of America. He never truly saw you. Know that!

Look beyond his death gaze, far beyond his platitudes of freedom, equality, and justice made for all. These statements will be said in earnest, and at first, you may trust him. Know such freedoms, equalities, and justifications inevitably crumble, for they are spoken on his terms, as they have driven centuries of people to their deaths, meaning what has driven mass dehumanization and degradation of our people always started with the written word of conquerors. Abandon allegiance!

Look beyond the space between his arms, and then beyond the canyons, redwood forests, snow-capped mountains, bonfires, and fog, beyond the old, majestic wildebeests shedding their antlers after winter. Look beyond the beauty of this country, *his* country, and now by war, displacement, colonization, *your* country.

Look beyond the beauty of your hand meeting his hand. Believe him when he says your hand is warm. Know this means that you possess the warrior spirit of an ancestor who he will never know. This is your writing hand, your colored hand, your once called savage hand, once bombed out hand, once monkey hand, once lotus hand, once Gook hand, Jap hand, Chink hand.... Need this hand go on? Must it go on? Sister-poet, choose!

You must go on without him. Write your warmth, that sacred instinct kept *despite* his death touch, pulling you for centuries into the parasitic betterment of Man. This is another way of saying that you no more should owe him any reminder of living beside the sun. You no more should owe him any of your culture, pain, or liberation, in every singular sense of those words. These are your words now. This is your tongue, your rage, your dark blood coursing through the page. Let it spill, but not into his empty hands.

Sister-poet, look away! Do not meet his gaze. Respond at minimum, a smile. Then remove yourself from his white space, no matter how invitingly anti-racist, anti-misogynistic his *still* white hands may seem. Know that loving him for this is not the truth and not the truth!

Let your knowing chest ache. Let it tear away your soft fern nature. Get some sleep.

Rest your heart, and know your dreams are sacred, too. Make every effort to remember them. Keep them close, for dreams carry the maps to your survival.

Sister-poet, this will hurt. So bite down. Let it fall, your spirit, let it break. Then let it rise.

Carol Smallwood

BROODING BEFORE WRITING

"Live first, write afterwards."
—John Galsworthy, *Glimpses & Reflections*

In an era of multi-tasking and mobile technology, we have little down time in which to reflect, to mull things over. But this kind of time is crucial for writers: we need time to daydream, drive without talking on phones. Poetry especially needs this brooding time for illusive images on the wing. I do not understand how mulling works because the mind has millions of connections and science is but on the frontier regarding how the mind works. I just know enough to respect its complexities and be open to it. For years the color of spring grass after a long rain, the brilliance of the emerald, made me want to capture it in words. Finally this spring a poem came easily and was accepted the first time I sent it out. The triolet still seems like it came from someone else when I read the hard copy issue. There was something awesome that connected with the mystery of renewal that I was trying to capture and struggled with every spring for years until the time was right.

The more acquainted I become with writing the more I am becoming convinced that it isn't the actual time spent writing, but all the rest of the time seemingly unconnected with it—we just can't say we write two to eight hours a day. We may read with envy that writers produced work in an amazingly short time, but it is because they have thought about, mulled it over long before a word was actually written. *The Old Man and the Sea* was composed in a short time because Hemingway was ready for it, had lived with it. It was ripe and the words didn't need to be fought for, changed, revised. I remember being amazed years ago at how quickly he wrote it, but understand better now. The very mysterious creative writing process reminds me of black holes made in space when stars die that scientists cannot explain: equations crumble in efforts to understand them.

It was hard to imagine how writers wrote without word processors until seeing the handwritten manuscript of Nobel Prize winner John Galsworthy—his first page of *The Patrician* with only a change here and there. Galsworthy related getting "the germ" of the book from a young politician's face he saw at a dinner-party: "It intrigued me profoundly, set me to sorting old impressions, and ruminating…" The book was published three years later. When words fall into place as if they are being dictated as they did in Galsworthy's case, chances are it involved ruminating. *The Patrician* was published after several novels, short stories, and plays, when Galsworthy was forty-four. His handwriting marched on with few revisions. It was confirmed when I read his preface to *Villa Rubein and Other Stories*: "I never saw, in the flesh, either de Maupassant or Chekov—those masters of such different methods entirely devoid of didacticism—but their work leaves on me a strangely potent sense of personality. Such subtle intermingling of seer with thing seen is the outcome only of long and intricate brooding, a process not too favoured by modern life, yet without which we achieve little but a fluent chaos of clever insignificant impressions, a kind of glorified journalism, holding much the same relation to the deeply impregnated work of Turgenev, Hardy, and Conrad, as a film bears to a play."

Brooding can also describe sitting on eggs to keep them warm, waiting for them to hatch. Snatches of conversation, an image, a quotation, diary entry, an expression on someone's face, a setting, can all be tucked away until they are ready to hatch into a poem, short story, essay, novel, article, or play. We are hatchers of multiple ideas, keeping them going like jugglers until one cannot be ignored, appears full grown like Athena.

Sometimes these incubating bits appear to have no connection, will not come together. Don't force them into a piece of writing, just let them sit and grow. Seemingly contradictory, opposite ideas often spark the best work. The most interesting characters are those with conflicts that tear them apart and in the process let us see ourselves. As readers we enjoy piecing clues together in a mystery. Sir Arthur Conan Doyle's stories present an atmosphere as thick as London fog in which we eagerly join glimpses in English life when the empire played a large part in British life. There is the fascinating pull between staid Watson and moody Holmes and I still envy Irene Adler in *A*

Scandal in Bohemia for being esteemed by Holmes as "the woman." Lines have become famous such as the dog not doing anything in the night, and Holmes noting: "That was the curious incident." Doyle's readers can only rejoice that his slow early medical practice was such that it allowed him to mull his stories into being.

Brooding and hatching. Athena appearing fully formed. I also think of Native American dream catchers, used to assure good dreams to those who sleep under them. Or the volcano eruption in Iceland not long ago that happened under a glacier, melted water accumulating till it finally broke through. Doris Lessing, who was awarded the 2007 Nobel Prize in Literature observed, "I usually spend a very long time thinking about it. Sometimes years. You know when you are able to write it. The work goes in before you start, really. You can have variations of the pattern, but the whole book must be there." Lessing was the oldest person to receive the Nobel Prize in Literature.

It is reassuring that no matter what we write, it makes us better writers: our work is not wasted even if tossed out. Make it a habit to jot down dreams soon as you awake as they can be the raw material of a lifetime.

Writers are very fortunate that writing is always possible no matter the time of the day, how old we are, where we live, how much money we have. Some writers don't even need a room of their own. I had one writing professor who wrote with the loudest music possible, drinking strong coffee in a busy campus restaurant. No matter what writing you do, don't depend entirely on your spell checker as we've all had experiences like: "Eye want to right well" going through the spell checker.

The more swings you take the greater your chances of hitting the ball—in other words, try different types of writing. Each genre will hone your writing skills in a different way, keep you from falling into a rut, and make you more aware of different aspects of those magical, illusive things called words.

Some writing may depend on your stage in life—only now I've had the courage for poetry. Poetry had always been too mysterious, an unreachable niche until I asked myself what I had to lose by trying.

Quotations provide inspiration as well as give that special touch to your writing and conversation. Copying them in your own hand or typing them is an excellent way to appreciate and acquire the unique taste of master stylists. Start your own collection and use them often. Have them on hand when you need them—the more they become a part of you, the more likely you will use them naturally.

Anaïs Nin observed, "It is the function of art to renew our perception. What we are familiar with we cease to see. The writer shakes up the familiar scene, and as if by magic, we see a new meaning in it." Eggs take time to hatch—brooding is a process that can't be hurried but fortunately, we can sit on several eggs at a time.

Tanis MacDonald

MADSKILLS FOR THE TWENTY-FIRST CENTURY: WRITING OUT OF LINE

Admitting to being aware of class—even introducing the subject—is a class betrayal in twenty-first century North America where capitalism is supposed to bestow middle-class privilege on everyone, or judgily, on everyone who tried hard enough to bootstrap themselves, as though those opportunities were not heavily influenced by race and class and region and history. Many things about class that need saying are its obvious truths: you will always be a product of where you came from, but you needn't be only that. There's a cliché lurking in there, about the ways that you could, given a certain amount of "success," embody against your wishes (or maybe align with them) the local kid who makes good. But the force of twenty-first century modernity all but insists that we live rootlessly and transiently upon the earth, yet somehow maintain connections with communities that are being made and re-made, so to an extent that is a bit bewildering, still we are also socially required—on pain of being found "cold" or "disconnected"—to be nostalgic about remembering our roots.

I have felt for a long time that the lived contradiction between the often-required far-flungness and the expected nostalgia is deeply disquieting. There are good practical reasons for moving far from one's homeplace, some of which are entwined with capitalism and colonialism. We move to where the work is despite the fact that it takes us away from our families and cultural heritage and home environments. We listen to capitalist rhetoric about upward mobility and colonial rhetoric about a united country and it's easy to believe that kind of identity—young upwardly mobile person on the move across the country—will stand in for family. It's insidious, and it replaces other thoughts we might have had about loyalty or duty or service to the community. Or maybe it doesn't. My students who have First Nations heritage often refer to needing to go home for ceremonies, for family occasions, for community celebrations or service work. So do students from other backgrounds that haven't been eroded by North American service to colonial capitalism. I admire their sense of belonging and their ongoing material evidence of community, because my own roots were so easily yanked up by a combination of cultural colonialism and creative ideology of elsewhereness.

When I was young, the party line was that if you wanted to make art (be an actor, writer, painter), then you had to leave your small city or town to be taken seriously. Goddess knows I was determined to be taken seriously at all costs. The irony of this is profound, considering that the small city I was from fostered a thriving arts community including a strong film group, an internationally acclaimed ballet school, two literary magazines, many local galleries and at least five professors of creative writing who were widely published authors and great instructors. But it also was a time when the grouchy snobbery of excuse-makers owned the surface level of the public discourse, and when you are a newbie to the scene, when you are looking for direction, you might get—and befriend—some bad advice. I didn't know anyone, and didn't even know that such local resources existed, so *hello, bad advice! Nice to meet you! Will you be my constant companion for years?* There's no formula for figuring out who to listen to, and who to trust, which is another reason why maintaining and participating in a broad and deep artistic community is so important. I wish I could tell you that artistic communities are by definition heavens on earth and all artists are benevolent: alas, no. Artists have every human frailty everyone else has, and sometimes they have given themselves special license to air those frailties to the detriment of others. While "others" includes just about everyone, it most especially includes beginner artists who are vulnerable to the machinations of power, or to just plain bad advice.

Pursuing an artistic path may mean staying home (or moving back after some time away) and making your home place's art scene more vibrant. It may also mean creating alone for a while, or a long time. While I often stress the vitality of community for a beginning artist, the ability to be solitary, to shut out the world, to drop a personal cone of silence onto your practice and just do the work without reward or feedback are valuable skills. They are also skills that are nearly unexplainable to others, and many will chafe against your ability to turn to your practice because others—non-artists—will have no context for understanding it. Others may refuse to acknowledge its value. And in our super-connected twenty-first century, the ability to be alone and solitary for the purposes of making art is a madskill. "Alone" is relative, of course: many of us make art in houses full of people and noise. Solitary is a state of mind, a practice, a discipline.

Focus is a madskill.

Patience is a madskill.

Observation is a madskill.

Generosity is a madskill.

Showing up is a madskill.

When I was a young artist, it was drummed into me that I should look to the process for my reward, and I was guided by that for a long time. It's decent advice, especially when you are starting out, because it's true that the immediate rewards will be few at first: intelligent eyes on your work, someone who says "this is good!," a reading or installation or performance with a small audience. My instructors and mentors and senior peers advised—strongly—that we concentrate on feeding our artistic practices and not our often-fragile egos, and when you are beginning, this can be a fine distinction. To delight in the process for its own sake is the madskill of cultivating aloneness. To practice patience with yourself will bolster you in lean times, and there are always going to be lean times, financially or psychologically. The process is the reward. Except when it's not. If the process was all the reward anyone needed, why would anyone publish? Sing for an audience? Act in a play? For me, six books and thirty years of magazine and journal publishing into the game, I will say that having faith in an audience—in readers out there, who may not be shouting about my latest book on Twitter—is a madskill. Everyone needs their own proportion of process and audience as reward. I don't know what your proportion will be like, but you can reasonably expect it to shift throughout your artistic life. And fair warning: when you are a beginning artist, the shock of having an audience can be as great as the delight of it.

Being public is a madskill.

Being private is a madskill.

An extremely smart friend once told me that she was trying to calculate what kind of encouragement would be enough for her, how much would cause her to say, "I get it. I'm worthy. That's enough." She pictured a concert scenario: a stadium of people cheering, howling their approval, roaring out their love for her and her work, and even as she pictured it, she thought "it's not enough." She also knew that the chances of getting that arena full of people cheering for her were slim; she wasn't a rock star or a professional athlete. It's a fact that sometimes we write for love, for approval, or for admiration. We write to be seen. This is may not be 100 percent psychologically healthy but it is perfectly normal. And there needs to be something else driving your art, because not everyone will love you, not everyone will approve of or admire you. Some people may even think your work is bad. Others may love your writing, though, or sit up and take notice: say, "Wait—what's this?" And that's who you are looking for, and who you are writing to, at least at the start: your people, your peers, your readers.

Listening to praise is a madskill.

Finding your people is a madskill.

Your relationship to money and power will always dictate how you look at the world. It's not as though people don't change, or remake themselves, or as it is popular to say, "re-invent themselves." That's true enough as far as appearances or tastes or experience goes (and this may make up 99 percent of what people know about you) but that doesn't necessarily mean that having a steady paycheck will make you completely relaxed about your bank account if you have grown up in a low-income environment, or—to keep things literary—that having a book published will make you supremely confident in your artistic ability. (One of my students on reading David Sedaris's frequent self-criticisms in *Theft By Finding: Diaries 1977-2003*: "Why is he so down on himself? He's a published author!") Why indeed.

Some things about growing up in the striving class just never go away. And that's not a bad thing. I propose to you that the outsider perspective is a good platform for anyone who wants to make art. Who better to offer different views, to change structures, to address different material, to offer new perspectives than someone on the outside? Who knows better what makes—and unmakes—a life than those of us who live outside the structures of privilege? This is all relative, of course; if you're white, you have instant structural privilege in many ways, but may have less in other ways if you're female, working-class, LGBTQ+, or disabled. Some of my privilege is hard-won, gained through risk and determination and pursuit of goals beyond my parents' imagining, and some I was born with. It's crystal clear that many people—maybe you—will have grown up less privileged than I did, and I want to articulate an open secret about art, which I hear my students ask, sometimes explicitly but more often implicitly, whenever they talk to me about creative work. One of the most consistent questions I hear from beginner writers is about what will be "allowed" in the literary world: will they be *allowed* to write? So much has already indicated strongly to them that art is for other people. There is also the closely related opposite: you may make art, but only under certain approved circumstances. You may sing, but only in the church choir. You may join a taiko group, but may not drum for a rock band. You may write genre fiction, but don't even think of going to some pretentious poetry reading.

Perspective is more than a madskill. It's a heroskill.

If you want good evidence, take a look at the giants in your field and work to see past the press kit. I guarantee you that they were uncool geeks in adolescence. David Bowie was waif-thin with a working-class accent, bad teeth, and mismatching eyes that he got from being beat up by other kids. He turned that oddness into Ziggy Stardust and other personae, but he was as geeky as all of us, and maybe even more. Check out his mime routine—dressed all in white—from his short film *Love You till Tuesday* from 1969 if you need proof of a terrific record of geekiness. You can still see the boy who was trying to figure out how to make art, who made a public misstep on his way to supreme coolness. Bowie is a great example of someone who drew from all the arts, including poetry, to write, using an avant-garde poetic technique—the cut-up—to write songs.

Love for our milieu saves us again and again.

Flexibility and adaptation are madskills you may already have if you are in the least out of line. Artists are adept at finding their art—and reasons to practice their art—everywhere. Part of your art is finding out where it lives in the world, even and especially where it lives in your small and sometimes stifling homeplace, what Richard Hugo calls "the triggering town" in his book of the same name. Sometimes you've got to work with what's in front of you. How can you work with what the other people offer and adapt it to your own artistic practice? Many fiction writers find their prose gets stronger after they study poetry. Many painters find the study of music changes how they "see." Working with whatever (and whoever) is in front of you sharpens your own skills at articulation. Want to strengthen your own vision? Try explaining it to someone else. Want to extend your vision? Try collaborating with another artist's practice. Sometimes—and maybe sooner than you expected—you will be the confident one, and others will be newer to the practice or more hesitant than you. You have to be brave to be generous, to pay attention to someone's work when you don't see yourself in it. Have faith that your generosity will create a more forgiving world, a bigger practice, many possibilities in a small place.

If it's brave to be generous, it's goddamned heroic to take leadership, to allow someone else's artsy geekiness into your protective circle, to dare to associate with uncoolness. You may be the one to grant permission. I can still remember C., the poet in my first workshop who spent a lot of time writing me feedback on one of my poems. The poem, for the record, was not very good, though it did represent the extent of my abilities at the time, and I had worked hard on it. Hers was a generous gift of attention, for she was far and away the best poet in the room and I was blown away that she would spend so much time on my poem. I saved the copy of the poem that she wrote all over for years and read it whenever I felt like I was going nowhere fast. I thanked her for it at the time, but she left the workshop a few weeks later and she never knew how important that piece of paper was to me for years.

Free the madskill you want to be in the world. Artists have to be good at deferring gratification. As a poet, I practice short written forms; I can draft a poem in a day, polish it over a few months, and send it out to a journal. If that seems like a long time to you, remember that it is lightning fast compared to writing a short story or a personal essay, and like a blink of an eye for a novelist. Artists are playing the Long Game. We learn to be happy with a day's work because most days that is all we have. It is a good way to live in the twenty-first century when so few people see the material evidence of their work. What can you show as your work; what have you "made" today? Art is very good for this if you know how to see progress in your own work, and that too is a valuable skill to develop. Craftspeople have known this for centuries. But then again, I remember being a young performer and listening to two young men arguing about whether acting was an art or a craft, and I remember thinking that this conversation was not about acting, or art, or craft. It was about ego. Which, for the record, is not a craft.

When you are an out-of-line writer, out of step with those around you and living far from the big city and its opportunities, one result of this aloneless may be a kind of sameness that haunts your work. Many beginning writers are fascinated by their own perspective mostly because they have been told they will never be allowed it. If you are a beginning writer and find yourself writing the same thing over and over, painting the same subjects, singing in the same style, don't worry. This is the forging of an aesthetic and the perfection of a mode. But—and this is a major caveat—when someone offers you a chance to do something different, take it. Inviting a beginning artist into the space of risk is an act of generosity and there's nothing quite like being allowed to experiment under the tutelage of senior artists. As I say to my students when I ask them to write outside of their comfort zone, just try it for a week; it won't take anything away from your usual practice and it might end up enhancing it.

The discovery of oneself as a creative source combined with the permission to create art can break the logjam of fear and those who witness the resulting deluge can be very surprised by the changes in that person. This is true for everyone at the start of any artistic practice, but it's doubly important for out-of-line artists to understand their internal resources because they will need to rely on them so much in their small place. It's not unlike coming out; the permission to be oneself is much the same. Of course, sometimes the two actions, coming out as an artmaker and coming out as LGBTQ+, or as a mental health consumer/survivor, or an assault survivor, or an addict, or any combination of these can happen temporally close to one another. Permission works that way. That said, there are many people who live private lives while being public artists. Artistic revelation does not necessarily scorch everyone around you with the blinding light of truth and reveal all. But keep an eye out for your impulse to say the whole truth because it may occur to you. It may occur to you a lot.

Permission is a madskill, a gift, the spring we drink from.

Ben White

WARRIOR POETS AND SUBVERSIVE POETRY: THE POEMS THAT STAND IN FRONT OF THE TANK

> "I believe that if someone chooses art as their subject, but [does] not criticize the issues of their society, they have betrayed themselves, their conscience, and their society."
> —Atena Farghadani

Warrior-poets are those literary artists who have served in the military and have gone to combat for their country. The battlefield experiences give these poets a voice that offers credibility to the war ideology that often counters the ideals of governments, societies, and citizenries. Warrior-poets, no doubt, are a subset of poets. However, in describing their experiences by using the literary art, their voices enter the social realm with perspectives differing from those of social norms. The depiction of war is taken from real experiences, not filtered through a Hollywood lens, and honestly depicts the attitudes and actions of people who lived through the events.

Because the poems of warrior-poets derive from personal experience and do not necessarily require imagination's interventions, they enable the reader to see the realities of war from firsthand witnessed accounts. Though they may not always be anti-war poems, the honesty and brutality depicted in these poems leave readers with a potential obligation to question individual values and beliefs, and subsequently assume an anti-war stance. The poetry that warrior-poets provide is not simply personal or political, but becomes eyewitness documentation augmenting historical events with credible perspectives that have the capacity to criticize, challenge, and subvert socially accepted truths and associated sentiments.

A nation's collective emotional intelligence is conditioned by expectations projected by and upon citizens and that subsequently evokes rationally developed responses to social situations. The emotions of the citizenry subsist on objects, events and thoughts by which *proper* affectations are defined, categorically accepted, and, upon acceptance, further perpetuated to assume a social state of national normalcy. The sentimentality of a society is a predictable construct of culture. Warrior-poets have the experiential capacity to challenge the preconditioned predictability by initiating counter-sentiments based on counter-facts that create cognitive dissonance among readers.

In America, the anti-war stance has become synonymous with anti-country. This is a jingoistic, cant position, as well as a manifestation of belief that a democratic, freedom-based country can do no evil in the world, and all the actions America takes are against the evils committed by other countries. The principles of cultural identity that American society applies are genuinely and inherently positive, so the social image that is projected by that identity is based on the ideals of goodness and righteous behaviors.

Put into simple terms, America going to war is a consistent extension of the nation's obligated effort to defend freedom, liberty, and the fundamental way of life that is perpetuated by social and political rhetoric aimed at increasing the hegemony necessary to continue the subjugations of global resources. There are no perceptions in mainstream American society that are not influenced—perhaps blinded—by the ideals of this global defense. These perceptions are rarely questioned, and even more rarely are they criticized. America is good and just and righteous, and populated by people who are good and just and righteous who are democratically represented by elected officials who are good and just and righteous. America's social system and its politics are above reproach. Consequently, the decisions made by the country's government are by definition, by default, and by association also above reproach.

To criticize any aspects of American society equates to criticizing the perfection and foundational ideals that Americans have used to create their identity and project their image around the globe. The worldview of Americans is extremely ethnocentric, and the ethnocentricity is exaggerated by generalized statements such as "everyone wants to come here," "America is the land of opportunity," and "everyone wants to live the American Dream."

The defense of these idealistic concepts has historically come down to the United States military; that five-branch organization that has been perfected by practicing the constant defense of the nation since the Revolutionary

War. Evidently there is credence to the aphorism "practice makes perfect." (Consider America's consistent battlefield history contained in Appendix I.)

With a few exceptions and setbacks, the United States military claimed victory in all of the 111 conflicts listed in Appendix I. Consequently, in every one of those conflicts, American lives were lost (sometimes on both sides). In a practice that alleviates questioning the war-mobilization decisions, those conflicts and individual lives were often glorified with monuments and generalized statements such as "freedom isn't free," "the ultimate sacrifice for God and country," and "on behalf of a grateful nation."

However, there is very little sentimentalized nationalism, glory, or romance in war. For instance, Randall Jarrell, a World War II veteran and warrior-poet, wrote a poem, "The Death of the Ball Turret Gunner," which counters the glorified sentimentality of war. The notions of noble sacrifice, freedom, God, or country are replaced by a dominating image of being unceremoniously washed out of a Plexiglas bubble with a U.S. Army-issued hose:

> From my mother's sleep I fell into the State,
> And I hunched in its belly till my wet fur froze.
> Six miles from earth, loosed from its dream of life,
> I woke to black flak and the nightmare fighters.
> When I died they washed me out of the turret with a hose.

Meanwhile, however, the harshness of this kind of warrior-poet poetry is overlooked, and the personification of America's power is erected along with its war memorials to project another aphorism: might makes right. Subsequently, the post-victory subjugation of other nations has led to additional conflicts in which the personification of power is manifested in additional deployments to maintain the fragile-most spoil of war: world peace. That jingoistic nature and cant position of America becomes an unquestioned and unchallenged social value. Returning home to share what they have witnessed, warrior-poets provide counter-facts to argue against that accepted normalcy and its overly romanticized sentiments towards war.

All artists—if not all citizens—are in the position to be society's conscience. However, many poets refuse to criticize society's norms and continue to operate in the acceptable range that has diluted avant-garde creativity, In her 2015 essay, "Delusions of Whiteness in the Avant-Garde," Cathy Park

Hong points out that this makes it more difficult to distinguish avant-garde creativity from the mainstream. However, now that only one percent of the nation serves in the military, it is not a mainstream experience to have been in combat. The dominant sentimentality of the majority is established by secondhand information and corresponding assumptions. The opportunity for warrior-poets to assume a subversive stance and criticize the social issues of constant troop mobilization is greater than it may have ever been before because their insights, worldviews, and perspectives are unique. This gives them an undermining edge against the majority's social perceptions. Ninety-nine percent of the population may know "war is bad," but someone with the credibility of having seen war firsthand offers the unique perspectives to point out why it is bad, present what about it is bad, and to shake away social sentimentality about glory, honor, duty, and service; if, that is, the civilian population is open to reading, analyzing, and recognizing warrior-poets as *witnesses* and *participants* (not bystanders) of history.

It may not always require the perspective of a warrior-poet to make the legitimate points that attack or subvert the social perspective. Stephen Crane used his imagination to fictionally characterize the experiences of Henry Fleming in *The Red Badge of Courage*, a book considered to be an American war-literature classic. However, this book may not be as much of a criticism of war as it is a philosophical declaration of the existential nature of humanity. To maintain public readership, Crane may have used more imagination as a war correspondent to depict battles so patriotic subscribers would continue to follow the war effort in Cuba. It is Crane's experiences in Cuba that give him more insight into the anti-war position that challenges the public view.

Crane was not in the military, but when he was a war correspondent in Cuba, he wrote, "War is Kind." The excerpt below depicts the brutality of what happens to soldiers, but consoles the now fatherless child (in this excerpt; a lover and a mother in other parts) by telling the babe not to weep, for war is kind.

> Hoarse, booming drums of the regiment,
> Little souls who thirst for fight,
> These men were born to drill and die.
> The unexplained glory flies above them,
> Great is the battle-god, great, and his kingdom—
> A field where a thousand corpses lie.

Do not weep, babe, for war is kind.
Because your father tumbled in the yellow trenches,
Raged at his breast, gulped and died,
Do not weep.
War is kind.

In other words, death is kind enough to provide a better option than having to live in a world where humans go to war, so war offers individual soldiers its own solution. This existential approach provides Crane a nihilistic perspective of a society that raises men "born to drill and die" for a great battle-god's kingdom "where a thousand corpses lie." This sardonic (yet subtle) twist of "war is bad" forces the members of society (or at least those members who read) to look at themselves through a lens that offers a closer look at their beliefs. It challenges society to criticize its own take on the glory and honor they expect to emerge from war and transition from the jingoistic to the realization of the tragic.

Another example of a poet who knows society should understand the fullest ramifications of saying "war is bad" is Demetria Martinez and her poem "Rules of Engagement."

Today I was told that the words
War is bad
Make for
Bad poetry.
OK.
Then consider
This poem
Dispensable,
Depleted
As uranium,
A poor poem,
A colored poem,
Drafted,
But not finished,
Out on a missing
Limb.
Nothing

But a little ink
Shed in the killing
Fields of the university
Writing workshops.

In this poem, Martinez advocates for the subversive poet. The "war is bad" poet who is directly saying the obvious in the most direct, concise way, is often reprimanded in workshops for not being poetic enough, too reliant on clichés, and not meeting the acceptable standards of what a poem is supposed to contain (or not contain) to be considered *good*.

This poem (itself, perhaps at first glance, not a "good poem" by workshop standards) attacks the heart of poetry defined in the governing society of universities where writing workshops don't allow the cliché, the obvious, or the declarations of the simplest ideas. These killing fields are brutal, but Martinez offers a subversive poem to undermine the brutality by letting the bad, war-is-bad poetry, lay down its arms and shed its ink to stink up the high-brow discussion of what makes *good poetry*. The depleted uranium of the poem hovers in the waste site as a reminder of what people—even poets—should consider.

And at the core of the poem, "war is bad." Admittedly not a complete poem, and a poem "out on a missing limb," but one discarded because of the use of three words that aren't poetically strong enough to even criticize a basic issue of society.

But Martinez' poem is operating on another tactical level. She has taken the instance of workshop feedback to make the poem viable. Her images use the language of war to support the war is bad idea. Consider: "Dispensable"—men are dispensable in war. (For instance, 2,499 dead Americans on June 6, 1944, during one of the most celebrated events of American history.) "Depleted as uranium"—there's no greater badness than a nuclear war. "A poor poem"—an allusion to the socio-economic status of those veterans sent to Vietnam. "A colored poem"—an allusion to the minorities sent to Vietnam. "Drafted"—an allusion to how the poor minorities could not escape being sent to Vietnam. "Out on a Missing Limb"—missing limbs are too often the result soldiers realize in combat. "A little ink"—all it takes to innocently say, war is bad. "Shed in the killing"—like innocence lost. "Fields"—completing the enjambment of "killing/fields" comparing workshops to combat zones.

So Martinez very effectively defends poets. And she also, subsequently, speaks for soldiers who already know war is bad, but who need advocates to reinforce the sentiment, and to provide the warrior-poet with a ground zero where points can explode into criticism that has the potential to bring about social reform(s).

The glory of war has been exemplified by politicians sending children into harm's way, urging citizens to get behind and support the troops responsible for defending freedom. The political rhetoric is, however, countered by the clichéd sentiment that war is bad. Given the contracts awarded to the military-industrial complex in America, "war is bad" is analogous to "just saying no" in the war against drugs; perhaps the second largest industry when it comes to government contracts and deployment of resources. It is understood that war is bad, but defending freedom counters the sentiment with a Charlie-checkmate maneuver stating that only anti-patriots and subversives would bring the war-is-bad-sentiment into the conversation in the first place. In simpler terms, "war is bad" is countered by behaviors acting upon the understanding that war is profitable.

The danger of being perceived as an anti-patriot and/or a subversive keeps people from criticizing the issues of society or from admitting openly that profit is behind the politics of war. Other issues are more open to being critiqued and are subject to more open discussion such as the disparities among races, equal citizenship, genders, and even, to some extent, religious perspectives. These are accepted areas that can be part of the American conversation. Racists, feminists, sexists, and even a religious extremist (given the "right" religion) are all tolerated in American society with generalized comments such as "debate is healthy," "we must learn to manage diversity," and "the constitution provides everyone the right of Freedom of Speech." However, when a person goes beyond the war-is-bad sentiment, that person is perceived as being unpatriotic and as participating in the rebellious act of weakening the dearest principles of defending freedom.

In *The Lover of a Subversive is Also A Subversive*, Martin Espada does not see men and women as dreams or dots, and presents the "proposition that the people who inhabit the unspoken places are not only subjects, but poets themselves" who have the "moral and literary authority to speak." However, in so speaking, those people and poets become the subversives who tell the story of the unspoken, forgotten places, the untold histories, the unseen perspectives, and the otherwise meaningless events upon which counter-facts are built.

Major General Smedley Butler, a two-time recipient of the Medal of Honor, served in the United States Marine Corps and was sent to China, Mexico, and Central America on military expeditions. When he retired, one primary reason he gave was that he was tired of being a thug for American businesses. General Butler's 1935 essay, "War is a Racket" capitalizes on the literary authority to speak, and ultimately he stands as a champion for all warrior-poets who write poems from their legitimate perspectives of lived (otherwise and elsewhere unspoken) experience.

General Butler presents a critically accurate depiction of what American history had been (and arguably continues to be) about. War is a racket, and he had been a participant. Although not necessarily from a poetic perspective, General Butler still had credible experience that needed a literary outlet. In his essay, he criticized the patriotism that American companies suddenly felt when they transitioned from making steel rails to making battle armaments; touting loyalty to the country while watching the profits soar; and selling mosquito nets for soldiers in France. (Mosquito nets that would not have provided much benefit and that never made it to France.) He also criticized the propaganda that made young men readily accept conscription so as not to appear unpatriotic (or less manly): "we used propaganda to make the boys accept conscription. They were made to feel ashamed if they didn't join the army." And finally, General Butler struck out at the heart of democratic-capitalistic thought: "If we put [people] to work making poison gas and more and more fiendish mechanical and explosive instruments of destruction, they will have no time for the constructive job of building greater prosperity for all peoples." General Butler finishes his essay, not by saying "war is bad" or even the more military sounding "war is hell!" He ends his essay with a resounding "to hell with war!"

Sadly, however, the "War is a Racket" essay could not stop America's propensity for war. Six years later, America was back to manufacturing the tools necessary to defend freedom. This time, however, it took a direct hit on an American facility to motivate the citizens to mobilize. It would be another area to research to see how General Butler's essay affected America's mindset toward going to war, but going to war has needed more drastic incentives (attacks on American territories, communist missiles 90 miles away, steady fear-mongering rhetoric, and the idea of weapons of mass destruction) to motivate America to mobilize troops. (Mobilization has continued to be profitable.)

Critical thinking leads to being able to criticize analytically with solutions and improvement in mind. America's overall mindset (stemming from the identity and projected image) is that it is better to be best than it is to get better. The process of getting better indicates being less than perfect, and that undermines the mindset based on power and righteous justice that America likes to think it represents in the world.

The socially established and socially accepted norms allow some criticism to take place within the realm of expected reason. The limits of allowance rarely extend to criticism (or even thoughtful analysis) of America's combat culture (and its sister gun-culture). Criticism of the issues will lead to labels that people want to avoid or embrace, but very few are brave enough, willing enough, or strong enough to fight against the label that comes with the perception of being unpatriotic, even when it stems from being humane and peaceful. Being humane and peaceful doesn't play well in a kingdom that constantly projects a need to protect its freedom.

If a two-star general cannot apply his credibility to making social change, artists will have an even more difficult time criticizing the social issues beyond taking the stances that lead to socially accepted labels. Criticizing the social issues that social culture expects to be criticized is not really an act of criticizing social issues.

Poetry is itself a criticized, under-appreciated art form. Publishers often include a "no poetry please" request in the calls for submissions. Some of the reasons behind that excluding request are self-induced by poets who are unwilling—perhaps unable—to go out on their own "missing limb" and have anything different to present in their poetry. Readers are often heard saying, "I don't get it," so publishers do their readers a favor by requesting literary art those readers will "get."

In his essay, "What is Literature?" Sartre wrote, "[p]oets are men who refuse to *utilize* language." The quest for truth, however, is dependent on the utilization of language, and consequently, if truth is indeed worth seeking, then poets have excluded themselves from the search. Poets, Sartre wrote, do not "aim to discern or expound the true," and are left not speaking while at the same time not remaining silent. At best, poets trying to gain a presence in the midst of utilitarian language have to "try to retrieve words from it in odd little groups, as for example 'horse' and 'butter' by writing 'horses of butter.'" "Horses of butter" may describe the poets and their poetry that easily melt away in a herd of rejection notices.

Still, there is a history of soldiers—warrior-poets; or perhaps cavalry poets riding their own wild horses of butter—who established a tradition of writing against the conditioned sentiments of a nation at war. The counter-establishment of subversive poetry and poetry of witness is rich in perspectives that oppose affectations of response designed to perpetuate the support of decisions to mobilize the forces. It is important to point out, at this juncture, that not all "war poetry" is written by warrior-poets.

For instance, Rupert Brooke was a World War I poet who wrote a very patriotic sonnet called "The Soldier."

> If I should die, think only this of me:
>   That there's some corner of a foreign field
> That is forever England. There shall be
>   In that rich earth a richer dust concealed;
> A dust whom England bore, shaped, made aware,
>   Gave, once, her flowers to love, her ways to roam;
> A body of England's, breathing English air,
>   Washed by the rivers, blest by suns of home.
>
> And think, this heart, all evil shed away,
>   A pulse in the eternal mind, no less
>   Gives somewhere back the thoughts by England given;
> Her sights and sounds; dreams happy as her day;
>   And laughter, learnt of friends; and gentleness,
>   In hearts at peace, under an English heaven.

However, to call Brooke a warrior-poet would be a misnomer. He shared no combat experience with soldiers in trenches, and wrote "The Soldier" based on observations he made from the deck of the ship to which he was assigned. It is a romanticized view of combat, sentimentalizes the sacrifice for God and King, and champions the colonialism of the previous century with an ethnocentric idea of richer, English earth. Joanna Scutts (2015), in her *New*

Yorker article, writes that Brooke is "famous mainly for one sonnet, "The Soldier," and its patriotic sentiment of making some foreign field "forever England." However, she continues to point out that Brooke "was a minor celebrity before he died and a monstrous one afterward, holding on, to this day, to his fame and a rather tattered glory." Scutts proposes that Brooke should have died out along with other war-romanticizing poets.

Juxtaposed with the poetry of Wilfred Owen, Brooke's romanticism and patriotic sentimentality of the battlefield pale in comparison with the grit of Owen's hard-hitting description of what a combat soldier is more likely to experience.

> If in some smothering dreams, you too could pace
> Behind the wagon that we flung him in,
> And watch the white eyes writhing in his face,
> His hanging face, like a devil's sick of sin;
> If you could hear, at every jolt, the blood
> Come gargling from the froth-corrupted lungs,
> Obscene as cancer, bitter as the cud
> Of vile, incurable sores on innocent tongues,—
> My friend, you would not tell with such high zest
> To children ardent for some desperate glory,
> The old Lie: *Dulce et decorum est*
> *Pro patria mori.*

This poem, although written within the confines of traditional rhyming schemes, deviated from the romanticized depiction of war. Flung into a wagon with a writhing face is a long way from Brooke's "The Soldier" calling for the continuation (if not stagnation) of proud English culture. Owen's poem also challenges the content and sentiment of older English works. Consider Tennyson's "Charge of the Light Brigade" and his "noble six hundred":

> Theirs not to make reply,
> Theirs not to reason why,
> Theirs but to do and die:
> Into the valley of Death
> Rode the six hundred.

Cannon to right of them,
Cannon to left of them,
Cannon in front of them
    Volley'd and thunder'd;

Tennyson's poem is based on a cavalry charge in the Crimean War; a very unpopular war. The poem may have been one of the first instances of being against the war, but being for the troops (a sentiment made popular recently in America's involvement in the Middle East). Tennyson, as an English subject felt a strong sense of duty for Queen Victoria's society (in which he was one of the three most famous people), and by honoring the 600 soldiers, he reminded his fellow countrymen to "honor the charge they made."

However, "to do and die" without reply or questioning why leaves no room for Owen's poetry because he had seen, firsthand, the physical effects of war, and called out the social norms by identifying an "old lie." The "old lie" couldn't compete with the sobering images of faces "sick of sin," the sounds of "gargling from the froth-corrupted lungs," and the realization of losing innocence with the "vile, incurable sores" on tongues that can no longer speak of "desperate glory." In one of Owen's first letters from the front (sent to his mother) he states, "There is a fine heroic feeling about being in France..." His experiences in the trenches of France would, however, make him shift his perspective from heroic to realistic. His insights into the reality of war changed the poet's role from romanticizing war like Tennyson (who read about the war in newspapers) and Brooke (who was in the Navy and never saw combat; ultimately dying of blood poisoning from an insect bite) to describing war in scenes of honest brutality based on firsthand experiences.

Owen's fellow warrior-poet, Siegfried Sassoon, also saw and wrote about the effects the war had on the attitudes of soldiers. Consider the actions taken in the sonnet "Attack" suddenly complemented with the attitude in the last two lines:

At dawn the ridge emerges massed and dun
In the wild purple of the glow'ring sun,
Smouldering through spouts of drifting smoke that shroud
The menacing scarred slope; and, one by one,
Tanks creep and topple forward to the wire.

The barrage roars and lifts. Then, clumsily bowed
With bombs and guns and shovels and battle-gear,
Men jostle and climb to, meet the bristling fire.
Lines of grey, muttering faces, masked with fear,
They leave their trenches, going over the top,
While time ticks blank and busy on their wrists,
And hope, with furtive eyes and grappling fists,
Flounders in mud. O Jesus, make it stop!

There is nothing to glorify, no patriotism or anything necessarily heroic in praying in "O Jesus, make it stop" as "hope... flounders in the mud." This is the soldier's perspective written from a subversive stance against the propaganda of social norms that had motivated young boys to patriotically volunteer to go to war. Sassoon's subversive stance did not stop at poetry as he wrote an open letter to the War Department refusing to fight any more and saying the war was merely being prolonged by forces that could stop it if they chose to. Sassoon's subversive pacifism (later taken up by philosopher Bertrand Russell, who urged the letter be read before the House of Commons) led him to expect a court-martial, but fellow poet Robert Graves intervened and convinced the chain of command that Sassoon needed to be hospitalized for shell-shock. In the hospital, Sassoon continued to write anti-war poems that graphically undermined the concepts of glory, honor, King and country. Many of these poems were published in *The War Poems of Siegfried Sassoon* and received strong public reactions. The Poetry Foundations' biography of Sassoon states, "Some readers complained that the poet displayed little patriotism, while others found his shockingly realistic depiction of war to be too extreme."

The social norm is to think that patriotism is an inherent characteristic of soldiers. It may be a correct thought, albeit too subjective to state as an absolute because the definition of the word "patriotism" differs in the application. Whereas the general population would take patriotism to be flag-waving and government-championing, a warrior-poet may apply a greater amount of patriotism by criticizing the issues facing society, or facing the society formed by his fellow soldiers. Having seen the absolute worst in men, the warrior-poet is in the best position to make points that could lead to social reforms. Warrior-poets not only demonstrate patriotism and a love for country, they also offer passionate insights into the truths held by social norms. Warrior-poets hold the counter-facts in their poetry to be brought forth against social truths. These counter-facts are formed by lived-through experiences.

In *Nine Gates*, Jane Hirshfield writes, "Passion for truth is an idea with more than one face. It includes the determination to look closely and long, to be unsatisfied with the secondhand and assumption." The concepts of what makes an act heroic are handed down as cultural artifacts. Heroism is the truth society expects from soldiers, but often speaking of heroism is just a way to cover up the realities—the truths—of war. Sassoon's "The Hero" makes the point:

> "Jack fell as he'd have wished," the mother said,
> And folded up the letter that she'd read.
> "The Colonel writes so nicely." Something broke
> In the tired voice that quavered to a choke.
> She half looked up. "We mothers are so proud
> Of our dead soldiers." Then her face was bowed.
>
> Quietly the Brother Officer went out.
> He'd told the poor old dear some gallant lies
> That she would nourish all her days, no doubt
> For while he coughed and mumbled, her weak eyes
> Had shone with gentle triumph, brimmed with joy,
> Because he'd been so brave, her glorious boy.
>
> He thought how "Jack", cold-footed, useless swine,
> Had panicked down the trench that night the mine
> Went up at Wicked Corner; how he'd tried
> To get sent home, and how, at last, he died,
> Blown to small bits. And no one seemed to care
> Except that lonely woman with white hair.

The social understanding that one should not speak badly about the dead perpetuates the concept of heroism, while the realities of war are swept away beneath the rugs of belief. Dying in war alleviates the truth, and allows myths to filter back into the accepted values of patriotic memorial. Sassoon's poem forces the reader to consider that "Jack" was not a hero, not a squared-away soldier, and did not fall "as he'd have wished" as his mother thought. In fact, mothers may not be proud of their dead soldiers, and would more likely want to have their sons at home than celebrated and memorialized beneath a government-provided marker. The gallant lies are really no replacement for the loss of sons, but the social norms are quick to hand out flags, award medals, and ceremoniously shoot rifles in the air in an effort to keep society from critically thinking about the mistakes, bad decisions, and secondary agendas it took to go (and stay) at war. In "The Poet as Hero," soldiers who had died in the misled, wrongly planned, poorly strategized war of attrition, are remembered by Sassoon:

> But now I've said good-bye to Galahad,
>   And am no more the knight of dreams and show:
> For lust and senseless hatred make me glad,
>   And my killed friends are with me where I go.
> Wound for red wound I burn to smite their wrongs;
>   And there is absolution in my songs.

In absolution, Sassoon points out society's sins. If he, as a warrior-poet, wasn't patriotic in the sense of wanting his country to do better than had been shown in World War I, he wouldn't need to point out political/military sins, absolve any wrongs, or remember the wasted lives of soldiers. England's experience in World War I would have long-lasting effects on the country's politics. Whether or not English Prime Minister Neville Chamberlain's "peace with honor" approach in the 1930's was an extension of the WWI experience (as presented by Owen, Sassoon, or others) is a topic for a separate debate, but the social stance towards war had certainly been changed by the war and the experiences of which warrior-poets wrote.

The devastation of the First World War was not only experienced by English warrior-poets. On the opposing side of no man's land, Germany and Austria had prepared for what Austrian writer, Stefan Zweig, called a "manly adventure." In an essay, "Stefan Zweig or Liberalism as Fate," Jose Maria Lassalle says of Zweig (even after he was moved away from the front lines) that "he soon became aware of the disaster the war would be, not only for Austria but for all of European civilization."

The war poetry written by these combat soldiers (combined with essays like Butler's "War is a Racket") forced—and forces—the readers of warrior-poet poetry to reconsider the historically romanticized perspectives of war. The 20th century would offer many more opportunities for poets to learn from Owen and Sassoon, and contribute their own insights into the actualities of war.

As alluded to above, mobilizing a nation into a full-scale war took more than coaxing Congress (as Wilson did in WWI) based on submarine warfare in the Atlantic. America's entry into World War II would take more provoking. A pre-war Gallup poll showed 88 percent of Americans did not want to enter the war in Europe. Japan was lured into attacking Pearl Harbor in response to political decisions by President Roosevelt:

> ... freezing her assets in America; closing the Panama Canal to her shipping; progressively halting vital exports to Japan until we finally joined Britain in an all-out embargo; sending a hostile note to the Japanese ambassador implying military threats if Tokyo did not alter its Pacific policies; and on November 26th—just 11 days before the Japanese attack—delivering an ultimatum that demanded, as prerequisites to resumed trade, that Japan withdraw all troops from China and Indochina, and in effect abrogate her Tripartite Treaty with Germany and Italy.

Yet, patriotic poetry still operates as if America was provoked. Consider Roger Hancock's 2010 poem, "Pearl Harbor Day" (one of many poems by the Patriot Poet at http://www.poetpatriot.com):

> World War Two drew in America,
> when Japan attacted (sic) Hawaii.
> Surprise attack in morning hours,
> woke the sleeping American giant.

Or Hancock's patriotism filled, "Surprised Infamy":

> A Nation's Infamy,
> attack within America.

Surprise attack,
wounds or kills four thousand,
early on that dreadful morn.
Sounds of planes overhead,
alarms ring, howl, screech,
rude awakening from dead of sleep.
Battle-stations, orders called,
unexpected confusion, duty calls.
One hundred planes overhead,
Japan's last emperor ordered,
attack that lives in infamy.
American battleships... five,
American destroyers... three,
four hundred planes all destroyed.
News spreads as wildfire.
"Pearl Harbor Attacked!"
President Roosevelt pledges,
"...triumph. So help us God."
America sleeps no more,
Two fronts fought 'til victory,
domination interests quelled.
December 7, remembrance,
Pearl Harbor attack,
Felt around the world.

Hancock is not a veteran, and his imagination is fueled by social standards of patriotic sentiment, providing words for those who have none. He provides no witness to the events, and is in danger of misrepresenting—if not misappropriating—the authenticity of history. It is with remembrance of this kind that a society can reject critical thinking, hold on to its romanticized truths, wave patriotic flags, and ultimately forget the past.

Thomas McGrath, on the other hand, was a veteran of World War II and provides a more realistic perception of what the war (and fighting in it) was like in his poem, "Remembering That Island" which ends with a counter-fact to social truth:

I see the vast stinking Pacific suddenly awash
Once more with bodies, landings on all beaches,
The bodies of dead and living gone back to appointed
    places,
A ten year old resurrection,
And myself once more in the scourging wind, waiting,
    waiting
While the rich oratory and the lying famous corrupt
Senators mine our lives for another war.

It requires a subversive tone to declare that "Senators mine our lives for another war" when senators are elected to represent the people—not mine their lives. In his testimony before the House Committee of Un-American Activities, McGrath stated, "The view of life which we receive through the great works of art is a privileged one—it is a view of life according to probability or necessity, not subject to the chance and accident of our real world and therefore in a sense truer than the life we see lived all around us."

The truer than life experiences may not be what a society or an individual expects. James Dickey's poem, "The Firebombing," personalizes the scene; not knowing what exactly to feel because "death will not be what it should."

Gun down
The engines, the eight blades sighing
For the moment when the roofs will connect
Their flames, and make a town burning with all
American fire.
                        Reflections of houses catch;
Fire shuttles from pond to pond
In every direction, till hundreds flash with one death.
With this in the dark of the mind,
Death will not be what it should;
Will not, even now, even when
My exhaled face in the mirror
Of bars, dilates in a cloud like Japan.
The death of children is ponds
Shutter-flashing; responding mirrors; it climbs

The terraces of hills
Smaller and smaller, a mote of red dust
At a hundred feet; at a hundred and one it goes out.
That is what should have got in
To my eye

And shown the insides of houses, the low tables
Catch fire from the floor mats,
Blaze up in gas around their heads
Like a dream of suddenly growing
Too intense for war. Ah, under one's dark arms
Something strange-scented falls—when those on earth
Die, there is not even sound;
One is cool and enthralled in the cockpit,
Turned blue by the power of beauty,
In a pale treasure-hole of soft light
Deep in aesthetic contemplation,
Seeing the ponds catch fire
And cast it through ring after ring
Of land: O death in the middle
Of acres of inch-deep water!

The power of the plane's eight blades, and the subsequent fiery explosions
perform exactly as designed, burning the town with "all/American fire."
Presenting the fire as all-American, Dickey brings in the jingoistic attitude
of the absolute righteousness of bombing a town. The pilot, upon seeing the
destruction, has an emotional response knowing he has destroyed the town,
killed children, and laid to waste a countryside. However, the emotions are
layered in the subjectivity of meeting one's obligations, destroying against
one's morals, admiring the absolute power of technological capabilities, and
struggling with the guilt of killing and the guilt of admiring the ability. It's
a guilt for not feeling guilty for being guilty. This is a very effective challenge
to the simple, idealistic concepts of war glory.

The "… triumph. So help us God" sentiment of Hancock's poetry goes
hand-in-hand with America's self-perception, and the victory in World War
II established "The Greatest Generation." However, by declaring a greatest

generation, America (by definition) is in decline. To defend herself from this decline, America mobilized troops to the Republic of Korea and Vietnam. Those two conflicts provided senators lives to mine for another war. The momentum of victory may have been felt and may have persuaded subsequent generations to join the military, but upon enduring combat in those conflicts, other generations of warrior-poets emerged.

Asking three simple questions in his poem, "Sure," William Wantling, a Korean War veteran raises doubt about getting back to a "normal" life while pointing out that too much has been lost to the experiences of defending that society against communism.

> but
> can you be a
> pacifist
> after you've killed
> too many
> & if one is too many
> where do I stand
> with my score?
> what I wouldn't
> give to go back, to
> start all over
>
> and you?

This expands the warrior-poet from not only experiencing and writing about war, but also returning from war with the changes in personality, beliefs, and values that have occurred. Doubtless, there are life experiences that change people, but the combat experience changes veterans in a way that challenges the idealism of the society they are fighting for. Korea may be a "forgotten war," but the experiences the veterans lived through cannot be forgotten, and are barriers in the way of returning to the idyllic nature of American society. (Wantling himself ended up in prison on drug charges.)

An excerpt from Keith Wilson's poem, "The Captain," helps understand why the return to idyllic America is difficult; if not impossible.

& what happened to his eyes
the changes when he spoke of their raids
of villages flaming, women and children
machinegunned as they ran
screaming from their huts:

The gunning down of women and children is rarely documented in history books or in school lessons. Neither do these episodes make it onto recruiting posters. Honesty (or dishonesty) in advertising is only relevant when selling beauty products; it is not a necessary aspect of recruiting young people into the military.

However, the truer view of service is present in the work of warrior-poets. Though a country may stereotype the honorable nature of military duty, the combat soldier is put in situations in which behaviors, thoughts, reactions, and even language are less than honorable. In his book, *Interrogations*, Leroy V. Quintana, a Vietnam veteran, poetically documents many episodes in which the American ideal of her soldiers fell disturbingly short of the stereotype. Consider the poem, "Johnny Johnson."

The last thing anybody would've called Johnny
Was a gung ho GI. He hated the Army.
He had a brother in Nam
So really didn't have to be in the war.
The last I heard of him
He was sporting a large necklace of rotting ears,
His M-16 steady on Rock 'n Roll.

"Sporting a necklace of rotting ears" is not an ideal picture of a soldier serving his country honorably. Quintana's honest depiction of Johnny's mindset in the jungles of Vietnam with "his M-16 steady on Rock 'n Roll" (i.e., set on the automatic setting to fire as many rounds as possible with one squeeze of the trigger) is a subversive undermining of the idealistic—if not naïve—perception of an infantryman's behavior in combat.

Released from the constraints of American society, Johnny is free to let his individual nature emerge, giving Quintana what McGrath called "a view of life according to probability or necessity" and a view "truer than the life we see lived all around us." Quintana's poems challenge the home-front definitions of what it means to serve in America's wartime military. For instance, doing one's duty is a romanticized notion replaced by doing what one has to do to survive. In "Booker," a soldier is "in the boonies up north/long enough to get jungle rot on both feet/on purpose..." to get some hospital time and hopefully be sent back "to the world." Instead, upon hearing he was headed "to the DMZ, he said, no,/not Demilitarized, baby,/that's Dead Marine Zone."

Doing what a soldier has to do to survive is often less than romantic, and Quintana's poems point that out clearly; "better/KP than KIA" a sergeant would say in "Sergeant Sterling." In "Recondo Sergeant," the experienced sergeant told the reconnaissance patrol "one way of keeping warm during monsoon/was to piss in our pants." But Quintana's poems often address more than the individual soldier's necessity to survive. There is an undercurrent of unethical—illegal—behaviors that are expected and accepted by the witnesses. These poems of witness are powerful and present strong evidence of the subversive nature of Quintana's poems that challenge and undermine the social norms that keep a certain, accepted truth satisfied with the secondhand and assumption. In "Interrogations," an interrogator, faced with "a gook who wouldn't talk," wired the man's genitals to a piece of electronic gear, "cranked like crazy." The person would talk then, "in Vietnamese, English/or Greek." In "POW," a Special Forces captain promises a prisoner that he will take him out and "put a .45 to his head." The next morning, there was "not a trace" of the POW and that left "everybody shaking their heads in admiration./The captain sure was a man of his word all right."

Doug Anderson, a combat medic in Vietnam, also writes poems that are very honest depictions of combat episodes that would challenge the idealistic perceptions of socio-political entities, as well as the general public, in America. In "Mamasan," Anderson captures a mindful moment that summarizes the war experience:

> We ride on tanks over the new rice,
> break down the dikes so the dirty water
> runs in with the clear. They run beside us,
> little claw gestures toward their mouths,
> *This is what we eat you are running over.*

We look back without expression.
Mamasan stands in front of the lead tank,
hoe raised over her head.
It is not her time to die. The tank stops,
driver comes out of the hatch to look.
Mamasan makes a sound like an old hinge,
shuffles forward,
breaks the tank's searchlight with her hoe.

The actions of an uncaring tank crew rolling through the livelihood of local farmers reveals an attitude of military members far from the stereotyped, romanticized mobility of great army. The human understanding of destroying the rice dikes being a less-than positive thing to do is juxtaposed with the soldier's understanding of having to maintain a sense of inhumanity. It's war, and the rice dikes are merely one more casualty. This creates a tension in the poem between the soldiers and the farmers suddenly represented by the most human of all beings, the Mamasan. Running along beside the tanks, with their destructive power and invincibility, she becomes a spokesperson for the farmers, but also for humanity. The soldiers are destroying the fields that feed the locals and in no universe should this be acceptable.

Soldiers are expected to deploy, do their jobs, complete their missions, and return home where, in Vietnam veteran vernacular, "the rest is gravy." But in Quintana's poem "Jimmy," that idea is quickly eradicated:

Jimmy was always alone since that day
the VC surrounded his recon team
and he was the one the chopper brought back alive.
His eyes. Those so green, so weary
such inexplicably shattered eyes.
His life awarded him posthumously.
He would haunt himself forever.

There's no gravy in this poem. It is a simple seven-line challenge to anyone who thinks war ends for the soldier when the rotation back to the States comes due or when discharge comes down through channels. It is a hard re-acclimation into a society where truth is tainted by a lack of facts.

The acquired counter-facts, however, permeate the lives of warrior-poets. Quintana's poem, "An Open Letter to President Bush," resurfaces his subversive position to not only question the president's decision, but to also re-introduce his own experiences and argue against the social truths by pointing out that President Bush "might not/make war/seem so unbelievably/easy." There may be nothing more subversive than writing an open letter to a standing president that disagrees with a pending decision. In this case, it is the first President Bush, and the war against Iraq being considered in the liberation of Kuwait; i.e. The Gulf War. Quintana's language in this poem is not as concise or as direct as the language he uses in many of his other poems, but still the language works here; because first, it is the language of a letter, and secondly it is the language of a parent, a veteran, and a citizen with a sense of urgency to stop the decision.

It would take a catastrophic event to pull America back into a long-term war with people's initial support. This support was garnered by fear and lies; another "old lie" full of propaganda using patriotism to get young men to join the military and fight terrorists for what they did on September 11, 2001. The War on Terrorism deployed American troops into Iraq and Afghanistan ready to reclaim the glory of "The Greatest Generation." It didn't take long for artists to emerge with subversive counter-facts to point out the futility of the effort. Bloggers like Colby Buzzell captured the gruesome realities, and poets like Brian Turner emerged with a warrior-voice to write poems of witness based on actual episodes. Turner's "Here, Bullet" (from the collection of the same name) invites a bullet to enter his body because that is "where the world ends, every time." As American civilian society was often oblivious to the war, daily routines went uninterrupted, and the "old lie" permeated the idealistic regions of service. Yellow ribbons went up, and again Tennyson-type sentiment went out to not support the war, but always support the troops. There was very little understanding of, and perhaps very little interest in, what soldiers faced on a day-to-day basis. The hardships of being deployed numerous times into a war where the front lines kept shifting offered very little decrease in the pressure, anxiety, or daily tensions of the effort while American society kept pace with normal routines without sacrifice.

With no thought about the innocence being lost, killing was part of the duty, and the duty was expected without very much concern from the home-front at all. The resultant mindset of an all-volunteer military is no one should fight who doesn't want to. Of course, this disregards many reasons people join the military. But one reason at the bottom of the list—if people knew the fullest extent of what fighting entails—would be to kill. Turner writes:

> Sadiq
> *It is a condition of wisdom in the archer to be patient*
> *because when the arrow leaves the bow, it returns no more*
> —Sa'di
>
> It should make you shake and sweat,
> nightmare you, strand you in a desert
> of irrevocable desolation, the consequences
> seared into the vein, no matter what adrenaline
> feeds the muscle its courage, no matter
> what god shines down on you, no matter
> what crackling pain and anger
> you carry in your fists, my friend,
> it should break your heart to kill.

"It should break your heart to kill." And it does; at least for those who have killed, or who have had to watch others kill. However, America remains a warring nation not interested in "peace with honor," and, paradoxically, stays able to govern in a global environment with ideas like "disarmament through armament" presented grandly and accepted by still-occupied countries. The "shock and awe" bombardment of Baghdad spoke volumes about the American culture; a culture slow to interject with diplomacy. The passion for American truth is content on the secondhand and the assumptions that maintain a status quo. The more critical understanding of global events (cause-and-effect events) is lost on the general public that is emerging as the most-entertained and least-informed citizenry in the history of civilization.

Those artists who heed Atena Farghadani's call to criticize the social issues must attack the issues in such a way that leads to social reform. Otherwise, the criticism is a continuation of betrayal that will not allow society to become better on its genuine path to being the best. In Farghadani's sense of betrayal, societies maintain a silent desire not to be betrayed because the individual sub-systems and human entities within the overall system do not want to be criticized, and have mechanisms in place to ensure they are not criticized. (Farghadani is in a Tehran prison serving a twelve-year sentence because her art offended the Iranian government.)

Warrior-poets are poets of witness who have the capacity to write from a more honest, realistic perspective. The issues of society need to be criticized because only through criticism can perfection emerge. Again, McGrath's testimony gives the strength to find perfection to artists and their works of art: "The view of life which we receive through the great works of art is a privileged one—it is a view of life according to probability or necessity, not subject to the chance and accident of our real world and therefore in a sense truer than the life we see lived all around us." The artist, the literary artist, the poet, and especially the warrior-poet have the capacity to see beyond chance and accident. They provide a view truer than the life society accepts. Society should listen to the criticism, for the counter-facts of truth are in there hiding. In the introduction in *Against Forgetting*, Carolyn Forché writes, "one has to be willing to accept the trauma" associated with personal and social issues.

APPENDIX 1

America's battlefield history:

The Revolutionary War, Chickamauga War, Northwest Indian War, The Whisky Rebellion, The Quasi-War, The First Barbary War, Tecumseh's War, The War of 1812, Creek War, The Second Barbary War, The First Seminole War, Texas Indian Wars, The Arikara War, The Aegean Sea Anti-Piracy Operations, The Winnebago War, The First Sumatran Expedition, The Black Hawk War, The Second Seminole War, The Patriot War, The United States Exploring Expedition, The Second Sumatran Expedition, The Capture of Monterey, The Mexican-American War, The Cayuse War, The Taiping Rebellion, The Apache Wars, The Bombardment of Greytown, The Puget Sound War, The First Fiji Expedition, The Rogue River Wars, The Third Seminole War, Yakima War, The Filibuster War, the Second Opium War, The Utah War, The Navaho Wars, The Second Fiji Expedition, The First and Second Cortina Wars, The Paiute War, The Reform War, The American Civil War, The Bombardment of Qui Noh'n (Vietnam), The Yavapai Wars, The Dakota War of 1862, The Colorado War, The Shimonoseki War, The Snake War, The Powder River War, Red Cloud's War, Siege of Mexico City, The Formosa Expedition, The Comanche Campaign, The United States Expedition to Korea, The Modoc War, The Red River War, The Las Cuevas War, The Great Sioux War of 1878, The Buffalo Hunter's War, The Nez Perce War, The San Elizario Salt War, The Bannock War, The Cheyenne War, The Sheep-eater Indian War, Victorio's War, The White River War, The Egyptian Expedition, The Pine Ridge Campaign, The Garza Revolution, The Overthrow of the Kingdom of Hawaii, The Brazilian Naval Revolt, The Yaqui Wars, The Second Samoan Civil Wars, The Spanish American War, The Philippine-American War, The Moro Rebellion, The Boxer Rebellion, The Crazy Snake Rebellion, The Border War, The Negro Rebellion (Cuba), The Occupation of Nicaragua, The Bluff War, The Occupation of Haiti, The Sugar Intervention (Cuba), The Occupation of the Dominican Republic, World War One, The Russian Civil War, The Bombardment of Samsun (Turkey), The Posey War, World War Two, The Korean War, The Lebanon Crisis, The Bay of Pigs Invasion (Cuba), The Dominican Civil War, The Vietnam War, Shaba II, The Multinational Force in Lebanon, The Invasion of Grenada, The Tanker War (Persian Gulf), The Invasion of Panama, The Gulf War, Iraqi No-Fly Zones, The Somali Civil War, The Intervention in Haiti, The Bosnian War, The Kosovo War, The War in Afghanistan, The Iraq War, The War in Pakistan, Operation Ocean Shield, The Libyan Civil War, and The War on ISIL.

And when there wasn't an active conflict in which to be involved, America had a forty-plus-year Cold War against communism with the Soviet Union.

REFERENCES

Anderson, Doug. "Mamasan." *The Moon Reflected Fire*. Farmington, ME: Alice James Books, 1994.

Brooke, Rupert. "The Soldier." Poets.org. Academy of American Poets.

Butler, Smedley. "War Is a Racket." www.ratical.org/ratville/CAH/warisaracket.html. 1935.

Crane, Stephen, and Joseph Katz. "War Is Kind." *The Complete Poems of Stephen Crane*. Ithaca, NY: Cornell UP, 1972.

Dickey, James. "The Firebombing." *Buckdancer's Choice*. Middletown, CT: Wesleyan UP, 1965.

Farhgadani, Atena, www.zenpencils.com/comic/atena. 2015.

Forché, Carolyn, ed. *Against Forgetting: Twentieth Century Poetry of Witness*. New York: W. W. Norton, 1993.

Espada, Martin. *The Lover of a Subversive Is Also a Subversive: Essays and Commentaries*. Ann Arbor, MI: The University of Michigan Press, 2010.

Hancock, Roger. "Pearl Harbor." PoetPatriot.com. 2010.

Hancock, Roger. "Surprised Infamy." PoetPatriot.com. 2010.

Hirshfield, Jane. Nine Gates: Entering the Mind of Poetry: Essays. New York: HarperCollins, 1997.

Hong, Cathy Park. "Delusions of Whiteness in the Avant-Garde." Lana Turner Journal. 2015.

Jarrell, Randall. "The Death of the Ball Turret Gunner." New York: Farrar, Straus and Giroux, 1981.

Lassalle, Jose Maria. "Stefan Zweig or Liberalism as Fate." 2003.

Martinez, Demetria. "Rules of Engagement." *The Devil's Workshop*. Tucson, AZ: The University of Arizona Press, 2002.

McGrath, Thomas. "'Remembering That Island." *The Movie at the End of the World: Collected Poems*. Athens, OH: Ohio University Press, 1973.

McGrath, Thomas. "Thomas McGrath's Statement to HUAC."

Owen, Wilfred. "Dulce Et Decorum Est." Poetry Foundation. Poetry Foundation.

Perloff, James. "Pearl Harbor: Hawaii Was Surprised; FDR Was Not." Pearl Harbor: Hawaii Was Surprised; FDR Was Not. 2014.

Poetry Foundation. "Siegfried Sassoon." https://www.poetryfoundation.org/poets/siegfried-sassoon.

Quintana, Leroy V. "Johnny Johnson." *Interrogations*. Chevy Chase, MD: Burning Cities Press, 1990.

Quintana, Leroy V. "Booker." *Interrogations*. Chevy Chase, MD: Burning Cities Press, 1990.

Quintana, Leroy V. "POW." *Interrogations*. Chevy Chase, MD: Burning Cities Press, 1990.

Quintana, Leroy V. "Sergeant Sterling." *Interrogations*. Chevy Chase, MD: Burning Cities Press, 1990.

Quintana, Leroy V. "Recondo Sergeant." *Interrogations*. Chevy Chase, MD: Burning Cities Press, 1990.

Quintana, Leroy V. "Interrogations." *Interrogations*. Chevy Chase, MD: Burning Cities Press, 1990.

Quintana, Leroy V. "Jimmy." *Interrogations*. Chevy Chase, MD: Burning Cities Press, 1990.

Quintana, Leroy V. "An Open Letter to President Bush." *Interrogations*. Chevy Chase, MD: Burning Cities Press, 1990.

Sartre, Jean. "What Is Literature." *What Is Literature? and Other Essays*. Cambridge, Mass.: Harvard UP, 1988.

Tennyson, Alfred. "The Charge of the Light Brigade." 1870.

Turner, Brian. "Here, Bullet." *Here, Bullet*. Farmington, Maine: Alice James Books, 2005

Scutts, Joanna. "The True Story of Rupert Brooke - The New Yorker." The New Yorker. 23 Apr. 2015.

Sassoon, Siegfried. *The War Poems of Siegfried Sassoon*. London: Faber and Faber, 1983.

Wantling, William. "Sure." *The Source*. Dust Books, 1966.

Wilson, Keith. "The Captain." *Graves Registry*. Clark City Press, 1992.

J.G. McClure

WHY I WRITE, OR, IT'S THE END OF THE WORLD AS WE KNOW IT AND I FEEL (SORTA) FINE

I remember as a kid going to a science museum somewhere in Missouri. They had an exhibit—basically a rickety computer with MS Paint hooked up to a radio transmitter. The idea was this: you'd draw a picture, the transmitter would transmit it upward, and *voila*, your masterpiece would travel out among the stars, waiting for distant life-forms to receive it. Whether this actually happened or whether it's merely a cocktail of youthful misunderstanding and nostalgia is beside the point. I remember it, and I remember the conviction that aliens would discover my rudimentary stick figure family and feel a pang of pathos for life on our little rock.

This was a great deal of pressure. If the drawing was bad, what would that say about our society? The aliens who found my little sketch—the lines rough, the colors off—might decide not to visit us after all. Or worse, they might rain fiery death down on us all for my grave sins against representational art. (My sketches were not good. If that turns out to be what dooms our world, I apologize.)

A 2015 piece in *Esquire*, entitled "When the End of Civilization Is Your Day Job, or, Ballad of the Sad Climatologists," explores the "pre-traumatic stress" experienced by climate researchers: the prevailing sense of apocalypse among the folks who know apocalypse best. The story describes "the gradual shift from hope of prevention to plans for adaptation" to an Earth so unrecognizable that we shouldn't even call it Earth anymore. (One writer proposes "Eaarth.") Even the "optimists" of the story speak of glacial melt, rising sea levels, and the obliteration of coastal cities worldwide as a foregone conclusion. As one researcher puts it, "We're fucked." Some of the less-hopeful scientists have moved into the woods (as far inland as possible) and set up off-grid cabins to wait out the end of days.

Of course, apocalyptic predictions are nothing new. Christianity has argued that we're living in the latter days pretty much since its inception. (Odd, then, that the GOP-Fundamentalist Complex so vehemently denies climate change—this is what they've been waiting for!) And it's no secret that everyone who lives dies—we each face our own private End of Days.

But our contemporary vision of the end seems different in that it erases the traditional hopes of immortality. The tormentedly atheist *Generación de '98* poet and playwright Miguel de Unamuno famously said that there are only three ways to cheat death: plant a tree, raise a kid, or write a book. For a long time I've put all my hopes in the book category. I'm certainly not the first: Shakespeare is full of boasts about how his poems will immortalize him and/or his beloved:

> Nor shall Death brag thou wander'st in his shade,
> When in eternal lines to time thou grow'st:
> So long as men can breathe or eyes can see,
> So long lives this, and this gives life to thee.

This is a species of immortality, but a deeply contingent one: when humans *can't* breathe anymore, the beloved finally, truly dies. At the time of writing, that wasn't a great concern. But now that we live in a world in which it is taken as a matter of course that on certain days it isn't safe to breathe the air (see Beijing or Los Angeles), the line has a new and unintended sense of menace.

There are countless examples, each equally contingent. Take Keats's fears that he may cease to be, Romanticism at large, Gilgamesh's tower, Beowulf's eulogy. Or take the oft-anthologized Aztec song "No acabarán mis flores" as translated by Miguel León-Portilla:

> No acabarán mis flores,
> No acabarán mis flores,
> no cesarán mis cantos.
> Yo cantor los elevo,
> se reparten, se esparcen.
> Aun cuando las flores
> se marchitan y amarillecen,
> serán llevadas allá, al interior de la casa
> del ave de plumas de oro.

The argument is familiar: even when flowers wither, *my* flowers (poems) will not end; they will be carried up into the house of the golden-feathered bird. This comes from an oral tradition: the singing of the poem is what allows it to transcend and endure. But today, when shifting climates stunt the flowers and drive the birds extinct (Jonathan Franzen has argued in the *New Yorker* that at this stage we should treat conservation as a kind of palliative care: give the birds preserves on which to die out a little more comfortably), how much comfort is left in this boast? Who sings the songs once we can't breathe the air?

There's a moment I love in *Futurama*. Fry, our lovable but dopey hero who has awoken thousands of years in the future, comes upon the dusty ruin of the Statue of Liberty. He falls to his knees à la Charlton Heston in *Planet of the Apes*, and cries, "No! They did it! They blew it up!" But then something dark and wonderful happens: the camera begins to pan out, revealing more and more ruined Statues of Liberty:

> And then the apes blew up *their* society too! How could this happen? And then the birds took over and ruined *their* society! And the cows—and then, I don't know, is that a slug maybe?

The implication is hilariously, devastatingly cyclical: history repeats itself, side by side, again and again, leading always to the same grim end. Ecocritics often call for the dismantling of our anthropocentric worldview—*Futurama* here argues that even if we manage to decenter humanity, the end is still nigh: once the cows get smart enough, they'll find a way to ruin the planet too.

Of course, not all climatologists think it's too late for us to make the changes necessary to keep the Earth livable for us, and it has been rightly pointed out that throwing up our hands and saying we're fucked doesn't do any good. I want to believe that the world's politicos will be able to set aside their squabbles and establish real sustainability legislature. I'm hoping for the best—but I'm expecting the worst. (A pretty common attitude, it seems—just look at the nihilistic GOP Presidential Debate Drinking Game articles around the web, including one from *TIME*!)

The first book about poetry that I ever read was Mary Oliver's *A Poetry Handbook*. It's heady stuff for a teenage undergraduate, and it made me feel that meaningful writing was at once impossible and crucial. I most remember Oliver writing, "I like to say that I write poems for a stranger who will be born in some distant country hundreds of years from now.... It reminds me, forcefully, that everything necessary must be on the page." Perhaps truly getting everything necessary on the page is impossible. Perhaps art depends on some shared frame of reference—Homer's "winedark sea" is beautiful because we know wine and we know seas. Flash forward a few millennia from where we stand today, and maybe that framework simply won't exist anymore. Maybe we simply won't exist anymore.

But the poet John Skoyles has spoken of "illusions that serve me well." That is, those ideas that, true or not, allow him to keep going. Here's mine: I want poetry that preserves us, warts and all.

If it is in fact too late for us, then when the slug-monsters inherit the Earth or aliens show up to terraform our barren planet, I want them to know what we were, how we lived.

Maybe then they'll feel that pang of pathos I hoped for as I beamed my stick figures into space as a boy. Maybe, as they come to know us in all our triumphs and our failings, we can be a beauty and a warning—and the ruin can end with us.

SUGGESTED READINGS

Tanis MacDonald—
One! Hundred! Demons! by Lynda J. Barry
The Triggering Town: Lectures and Essays on Poetry and Writing by Richard Hugo
"The Near Transitive Properties of the Political and the Poetic: Erasure" by Solmaz
   Sharif
"Twenty-Two Poem Hacks." by Carmen Giménez Smith
The Misfit's Manifesto by Lidia Yuknavitch

Christine Riddle—
A Room of One's Own by Virginia Woolf
The Writing Life by Annie Dillard

David Shumate—
The Triggering Town: Lectures and Essays on Poetry and Writing by Richard Hugo
The Poetry Home Repair Manual: Practical Advice for Beginning Poets by Ted Kooser
One Hundred Poems from the Chinese and *Love and the Turning Year: One Hundred
   More Poems from the Chinese* translated by Kenneth Rexroth

Rishi Dastidar—
An Introduction to English Poetry by James Fenton
101 Sonnets from Shakespeare to Heaney edited by Don Paterson
The Hatred of Poetry by Ben Lerner

Kyle Flak—
"Personism: A Manifesto" by Frank O'Hara
"The Art of Poetry" by Kenneth Koch
The Paris Review interviews
The Poets on Poetry series from University of Michigan Press

Michelle Bonczek Evory—
"Writing Off the Subject" by Richard Hugo
"A Way of Writing" by William Stafford
The Poet's Companion: A Guide to the Pleasures of Writing Poetry by Kim Addonizio
   and Dorianne Laux

The Sounds of Poetry by Robert Pinsky
The Life of Poetry by Muriel Rukeyser

Jennifer Moore—
The Art of the Poetic Line by James Longenbach
The Art of Description by Mark Doty
A Primer for Poets and Readers of Poetry by Gregory Orr
Bird by Bird: Some Instructions on Writing and Life by Anne Lamott
Madness, Rack, and Honey by Mary Ruefle

Michael Angel Martín—
The Essential Haiku: Versions of Basho, Buson, & Issa by Robert Hass
Responses: Prose Pieces, 1953-1976 (1976 / 2000) by Richard Wilbur
Finders Keepers by Seamus Heaney
The Poem's Heartbeat by Alfred Corn

David M. Harris—
The Ode Less Traveled by Stephen Fry
The Book of Forms by Lewis Turco
Patterns of Poetry by Miller Williams
The Triggering Town: Lectures and Essays on Poetry and Writing by Richard Hugo
Princeton Encyclopedia of Poetry & Poetics
A Poet's Glossary by Edward Hirsch
A rhyming dictionary: there are plenty of good ones.

Michael Collins—
The Flexible Lyric by Ellen Bryant Voigt
Poets Teaching Poets: Self and the World edited by Ellen Bryant Voigt and Gregory
    Orr
The Demon and the Angel: Searching for the Source of Artistic Inspiration by Edward
    Hirsch
After Confession: Poetry as Autobiography edited Kate Sontag and David Graham
Real Sofistikashun: Essays on Poetry and Craft by Tony Hoagland

Rob Carney—
The Triggering Town: Lectures and Essays on Poetry and Writing by Richard Hugo
The Poetry Home Repair Manual: Practical Advice for Beginning Poets by Ted Kooser

Melanie Faith—
The Poet's Companion: A Guide to the Pleasures of Writing Poetry by Kim Addonizio
The Poetry Dictionary by John Drury
Ordering the Storm: How to Put Together a Book of Poems by Susan Grimm
Poemcrazy: Freeing Your Life with Words by Susan G. Wooldridge

Nancy Scott—
Handbook of Poetic Forms by Ron Padgett
The Crafty Poet: A Portable Workshop by Diane Lockward
Best Words, Best Order: Essays on Poetry by Steven Dobyns
Real Sofistikashun: Essays on Poetry and Craft by Tony Hoagland

Jenny Ferguson—
The Art of Attention: The Poet's Eye by Donald Revell
The Art of Intimacy: The Space Between by Stacey D'Erasmo
The Art of Recklessness: Poetry as Assertive Force and Contradiction by Dean Young
The Art of Syntax: Rhythm of Thought, Rhythm of Song by Ellen Bryant Voigt
The Art of the Poetic Line by James Longenbach

Whitney Sweet—
Mentor Me: Instruction and Advice for Aspiring Writers edited by Heidi Stock
The Writing Life by Annie Dillard
"The Figure a Poem Makes" by Robert Frost

Barbara Perry—
Writing Down the Bones: Freeing the Writer Within and *Thunder and Lightning: Cracking Open the Writer's Craft* by Natalie Goldberg

Norman Minnick—
ABC of Reading by Ezra Pound
De/Compositions by W. D. Snodgrass
Work toward Knowing: Beginning with Blake by Jim Watt
New & Selected Essays by Denise Levertov
Selected Letters of John Keats

Dike Okoro—
Letters to a Young Poet by Rainer Maria Rilke
Very Young Poets by Gwendolyn Brooks
West African Verse by Donatus Ibe Nwoga
The Poetry Home Repair Manual: Practical Advice for Beginning Poets by Ted Kooser
A Poetry Handbook by Mary Oliver

Emily Stoddard—
Nine Gates: Entering the Mind of Poetry by Jane Hirshfield
In the Palm of Your Hand: The Poet's Portable Workshop by Steve Kowit
Poemcrazy: Freeing Your Life with Words by Susan Goldsmith Wooldridge
"Learning the Poetic Line" by Rebecca Hazelton
"Message to Poets" by Thomas Merton

Jason McCall—
The Teachers and Writers Handbook of Poetic Forms by Ron Padgett

Tara Skurtu—
"On Fear" by Mary Ruefle
The Sounds of Poetry and *Singing School: Learning to Write (and Read) Poetry by Studying with the Masters* by Robert Pinsky
The Making of a Poem: A Norton Anthology of Poetic Forms by Mark Strand and Eavan Boland

David Bergman—
Studies in the History of the Renaissance by Walter Pater
Pleasures of the Text by Roland Barthes
Twentieth Century Pleasures by Robert Hass

John Langfeld—
Anything by Stephen Dunn

Kelly Cherry—
MLA Handbook, 8th edition. Because grammar and punctuation still matter.
Making Your Own Days: The Pleasures of Reading and Writing Poetry by Kenneth Koch
Why I Write by George Orwell
Rhyme's Reason: A Guide to English Verse by John Hollander
The Art of Syntax: Rhythm of Thought, Rhythm of Song by Ellen Bryan Voigt

J.G. McClure—
The Poet's Companion: A Guide to the Pleasures of Writing Poetry by Kim Addonizio and Dorianne Laux
A Poetry Handbook by Mary Oliver
The Art of the Poetic Line by James Longenbach
The Art of Syntax by Ellen Bryant Voigt
"The Four Temperaments of Poetry" by Gregory Orr

Stacey Balkun—
Letters to a Young Poet by Rainer Maria Rilke, translated by Stephen Mitchell
The Art of Daring by Carl Phillips

Zoë Brigley—
Sunbathing in the Rain: A Cheerful Book About Depression by Gwyneth Lewis
The Poetics of Dislocation by Meena Alexander

Language for a New Century: Contemporary Poetry from the Middle East, Asia, and Beyond edited by Tina Chang, Nathalie Handel, and Ravi Shankar.
The Cambridge Introduction to Creative Writing by David Morley

Chaun Ballard—
A Poet's Glossary by Edward Hirsch
Writing Poems by Robert Wallace and Michelle Boisseau
Can Poetry Matter? Essays on Poetry and American Culture by Dana Gioia

Michael Rather, Jr.—
Western Wind: An Introduction to Poetry by David Mason and John Frederick Nims
On Poetry & Craft by Theodore Roethke
The New Book of Forms: A Handbook of Poetic by Lewis Turco
The Art of Recklessness by Dean Young
A Test of Poetry by Louis Zukofsky

John Robinson—
Fables of Identity: Studies in Poetic Mythology by Northrop Frye
Claims for Poetry edited by Donald Hall
"Feeling into Words" by Seamus Heaney
The Triggering Town: Lectures and Essays on Poetry and Writing by Richard Hugo
On Poetry & Craft: Selected Prose of Theodore Roethke by Carolyn Kizer

Jaydn DeWald—
A Field Guide to Contemporary Poetry and Poetics edited by Stuart Friebert, David Walker, and David Young
"Traveling Between Languages" by Chen Li, translated by Chang Fen-Ling
The Cracks between What We Are and What We Are Supposed to Be: Essays and Interviews by Harryette Mullen
The Uncertain Certainty: Interviews, Essays, and Notes on Poetry by Charles Simic
The Art of Recklessness: Poetry as Assertive Force and Contradiction by Dean Young

Nathan McClain—
Best Words, Best Order by Stephen Dobyns
The Flexible Lyric and *The Art of Syntax* by Ellen Bryant Voigt
"The Four Temperaments" by Gregory Orr
The Art of the Poetic Line James Longenbach

Thom Tammaro—
The Winged Energy of Delight: Selected Translations by Robert Bly
Writing Down the Bones: Freeing the Writer Within by Natalie Goldberg

The Triggering Town: Lectures and Essays on Poetry and Writing by Richard Hugo
Writing the Australian Crawl: Views on the Writer's Vocation by William Stafford
Wingbeats: Exercises and Practice in Poetry edited by Scott Wiggerman and David
　Meischen

Victoria L. Davis—
Writing Down the Bones: Freeing the Writer Within by Natalie Goldberg
The Poet's Companion: A Guide to the Pleasures of Writing Poetry by Kim Addonizio
　and Dorianne Laux

Natalie Homer—
Ordinary Genius: A Guide for the Poet Within by Kim Addonizio
Spreading the Word: Editors on Poetry edited by Stephen Corey
The Art of the Poetic Line by James Longenbach

C. Kubasta—
The Practice of Poetry edited by Robin Behn & Chase Twichell
Break, Blow, Burn by Camille Paglia
My Unwritten Books by George Steiner

Kevin Pilkington—
Best Words, Best Order by Stephen Dobyns
Writing Well by Donald Hall
The Triggering Town: Lectures and Essays on Poetry and Writing by Richard Hugo
Fables and Distances by John Hines
On Writing Well by William Zinsser

Daniel Bosch—
Ways of Seeing by John Berger
The Missing Pieces by Henri Lefebvre
"Landays" by Eliza Griswold
Junket is Nice by Dorothy Kunhardt

James B. Nicola—
Poets on Poetry: Sixteen Famous Poets Consider Their Art edited by Charles Norman
The Poetry Home Repair Manual: Practical Advice for Beginning Poets by Ted Kooser
Poetry for Dummies by John Timpane
Poetic Meter and Poetic Form by Paul Fussell
The Making of a Poem: A Norton Anthology of Poetic Forms by Mark Strand and
　Eavan Boland

Robbie Gamble—
The Poetry Home Repair Manual: Practical Advice for Beginning Poets by Ted Kooser
The Triggering Town: Lectures and Essays on Poetry and Writing by Richard Hugo
Madness, Rack, and Honey by Mary Ruefle
Why Poetry by Matthew Zapruder
The Poem is You by Stephanie Burt

Helen Ruggieri—
Writing the Australian Crawl and *You Must Revise Your Life* by William Stafford
Narrow Road to the Deep North by Basho
Two Essays on Analytical Psychology by Carl Jung
On Poetry and Craft by Theodore Roethke

Linda Simone—
The Triggering Town: Lectures and Essays on Poetry and Writing by Richard Hugo
The Practicing Poet: Writing Beyond the Basics edited by Diane Lockward
Bird by Bird: Some Instructions on Writing and Life by Anne Lamott
Ordering the Storm: How to Put Together a Book of Poems edited by Susan Grimm
Handbook of Poetic Forms edited by Ron Padgett

Laura M Kaminski—
Writing Poetry from the Inside Out by Sandford Lyne
The Tao of Writing: Imagine, Create, Flow by Ralph L Wahlstrom
The Book of Forms: A Handbook of Poetics by Lewis Putnam Turco

Joan Leotta—
How Does a Poem Mean? by John Ciardi
Ghazal Cosmopolitan: The Culture and Craft of the Ghazal by Shadab Zeest Hashmi

Katie Manning—
A Poet's Guide to Poetry by Mary Kinzie
Poets Teaching Poets: Self and the World edited by Gregory Orr & Ellen Bryant Voigt
Lofty Dogmas: Poets on Poetics edited by Deborah Brown, Annie Finch, and Maxine
    Kumin
Classic Writings on Poetry edited by William Harmon
Letters to a Young Poet by Rainer Maria Rilke

Tasha Cotter—
Bird by Bird: Some Instructions on Writing and Life by Anne Lamott
The Poetry Handbook: A Dictionary of Terms by Babette Deutsch
A Poetry Handbook by Mary Oliver

Writing Down the Bones: Freeing the Writer Within by Natalie Goldberg
Still Writing by Dani Shapiro

Nancy Reddy—
Object Lessons by Eavan Boland
The Poet's Companion: A Guide to the Pleasures of Writing Poetry by Kim Addonizio
  and Dorianne Laux

Marina Blitshteyn—
Women in Praise of the Sacred: 43 Centuries of Spiritual Poetry by Women edited by
  Jane Hirshfield
Paul Celan: Poet, Survivor, Jew by John Felstiner
Recollections of My Life as a Woman by Diane Di Prima
The Book of Forms by Lewis Putnam Turco
Selected Prose, Daybooks, and Papers by George Oppen

Leonard Franzén—
The Hatred of Poetry by Ben Lerner
What is Art and 100 Other Very Important Questions by Ernst Billgren

Abayomi Animashaun—
"Tradition and the Individual Talent" by T.S. Eliot
Triggering Town: Lectures and Essays on Poetry and Writing by Richard Hugo
You Must Revise Your Life by William Stafford
The Making of a Poem: A Norton Anthology of Poetic Forms by Mark Strand and
  Eavan Boland
Novices: A Study of Poetic Apprenticeship by Clayton Eshleman

Aaron Brown—
Ambition and Survival: On Becoming a Poet by Christian Wiman
The Art of the Poetic Line by James Longenbach
Mystery & Manners by Flannery O'Connor
The Hatred of Poetry by Ben Lerner
Nineteen Ways of Looking at Wang Wei by Eliot Weinberger

Ashton Kamburoff—
A Broken Thing: Poets on The Line edited by Emily Rosko & Anton Vander Zee
Blue Notes: Essays, Interviews, and Commentaries by Yusef Komunyakaa
The Hatred of Poetry by Ben Lerner
Proofs & Theories by Louise Glück
The Art of Daring by Carl Phillips

Christine Beck—
The Poetry Home Repair Manual: Practical Advice for Beginning Poets by Ted Kooser
Imaginative Writing, The Elements of Craft by Janet Burroway
America's Favorite Poems edited by Robert Pinsky and Maggie Dietz
The Poets Laureate Anthology edited by Elizabeth Hun Schmidt

Jessamine Price—
The Art of Syntax: Rhythm of Thought, Rhythm of Song by Ellen Bryant Voigt
"Poetry" by Rita Gabis
Writing Down the Bones: Freeing the Writer Within by Natalie Goldberg
"Poetry and Ambition" by Donald Hall
"Some Thoughts on the Integrity of the Single Line in Poetry" by Alberto Rios

J.S. Watts—
How To Publish Your Poetry by Peter Finch
Writers' Guidelines by J.C.R Green
Annual *Writers' & Artists' Year Book*
The Journals of Sylvia Plath

Diana Rosen—
Finding What You Didn't Lose, Expressing Your Truth and Creativity Through Poem-Making by John Fox
Elements of Eloquence, Secrets of the Perfect Turn of Phrase by Mark Forsyth
Writing Begins with the Breath, Embodying Your Authentic Voice by Laraine Herring
The Crafty Poet and *The Crafty Poet II* by Diane Lockwood
The Triggering Town: Lectures and Essays on Poetry and Writing by Richard Hugo

Amy Miller—
"Why You Should Aim for 100 Rejections" by Kim Liao
"8 Reasons Your Submission Strategy Sucks" by Becky Tuch
Anne Sexton: A Self-Portrait in Letters edited by Linda Gray Sexton and Lois Ames
Bird by Bird: Some Instructions on Writing and Life by Anne Lamott
An Introduction to Poetry edited by X. J. Kennedy & Dana Gioia

Darby Price—
The Poet's Companion: A Guide to the Pleasures of Writing Poetry by Kim Addonizio
and Dorianne Laux
Bluets by Maggie Nelson
Sleeping with the Dictionary by Harryette Mullen
Delusions, Etc. by John Berryman
Deepstep Come Shining by C.D. Wright

Megan Merchant—
"Personism: A Manifesto" by Frank O'Hara
The Crafty Poet: A Portable Workshop by Diane Lockward
On Being Stuck: Tapping Into the Creative Power of Writer's Block by Laraine Herring
Ordinary Genius: A Guide for the Poet Within by Kim Addonizio
i: six nonlectures by e. e. cummings

Claudia F. Savage—
A Poet's Glossary by Edward Hirsch
The Art of Recklessness: Poetry as Assertive Force and Contradiction by Dean Young
The Riot Inside Me: More Trials and Tremors by Wanda Coleman
Coming After: Essays on Poetry by Alice Notley, especially the essay "Voice"
"Putting Everyday Words into the Nuclear Reactor" by Monica Youn

David S. Maduli—
"Painting a Body of Loss and Love in the Proximity of an Aesthetic" and "Ethics and
   Narrative: the Human and Other" by Chris Abani

John Guzlowski—
Writing Down the Bones: Freeing the Writer Within by Natalie Goldberg
Letters to a Young Poet by Rainer Maria Rilke
Song of Myself by Walt Whitman
Writing Poems by Robert Wallace
The Practice of Poetry by Robin Behn

Duane L. Herrmann—
Another Song, Another Season by Roger White
The Collected Poems of Robert Hayden by Robert Hayden
Down of a Thistle by Margaret Danner
Tahirih: A Portrait in Poetry by Tahirih

Stephen Page—
Creating Poetry by John Drury
Haiku Moment: An Anthology of Contemporary North American Haiku edited by
   Bruce Ross

Kari Treese—
Poetry's Old Air by Marianne Boruch
The Making of a Poem: A Norton Anthology of Poetic Forms by Mark Strand and
   Eavan Boland
Light up the Cave by Denise Levertov

Gillian Parrish—
"American Encounter" and "Statement of Principles" by Jerzy Grotowski
An Exaltation of Forms: Contemporary Poets Celebrate the Diversity of Their Art by Annie Finch & Katherine Varnes
What is Found There: Notebooks on Poetry and Politics by Adrienne Rich
Convictions Net of Branches: Essays on the Objectivist Poets and Poetry by Michael Heller
Diffusion of Distances: Dialogue Between Chinese and Western Poetics by Wai-Lim Yip

Kathryn Hummel—
The Anthologist: A Novel by Nicholson Baker
Break every rule: Essays on language, longing, and moments of desire by by Carole Maso
"When we dead awaken: Writing as re-vision" by Adrienne Rich

José Angel Araguz—
A Natural History of Chicano Literature by Juan Felipe Herrera (talk available on YouTube)
Best Words, Best Order by Stephen Dobyns
Elegies in Blue by Benjamin Alire Saenz
Letters to a Young Poet by Rainer Maria Rilke
A Formal Feeling Comes: Poems in Forms by Contemporary Women edited by Annie Finch

Jon Hoel—
Proofs and Theories: Essays on Poetry by Louise Glück
The Anxiety of Influence by Harold Bloom
Madness, Rack, and Honey by Mary Ruefle
Equipment for Living by Michael Robbins

Todd Davis—
A Poetry Handbook by Mary Oliver
Still Life with Oysters and Lemon: On Objects and Intimacy by Mark Doty
The Triggering Town: Lectures and Essays on Poetry and Writing by Richard Hugo
Writing the Australian Crawl: Views on the Writer's Vocation by William Stafford
Madness, Rack, and Honey by Mary Ruefle

Noah Davis—
A Poetry Handbook by Mary Oliver
The Poet's Companion: A Guide to the Pleasures of Writing Poetry by Kim Addonizio

Kari Wergeland—
Best Words, Best Order: Essays on Poetry by Stephen Dobyns
The Making of a Poem: A Norton Anthology of Poetic Forms by Mark Strand and
  Eavan Boland
The Poem's Heartbeat: A Manual of Prosody by Alfred Corn
A Poetry Handbook by Mary Oliver
The Triggering Town: Lectures and Essays on Poetry by Richard Hugo

Guillermo Cancio-Bello—
Stepping Stones by Seamus Heaney
The Essential Haiku: Versions of Basho, Buson, and Issa by Robert Hass
A Little Book on Form: An Exploration into the Formal Imagination of Poetry by
  Robert Hass
Seven Brief Lessons on Physics by Carlo Rovelli
The Family Evaluation by Murray Bowen & Michael Kerr

Sophia Terazawa—
This Bridge Called My Back: Writings by Radical Women of Color edited by Cherríe
  Moraga and Gloria E. Anzaldúa
Women, Native, Other by Trinh T. Minh-ha
Poetics of Relation by Édouard Glissant
Borderlands/La Frontera: The New Mestiza by Gloria E. Anzaldúa
Dictée by Theresa Hak Kyung Cha

Carol Smallwood—
How to Write Classical Poetry: A Guide to Forms, Techniques, and Meaning edited
  by Evan Mantyk & Connie Phillips
*You Can Be A Winning Writer: The 4 C's Approach of Successful Authors—Craft,
  Commitment, Community and Confidence* by Joan Gelfand

Ben White—
Against Forgetting: Twentieth Century Poetry of Witness edited by Carolyn Forché
Nine Gates: Entering the Mind of Poetry : Essays by Jane Hirshfield
"Delusions of Whiteness in the Avant-Garde" by Cathy Park Hong
Interrogations by Leroy V. Quintana
What Is Literature? and Other Essays by Jean Sartre

CONTRIBUTORS

Tanis MacDonald is a poet, scholar, and editor. She is the author of three books of poetry with the fourth, *Mobile*, forthcoming with Book*hug Press in 2019. Her book of essays, *Out of Line: Writing Outside of the Big City* was published by Wolsak and Wynn in Spring 2018. She is the co-editor of *GUSH: menstrual manifestos for our times* (Frontenac Press, 2018), and has taught an entire generation of creative writers across Canada. She is Professor in the Department of English and Film Studies of Wilfrid Laurier University in Waterloo, Ontario, Canada.

Christine Riddle is a retired nurse and published poet who lives with her husband on Alabama's Gulf Coast. She is a member of the Pensters Writing Group of Fairhope, AL, the Alabama Writers' Conclave, and the Alabama State Poetry Society, from which she has won several awards. She enjoys writing essays, creative non-fiction, and lucid poetry. She may be reached at christineriddle234@gmail.com.

David Shumate is the author of three books of prose poems published by the University of Pittsburgh Press: *Kimonos in the Closet* (2013), *The Floating Bridge* (2008) and *High Water Mark* (2004), winner of the 2003 Agnes Lynch Starrett Poetry Prize. His poetry has appeared widely in literary journals and has been anthologized in *Good Poems for Hard Times*, *The Best American Poetry*, and *The Writer's Almanac* as well as in numerous other anthologies and university texts. He was awarded an NEA Fellowship in poetry in 2009 and a Creative Renewal Fellowship by the Arts Council of Indianapolis in 2007. Shumate is poet-in-residence emeritus at Marian University and a lecturer in Butler University's MFA program. He lives in Zionsville, Indiana.

Rishi Dastidar's poetry has been published by *Financial Times, New Scientist,* Tate Modern and London's Southbank Centre amongst many others. A fellow of The Complete Works, the Arts Council England funded programme for poets of colour, he is a consulting editor at *The Rialto* magazine, a member of the Malika's Poetry Kitchen collective, and serves as chair of the London-based writer development organization Spread The Word. His debut collection *Ticker-tape* is published in the UK by Nine Arches Press, a poem from which was included in *The Forward Book of Poetry 2018*.

Kyle Flak is the author of *Sweatpants Paradise* (Gold Wake Press, 2019), *I am Sorry for Everything in the Whole Entire Universe* (Gold Wake Press, 2017), and various other little books and chapbooks of poetry. Some of his favorite things include: warm toast with peanut butter on it, the movie *American Graffiti*, Lake Superior, long walks where he wanders around aimlessly, and songs by The Beach Boys.

Michelle Bonczek Evory is the author of *The Ghosts of Lost Animals*, winner of the 2018 Barry Spacks Poetry Prize (Gunpowder P, forthcoming), three chapbooks of poetry, and the Open SUNY Textbook *Naming the Unnamable: An Approach to Poetry for New Generations*. Her poetry is featured in the *Best New Poets* Anthology and has appeared in over eighty journals and magazines, including *Crazyhorse, cream city review, Green Mountains Review, Orion Magazine, The Progressive*, and *Wasafiri: The Magazine of International Contemporary Writing*. In 2015, she and her husband poet Rob Evory were the inaugural Artists in Residence at Gettysburg National Military Park. She holds a PhD from Western Michigan University; an MFA from the Inland Northwest Center for Writers at Eastern Washington University; and an MA from SUNY Brockport. She teaches literature at Western Michigan University, and mentors poets at The Poet's Billow (thepoetsbillow.org).

Jennifer Moore was born and raised in Seattle. She is the author of *The Veronica Maneuver* (The University of Akron Press, 2015) and *Easy Does It* (The University of Akron Press, 2021). Her poems have appeared in *Crazyhorse, Bennington Review, DIAGRAM, The Cincinnati Review*, and elsewhere. An associate professor of creative writing, she currently serves as Director of the School for the Humanities and Global Cultures at Ohio Northern University and lives in Bowling Green, Ohio.

Michael Angel Martín has poems and essays in or forthcoming in *Kenyon Review—KR Reviews, America magazine, Anglican Theological Review, Modern Literature, Green Mountains Review, Apogee, Dappled Things, Ruminate, Presence, Pilgrim*, and elsewhere. He lives in Miami, FL, with the poet Annik Adey-Babinski and their cat Tina.

Until 2003, **David M. Harris** had never lived more than fifty miles from New York City. Since then he has moved to Tennessee, acquired a daughter and a classic MG, and gotten serious about poetry. All these projects seem to be working out pretty well. His work has appeared in *Pirene's Fountain* (and in *First*

Water, the Best of Pirene's Fountain anthology), *Gargoyle*, *The Labletter*, *The Pedestal*, and other places. His first collection of poetry, *The Review Mirror*, was published by Unsolicited Press in 2013. Before getting an MFA and becoming a teacher, Harris worked in book publishing as an editor and other jobs, in film production as a still photographer and script supervisor and, for part of one summer, in an ice cream hardening room. He has published a novel, essays, short fiction, and reviews, and has written two feature films.

Michael Collins' poems have received Pushcart Prize nominations and appeared in more than 70 journals and magazines. He is also the author of the chapbooks *How to Sing when People Cut off your Head and Leave it Floating in the Water* and *Harbor Mandala* and the full-length collections *Psalmandala* and *Appearances*, which was named one of the best indie poetry collections of 2017 by Kirkus Reviews.

Rob Carney is originally from Washington state. He is the author of five books of poems, most recently *The Book of Sharks* (Black Lawrence Press, 2018). In 2014 he received the Robinson Jeffers/Tor House Foundation Award for Poetry. His work has appeared in *Cave Wall*, *Columbia Journal*, *Dark Mountain: Uncivilised Poetics* (Issue 10), *Sugar House Review*, and many others. He is a Professor of English and Literature at Utah Valley University and lives in Salt Lake City. rob.carney@uvu.edu.

Melanie Faith is an English professor, tutor, auntie, and photographer. Recent publications include a poetry collection, *This Passing Fever* (Future Cycle Press 2017), and two craft books for writers called *In a Flash* and *Poetry Power* (both Vine Leaves Press 2018). Read more about her writing, photography, and publications at: https://www.melaniedfaith.com/blog.

Nancy Scott has been managing editor of *U.S.1 Worksheets*, the journal of the U.S.1 Poets' Cooperative in Central Jersey, for more than a decade. She is the author of nine collections of poetry and one novella, *Marriage by Fire* (Big Table Publishing Company, 2018), which combines short stories, poetry and prose poems. She frequently writes about people and place and social justice issues. Scott worked for the State of New Jersey for twenty years, first on behalf of abused and neglected children, and then to assist homeless families find permanent housing in the community. Find a sample of her poems and other information at www.nancyscott.net.

Jenny Ferguson is Métis, an activist, a feminist, an auntie, and an accomplice with a PhD. She believes writing and teaching are political acts. *Border Markers*, her collection of linked flash fiction narratives, is available from NeWest Press. Her recent lyric essays can be found at *The Malahat Review* and *The Account*. She is the creative nonfiction editor and à la carte blog editor for *carte blanche*, where she welcomes pitches for blog posts from BIPOC, QT2S, and disabled writers, as well as writers from other marginalized communities.

Whitney Sweet is a poet and writer of fiction. Her work has been included in *A&U Magazine* as well as the *Mentor Me: Instruction and Advice for Aspiring Writers* anthology and *Another Dysfunctional Cancer Poem Anthology*. She is the winner of the 2014 Judith Eve Gewurtz Memorial Poetry Award. She is the creator and editor of T.R.O.U. Lit. Mag, a literary magazine dedicated to love and diversity. Whitney holds an MA in Communication and Culture from York University as well as a BA in Creative Writing and English. www.troumagazine.com; www.whitneysweetwrites.com for more about the author.

Barbara Perry, MFA School of the Art Institute of Chicago, is an Illinois Arts Council Poetry Fellow. She has been a finalist six times for her first collection of poetry by journals such as *Tupelo Press, Pleiades Press, Arts and Letters*, and *The Faulkner Society*. She was honored with a *Whitney Museum of American Art Independent Graduate Studies Award*, an *Andrew W. Mellon Foundation Fellowship* Honorable Mention, and has shown her video poems at *The International Art Expo/Chicago* and the *Olympia Media Exchange/Tokyo*. She practices Buddhism to unconditionally accept her mind, a good thing for any poet.

Norman Minnick was born in Louisville, Kentucky. His first collection of poems, *To Taste the Water*, won the First Series Award for Poetry and was published by Mid-List Press. His second collection, *Folly*, was published in 2013. He is the editor *of Between Water and Song: New Poets for the Twenty-First Century* (White Pine Press, 2010). For more information, visit www.buzzminnick.com.

Dike Okoro is a poet, essayist, short story writer and editor. He is the recipient of a 2017-18 Newberry Scholar-in-Residence Award and was shortlisted for the 2016 Cecile De Jongh Literary Award. He received his PhD in English from the University of Wisconsin Milwaukee and holds both an MA in English and an MFA in Poetry from Chicago State University. Okoro's edited books include *Speaking for the Generations: Contemporary Short Stories from Africa* (AWP, 2010); *We Have Crossed Many Rivers: New Poetry from Africa* (Malthouse/ABC, 2013); and *Echoes from the Mountain: Selected Poems by Mazisi Kunene* (Malthouse/ABC, 2007). He is the author of two poetry collections: *In the Company of the Muse* (2016) and *Dance of the Heart* (2007). He is a professor of English at Harris-Stowe

State University, where he also serves as editor of the Africana Studies Journal and coordinator of the Sigma Tau Delta/International English Honor Society.

Emily Stoddard's writing has appeared in *Tinderbox Poetry Journal, New Poetry from the Midwest, Rust+Moth, Menacing Hedge, Hermeneutic Chaos, Gravel,* and elsewhere. She is an affiliate of the Amherst Writers & Artists Method and founder of Voice & Vessel, a writing studio. She leads workshops and supports creative spirits online and in Michigan. More at www.emilystoddard.com.

Jason McCall is an Alabama native, and he currently teaches at the University of North Alabama. He holds an MFA from the University of Miami, His collections include *Two-Face God* (WordTech Editions); *Dear Hero,* (winner of the 2012 Marsh Hawk Press Poetry Prize); *Silver* (Main Street Rag); *I Can Explain* (Finishing Line Press); and *Mother, Less Child* (co-winner of the 2013 Paper Nautilus Vella Chapbook Prize). He and P.J. Williams are the editors of *It Was Written: Poetry Inspired by Hip-Hop* (Minor Arcana Press).

Tara Skurtu is a two-time Fulbright grantee and recipient of two Academy of American Poets prizes and a Robert Pinsky Global Fellowship in Poetry. She is the author of the chapbook *Skurtu, Romania* and the full poetry collection *The Amoeba Game.*

David Bergman is the author of *Gaiety Transfigured, The Violet Hour: The Violet Quill and the Making of Gay Culture,* and *The Poetry of Disturbance.* His latest book of poetry is *Fortunate Light.*

John Langfeld, a retired musician and arts educator living in Westchester, IL, has been writing in various genres since 1981. Langfeld's first book of poetry, *There's a Brevitist Loose in the Condensory* [or] *If You Want Your Heart Broken, Read Somebody Else,* was self-published in May 2014. Since then, Langfeld's stories and poems have been published in print and online media.

Kelly Cherry is the author of 27 books, 11 chapbooks, and 2 translations of classical drama. Most recent: *Quartet for J. Robert Oppenheimer* (poetry). A former Poet Laureate of Virginia. She is also a member of Poets Corner, Cathedral Church of St. John the Divine, NYC, and a recipient of NEA, USIA, Rockefeller, Bradley Lifetime Award, Weinstein Award, others. Her publications have also appeared in prize anthologies. Cherry is a Eudora Welty Professor Emerita of English and Evjue-Bascom Professor Emerita in the Humanities, University of Wisconsin Madison. Eminent Scholar, UAH, 2001-2005. More info and details on Wikipedia/Kelly Cherry.

J.G. McClure holds an MFA from the University of California–Irvine. His poetry and prose appear widely, including in *Gettysburg Review, Green Mountains Review, Birmingham Poetry Review, Nashville Review, The Pinch, The Southern Poetry Anthology,* and *Best New Poets.* He is the author of *The Fire Lit & Nearing* (Indolent Books 2018) and the translator of *Swimming* (Valparaíso Ediciones 2019). A three-time Pushcart Prize nominee, he is a book reviewer for numerous journals and teaches a variety of online writing workshops. More info is available at www.jgmcclure.com.

Stacey Balkun is the author of *Eppur Si Muove, Jackalope-Girl Learns to Speak,* & *Lost City Museum.* Winner of the 2017 Women's National Book Association Poetry Prize, her work has appeared in *Crab Orchard Review, The Rumpus, Muzzle, Bayou,* and others. Chapbook Series Editor for Sundress Publications, Stacey holds an MFA from Fresno State and teaches poetry online at The Poetry Barn and The Loft.

Zoë Brigley (Thompson), originally from Wales, is Assistant Professor in English and Sexuality Studies at the Ohio State University. She has three poetry collections, *The Secret* (2007), *Conquest* (2012) and *Hand & Skull* (2019). She is editor of *Feminism, Literature, and Rape Narratives* (2010). Her first collection of essays, *Notes from a Swing State,* is out in 2019. Most recently, her poems have been accepted by *Chicago Review, Copper Nickel, Australian Book Review, Orion,* and *Poetry Ireland Review.*

Raised in Missouri and California, **Chaun Ballard** is an affiliate editor for *Alaska Quarterly Review,* a Callaloo fellow, and a graduate of the MFA Program at the University of Alaska, Anchorage. For eight years now, he and his wife have been teaching in the Middle East and West Africa. Chaun's chapbook, *Flight,* is the winner of the 2018 Sunken Garden Poetry Prize (Tupelo Press, 2018). His poems have appeared or are forthcoming in *ANMLY (FKA Drunken Boat), Borderlands: Texas Poetry Review, Chiron Review, Columbia Poetry Review, Frontier Poetry, International Poetry Review, Pittsburgh Poetry Review, Rattle,* and other literary magazines. His work has received nominations for both Best of the Net and a Pushcart Prize.

Dr. Michael G. Rather, Jr. (M. Rather, Jr.) has had poetry appear in *West Texas Review, Concho River Review, Cypress Branches, Borderlands, Delinquent, Rio Grande Review, Flyways, Reed,* and *The Greensboro Review.* His poetry has also been published as limited edition broadsides through Yellow Flag Press. His critical work has appeared in the *CLCWeb* through Purdue University. He has a PhD in English from the University of Louisiana at Lafayette and an MFA in Creative Writing with a focus in Poetry from McNeese State University. He teaches composition at SOWELA Technical Community College.

John Timothy Robinson is a traditional, mainstream citizen and ten-year educator for Mason County Schools in Mason County, WV, who holds a Regent's Degree. John's poetry has appeared in fifty-eight journals since August 2016, the United States, Canada and the United Kingdom, electronic and print. He has also published several literary critical essays. As a printmaker, John has published forty photo and art images which have appeared in eleven journals and websites in the United States and Italy.

Jaydn DeWald is a writer, teacher, jazz bassist, and the author of three limited-edition chapbooks, *The Rosebud Variations: And Other Variations* (Greying Ghost, 2017); *In Whose Hand the Light Expires* (Yellow Flag Press, 2018); and *as counterpoint to this compressed mass a longing* (forthcoming from Sutra Press). His poems, stories, and critical essays have appeared in *Best New Poets 2015*, *Brilliant Corners: A Journal of Jazz & Literature*, *The Collagist*, *south: a scholarly journal*, *West Branch*, and many other publications. He's a PhD candidate at the University of Georgia.

Nathan McClain is the author of *Scale* (Four Way Books, 2017), the 2017 Gregory Pardlo Frost Place Poetry fellow, and a recipient of scholarships from the Sewanee Writers' Conference and the Bread Loaf Writers' Conference. His poems and prose have recently appeared or are forthcoming in *New York Times Magazine*, *Academy of American Poets Poem-a-Day*, *The Rumpus*, *upstreet*, and *Tinderbox*. He teaches at Hampshire College.

Thom Tammaro retired from Minnesota State University Moorhead in 2017, where he was Professor of English and co-founder and director of the MFA in Creative Writing Program. His collections of poems include, *23 Poems*, *Holding on for Dear Life*, *When the Italians Came to My Home Town*, *31 Mornings in December*, and *Minnesota Suite*. He is co-editor of nine anthologies, among them *Visiting Bob: Poems Inspired by the Life and Work of Bob Dylan* and *Visiting Emily: Poems Inspired by the Life and Work of Emily Dickinson*.

Victoria L. Davis lives in Seagrove, North Carolina, with her loving husband. She believes in the power of poetry and its ability to climb the most divisive walls. Her previous publications include individual poems in *Snapdragon* and *Minerva Rising*. Her hope is that she honors the Christ-centered legacy of her late mother, whose life itself was the most intricate of poems.

Natalie Homer has an MFA in poetry from West Virginia University. Her poetry has been published or is forthcoming in *The Journal, Blue Earth Review, The Pinch, The Lascaux Review, Ruminate, The Minnesota Review, Salamander,* and elsewhere.

C. Kubasta writes poetry, prose & hybrid forms. Her favorite rejection (so far) noted that one editor loved her work, and the other hated it. She is the author of two poetry chapbooks: *A Lovely Box,* which won the 2014 Wisconsin Fellowship of Poets Chapbook Prize, and *&s;* and the full-length collections, *All Beautiful & Useless* (BlazeVOX) and *Of Covenants* (Whitepoint Press), and the novella *Girling* (Brain Mill Press). Her most recent book is the novel *This Business Of The Flesh* (Apprentice House). She teaches English and Gender Studies, is active with the Wisconsin Fellowship of Poets, and works with Brain Mill Press. Find her at ckubasta.com. Follow her @CKubastathePoet.

Kevin Pilkington is on the writing faculty at Sarah Lawrence College. He is the author of nine poetry collections and a novel. His latest collection, *Where You Want to Be: New and Selected Poems* was published by Black Lawrence Press and was a 2017 IPPY Award winner.

Daniel Bosch is the student of poets and translators A. McA. Miller, Edward Snow, Richard Howard, and Derek Walcott. His collection *Crucible* was published by Other Press in 2002; his *Octaves* at Beard of Bees.com in 2014. "Cover Letter: Toward a New Creative Writing" was first published at *3:AM*. He teaches reading and writing at Emory University.

James B. Nicola's poems have appeared stateside in such publications as the *Antioch, Southwest* and *Atlanta Reviews, Rattle, Tar River,* and *Poetry East,* and in many journals in Europe and Canada. His poetry collections are *Manhattan Plaza* (2014), *Stage to Page: Poems from the Theater* (2016), *Wind in the Cave* (2017), and *Out of Nothing: Poems of Art and Artists* (2018). His poems have received a Dana Literary Award, two *Willow Review* awards, six Pushcart Prize nominations, and a People's Choice award from *Storyteller* magazine. He has been the featured poet in *Westward Quarterly* and *The New Formalist*. His nonfiction book *Playing the Audience: The Practical Actor's Guide to Live Performance* won a *Choice* magazine award. Lately Nicola has been conducting both poetry and theater workshops at libraries, literary festivals, schools, and community centers all over the country, most notably the Kennedy Center/American College Theater Festival.

Robbie Gamble received his MFA in poetry from Lesley University. His poems and essays have appeared in *Solstice, Writers Resist, Mass Poetry, Poet Lore,*

RHINO, and *Carve*. He works as a nurse practitioner caring for homeless people in Boston, Massachusetts.

Helen Ruggieri has had work in over a hundred magazines and anthologies. She has been rejected by more than a hundred more.

Linda Simone is the author of *The River Will Save Us* (Kelsay Books); *Archeology* (Flutter Press); the award-winning *Cow Tippers* (Shadow Ink Publications); and *Moon: A Poem* (Richard C. Owen Publishers). Her essays and Pushcart-nominated poems appear in print and online journals and anthologies. She is honored to be one of 30 poets selected for San Antonio's 2018 Tricentennial chapbook and exhibition. New York born and bred, Simone relocated to San Antonio in 2015. www.lindasimone.com.

Laura M Kaminski (Halima Ayuba) grew up in Nigeria, went to school in New Orleans, and currently lives in rural Missouri. She serves on the editorial teams of two online journals, *Right Hand Pointing* (USA) and *Praxis Magazine Online* (Nigeria). She is also the author of several chapbooks and poetry collections, including *Anchorhold* (2016) and *Considering Luminescence* (2015). Her most recent collection is *The Heretic's Hymnal* (Balkan Press, 2019).

Joan Leotta has been playing with words on page and on stage since childhood. She is a story performer, poet, and writer of mystery and historical fiction, whose books include a collection of short fiction and tales of strong women (Legacy of Honor series). Joan's poems and other writings appear in many journals, magazines and newspapers. Her first chapbook, *Languid Lusciousness with Lemon,* was published 2017 by Finishing Line Press. When she is not writing or re-writing, Joan is often at the beach.

Katie Manning is the founding editor-in-chief of *Whale Road Review* and an associate professor of writing at Point Loma Nazarene University in San Diego. She is the author of *Tasty Other*, which won the 2016 Main Street Rag Poetry Book Award, and four chapbooks, including *The Gospel of the Bleeding Woman*. Her poems have appeared in *The American Journal of Nursing*, *New Letters*, *Poet Lore*, *Stirring*, *THRUSH*, *Verse Daily*, and many other journals and anthologies. Find her online at www.katiemanningpoet.com.

Tasha Cotter is the author of the poetry collection *Some Churches* (Gold Wake Press, 2013) and the chapbooks *That Bird Your Heart* (Finishing Line Press, 2013) and *Girl in the Cave* (Tree Light Books, 2016). Winner of the 2015 Delphi Poetry Series, her work has appeared in journals such as *Contrary Magazine*, *NANO fic-*

tion, and *Thrush*. She makes her home in Lexington, Kentucky where she works in higher education and serves as the president-elect of the Kentucky State Poetry Society. You can find her online at www.tashacotter.com.

Nancy Reddy is the author of *Double Jinx* (Milkweed Editions, 2015), a 2014 winner of the National Poetry Series, and *Acadiana* (Black Lawrence Press, 2018). Poems have appeared or are forthcoming in *Pleiades, Blackbird, The Iowa Review, Smartish Pace*, and elsewhere. The recipient of a Walter E. Dakin Fellowship from the Sewanee Writers' Conference and grants from the New Jersey State Council on the Arts and the Sustainable Arts Foundation, she teaches writing at Stockton University in southern New Jersey.

Marina Blitshteyn is the author of *Two Hunters* (Argos Books, 2019). She holds a BA from SUNY Buffalo and an MFA from Columbia University. Prior chapbooks include *Russian for Lovers, $kill$, Nothing Personal*, and *Sheet Music* (Sunnyoutside Press). She works as an adjunct assistant professor of composition and rhetoric and hybrid forms.

Leonard Franzén (1987) lives in Malmö, Sweden. He holds a BFA in creative writing from Lund University and his work has appeared in Swedish and American poetry journals. He is the author of *Ex-kille* (Carl Lindsten Bokförlag, 2018) and *Man går på IKEA själv och allt gör ont allt luktar björk och kartong en man i stentvättade jeans stirrar på en matta i en kvart man står på håll och betraktar hur hans byxor skär in i röven det finns en slags symbolik i allt* (AFV Press, 2017).

Abayomi Animashaun is the author of two poetry collections, *The Giving of Pears* and *Sailing for Ithaca*, and editor of two anthologies, *Others Will Enter the Gates: Immigrant Poets on Poetry, Influences, and Writing in America* and *Walking the Tightrope: Poetry and Prose by LGBTQ Writers from Africa*.

Aaron Brown is the author of the poetry collection, *Acacia Road*, winner of the 2016 Gerald Cable Book Award (Silverfish Review Press, 2018) and of the memoir, *Less Than What You Once Were* (Unsolicited Press, 2022). He has published work in *Michigan Quarterly Review, Image, World Literature Today* online, *Waxwing*, and *Transition*, among others, and he is a contributing editor for *Windhover* and blogs regularly for *Ruminate*. Brown grew up in Chad and now lives in Texas, where he is an assistant professor of English and directs the writing center at LeTourneau University. He holds an MFA from the University of Maryland. www.aaronbrownwriter.com

Ashton Kamburoff is from Cleveland, Ohio, and he currently lives in Smithville, Texas, where he serves as the 2017-2018 L.D. and LaVerne Harrell Clark Writer in Residence. A Round Top Poetry Scholar, he holds an MFA from Texas State University and his work has appeared in *Rust + Moth*, *Crab Creek Review*, and *The Naugatuck River Review*, where his poem "Revising The Hexes" was selected by Kaveh Akbar as a finalist for the "2017 Narrative Poetry Contest." He is the poetry editor for *Opossum* and *Profane Journal*.

Christine Beck holds a Master of Fine Arts in Creative Writing degree from Southern Connecticut State University and is the author of *Blinding Light* (Grayson Books 2013), *I'm Dating Myself* (Dancing Girl Press 2015), and *Stirred, Not Shaken* (Five Oaks Press 2016). She is the poetry editor of *The Perch*, a journal of The Yale Program for Recovery and Community Health. Christine teaches poetry, creative writing and literature at The University of Hartford and in private workshops. She is a former president of the Connecticut Poetry Society and currently directs its monthly series at which poets moderate a discussion about a well-known poet at the Hartford Public Library. She was Poet Laureate of the town of West Hartford, CT from 2015-17. More information about her many activities is on her website—www.ChristineBeck.net.

Jessamine Price's uncommon first name comes from a Tennyson poem. She wrote poetry for thirty years before beginning to publish it in 2017. Her poems have since appeared in publications such as *Rattle, Delmarva Review,* and *Rust + Moth*. She won first place in the 2018 Global Commemoration of Nanjing poetry contest judged by Grace Cavalieri. She's also a published essayist with an MFA from American University and an M.Phil. in history from Oxford. Her hometown is in Virginia, but she currently teaches in South Korea.

J.S. Watts is a British poet and novelist. Her work appears in publications in Britain, Ireland, Canada, Australia, New Zealand, and the States and has been broadcast on BBC and Independent Radio. She has edited magazines and anthologies. To date, J.S. has published seven books: poetry collections, *Cats and Other Myths* and *Years Ago You Coloured Me*, plus multi-award nominated poetry pamphlet *Songs of Steelyard Sue* and her most recent pamphlet, *The Submerged Sea*. Her novels are *A Darker Moon*—dark fiction, *Witchlight* and *Old Light*—paranormal. See: www.jswatts.co.uk.

Diana Rosen is a journalist and the author of thirteen non-fiction titles on food, beverage, and other lifestyle topics. She contributes to several online websites on tea and blogs for the Los Angeles Public Library Docents. More than sixty of her poems, haiku, flash fiction, and essays have appeared in print or online in journals, books, and anthologies. Red Bird Chapbooks accepted her manuscript for publication in 2019. She lives and works in Los Angeles.

Amy Miller's full-length poetry collection *The Trouble with New England Girls* won the Louis Award from Concrete Wolf Press, and her poetry and essays have appeared in journals ranging from *Asimov's Science Fiction* and *Fine Gardening* to *Gulf Coast, Nimrod, The Poet's Market,* and *ZYZZYVA.* She lives in Oregon, where she works as an editor and print production manager.

Darby Price earned her MFA from George Mason University, where she was a Heritage Fellow and the Poetry Editor for *Phoebe.* In 2014, she was named a Finalist for the Wisconsin Institute for Creative Writing Fellowships and a Semifinalist for the Provincetown Fine Arts Work Center Fellowships. Darby is now a Lecturer at UC Irvine and a volunteer for WriteGirl Los Angeles. Her interviews and book reviews have appeared in *The Collagist* and *The Southeast Review,* and her poetry has appeared in *Zócalo Public Square, Beloit Poetry Journal, Cimarron Review, Redivider, Sierra Nevada Review,* and *PANK,* among others.

Megan Merchant lives in the tall pines of Prescott, AZ with her husband and two children. She is the author of three full-length poetry collections with Glass Lyre Press: *Gravel Ghosts* (2016), *The Dark's Humming* (2015 Lyrebird Award Winner, 2017), *Grief Flowers* (2018), four chapbooks, and a children's book, *These Words I Shaped for You* (Philomel Books). She was awarded the 2016-2017 COG Literary Award, judged by Juan Felipe Herrera, the 2018 Beullah Rose Poetry Prize, and most recently, second place in the Pablo Neruda Prize for Poetry. She is an Editor at The Comstock Review and you can find her work at meganmerchant.wix.com/poet.

Claudia F. Savage is part of the performance duo Thick in the Throat, Honey. Her latest collection of poetry is *Bruising Continents* (Spuyten Duyvil) with recent work in *BOMB, Denver Quarterly, Columbia, Nimrod, Water-Stone Review,* and *Anomaly* (the interview series "Witness the Hour: Arab American Poets Across the Diaspora"). She is a 2018-2021 Black Earth Institute Fellow and her collaboration, *reductions,* with visual artist Jacklyn Brickman, is forthcoming in 2020. Her poetics are influenced by rabid reading, Alice Coltrane, and long hikes in drippy forests. She teaches privately and lives with her husband and daughter in Portland, OR. www.claudiafsavage.com.

David S. Maduli is a father of two, veteran public school teacher, deejay, and the author of the chapbook *00:33:33 (thirty-three and a third)* (Zoetic Press, 2018). An alumnus of the VONA/Voices, Las Dos Brujas, and Napa Valley Writers' workshops, he was the recipient of the Joy Harjo Poetry Prize in 2011. Born in San Francisco and raised all over, he is a longtime resident of Oakland, California.

He completed his MFA in Creative Writing at Mills College with a fellowship in Community Poetics.

John Guzlowski's writing appears on Garrison Keillor's *Writers Almanac* and in *Rattle, Ontario Review, North American Review,* and many other journals here and abroad. His poems and personal essays about his Polish parents' experiences as slave laborers in Nazi Germany and refugees making a life for themselves in Chicago appear in his memoir *Echoes of Tattered Tongues* (Aquila Polonica Press). *Echoes of Tattered Tongues* received the 2017 Benjamin Franklin Poetry Award and the Eric Hoffer Foundation's Montaigne Award. He is also the author of the Hank and Marvin noir mystery series.

Duane L. Herrmann a fifth generation Kansan, farming on a tractor by age 13. His connection to the land is reflected in his writing. Internationally published, award-winning poet and historian, his work is published in a dozen countries in four languages. He's received the Robert Hayden Poetry Fellowship, the Ferguson Kansas History Book Award, inclusion in Kansas Poet's Trail, Map of Kansas Literature and *American Poets of the 1990s.* He has authored seven collections of poetry, *No Known Address, Family Plowing, Gedichte aus Prairies of Possibilities, Remnants of a Life, Prairies of Possibilities, Ichnographical:173, Praise the King of Glory*; a collection of short stories, *Institor Gleg*; and a science fiction novel, *Escape from Earth: Murder on Makana.* Despite a traumatic childhood with dyslexia, ADHD, and PTSD.

Stephen Page is part Apache and Shawnee. He was born in Detroit. He is the author of three books of poetry—*A Ranch Bordering the Salty River, The Timbre of Sand,* and *Still Dandelions.* He holds two AA's from Palomar College, a BA from Columbia University, and an MFA from Bennington College. He also attended Broward College. His literary criticisms have appeared regularly in the *Buenos Aires Herald, How Journal, Gently Read Literature, North of Oxford,* and the *Fox Chase Review.* His fiction has been published in *Quarto, The Whistling Fire,* and *Amphibi.* He is the recipient of The Jess Cloud Memorial Prize, a Writer-in-Residence from the Montana Artists Refuge, a Full Fellowship from the Vermont Studio Center, an Imagination Grant from Cleveland State University, and an Arvon Foundation Ltd. Grant. He loves long walks through woodlands, spontaneous road trips, his wife, and throwing cellphones into lakes.

Kari Treese is a mathematics teacher and writer in California. She received a Master of Education from UCLA and is pursuing an MFA at Mills College in Oakland, CA. Her work has appeared in *The Los Angeles Review, Crab Fat, The Fem, Lunch Ticket,* and *Pacifica Review.*

Gillian Parrish spent some early years in the UK, some later ones in China and South Asia, and now lives in the brick and sycamore city of St. Louis, where she studied at Washington University and teaches as an assistant professor at Lindenwood University. Work has appeared in anthologies from Wesleyan Press and Black Lawrence Press. She is the author of two books of poems, supermoon and of rain and nettles wove (Singing Horse Press), and co-translator of a collection of poetry by Chinese poet Yang Jian. She serves as the mothership of spacecraftproject, a journal that features interviews with artists and new work by writers from around the world.

Kathryn Hummel is a writer, mixed-media artist and multidisciplinary researcher from South Australia. She is the author of *Poems from Here, The Bangalore Set, splashback, The Body That Holds* and *A Few Franks for Dearest Dominic*, as well as the recent *Lamentville* and print edition of *splashback*. Kathryn's work has been published, performed, translated and anthologized around the world. Recipient of the NEC/*Meanjin* Essay Writing Competition prize and the Melbourne Lord Mayor's Dorothy Porter Award, Kathryn's writing has been nominated for the Pushcart Prize, among others. Kathryn holds a PhD in Social Sciences and edits non-fiction and travel writing for Australian creative arts journal *Verity La*.

José Angel Araguz is a CantoMundo fellow and the author of seven chapbooks as well as the collections *Everything We Think We Hear, Small Fires, Until We Are Level Again*, and, most recently, *An Empty Pot's Darkness*. His poems, prose, and reviews have appeared in *Crab Creek Review, Prairie Schooner, New South, Poetry International*, and *The Bind*. Born and raised in Corpus Christi, Texas, he runs the poetry blog The Friday Influence and composes erasure poems on the Instagram account @poetryamano. A faculty member in Pine Manor College's Solstice Low-Residency MFA program, he also reads for the journal *Right Hand Pointing*. With an MFA from New York University and a PhD from the University of Cincinnati, José is an Assistant Professor of English at Suffolk University in Boston where he also serves as Editor-in-Chief of *Salamander Magazine*.

Jon Hoel is a New England poet who studied English at the Massachusetts College of Liberal Arts in the Berkshires and poetry in the MFA at Sarah Lawrence College. He's had poems published in several journals and has a book of essays on Andrei Tarkovsky coming out next year via Columbia University Press. He lives in New York City.

Todd Davis is the author of six full-length collections of poetry, most recently *Native Species* and *Winterkill*, both published by Michigan State University Press. He edited the nonfiction collection *Fast Break to Line Break: Poets on the Art of Basketball* and co-edited the anthology *Making Poems*. His writing has won the Gwendolyn Brooks Poetry Prize, the Chautauqua Editors Prize, and the Fore-Word Magazine Book of the Year Bronze and Silver Awards. His poems appear in *American Poetry Review, Alaska Quarterly Review, Barrow Street, Iowa Review,* and *Gettysburg Review.* He teaches environmental studies and creative writing at Pennsylvania State University's Altoona College.

Noah Davis' manuscript *Of This River* was selected for the 2019 Wheelbarrow Emerging Poet Book Contest from Michigan State University's Center for Poetry. Davis is a MFA candidate in poetry at Indiana University and his poetry is published in *Best New Poets, Orion, North American Review, Atlanta Review, Water~Stone Review,* and *Chautauqua,* among others. Davis has received Pushcart Prize nominations from *Poet Lore* and *Natural Bridge.* Davis was also a Katharine Bakeless Nason Fellow at the Bread Loaf Writer's Conference and the recipient of the 2018 Jean Ritchie Appalachian Literature Fellowship from Lincoln Memorial University.

Kari Wergeland, who hails from Davis, California, is a librarian and writer. Her work has appeared many journals, including *The Delmarva Review, New Millennium Writings, Pembroke Magazine,* and *Broad Street.* Her chapbook, *Breast Cancer: A Poem in Five Acts* was recently released from Finishing Line Press. Meanwhile, her long library career has taken her into libraries up and down the West Coast. At some point in all of this, she served as a children's book reviewer for *The Seattle Times.*

Guillermo Cancio-Bello is a poet and psychotherapist living in Miami, Florida with his wife and two dogs.

Sophia Terazawa is a poet of Vietnamese-Japanese descent. She is the author of two chapbooks: *Correspondent Medley* (winner of the 2018 Tomaž Šalamun Prize, forthcoming with *Factory Hollow Press*) and *I AM NOT A WAR* (a winner of the 2015 Essay Press Digital Chapbook Contest). Her poems appear in *The Seattle Review, Puerto del Sol, Poor Claudia,* and elsewhere. She is currently working toward the MFA in Poetry at the University of Arizona, where she also serves as poetry editor for *Sonora Review.*

Carol **Smallwood** returned to college to take creative writing classes and has founded humane societies. Her 2018 books include: *In the Measuring* (Shanti Arts); *A Matter of Selection* (Poetic Matrix Press, 2018); *Genealogy and the Librarian* (McFarland, 2018); and *The Relevant Librarian* (McFarland, 2018). A recipient of the Albert Nelson Marquis Lifetime Achievement Award, she's a literary reader, judge, and interviewer.

With 22 years of military service (PFC, Spec4, SN, PO3, ENS, LTjg, LT, LCDR) and 26 years of education (AA, BA, BA, MBA, MA, MFA, EdD), **Ben White** is the author of the book-length poem, *Buddha Bastinado Blues*, the e-novel, *The Kill Gene*, and a novella, *The Cuban*. He received his MFA from the University of Tampa thinking he was a poet only to find out he is not a poet at all. He is a witness; what he writes is testimony.

ACKNOWLEDGMENTS

Many thanks to the contributors whose wonderful essays taught me so much about poetry and contributed immensely to my growth as a poet. Also, thanks to Kim Stafford, Fred Marchant, Joe Harrington, Folabo Ajayi, and Tara DaPra for believing in this project. And, I'm beyond grateful to Angela Leroux-Lindsey, Gina Keicher, and Diane Goettel for their encouraging words, faith, and hard work; without them this anthology would not be possible.